THE MODERN HISTORY OF CHINA

The Praeger Asia-Africa Series

THE PRAEGER ASIA-AFRICA SERIES
Editor: Bernard Lewis

Other volumes in the series:

THE MODERN HISTORY OF JAPAN
W. G. Beasley

A MODERN HISTORY OF THE SUDAN
P. M. Holt

A MODERN HISTORY OF SOVIET GEORGIA
D. M. Lang

THE MODERN HISTORY OF SOMALILAND
I. M. Lewis

THE MODERN HISTORY OF CEYLON
E. F. C. Ludowyk

THE MODERN HISTORY OF CHINA
Henry McAleavy

THE MODERN HISTORY OF LEBANON
K. S. Salibi

THE MODERN HISTORY OF
SOVIET CENTRAL ASIA
Geoffrey Wheeler

THE MODERN HISTORY
OF
CHINA

HENRY McALEAVY

FREDERICK A. PRAEGER, *Publishers*

NEW YORK · WASHINGTON

BOOKS THAT MATTER

Published in the United States of America in 1967
by Frederick A. Praeger, Inc., Publishers
111 Fourth Avenue, New York, N.Y. 10003

CONTENTS

ILLUSTRATIONS

(Between pages 214 and 215)

ACKNOWLEDGEMENTS

The author and publishers would like to thank the following for supplying photographs for use in this volume. Plates 13, 19, 22, Radio Times Hulton Picture Library; Plates 20, 28, 29, 32, 33, 34, 37, Camera Press Ltd; Plates 23, 26, 27, Keystone Press Agency Ltd; Plate 25, The Associated Press of Great Britain Ltd; Plates 36, 38, 39, United Press International (UK) Ltd.

CHAPTER I

TRADITIONAL CHINA [1]

China in 1840 – the Confucian family system – Supernatural religion: Buddhism, Taoism, Islam

---

China in 1840

ON 7 April 1840, the British Parliament found itself discussing the affairs of China. The occasion was serious enough. There could be no doubt that Queen Victoria was in effect at war with the Emperor Tao Kuang, and Her Majesty's Government had to answer to the country for its responsibility in the matter. Yet somehow the House of Commons was conscious of a tang of fantasy in the air. More than anything else it was the names that were to blame. Not that Westminster was unused to the mention of Asiatic persons and places: but these elusive monosyllables had an outlandishness all their own. It soon appeared that the most erudite member of the Government, the omniscient Secretary at War, Mr Thomas Babington Macaulay, was in this particular matter no better off than his fellows, and he had the honesty to confess it. 'What does anybody here know of China?' he demanded. 'Even those Europeans who have been in that empire are almost as ignorant of it as the rest of us. Everything is covered by a veil, through which a glimpse of what is within may occasionally be caught, a glimpse just sufficient to set the imagination at work and more likely to mislead than to inform.'[1]

It was the voice of common sense and after more than a hundred and twenty years, as we try to discern what lies behind the curtain of propaganda, we may be forgiven for thinking that it has lost none of its cogency. Did China in 1949 for the first time pass into the hands of her own people, who since then, under leaders of genius, have been taking her along the road towards industrialization and prosperity? Or has she been transformed into an insect society, an anthill, ruled by a callous oligarchy, who to maintain their power deliberately keep their subjects in a condition of semi-starvation and look with equanimity at the prospect of nuclear war? Both these schools of thought, and a dozen others besides, can boast their distinguished partisans, and it is small wonder if an ordinary man is tempted to shrug his shoulders and let the matter rest. Yet it does not need much foresight to recognize that China is likely to have an increasing influence, unwelcome though this may be, on the lives of all of us, and it would not be in human nature to stay incurious before such a conundrum. But no investigation into the People's Republic will be profitable unless it is based on an understanding of that Empire concerning which Macaulay was so candid in disclaiming knowledge. He and his colleagues could perhaps afford their ignorance. The war they were debating was to usher in a new era in the course of which China would be degraded to a subordinate place among the nations and her ancient status and privileges so dimly remembered that when in our own time she is trying to reassert them the attempt can without manifest absurdity be represented as a threat to the peace of the world. It is this period of humiliation which forms the main theme of the pages that follow, but it would not be inopportune first of all to glance at the Old China as she enjoyed the last secure years of her traditional existence.

In 1840, the heart of the Chinese Empire, and indeed of all Eastern Asia, was China proper, stretching from the Great Wall to the borders of Vietnam and Burma, and from the Pacific Ocean to the Tibetan and Mongolian marches. It had a population of three hundred and fifty million people. Around the periphery of this vast land was a string of dependencies, inhabited largely by peoples not of Chinese blood and either administered from Peking or possessing internal autonomy but acknowledging Chinese suzerainty. The dominions making up the former group constituted with metropolitan China an empire far more extensive than the People's Republic of today, for besides Tibet and Sinkiang they included Outer as well as Inner Mongolia, while the frontiers of Manchuria reached across the Amur River to the Stanovoi Mountains, enclosing an area of what is now Soviet territory equal to that of France and Germany together. In the second or autonomous

2

class came such states as Burma, and, closer at hand and thoroughly permeated by Chinese culture, Korea and Vietnam whose rulers paid regular tribute to Peking and felt their title to their thrones to be incomplete without the ratification of their overlord the Chinese emperors. The Loochoo Islands were numbered in the same category. Japan, although never losing her political independence, owed an incalculable debt to China in the sphere of culture. This central position was expressed by the Chinese in the name they gave to their country, which they called Chung Kuo or 'The Middle Kingdom'. Looking out from it at neighbours patently inferior to themselves in all the arts of civilized life, they had become accustomed to the notion that their predominance was part of the order of nature.

It would have surprised them to learn that their good opinion of themselves was not universally shared. On the other side of the world, Thomas De Quincey confided to his journal for May 1818:

> I have often thought that if I were compelled to forego England and to live in China, I should go mad. The mere antiquity of Asiatic things, of their institutions, etc. is so impressive that the vast age of the race and name overpowers the sense of youth in the individual. A young Chinese seems to me an antediluvian man renewed. In China, I am terrified by the modes of life, by the manners, and the barriers of utter abhorrence and want of sympathy, placed between us by feelings deeper than I can analyze. I would sooner live with lunatics, or brute animals.[2]

This idea of the ineffable antiquity of Chinese civilization has its political importance even today, for it continues to inspire in many people the same loathing and disgust that it aroused in De Quincey, and is one of the most potent ingredients in the myth of the Yellow Peril. It is as well at the start to dispel such horrors by declaring that compared with the ancient kingdoms of the Near East, China is a newcomer in the world with a pedigree not going farther back than the second millennium before Christ. To be united under one government she had to wait until 221 BC and a sizeable portion even of her metropolitan territory was not incorporated until well into the Christian era. But if in the matter of age she cannot claim any special seniority, she must nonetheless be conceded pre-eminence in other domains. Of all the nations that now exist the Chinese have the most original genius, in that their traditional way of life is almost entirely indigenous. Buddhism, which was introduced to China from India about the time that

Christianity came to Europe, is the most striking exception, but its significance must not be exaggerated. China never became in any real sense a Buddhist country, and Buddhism, unlike Christianity in the West, did not take the place of the native Chinese beliefs.

The great area, about a million and a half square miles, of China proper, and the striking geographical and climatic differences within it, from the arid plains of the north, with their almost Siberian winter, to the subtropical humidity of Canton, have created a wide variety of dietary and living conditions, with perceptible effects on the physical appearance of the inhabitants. The peasant from the banks of the Yellow River, reared on millet or wheat, is as a rule easily distinguishable by his height and build from the slighter native of the rice-growing south, and each of them will be jealously attached to his provincial origins. Even so, the Chinese are deeply conscious of their national and cultural unity. Here it is worth while to correct a mistake commonly made by foreigners. European merchants from the sixteenth century onwards, in reaching China by sea, made their first acquaintance with the south-eastern coast, a region, as it happens, divided by mountain ranges into valleys whose inhabitants, thanks to this isolation, speak languages as distinct from one another as English is from Dutch. Not surprisingly it was deduced from this that the whole of the country was in a similar condition. In fact, except for this narrow belt along the coast between Canton and Shanghai, there was a common Chinese spoken everywhere, but with regional variations of the degree found in the dialects of English or French and therefore in very rustic mouths often hard for strangers to follow. The pronunciation of Peking was the standard but no social stigma resulted from a provincial brogue, and today both Mao Tse-tung and Chiang Kai-shek have accents you could cut with a knife. The written characters were identical and the same books were read from Canton to Peking.

The Confucian Family System

The most enduring feature of this populous nation was a concept of society handed down from its forebears for over three thousand years. To the earliest farmers along the Yellow River it had been a matter of life and death to beget sons who would help in tilling the ground and would support their parents if these were lucky

4

enough to survive into old age. But in the course of centuries this simple form of insurance had been elaborated into a system of doctrine which regulated every aspect of human activity and formed the basis of the entire structure of the state. This development was due especially to the influence of Confucius – the name is a latinization of the Chinese K'ung Fu-tzu, or 'Master K'ung' – who lived between 551 and 479 BC at a time when China was divided into warring feudal principalities, and who in consequence saw it as the prime need of mankind to resolve the problems of peaceful coexistence and harmony with the universe. He found the answer in the virtue of *hsiao*, most inadequately translated by 'filial piety' and defined as 'to serve parents during their life and when they die to bury them and to sacrifice to them'. The last particular has led to the use by westerners of the term 'ancestor worship' which one would be well advised to eschew as misleading. In its origins, the practice of setting ritual meats before the tablets representing the dead progenitors was based on the notion that their spirits were nourished or appeased by such offerings, and it was always permissible to believe that the human personality survived the death of the body, for Confucius resolutely declined to discuss the subject. But his aversion towards supernatural topics did not encourage hope of immortality, and there is little doubt that in the early nineteenth century most educated men, and indeed a fair number of the peasantry, interpreted these 'sacrifices' as nothing more than an honour paid to the name of the dead.[3]

This posthumous extension of duty, however, had the most radical consequences in society. For if I am bound to celebrate the memory of my deceased parents, it follows that I ought to take steps to ensure the continuation of the cult when I am no longer alive to perform it. In other words, it is incumbent upon me to produce a son, who will in due course not only pay his own tribute to me but will assume my responsibility towards our common ancestors. Not to have a son was the most heinous of all forms of unfilial conduct. Marriage was thus a moral obligation, and failure by my wife to give me an heir was a strong reason, if I could afford it, to try and supply the deficiency from a concubine. As a last resort, I should at least adopt a successor who could sustain the part of a son.[4]

The ties created by this unavoidable domesticity extended far beyond parent and children. All descendants in the male line of a common ancestor were considered as kinsmen, and through five generations the relationship was nicely graded in order of proximity. To make the distinction clearer, the members of each generation, in addition to their surname, often had a common element in their personal names as well so that their place in the scale could be told at a glance. Juniors, reckoned by generations, and in the same generation by age, owed respect and obedience to their seniors, and the duty was enforced by the laws of the state, which punished more severely an offence by a junior towards a senior, and less severely one by a senior towards a junior, than in the case of two unrelated persons. The question was also important when it came to adoption, for the strict theory was that you must choose a successor from among your kinsmen of the generation immediately junior to your own, to which your natural son would have belonged. A cousin, for instance, would not do, while a nephew or a cousin's son would suit perfectly.

It was the Confucian ideal that families should stay undivided through the generations, contributing by their labours to their joint support. Such a group would retain its identity although its members were constantly changing, for, apart from birth and death, daughters would leave the family to marry while other girls came into it as brides. In most cases the land would provide a livelihood, though if a member went to work away from home he would remit to the family what was left from his earnings after he had paid for his keep. The affairs of the group were administered by the family head, who was usually the most senior male, though on occasion a younger member of outstanding ability might hold the post. But the family property was owned by all members jointly. If a junior was caught with his hand in the cash-box, he could not be accused of theft; his offence was the attempted misuse of family funds without authorization. The notion, then, of personal property was rather faint, group ownership being regarded as the normal mode, but this fact, which is not irrelevant to political developments in contemporary China, has for most foreign observers been obscured by another, namely that the obedience owed by sons rendered it impossible for them to restrain a parent who might be wasting the family estate. In most parts of the country, however, a father who wished to sell land would not find a buyer unless his adult sons joined in the conveyance.

6

Here and there a great household, unbroken for generations, existed as if to provide an example of perfection, but for the mass of the people human nature itself made the ideal unattainable and it was acknowledged to be the rule rather than the exception that after their parents had died sons should establish separate homes with their wives and children. Quarrels between daughters-in-law were usually alleged to be the reason, and it often happened that even during the parents' lifetime, and with their permission, married sons set up on their own. All sons, whether by wives or concubines, shared equally, and distribution of the estate was generally made by drawing lots. Girls were entitled to their keep until marriage and then to a dowry. When partition happened during the parents' life, the latter retained a portion of the estate for their own support, and this in turn was divided on their death between the sons.

Most of the rights and duties of kinship stayed unaffected by the separation, and the new families which had come into being on the division of the old one commonly found themselves joined by economic as well as moral ties. For even a poor household was likely to own some items of property which could not be broken into parcels; a fruit-tree, for instance; a set of agricultural tools; or perhaps a water-buffalo. The only sensible thing to do in such a case was to hold these objects in common. Richer people might have a shop or business which, instead of selling and dividing the proceeds, it would be more profitable to leave intact and manage jointly. In this way, as the new families formed a clan, so the clan often had its property, and when the clan was numerous and wealthy this could be very extensive indeed. The tablets of the common ancestors, instead of being kept in the house of one of the members, would be lodged in an elegant temple, for the maintenance of which land would be dedicated. Schools and other institutions would be founded. In the southern provinces especially clan organization was highly developed and undertook many of the functions of local government.

The relationships based on birth, between parents and children, brothers, and so on throughout the clan, were considered to be created by nature itself and indissoluble by man. Marriage, however, was put into a different category and was regarded as a contract which, in certain circumstances, could be terminated by the parties. This bald statement, however, would be misleading if

7

it suggested that divorce was treated lightly or was of frequent occurrence. On the contrary, it was thought to be one of the greatest of misfortunes, just as marriage – or at least the taking of a wife, as opposed to a concubine – in spite of the absence in it of any sacramental quality, was the most momentous transaction in a man's life and was surrounded by everything that could impress the mind with the solemnity of the event.

Wife and concubine were distinct not merely in degree but in kind, and as concubinage was limited in practice to a relatively small part of the population we can leave discussion of it until we have dealt with marriage proper. This, in the eyes of the State always, and in popular custom usually, was intended to be monogamous. The spouse had to be from a different clan from that of her husband, and in fact the general prejudice went further and forbade a union between partners bearing the same surname, even when no consanguinity was traceable and although the paucity of Chinese surnames at times rendered the prohibition inconvenient. Assent to the match was signified not by the parties themselves but by representatives called 'authorizers'; by parents, if alive, or otherwise by senior clansmen. When it was the parents who authorized the marriage, the consent of the parties was not necessary. Finally, when an auspicious day had been chosen, the bride was taken to her husband's family in a red sedan chair, usually attended by musicians. This ostentation, together with the use of matchmakers, fulfilled the purpose of publicity, for there was no registration by any government office. In the nuptial chamber the groom unveiled his bride and, in theory, looked upon her face for the first time.

There was no minimum age for the formation of a marriage, and as sexual consummation was not a requisite of validity, weddings between young children were quite common. Frequently a peasant boy of ten or less would be given a wife of eighteen or twenty who looked vigorous enough to be useful on the land. But the most quintessentially Chinese institution was posthumous marriage, which often occurred when one of the parties died during betrothal. A relatively humane form of this was when a dead girl was buried with her fiancé's family, and honoured as his first wife by the children of any marriage he contracted later. If the posthumous union was carried out on the young man's death the girl was condemned to enter his family as his widow, adopting a

8

son to perpetuate the fiction. Sometimes two dead children were dubbed husband and wife in this way, and offspring adopted for them. Such an arrangement showed the love of their families towards the deceased and a concern that their memory should be kept alive.

The groom's parents paid an agreed sum in money or goods to the family of the girl. In peasant society this was to all intents and purposes a bride-piece, but among people of standing it was a point of honour that on the marriage the gift should be handed back, together with the girl's dowry, to form a nest-egg for the young couple. This was kept apart from the general family property, and later, on partition, instead of being divided it passed intact to those for whom it was intended. Thus, even in a joint family, a son and his wife did not lose their identities in the mass, but made up a distinct 'apartment' of their own, as it was called, which in due course became a separate family.

The wife was deemed to form one person with her husband, and to share his rank in the household. True, during his life it was he who exercised the rights and powers of the parental status, but after his death his authority passed to the widow. At all times she was entitled to respect from her children equal to that enjoyed by her husband. To be sure, when a son was of an age to manage family affairs, it was more seemly that he should carry out this duty, but in the privacy of the home he was obliged to listen to his mother's injunctions. During her widowhood, for instance, there could be no partition of property without her consent. This high esteem paid to the mother must be particularly borne in mind if the history of the Court of Peking in the last half century of the Empire is to be at all intelligible.

We have already noticed that the idea of personal, as opposed to group property was very faint. It could be said that a father in relation to his sons had no personal property to which he could frustrate their hopes of succession, as a will could not defeat the claim of an heir-at-law, and therefore all he left at his death was liable to be divided accordingly. Yet, curiously enough, women were allowed some property of a personal nature. A wealthy bride's jewellery was looked upon as belonging to her. What was more important in ordinary families, a wife's savings from household expenses as well as certain part-time earnings from needlework and the like were deemed to be hers to dispose of as she wished, and she often left them to her daughters who, as we have seen, were not entitled to family property, beyond their claim to a dowry and maintenance until marriage. Besides this, it is worth remarking that in one respect a woman, on becoming a widow, gained a freedom that a man could never achieve. In theory, a widower, no matter what his age, could be obliged to take a second wife by his parents' orders. A widow, on the other hand, could not be forced to remarry against her will, either by her husband's parents or her own.

While the wife was chosen as a rule from a family of equal standing with that of the husband, a concubine, as might be expected with an institution found only among people of means, almost invariably came from humbler origins. She never shared her husband's status, but was reckoned simply as a member of his family. On a wife's death a concubine was not automatically elevated to fill the vacancy; an additional ceremony of marriage was required for such a promotion. There was no limit to the number of concubines allowed at one time, and of course no consent on the wife's part was necessary.

It was in the matter of divorce that the distinction between the two kinds of spouse became most obvious. Marriage and concubinage could both be terminated by mutual consent and in both unilateral repudiation was available only to the man. But whereas a wife could be put away only for cause, a concubine could be dismissed at will. The 'causes' to be alleged against a wife were seven in number, beginning with unchastity and continuing with such faults as not bearing a son and disobedience to parents-in-law. A characteristically Chinese touch was the provision that even these 'causes', except unchastity, could not be invoked in three cases; namely when a man had risen to eminence from modest beginning and wished to be rid of the wife of his youth, when a wife had shared with her husband the austerities of mourning for his parents, and last of all when the woman had no place to go. With regard to the first of these exceptions, it should be said that in the twentieth century when under the Republic the old law was no longer enforceable Chinese public opinion was much shocked by the actions of Sun Yat-sen and Chiang Kai-shek, each of whom dismissed his original wife to marry a younger and more sophisticated woman.

Quite apart from the strong social disapprobation of divorce, which has already been noticed, a wife in the upper classes was protected by the knowledge that any unjust repudiation would be resented as an insult to her own family, while among the peasantry she was too valuable an asset to be thrown away lightly. Even though a concubine rarely came from a family powerful enough to help her, once a son had been born even she had little reason to fear being abandoned. Like a wife, she sometimes had property of her own, and indeed – although the circumstances must have been most unusual – there has been found a deed-of-sale from the middle of the nineteenth century in which the vendor declares that he is parting with a piece of land in order to repay out of the purchase money the principal and interest of a loan made to him by his concubine. Finally as regards third persons, a concubine generally stood in the same relation to her husband as a wife. For instance, in the case of adultery, which was a crime, a concubine and her paramour were punished as severely as if a wife had committed the offence.[5]

Such, in its salient features, was the Confucian system of the family. The essential part of it, namely the veneration of ancestors, respect towards parents and seniors, and desire for sons, was common to all classes of Chinese society. But in other points it tended to be noticeably weaker the lower one descended in the social scale. It can be readily understood that a father whose only child was a daughter might be unwilling to lose her on marriage and it was not uncommon in those circumstances to stipulate that a son-in-law should himself move into the house. According to strict theory, the newcomer as an outsider was permanently debarred from the ritual succession, and a member of the clan must in addition be chosen for that purpose. Yet in a peasant family, such an extra adoption would be to the material detriment of the daughter, and the claims of natural affection were consequently permitted to override the law, with the result that in the following generation the daughter's sons were given her surname and were treated in all respects as if they had been born from the male line. Again, the law forbade a woman, who had been divorced for unchastity, to marry her paramour, yet in more rough and ready circles the prohibition was disregarded. Similarly, the dynastic codes provided severe punishment for those who sold or leased their wives to other men, and it would be hard to conceive of an action more repugnant to Confucian prejudices. But the mere fact that it was legislated against would suggest that it occasionally happened, and modern research has disclosed the customs which governed paternal rights over children born in such cases. Even so, we must remember that the sale of wives was practised in equivalent strata of English society until well into the nineteenth century.[6]

If Confucianism, as we have seen, preferred to avoid the discussion of the supernatural, it was not on that account less concerned with man's place in the universe. The elaborate doctrine of family relationship was considered to derive its validity from the principles regulating the cosmic process, to such an extent that any breach of the duties imposed by it would, unless properly expiated, throw disharmony into the rhythm of nature itself. But the matter did not rest there. Every aspect of human activity had its correspondence in the physical world and it was a wise precaution to make sure that business of moment should not be undertaken at a time or in a manner likely to disturb the concord. Astrologers calculated horoscopes and designated lucky and unlucky days, while another body of consultants, the geomancers, gave advice on the proper use and development of land, basing their opinion on what was called the 'wind and water' or the natural features of the terrain, interpreted in a highly technical manner. Sites for houses were chosen according to this science, and as an infelicitous building might bring misfortune not only to its occupier but to all the neighbourhood, the State, if necessary, enforced conformity to the rules. But it was in the selection of a grave that geomancy was specially important. Any method of disposal of the bodies of the dead other than burial was forbidden by law and it was a wretchedly poor family that did not make provision as adequately as it could for the interment. Coffins were often procured in advance and kept ready for use without any feeling of morbidity. In the course of centuries grave mounds dotted the countryside everywhere; and even when land had to be sold rights of way were retained to enable the former owners to make periodic visits to the tombs of their ancestors.

Supernatural Religion: Buddhism, Taoism, Islam

In the eighteenth century when accounts of the Confucian system became available in Europe, Voltaire and others praised China to the skies as a nation of philosophers, free from all taint of superstition and priestcraft, and a model to the world of how rational beings ought to manage their affairs. Certainly the sobriety and common sense of Confucius and his disciples must have made a deep impression on men who had not long since emerged from the horrors of the wars of religion and the black atrocities of the witchcraft trials. Yet if Voltaire had actually visited China he would have been forced to qualify his enthusiasm. Eighty years ago a Chinese Catholic priest amused himself by compiling a list of the divinities worshipped by his countrymen. There were spirits representing every natural phenomenon, the gods of fire, water, thunder, rain, wind, smallpox, as well as those who stood for objects of human artifice, such as the gods of city moats, of city walls, and of beds. Heroes of myth and history were asked to ward off sickness and danger, and their cult was often celebrated with a Mediterranean exuberance. A curious example of this process of deification could be observed a few years ago in Shanghai. About 1870 a foreigner opened a livery stable in the very middle of the International Settlement, opposite the Racecourse, and as a decoration put two statues outside the gate. These were lay figures of Chinese men in ancient dress, but nobody had the faintest idea whom they represented or indeed if they were intended to stand for anyone in particular. The years passed, motor cars came on the scene, and the stable was pulled down and shops erected in its place. Yet the images were allowed to stay, for they had become the centre of a thriving worship. Joss-sticks burning in front of them filled the air with the smell of incense and passers-by had to walk in the road to avoid tripping over the old women kowtowing on the pavement, not one of whom, it is safe to say, could have told you to whom or what she was praying. At last in 1948, by which time the statues had survived the International Settlement itself, and all Shanghai had returned to Chinese rule, the municipal authorities, on the grounds that the flaunting of such superstition under the noses of foreign visitors was harmful to national prestige, decided they must be taken away and dumped in a field outside the city. On the day of the removal, a large force of soldiers had to be called out to control the crowd, and for a while it was touch and go whether the affair would develop into a riot.[7]

It was on such polytheistic foundations that the organized religions were erected. The most important of these was the

13

Buddhist Church, which though never attaining the position it holds in Ceylon or Burma, had long since lost any stigma from its alien origin and was accepted as part of the ordinary background of life. No doubt it owed this easy naturalization to the fact that the Mahayana school of doctrine, which was the form of the faith introduced into China, with its pantheon of miracle-working bodhisattvas, all ready to lend an ear to the voice of distress, harmonized better with the pragmatical native temper than the more austere and authentic Buddhist tradition which told a man that salvation could come only from within himself. As with religions everywhere, it was the women who were its mainstay, and their influence ensured that when bereavement came to a house, the family of the deceased – provided their means ran to it – would hardly ever fail to have a requiem said to promote his posthumous welfare. In the Mahayana teaching, Nirvana was presented in the shape of a blissful paradise to which prayers and good works, after a cycle of transmigrations and purgatorial interludes, would convey the soul. The practice of the rites of Chinese Buddhism was to provide insurance against the risk of the theory's being true. So much is admitted in a little Catechism, published in 1919 with the hope of winning adherents. There are two initial dogmas which the convert must accept, says the pious author. These are that every man has a soul which survives death and that in due course this soul returns to attach itself to a new body. Unfortunately, he goes on, in China neither of these dogmas is much believed in.[8]

If the dubious possibility of a future state was provided for by Buddhism, this present life was chiefly under the patronage of another and more indigenous faith, namely that of the Taoists. The name is sufficiently well known in the West from the School of philosophy, said by legend to have been founded by Lao-tzu in the sixth century BC, which advocated harmony with nature, not, in the Confucian mode, by the maintenance of a planned social order, but by abstention from such endeavours and the surrender of oneself to the *Tao* or 'Way' of the universe. It was an attitude of mind as characteristically Chinese as its Confucian antithesis, and in the domain of art its inspiration was especially potent. But it would be a mistake to insist upon too close a connexion between the philosophy and the organized church. The organization of the Taoist faith came into being in the early centuries of the Christian era as a deliberate adaptation of the Buddhist establishment to suit the needs of the native religion.

The compliment was soon returned, and many purely Chinese features were incorporated in the local Buddhist practice, to such an extent that in many aspects the distinction between the two creeds would be hard to define. Generally speaking, however, the Taoists boasted that their adepts could acquire certain magical techniques which enabled them to control natural processes. They also preached a doctrine of rewards and punishments to be received in a future state, but it was essentially the former claim which attracted worshippers in search of panaceas for health and longevity.

These faiths, Confucian, Buddhist and Taoist, have sometimes been called the three religions of China, and if we leave aside the question of whether Confucianism may properly be termed a religion or not the statement is fair enough. But we must bear in mind that to the vast majority of people the three were in no sense mutually exclusive. To be sure, here and there a dyed-in-the-wool Confucian scholar would leave instructions that on his death no Buddhist rigmarole was to be chanted over his remains, but such bigotry was rare, and in one and the same family together with the observance of the Confucian duties, Taoist deities would be turned to in sickness, and Buddhist services would give consolation at a funeral. Even so, the more cultivated a household, the more likely it was that the resort to the supernatural would come primarily from the women, while the men watched tolerantly, grumbling now and then at the expense.

Provided that public order was not threatened, as happened occasionally when some local miracle-working cult got out of hand, the State, although itself committed to the support of Confucianism, did not interfere with Taoist or Buddhist beliefs as such. Yet both religions contravened one fundamental Confucian precept in that they tended to encourage men and women who took their doctrines seriously to abandon their filial duty and retire from family life into the seclusion of monasteries and convents. Such a practice, if carried to excess, would, it was felt, be a social evil and therefore during the seventeenth and eighteenth centuries, it had been regulated and discouraged by various statutes incorporated into the dynastic code. Finally, the general discipline of monks and nuns was in the hands of officers responsible to the state, and temples and monasteries could not be established without the government's permission.

Yet religious people of both faiths were found throughout the country; their celibacy often enough the object of scandal and ridicule, but even at their worst, contributing immeasurably to the charm and diversity of the Chinese scene, and at their best giving refreshment to minds parched with the aridity of life. For pious laypeople, Buddhism especially was a matter of abstaining from meat on certain holy days – permanent abstention was left as a rule to monks and nuns – and of acquiring merit by the performance of acts of charity. The scope of this virtue was deemed to extend to the brute creation, and the faithful would buy captive birds to set them free, or put fish back into the water. But none of these lay believers would have considered himself a Buddhist in the way a man will tell you he belongs to such and such a Christian church. In China, the only people who would have announced their faith so uncompromisingly were those who adhered to an alien religion.

The most important of these was Islam – Christianity we can leave until later – which seems to have been carried to the port of Canton by Arab merchants within a few years of the Prophet's preaching, but of which the main current flowed in during the following centuries by way of Central Asia. Besides the inhabitants of Turkestan, the Muslims of China proper, about ten million in number, could be divided into two classes – those who formed a local majority as they did in the north-west and in the south-western province of Yunnan, and those who were scattered as a minority throughout the rest of the country. Whatever tincture of foreign blood was at their origin, they were both now considered thoroughly Chinese in speech and race, but were distinguishable from the mass of their countrymen by their aversion to pork. Even this they turned to good account by opening restaurants which specialized in mutton and beef, and as they had no scruple in selling wine their establishments were well patronized. Mosques were found in all the main cities, and religious purity was maintained by an avoidance of intermarriage with pagans.

CHAPTER II

TRADITIONAL CHINA [2]

The vicissitudes of Empire – the Manchus and their dynasty – the machinery of government – the scholar-gentry – the peasants – manufacture and industry – commerce – the 'mean' classes

The Vicissitudes of Empire

THE notion of a peaceful society regulated harmoniously by laws drawing their authority from nature itself had been present with special urgency in the mind of Confucius because the world of the Warring Kingdoms which he knew formed so sharp a contrast with his ideal. He had been in his grave for two and a half centuries before one of these principalities, the state of Ch'in, defeated all its rivals and in the year 221 BC united the whole land in obedience to its ruler, who is known to history as the First Emperor. Even then, the new peace seemed worse than the old disorder, so abominable was the tyranny, and when in a few years the First Emperor was removed from the scene by death, the house he had destined to an eternity of power collapsed under rebel assault. Yet the throne passed intact into the hands of the most able of the insurgents and a fresh dynasty, that of the Han, ruled over the land. A pattern had thus been established for the future. From then on for two thousand years the normal condition of China was to be unity under an imperial government, but if such a government made itself insupportable whether by its exactions or its inefficiency it would sooner or later be overthrown and another dynasty would take its place. As regards efficiency, the great test from the earliest times was the maintenance of public works, in particular the damming and control of the Yellow River on which the economy of North China depended. This necessity was the chief reason why a strong central authority was regarded as essential to the general welfare. In fact, a dynasty on succeeding to the throne would correct the faults of its predecessor, and for a few generations prosperity would return. Then gradually decay would set in, and neglect and peculation between them would ruin the projects so laboriously devised, so that a vagary of the weather was sufficient to bring calamity. The peasantry, unable in such circumstances to bear the weight of taxation, would revolt, and if the dynasty was unable to regain its grip on the situation it too would disappear from the earth.

Of the most successful dynasties, whose names are known throughout the world, the T'ang, the Sung, the Ming, each reigned for about three centuries: the Han was even more enduring, for it lasted, with a brief usurpation in the middle, from 202 BC to AD 220. Other houses had a much shorter life: some of them moreover did not establish their authority over the whole country, and dynasties and anti-dynasties partitioned the land between them. This state of affairs was viewed as forming part of the rhythm of nature, and the most celebrated of Chinese historical novels *The Tale of the Three Kingdoms*, which describes just such a division at the fall of the Han, begins with the declaration that when the Empire has for ages been united, division must come at last, while after long division unity is equally inevitable. Perhaps the second part of this statement is the more important. During the rule of a dynasty, attention was not directed to what was to come after it – speculation of the kind would have been the blackest treason – but in a period of chaos, such as China passed through in the first half of this century, the sentiment that unity was bound sooner or later to prevail was of the greatest political significance.

A good Confucian, although not dissenting from the proposition that a corrupt regime might justifiably be overturned by its subjects, would have expressed the idea in another way. To him the essential function of the emperor was to be the mediator between mankind and an impersonal godhead called *T'ien* or Heaven in which resided the control of the forces of nature. When there was a dispute between rival claimants – as happened on the collapse of a dynasty – Heaven itself signified its preference by bestowing its Mandate on one of the candidates, and the choice was rendered manifest in the eyes of all the world by the victory of the favourite, who was thenceforward recognized to be the Son of Heaven. In its regularity and decorum his life should be attuned to the harmony of the universe, while any lapse from grace on his part created a discord of which the consequence was all too often drought, floods and other disasters. Even then the balance could be restored by imperial self-accusation and repentance, and the right order of the seasons would be resumed.

When the sovereign came to die, the Mandate was transmitted to his successor, who was appointed according to the principles of Confucian family law described in the last chapter. This meant that the throne must pass to a male of the imperial clan, who belonged to the generation immediately junior to that of the deceased ruler. Sons of course had a prior claim and by the early nineteenth century it had become the practice for a reigning emperor to make a secret nomination in writing of the son whom he considered most fit for the post and have the document made public at his death. If the emperor had no sons of his own, a successor would be chosen in the normal manner from nephews or remoter kinsmen, just as in the case of an ordinary adoption. The rule that he must come from the next generation was of great importance, and an infringement of it in 1875, as we shall discover, was regarded as a national disgrace.

Of the public works carried out by the First Emperor of a united China in the third century BC by far the most costly was the building, or rather the completion, of the Great Wall, for that extraordinary fortification already existed in bits and pieces. From remote antiquity the nomads of the northern wastes had proved themselves uncomfortable neighbours of the settled Chinese lands and defence against their incursions was recognized to be an urgent necessity. Even the Wall, with its fifteen hundred miles of battlements and turrets, was effective only so long as it was manned by the soldiers of a strong and determined government. That was certainly the case during Han times, and the flood of barbarism, deflected westwards by the rampart, rolled across the Eurasian continent to press upon the Roman Empire. But when the Han dynasty had fallen, and unity had for a while given way to chaos, the Wall was no protection and the northern provinces were not merely plundered but even occupied by invaders from beyond the pale. Often these newcomers were already tinctured by Chinese culture, and once established on the soil of the Middle

Kingdom their chieftains felt justified in accepting the celestial mandate and becoming the emperors of dynasties which appear in history with as good a title as their purely Chinese rivals who maintained themselves at a safe distance in the Yangtze Valley and beyond. In the thirteenth century even this bastion of cultural integrity was overrun, when the Mongols occupied the whole country, and Kublai Khan reigned as the undoubted Son of Heaven from Peking, now for the first time made capital of China. A hundred years later the house of Ming had expelled the aliens and the country was once again under native rule. Then as the generations succeeded one another, the seemingly inevitable putrefaction began to manifest itself. Affairs of state were entrusted to the management of eunuchs and palace women. Armies of rebellious peasants marched across the land until in May 1644 one of them seized Peking itself and its leader, following the immemorial tradition, took his seat on the Dragon Throne, conveniently left vacant by the suicide of the last Ming sovereign. But his self-confidence was premature, as it was not to a Chinese insurgent but to a Tartar prince from over the Wall that the unpredictable whim of Heaven vouchsafed the mandate of Empire.

The Manchus and their Dynasty

For many centuries the region foreigners call Manchuria had formed part of the periphery of the Chinese world, where it was known simply as the North-East. The most southerly portion of it was occupied by Chinese colonists while on the steppes of the western marches Mongol nomads wandered with their flocks. The rest of the country was inhabited by Tungus tribes who lived in the main by hunting and fishing. There was, however, no hard and fast cultural demarcation. Mongols and Tungus had intermarried freely, and to both peoples, especially their rulers, there had been frequent Chinese admixture. The Tungus living on the frontier of the Chinese domain had most clearly been influenced by Chinese civilization. They practised a fair amount of agriculture and their chiefs, who dwelt in walled towns or fortresses, often became rich by selling such articles of luxury as furs and pearls, as well as the finest ginseng, the greatly prized medicinal root, to the Chinese market. These chiefs were childishly vain of any marks of honour that the Chinese Court might condescend to bestow on them. In particular, they were very careful to have their accession to the chieftainship ratified by the emperor. The Chinese claimed sovereignty over the whole region and from time to time tightened the strictness of their control: for example the Ming dynasty, in the first vigour of its youth, had sent a fleet to the mouth of the Amur. But by the beginning of the seventeenth century, apart from the colonial areas of the south, Chinese rule in Manchuria amounted nowhere to more than a somewhat vague suzerainty, which Peking was content to maintain by encouraging the Tungus to dissipate their energies in inter-tribal conflicts.

One of the chieftains the Chinese condescended to patronize was a man named Nurhaci. By an adroit mixture of war and diplomacy Nurhaci gained a position which threatened to upset the balance of power, and the Peking government decided it was high time to give support to his rivals. They little knew with whom they were dealing. In 1616 Nurhaci proclaimed himself Khan, and two years later, declaring war on the Ming dynasty, marched against the Chinese settlers. Peking sent its best commanders to take the field, but Nurhaci seemed irresistible, and before his death in 1626 he had established his headquarters deep inside the Chinese zone in the city of Mukden.

By this time the Chinese colonists were aware of the futility of looking for support from their home government. Many of them chose to safeguard their wealth by transferring their allegiance to the invaders who were only too glad to make use of their services. So far the establishment created by Nurhaci was of an essentially military nature, consisting of eight companies, or 'banners', between which his warriors were distributed under the leadership of his sons. While the war should last, the banners were to be allies and to obey a supreme commander – Nurhaci during his lifetime, and after his death one of the banner-leaders elected to the post – but in peace it was intended that they should be to all intents and purposes independent. It seems that Nurhaci never contemplated the conquest of China, and that he felt this simple organization would be adequate to give his people the mastery of Manchuria. His son and successor Abahai, although elected according to plan, breathed from the beginning of his administration, a more sophisticated atmosphere and listened with pleasure to the Chinese renegades who recommended that his affairs were now sufficiently prosperous to require the setting up of an autocratic government on the Chinese pattern. As if to emphasize the break with the old tribal past, the conquerors in 1635 assumed the style of 'Manchus'. The origin of this word, which was to become so celebrated throughout the world, is obscure; but the most likely theory is that it was derived from the name of the Bodhisattva Manjusri, whose cult had long been practised among the Tungus. The regime too was given a fresh title and was proclaimed as the 'Ch'ing' or 'Pure' Dynasty.

Thus reshaped the Manchu power appeared more unshakeable than ever. In 1638, after a short campaign, the King of Korea was forced to withdraw allegiance from the Ming and to acknowledge Abahai as his suzerain. The subjugation of Inner Mongolia had been completed three years earlier. Meanwhile, south of the Wall, where the house of Ming was manifestly approaching its end, an even greater destiny beckoned. The difficulty was that a full-scale invasion of China could move only by way of the pass at Shankaikwan, where the Wall comes down to the sea, and this was comparatively easy for the Ming to defend.

As it happened, the garrison of this important post in 1644 was commanded by one Wu San-kuei, himself of Chinese colonial stock, whose family estates were now occupied by the Manchus. When in April of that year the news came from Peking that the Ming emperor was dead, and the capital in the hands of a peasant army, Wu found himself compelled to make a momentous decision. On the one hand the insurgent leader invited him, as a brother Chinese, to join the resistance against the common enemy from the north. On the other, the Manchu regime, which now counted as its subjects many of his old friends and associates, offered him the prospect of power and honour in an ordered society. Wu salved his conscience by asking the Manchu army to enter China to put down the rebellion and avenge the Ming; but he must have known that, once they had gained the pass, the invaders would never leave. The Manchus swept down on Peking, which they entered on 6 June 1644, and soon afterwards a Tungus Son of Heaven, the first of ten, was installed in the Forbidden City. This was not Abahai, who had died the year before, but his son Fu-lin, a child of six. Some bitter fighting lay ahead but in the course of a few years the country had accepted its new masters.

The dynasty so established was fated to be the last to rule over China, for it endured until it was replaced by a Republic in 1912, and certain Chinese today attribute a large share of the calamities of their nineteenth-century history to the fact that at the moment when China came face to face with the western world her throne was occupied by aliens whose interests were not those of her own people.

At the present time the Manchus are totally submerged in the general Chinese population, from whom they are indistinguishable in speech and appearance. Even three hundred years ago, at the time of the conquest, the Manchus, especially those of the upper class, were heavily influenced by Chinese habits. To complicate matters still further, the Chinese renegades who went over to the winning side – most of whom were Manchurian colonists, but some joined the victors as they passed south of the Wall – were incorporated into a banner organization of their own, and their status and that of their descendants was in many respects identical with that of the native Manchus. If to all this we add the speed of cultural assimilation which was well advanced by the early eighteenth century, we may be led to imagine that the Manchus as a race had little influence on the national development of China. Such an opinion, however, would be very far from the truth.

To begin with, the Manchus transformed the appearance of the country by compelling the male population to shave the front of the head, and to wear the hair in a queue. Official dress was altered from the Chinese style, which resembled the Japanese kimono, with robes folding across the front, to the skullcap and Tartar gown with high collar and fastening at the side. In the first year or two of the conquest, especially in that centre of traditional Chinese culture, the lower Yangtze Valley, the opposition to these measures was intense, and thousands of people from all walks of life chose to die rather than adopt the marks of servitude. A man could avoid the issue by entering a religious order, becoming either a Buddhist monk, when he shaved his head completely and wore no queue, or a Taoist priest, with long hair gathered into a topknot in the genuine Chinese mode. In fact, many officials and scholars who could not find it in their hearts to accept the new regime, yet who shrank from sacrificing their lives, did retire from the world. In South China in particular, the country people now and then still point out some lonely temple where three hundred years ago, at dead of night, clandestine societies met together to swear allegiance to the house of Ming. But, in a few decades the queue had become an accepted part of daily life, to such an extent that in the nineteenth century attempts by rebels and reformers to get rid of it at first provoked intense annoyance among the people at large. Indeed, as recently as fifty years ago, on the very eve of the revolution that was to overthrow the Manchus, students who had parted with their queues while studying abroad found it expedient, if they were to avoid being pelted in the streets, to buy artificial ones from the Shanghai barbers, who were in this way enabled to start a new and profitable line of business.

It often puzzles a foreigner, who has got to know the Chinese at home, and who has found them to be the most exuberantly human of all races, to understand how, in the nineteenth century, there should have arisen the peculiar fear and loathing that their very name still excites in some Europeans. The mystery becomes clearer if we call to mind the appearance of the stage Chinaman, as we saw him in the melodramas of our youth, with his sinister drooping moustache and obscene pigtail. It is difficult to imagine that a character in the authentically Chinese attire of the Ming dynasty would have aroused such emotions. But as compensation, if the Manchus are to blame for the rather disagreeable international image of the traditional Chinese male, they are entitled to claim credit for a legacy of a happier sort. During the 1920s, in Shanghai, some dressmaker of genius had the notion of adapting the Manchu robe, then still commonly worn by men, to the use of women. This was the origin of the enchanting, the outrageous, 'slit-skirt', now eschewed by Communist China for its frivolity, but the fashionable dress of Chinese women everywhere else. If you inquire the name of this garment, you will be told that, at least in standard Chinese, it is called the *ch'i pao* or 'banner robe'. One assumes that the ladies of Hong Kong or Singapore have other things on their minds than the story of Nurhaci. Nonetheless, they are paying their own tribute to the memory of the old Tungus chieftain and his warriors of three hundred and fifty years ago.

During the days of their power the Manchu leaders were resolute in disapproving of the most quintessentially Chinese of all women's adornments, namely the age-old habit of footbinding; and forbade the practice to their own women. The compression of the feet was so painful a procedure, at any rate in its initial stages, that one might have thought the Manchu ladies would have been only too grateful for being spared the suffering. In fact the perverse creatures envied the superior elegance of their Chinese sisters and from time to time it was necessary to promulgate a new statute threatening them with severe penalties if they should put the bandages on themselves or their daughters.

The Manchus never forgot that they had come into China from outside and had conquered the country by force of arms. Always in their minds were the examples of previous invaders who had succumbed to the enervating influence of Chinese culture. The strictest provisions were laid down for bannermen to keep up the exercise of the military arts, skill in which was made a condition of their privileged status and of the subsidies granted to them and their dependants. In time, however, the duty was largely evaded. One of the main instruments by which they hoped to preserve their separate identity was the Manchu language. This is totally different from the Chinese, belonging to the great family of languages called the Ural-Altaic group, represented in Europe by Lapp, Finnish and Hungarian, and is written in an adapted form of the Mongol script. Yet, whereas Mongol has maintained its vitality to the present day, Manchu as a spoken language was in full decline by the middle of the eighteenth century, and is said now to survive chiefly among a community in Turkestan who are descended from Manchu bannermen.

Until the end of the dynasty, despite the virtual loss of their language, the Manchus retained enough of their indigenous characteristics to create a social barrier between themselves and the Chinese. In law, intermarriage between the two races was forbidden, though the practical effect of this prohibition must not be exaggerated. It was never intended to apply to unions between members of the Chinese and Manchu banners; and probably its only result was to fortify Manchu families in their reluctance to give their daughters in marriage to ordinary Chinese civilians.

Manchu men, apart from the imperial family itself, were not all deterred by statute from taking Chinese concubines. The Emperor, in order that he should not beget a successor in whom an admixture of Chinese blood might arouse inconvenient sympathies, was strictly limited to a seraglio of Manchu and Mongol ladies: in other words no Empress of the last dynasty to rule over China was of Chinese stock. Yet the subject race, even if kept with such care out of the sovereign's bed, was intimately present in his daily life, for the three thousand or more eunuchs who pullulated throughout the courtyards of the Forbidden City were all Chinese – the gelding of bannermen for this purpose was not allowed. From his childhood, then, a Manchu Son of Heaven was surrounded by Chinese influence of the least desirable sort. The disastrous example of the Ming, however, during the last years of which the central administration was to all intents and purposes in the hands of the palace castrati, was at first sufficient to ensure that under the new dynasty a rigorous discipline should be imposed on these creatures, and it was not until the nineteenth century, in the period we are about to discuss, that history repeated itself and the eunuchs once again resumed their old intrigues and ambitions.

The Machinery of Government

The speedy acquiescence of the population at large in Manchu rule may be attributed to the universal desire for peace and order after the chaos of rebellion and civil war. From the beginning, the conquerors demonstrated that they welcomed the co-operation of Chinese officials, and were anxious not to disturb the established pattern of society. In general, the administrative structure and the laws of the Ming dynasty were taken over unchanged. All authority, legislative, judicial, and executive, resided with the Emperor himself and was exercised in his name by an elaborately contrived civil service, appointment to which was in the great majority of cases dependent upon the candidate's passing a state-controlled examination in the Confucian classics. In practice, the sovereign made decisions on matters of importance after conferring with his senior advisors. The mode of doing this varied over the years, but by the nineteenth century the Grand Council, originally created in 1730 for the purpose of supervising the conduct of a war in Central Asia had become the highest consultative body. Its members, however, had no joint responsibility, but merely gave their advice as individuals. The main branches of government were looked after by their respective ministries in Peking. One institution especially deserving notice was the Censorate, whose function was to denounce the failings not merely of officials but even on occasion of the Court and the Emperor himself.

China proper was divided into eighteen provinces: in recent times their number has been added to, but the original units, which were mostly created by geographical conditions, remain with only slight modifications. Each had its provincial administrators, headed by a governor. Thirteen of them were grouped in twos; in one case three; and every group was subject to the overriding authority of a governor-general. Of the rest, the importance of Chihli, the metropolitan province in which Peking was situated, and the great extent of Szechwan, on the upper reaches of the Yangtze, were recognized by their each being given a governor-general to itself. Beneath the provincial government came circuits or prefectures, and lowest of all the district or *hsien*, as it was called in Chinese. There were about fifteen hundred of these hsien altogether, with an average population in the early nineteenth century of two hundred thousand souls. The hsien magistrates as the immediate representatives of governmental authority to the people were the backbone of the administration and were vested with judicial and executive powers. Naturally they required a staff of clerks and other subordinates to assist them in performing their duties.

The most noteworthy alteration of this system after the Manchu conquest was that in the ministries and other central departments Chinese officials found that they had to share their posts with Manchu counterparts, while there were some councils of special importance into which Chinese did not make their way. The conditions of entering into government service were notably less rigorous in the case of Manchu candidates, and terms of employment more generous. But in spite of these pinpricks the Chinese aspirant to the mandarinate saw before him every prospect of a dignified and lucrative career.

Much care was taken to ensure that no provincial government should develop into a quasi-independent satrapy. A man was not allowed to take up an official post inside his native province, nor could a magistrate marry a girl from a family in his jurisdiction. At the same time, length of tenure was restricted to about three years, and changes of appointment were often even more frequent. Certain officers, while within the framework of a provincial administration, were directly answerable to Peking; these included commissioners of taxes, provincial judges, and inspectors of examinations.

This immense apparatus of government, equipped as it was with a copious literature of statutes and precedents, might well have seemed at first glance designed to regulate society with a thoroughness hardly equalled elsewhere. Yet such an impression would have been most superficial and would not have survived a closer acquaintance with the actual working of the machine.

The truth was that neither the Manchu dynasty nor any of its predecessors had achieved that degree of control which the most laissez-faire of Western politicians would have thought the minimum requirement for the existence of a state. To be sure, the penalties for crime were severe, and the use of torture in extracting evidence shocked European sensibilities, though even the so-called 'death of a thousand cuts' was less horrible than the hanging, drawing and quartering meted out not so long since to traitors in England. Dr Morrison, an Australian doctor who became *The Times* correspondent in Peking, found towards the end of the nineteenth century that there was no more cruelty in Chinese prisons than had been practised in the convict settlement of Botany Bay a few decades earlier. But this very severity was deliberately used to deter litigants from having recourse to the justice of the state. One of the greatest of Manchu emperors, K'ang Hsi, in an edict of 1692 ordered magistrates to make their courts so dreaded by the people that they would not think of carrying their quarrels before them. According to the Chinese view it was not an essential part of the government's function to settle civil disputes, which should be resolved by arbitration between the parties themselves. Indeed, there was no distinct civil procedure: in order to sue your neighbour for debt, say, you had in effect to accuse him of behaviour amounting to a crime. If you persevered, you might be listened to, but you were none the less a trouble maker, and woe betide you if you failed to make out your case, for you would then incur the penalty which would have been suffered by the other party if he had lost. It followed from this doctrine that legal advice to a private citizen was itself a crime against the public order; in the old China the only professional lawyers were clerks who had specialized in that branch of knowledge and who were therefore employed by magistrates and in government departments.[1, 2]

If the state was decidedly unwelcoming to ordinary litigants, it will be readily imagined that there was even greater reluctance to interfere in the affairs of a family or of a clan. As we have seen, a son or daughter could not invoke the aid of the courts against a parent; such an act would itself be the most serious of crimes. In the course of the centuries it had been established that a parent's powers of chastisement over a child did not include the right of putting it to death; such a sanction, in the event of gross insubordination, might be imposed by the court at the parent's complaint. But anybody familiar with the Chinese newspapers of the last years of the empire will have seen reports of cases where men or women accused of a particularly aggravated offence against family morals were put to death – sometimes by burial alive – without any interference on the part of the public authorities. Of course these sensational events were the exception and not the rule, but the most humdrum of families had a jurisdiction outside the sphere of government control, and the total effect was to create a very sizeable breach in the structure of state power. The Confucian doctrine was at the same time the guiding philosophy of the empire, however, so that the government did not consider the privilege accorded to family seniors to be in any sense derogatory to its own prestige. But no such excuse could be made for another kind of infringement of authority, namely that which proceeded from the usurpation of power by local grandees.

Here, in fact, we are confronted with a noteworthy disagreement among the historians. Generally speaking, modern Chinese scholars, especially those who incline to the Communist view, are anxious to prove that by the early years of the nineteenth century the greater part of the soil was owned by a small minority of proprietors, while, according to the province, from sixty to ninety per cent of the peasantry was landless, and obliged to rent the fields of others. Against this, some maintain that at least half the peasants owned their own land, although to be sure the number of those who were forced to sell their farms and become tenants of others increased considerably during the economic distress of the nineteenth century. It is not disputed that the great estates whose rise was favoured by this same distress were more often than not organized for self-defence, with tenants compelled to serve when necessary as members of the landowner's private army. Sometimes, particularly in South China, wealthy clans would even hire mercenaries to fight in their private feuds with rivals, and the local magistrates either pretended to ignore what was passing, or if they took cognizance of the matter at all, tendered their good offices as peacemakers. It is obvious that in such circumstances a peasant could have little hope of enjoying the protection of the state even against the most brutal outrages, and we can understand why, in the famous eighteenth-century novel, *The Dream of the Red Chamber*, a magistrate, newly arrived at his post, is thankful to receive a list of those powerful families of the place with whom it was inadvisable to interfere. In a word, the imperial government, even at the best of times, was very far from possessing a monopoly of force throughout its dominions.[3]

The Scholar-Gentry

Usually, though, the dynasty had sufficient community of interest with the great proprietors not to worry unduly about their local influence. The Manchus, after all, had been brought into the country by the territorial magnates in order to suppress the peasant risings at the end of the Ming dynasty and in the course of a few decades the richer landowners had become firmly attached to their rulers, who confirmed them in their privileges and relied on them to form the backbone of the civil service. In theory, the examinations which gave entry to an official career were open to almost every section of the population, but in practice the lengthy process of education gave a great advantage to the sons of families rich enough to support them and to pay their teachers, for all schooling was privately maintained. The successful candidate found his efforts well rewarded. The prestige conferred by an academic degree was reinforced in the most practical way by the exemption of the holder from any public obligation to manual labour, as well as from flogging and other degrading forms of corporal punishment if he got into trouble with the law. He also enjoyed a certain indulgence in the matter of taxes. What was not less important was that, even if he did not take up government office, he was acknowledged as a social equal by those who did, and was deemed to have the capacity to perform certain functions of local administration lying beyond the scope of government proper. In the countryside it was he and his fellows who as leaders of the community acted most frequently as arbitrators in civil disputes, and who supervised public works, while even the least efficient could earn a living by teaching. This envied class formed slightly more than one-hundredth of the population.

The Peasants

The next in order of Confucian esteem were the tillers of the soil, that eighty per cent or more of the people upon whose shoulders the elaborate structure of Chinese civilization was erected. In all probability the difference of tenure between peasant owners and their lessee neighbours was of smaller consequence than the burden imposed upon them by government taxation or landlords' rents. Rents paid to the landlords, out of which land tax was paid to the government by the landlord, was rarely less than fifty per cent of the crop, and on occasion as much as seventy per cent. A peasant proprietor, having to pay land tax directly, was very much exposed to the rapacity of dishonest officials and was often in no better position than his neighbour, the leaseholder. An important cause of agrarian poverty was the Confucian law which by giving equal shares on partition to all sons, tended to split the land into ever smaller lots. It has been calculated that in the north, an average farm was about three acres, and about half that size in the south. This meant that in a bad year, the owner was able to offer little as security against a loan and could only raise funds at such exorbitant rates of interest that he was from then on to all intents and purposes in bondage to the usurer.

This state of affairs was nothing new in China, but by the early nineteenth century another development was aggravating the situation to a dangerous extent. This was the phenomenal increase in the population which from about a hundred million on the eve of the Manchu conquest had in two hundred years risen to three and a half times that number. No doubt the long domestic peace had played some part in this multiplication, but, as in the case of the parallel development in Europe, another reason was to be found. Like the potato in the West, maize, introduced into China from the New World at the end of the sixteenth century, provided a fresh source of nutriment. Whatever the cause of population increase, the result was a decided pressure on the land, with consequent agrarian unrest, and by the 1830s uprisings in one part of the country after the other were being heard of with disturbing frequency. Yet even at his poorest, the Chinese peasant was no serf and the respect shown to him by Confucian tradition was more than an empty formula.

Manufacture and Industry

The artisan was reckoned next in the social scale. Each type of manufacture regulated its activities and protected its interests by means of its separate guild. Small-scale handicrafts were the most numerous but there were certain large enterprises in which modern Chinese scholars claim to discern the stirrings of capitalism. These included the great porcelain industry of Ching-te-chen in Kiangsi, silk spinning at Nanking and elsewhere in the Lower Yangtze Valley, paper making at various centres and iron smelting at Fatshan near Canton. Coal-mining was an important pursuit at Mentowkow not far from Peking. On the whole, Confucian prejudice was rather opposed to the expansion of industry, as tending to divert labour from the basic activity of farming, or sometimes as being injurious to the amenity of a place. The geomancers, for example, were able to prevent brewing or oil pressing from being carried on within twelve miles of the capital. A paper manufactory at Yangchow on the Yangtze was ordered to shut down because it had insulted the written word by using as material wastepaper with characters on it. The Manchu government, too, was not happy to see large numbers of workmen – especially of the rougher sort such as miners – congregated in one place where a storm might blow up at any time.[4]

These big undertakings were as a rule run by partnerships fashioned very closely on the model of clan ownership. Indeed it was from this original that all Chinese commercial partnership was derived. The earliest form of such association was created when on the partition of a family the brothers continued to hold a shop or business in common. Later people unconnected by blood began to contribute to a joint venture, sharing the profits and the liabilities proportionately to their stake in the firm.

Commerce

Merchants were in theory the least regarded of all the respectable classes of society, but the richest of them were able to maintain social links with the upper bureaucracy into which they strove to introduce their sons, either by the normal examinations or by purchase. Probably the most famous were those to whom the government had farmed out the salt monopoly. The city of Yangchow was their special headquarters and the luxury of their life was a household word. Pawnbrokers formed another prosperous class. In the middle of the eighteenth century there were about seven hundred pawnshops in Peking alone. When in 1798 the minister Ho Shun was put to death for malpractice it was discovered that he owned seventy-five pawnshops and forty-two banks; a striking instance of how officials set their money to work, and how ineffectual Confucian contempt of trade was in circumstances of the kind.[5]

Such were the divisions of the respectable, or free, population. The scholar-bureaucrats stood at the summit, their dignity indicated by the very costume they wore, but entry to their class was always open, and in spite of a poor boy's great disadvantage in schooling, enough peasants' sons succeeded in the examinations to support the theory of equal opportunity. Nor, when nobility was conferred by the state, was a hereditary peerage thereby created, for a title diminished by one degree each generation and even the most exalted honour was extinguished in five lifetimes.

The 'Mean' Classes

Here we come to a distinction which promises to be of fundamental significance. In all the collections of Chinese imperial codes down to and including that of the Manchu Dynasty we find reference to another kind of person, namely the 'mean' or unfree members of the community. First of these come the slaves, and one could, without difficulty and by relying simply on the most accessible compilation of Manchu statutes, construct a law of slavery almost as detailed as that of Rome itself. The various modes of acquiring the servile status, by judicial process as a punishment for certain heinous crimes, by sale, by birth, as well as methods of emancipation, are all listed and defined with the utmost clarity. As in Rome, slavery was transmissible at nativity, and marriage between free and unfree was prohibited. Such research might well gratify the academic student of law, but it would be almost totally futile as a step towards understanding the structure of nineteenth-century Chinese society. For law books,

in China as in Europe, are specially prone to the gathering of cob-
webs and the jurisprudence of slavery, by 1840, was largely a
dead-letter. A few years later, certainly, male slaves, in the proper
sense, could not be found, as transported criminals were merely
prisoners. Only among the female sex could slaves be said to survive; 'slave-girl' seemed the right term for a child who was openly
sold into bondage. Yet even in her case the expression may have
been too severe. For whatever her maiden status, she married a
free man – there was in practice no other sort of man available –
and her children were free. Indeed, if she was at all pretty, she
could hardly avoid the lecherous attentions of her master in which
case she probably became a concubine, whose sons were for most
purposes every bit as good as those of a wife.[6]

Besides the slave, the imperial codes mentioned another group
of 'mean' persons, whose occupations were thought to render
them unworthy of entering the official class. These consisted particularly of entertainers, such as musicians, actors and prostitutes,
and certain menial functionaries. Like the slaves, they and their
descendants to the third generation were barred from competing
at the examinations. Males among them were not allowed to
marry a woman from the respectable classes nor could their own
daughters become the wives or concubines of officials, though the
girls' marriage with non-officials was not forbidden. Undoubtedly
the government succeeded to a certain extent in having these
restrictions respected, for the bureaucracy and the ways of entry to
it were very much in the public eye. Yet even so there were many
notorious violations of the rules. To give only one example, in
1887 an eminent mandarin, Hung Shen, took as his concubine a
young prostitute named Sai-chin-hua. There was nothing secret
about the business; the girl was carried to his house in a bridal
procession through the streets of Soochow, though at the time he
was in mourning for his mother and was bound by law to abstain
not only from increasing his seraglio but even from sexual intercourse itself. A few months later, his mourning over, Hung was
appointed Minister to Germany and Russia. As his wife did not
wish to make the journey, he took Sai with him instead, and for
over two years the former prostitute presided as first lady over the
Chinese legations at Berlin and St Petersburg. True, later on some
of Hung's enemies tried to raise the matter against him but before
his death in 1893 the charges had been dropped. The explanation

probably is that Hung was regarded with favour by the all-powerful Empress Dowager, and with such protection he was able with impunity not so much to defy the law – that would imply some theatrical bravado which was not in his mind – as to ignore it.[7]

To sum up, one is justified in saying that while the Chinese state recognized and sanctioned the class structure of its society, there was nothing which resembled a caste system.

CHAPTER III

THE WEST BREAKS IN

*The Catholic missionaries – Sino-Russian treaties – British envoys –
the opium traffic – Commissioner Lin at Canton – the war with
Britain – the Treaty of Nanking*

The Catholic Missionaries

THERE was indirect contact between China and the West since
Roman times, and in the thirteenth century the Mongol subjugation of much of the Eurasian continent made it possible for European merchants and travellers to journey overland to the Far East.
On the collapse of the Mongol empire this route was impracticable, and Europeans had to wait for the great voyages of
discovery before they could renew a direct acquaintance with the
Chinese world. But by 1516 the Portuguese were at Canton – forty
years afterwards they had installed themselves in nearby Macao –
and from that time on the traffic was never to be interrupted. On
its commercial side it assumed at the start the pattern it was to
keep for almost three hundred years. Foreign traders were not
permitted to reside or carry on business inside the country, but
dealt at certain appointed places on the frontier, under government supervision. For seafarers these markets were at the coastal
ports, and by the middle of the eighteenth century had been
restricted still further by being confined to Canton alone.

The Catholic missionaries did not lag behind the merchants, and
were luckier than they had been in gaining entry beyond the frontier. Assuming the dress of a scholar, and taking infinite pains to
win the goodwill of influential people, the Jesuit Matteo Ricci in
1601 founded a mission in Peking itself. To most of the Chinese
who came into contact with them, he and his followers were not

36

so much propagandists of a religion as experts in certain useful techniques, especially as regards mathematics and astronomy. In a more warlike domain they tried to stiffen the Ming armies by introducing the employment of cannon, but in the event it was the Manchus who benefited from the lesson, for the new weapon was soon incorporated into their armament and helped them enormously in the gaining of their victory.

The mission survived the change of dynasty and before long the fathers were on terms of intimacy at the Manchu Court. At the Tribunal of Mathematics and the Observatory Jesuits were entrusted with the preparation of the calendar, a task of vital consequence in that agrarian society. Others kept in order the clocks which had been imported as presents from Europe. Jesuit artists and architects in the eighteenth century contrived for the emperor's pleasure a Summer Palace a few miles from Peking, which the Chinese thought to be one of the wonders of the world. About the same time, another member of the Order carried out the first scientific cartographical survey of the whole country.

Enjoying such esteem as they did, the Jesuits could hardly fail to make converts, and in fact for a time they were markedly successful, especially among the ruling class of Manchus towards whom, after the establishment of the new regime, they deployed their best efforts. To make things easier, they saw no reason why needless difficulties should be set in the way of the faith and allowed their converts to continue the Confucian custom of honouring ancestors, arguing that the practice had no religious significance whatever. Meanwhile, their rapid advance had earned them the enmity of rival orders, particular of the Dominicans, and complaints were made at Rome of the Jesuit laxity. For years this controversy over 'the Chinese rites' agitated Catholic theologians. On their side the Jesuits had an idea of genius; they persuaded the emperor K'ang Hsi himself to certify that their interpretation was the true one.

Even this expert testimony was of no avail, and in 1718 the Holy See forbade converts to venerate their ancestors. Of course the decision was a cruel blow to all that the Jesuits had stood for; not only did it force Chinese Christians to abjure the most cherished tradition of their race, but it was a gross insult to K'ang Hsi, who at once issued an edict condemning the foreign religion. Even so, the Jesuits continued to be tolerated as artists and technical advisers to the Court, until later in the century when their Order was dissolved by the Pope and their house in Peking taken over by the Lazarists. During the first decades of the nineteenth century, persecution became more frequent, and a number of priests functioning in the provinces were put to death. Newcomers, mostly French, continued to enter the country secretly from Macao and to minister to their communities, which were scattered across the land as far as Manchuria and numbered about a quarter of a million souls. Most astonishing of all, a solitary Lazarist priest kept up the tradition of his Jesuit predecessors and as a servant of the Chinese state worked at the Peking observatory until his death in 1838. Protestantism can claim no part of this heroic endeavour; its first missionary to China, Robert Morrison, did not arrive until 1807, nor did he ever get farther than Canton, while co-religionists who followed him found themselves similarly halted at the coast.

Perhaps the greatest work of the Catholic fathers, and particularly of the Jesuits, was their introduction of China to intellectual circles in the West. Thanks to their memoirs and translations, an educated European in the eighteenth century had very likely a juster appreciation of Chinese culture than his descendants today. Macaulay ought to have been ashamed of himself for having to make that confession of ignorance to the House of Commons; by spending a few hours in any good library he could without difficulty have got acquainted not with the Chinese politics of 1840, but with what was more important, the basic principles of Chinese society and government. In this, Voltaire and other men of the Enlightenment showed a finer perception.

Sino-Russian Treaties

While western tradesmen and missionaries were making the long voyage by sea, another kind of European began to arrive across the continent itself. By a strange coincidence, the Manchus had scarcely occupied the Dragon Throne when the news reached them that their own homeland was being invaded from the north. The aggressors were the Russian Cossacks who in the space of half a century, beginning with their crossing of the Urals in 1580, had traversed the whole extent of Siberia to the shores of the Pacific. Furs were the immediate incentive for these adventurers, but land settlement was another and so it was with special interest that the pioneers in Eastern Siberia heard of a great river not far to the south which flowed through fields of wheat into the sea. This was the Amur, and in 1643–4 a Russian party navigated it to its mouth, a success which encouraged the despatch of military expeditions with the aim of incorporating all the land north of the river into the Russian dominions.

The natives of the country were Tungus hunters and fishers, closely related in race and language to the Manchus, and indeed the latter, in the course of the great reorganization which preceded their conquest of China had taken care to reduce into obedience their Tartar kinsmen across the Amur as far as the Stanovoi Mountains. No attempt was made to garrison the country, with the result that the Russians encountered hardly any resistance and were able to slaughter or enslave the inhabitants almost at will.

The reports of the invasion were very confused and the Manchus probably believed that the troublemakers were simply an offshoot of one of the northern peoples who had plagued the frontier from time immemorial. For this reason their response to their subjects' appeals for help was somewhat perfunctory, and a force sent against the aggressors was heavily defeated. This, the first battle in history between Russia and China, took place in 1652 near the site on the northern bank of the Amur of the modern city which bears the name of Khabarovsk in honour of the Cossack leader of three centuries ago.

After so sharp a lesson, Peking viewed the matter in a more serious light. Even then the new dynasty had so much on its hands in China itself, where the conquest still required to be consolidated, that it was thirty years before it felt free to give its undivided attention to the far north. When it did so, it was clear at once that the Cossacks were no match for the armies that China could put into the field against them. Meanwhile, quite apart from its Siberian expansion, Moscow had for years been trying to establish diplomatic relations with Peking. Linguistic incomprehensibility was the chief stumbling block, until the Russian envoys thought of using the good offices of the Jesuit fathers. The accession of Peter the Great created a favourable atmosphere for negotiation, since the new Tsar, having a war on his hands in the Baltic, could not risk a conflict with China as well, and was eager to replenish his treasury with the Chinese silver he saw the chance of acquiring in return for Siberian furs. On the other side, the Emperor K'ang Hsi was just as anxious for peace with Russia so that he could be free to deal with the affairs of Central Asia. All these reasons finally brought commissioners of the two parties to a conference outside the Russian settlement of Nerchinsk, where in May 1689 China signed her first treaty with a European power. The part played by Jesuit interpreters in the transaction was acknowledged by the fact that the authentic text was in Latin.

This Treaty of Nerchinsk, modified by another agreement concluded at Kyakhta in 1727, governed Sino-Russian relations for a hundred and seventy years. Russia renounced her claim to the Amur lands and recognized as Chinese all territory north of the river to the Stanovoi Mountains. Caravans of licensed traders were to be allowed to make periodic visits to Peking, but commerce between the two nations was mainly to be carried on at the frontier markets of Nerchinsk and Kyakhta.

In the course of the war in Manchuria, a number of Cossacks who had either been captured or who had surrendered voluntarily had been sent to Peking and enrolled in the Manchu forces. By the treaty of 1727 China agreed to receive and maintain a Russian ecclesiastical mission to look after the spiritual needs of these expatriates. The foundation lasted to our own day and until a few years ago one of the strangest experiences for a visitor to Peking was to go to the church where the gorgeous orthodox ritual was celebrated in front of what in the course of more than two centuries of intermarriage had become to the eye a purely Chinese congregation.

Besides priests, this resident mission included a group of students who were permitted to remain in Peking up to eleven years to learn the Chinese and Manchu languages. In this way, by the middle of the eighteenth century the Russian government had at its disposal a group of experts thoroughly conversant with Chinese affairs. Although the mission was religious in character, and in no sense an embassy, it was inevitable that now and then it should be called upon to perform duties of a diplomatic nature.

Trade with China was of the utmost importance to the Russian development of Eastern Siberia. In return for their furs they got a supply of manufactured goods which their colonists and administrators required for the purposes of daily life. Even so, as the eighteenth century drew to its close Moscow began to repent of its bargain and to hanker once more after its old ambitions on the Amur. Nor was this surprising, for the policy of the Manchus towards their north-eastern dominions appeared specially designed to provoke Russian cupidity. The most effective means of safe-guarding Manchuria from foreign aggression would have been to see that it was properly developed and settled. But this would have meant permitting Chinese immigration from south of the Wall, and in proportion as the Manchus were conscious of the loss of their racial characteristics under the all-pervading influence of Chinese habits, so they determined to preserve at least their home-land as a sort of national sanctuary. Thus it was that in the middle of the eighteenth century, Chinese settlers were denied entry to Manchuria altogether, and although the ban which was to remain for a hundred years was never fully enforced it had the result of keeping the north-east relatively denuded of population. To make things worse, no garrisons at all were maintained north of the Amur, and it was thought sufficient to carry out periodic inspec-tions of the frontier. So the Russians saw a potentially rich country going to waste. True, in exchange for renouncing their own claims to it they had won the privilege of trade, but even this had its drawbacks for it was stipulated in the treaty that commerce be-tween the two countries should be restricted to the overland route, and applications by Russia to be allowed to send her merchant ships to Canton met with a very sharp refusal.

British Envoys

On the other side, the nations engaged in maritime traffic, of whom by the middle of the eighteenth century Britain was the chief, considered they too had ample reason for complaint. A few de-cades earlier their ships had been allowed to call at a number of places including Amoy, Foochow and Ningpo, and the memory made the present limitation to the one port of Canton all the more galling. Then again the regulations with which they had to comply were nothing if not vexatious. They could deal only with a group of licensed merchants called the Thirteen Hongs (*hong* is the Chinese for 'firm'), who were entrusted by the government not only with the entire management of international commerce at Canton but also with the handling of all communications between aliens and the local authorities. The foreign merchants were confirmed to a narrow ghetto outside the city, from which they were allowed out at intervals to stretch their legs and enjoy a breath of fresh air. Even this uncomfortable residence was available only in the trading periods of summer and autumn and with the approach of winter they had to withdraw to Macao. Foreign women were not permitted to come to Canton at all. To add to the sense of exclusion it was a crime for a Chinese to give language instruction to a foreigner, and the export of Chinese books was forbidden. Both these last provisions were occasionally circumvented. The fact that the circumvention was not without danger is shown by the anecdote concerning the Chinese teacher of Robert Morrison, the pioneer of Protestant missions, who is said to have visited his pupil carrying a pair of shoes, in order to pass as a shoemaker, and with a phial of poison he could swallow in case of arrest.[1]

One result of their being kept at arm's length was that foreigners were permitted to settle their disputes among themselves, but trouble arose when Chinese were injured, for then the authorities assumed jurisdiction, and neither the substantive law nor the procedure of Chinese courts was calculated to reassure the spirits of a defendant. Often enough the man involved was sent out of reach in time, but on several occasions foreigners were put to death for what in western eyes was no more than accidental homicide.

The trade so anxiously sought was until the end of the eighteenth century markedly one-sided, consisting essentially of the export of Chinese goods, such as silk, porcelain, rhubarb and tea, against payment in silver, for the manufactured goods of the seafaring nations did not find so ready a market in China as the Russian furs. Imports were hampered still further by the vagaries of customs dues. True, the rate fixed by the central government was very moderate, never rising above four per cent, but thanks to the manipulations of local officials the amount levied often came to twenty per cent, and there was always much undignified haggling.

Twice in the space of a quarter of a century Britain had tried to reach an agreement with China which would open the country generally to those goods for which Britain at the height of the Industrial Revolution was anxious to find as many markets as possible. The first attempt was made in 1793 when Lord Macartney was sent to Peking to congratulate the Emperor Ch'ien Lung on the occasion of his eightieth birthday. Voltaire's admiration for China still influenced European minds, and the old monarch was regarded as the very type of enlightened ruler who would not fail to realize that Britain too was a powerful and civilized state, and would consequently make no difficulty over granting her reasonable requests. These were: that a British ambassador should reside permanently at Peking, while his Chinese counterpart would be welcomed to London; that more ports should be opened to British trade; that tariffs should be fixed and published; and finally that China should grant British traders the use of some small island as a station in the same way as the Portuguese had Macao.

London could not have chosen a better man, for Macartney was highly intelligent, cultivated, and easy-going. Ch'ien Lung appreciated the envoy's urbanity and responded to it with courtesy, but the mission as such, except that it had come further, was to him no different from any of the tribute-carrying delegations to which the Court was accustomed. To be sure, Macartney made such heavy weather over the ritual of kowtowing that he was good-humouredly allowed to do obeisance by a simple genuflection, but that was as far as his demands could be met. The Chinese Empire, he was told, had all the products it wanted within its own borders and there was in consequence no need for barbarian trade. Given China's then economic structure this was no more than the truth. As a token of the Emperor's benevolence Britain and the other western nations could continue to avail themselves of China's abundance to supply their own requirements at Canton as before. It was a sad disappointment, and to the British Ch'ien Lung's words must have sounded like the boast of a megalomaniac. In 1816, London made another attempt to open the door by dispatching a second mission under Lord Amherst, but this time neither the ambassador nor the Emperor, Ch'ien Lung's son, had the tact of his predecessor and Amherst was expelled without an audience.

The Opium Traffic

If the chance of clothing North China in Yorkshire woollens seemed more remote than ever, the East India Company, who held the monopoly of British commerce at Canton, had at last found a way to achieve a more equitable balance of trade. Opium had been imported into China from an early date but in small quantities and as a medicine. It was not until well into the eighteenth century that the full possibilities of the commodity were realized, and the East India Company began to take advantage of its dominion in Bengal to cultivate the poppy. As the addiction gained ground, the demand for the narcotic increased. About 1750, the quantity imported did not exceed four hundred chests a year. By 1821 the figure was five thousand chests, and by 1839 forty thousand.

It was the social effects of this traffic that first aroused the government's attention, since the taste for the drug was especially prevalent among the official classes, who in their turn had acquired the habit from the wealthy merchants. In the metropolitan province, says a report of 1831, from the governor downwards there were very few mandarins indeed who did not, at least sometimes, smoke opium, and in 1835 the total number of addicts in the country was estimated at more than two million. Only the peasantry, it was thought, were free from the vice. But soon it was the economic rather than the moral danger that was causing concern. For the first time in history, the value of China's imports had become greater than her exports. During the twenty years ending in 1839 the discrepancy necessitated sending abroad a total of a hundred million ounces of silver. The treasury was alarmed by this outflow of wealth, but it was by the peasantry that the matter was felt most cruelly. Two kinds of currency were in use; silver and copper. The latter was employed in simple daily transactions, but taxation was estimated according to the former. Now the loss of so much silver in the opium trade meant that its value compared with that of copper was much increased, and in consequence farmers had to pay more copper cash to meet their land tax.[2, 3]

On several occasions the Peking government promulgated edicts forbidding the importation of opium, but for a variety of reasons the prohibition was ineffectual. In the first place, many, if not most of those whose duty it was to enforce the law were themselves addicts. Then again, the commerce was so profitable that it was not hard to find men who were willing to turn to smuggling, if the procedure so-called merited that name, for it was carried on with scarcely any pretence at secrecy. Merchants who were interested called on the foreign agents in Canton and, when the price had been agreed, were given a ticket with which they went in a launch to a storeship, lying at anchor off the coast, and claimed their opium. Once landed, the stuff was passed along a well-organized network till it reached its eventual customers.

There were Chinese who felt the absurdity of the situation and would have preferred to see the trade regulated since its suppression appeared impossible but it took courage to voice such an opinion. In 1836, however, one high official was brave enough to do so. He proposed that opium should be allowed into the country, and that it should be taxed as medicine, but that it must not be paid for in cash; Chinese goods should be exchanged for it instead. Addiction in officials was not to be tolerated, but a guilty party might avoid punishment by retiring from office. Ordinary citizens might deal in opium or smoke it with impunity. Further, the poppy should be cultivated in China, so that ultimately there would be no market for the foreign product.[4]

Some of those who shared these views, in particular certain members of the Canton administration, were now emboldened to express their approval publicly, and many more looked hopefully for a sign that the suggestion was going to be adopted. But the voice of austerity was not long in making itself heard. In 1838, another eminent mandarin in a memorial to the throne, delivered a scathing attack on his colleagues, whose corruption he blamed for the harm being done to the nation's health and prosperity.

There are opium-dens in every prefecture in the country, and they are kept as a rule by magistrates' constables and soldiers from the army, who gather together dissolute youngsters from rich local families to indulge in the pipe where they can't be seen. As most of the clerks in the magistracies share the same taste, they are sure to be protected. I beg Your Majesty to set a date a year from now after which all smokers who persist in their addiction will be put to death. For mark my words a man will bear the discomfort of a cure if he knows that by doing so he has earned the privilege of dying in bed, whereas indulgence in his craving will bring him to the execution-ground.[5]

The Emperor to whom the advice was addressed was Tao Kuang, a grandson of Ch'ien Lung, who on coming to the throne in 1821 had made it his first business to issue decrees against the use of opium, and now that somebody was at last proposing to enforce the law he thought the occasion deserved to be marked by a special degree of urgency. So he circulated the memorial to all governors of provinces and asked for their views. It was fairly clear which way the Emperor's own preference went. Even those with vested interests at stake hesitated to appear disrespectful both of the imperial will and the moral code, and contented themselves with warning of the need for prudence, or hinting that perhaps causes other than the opium trade were to blame for the economic crisis. In the light of what followed, it is highly significant that the most outspoken critic was Kishan, the Manchu governor-general of the metropolitan province, who declared:

> If a man is to fall foul of the law just for taking a pipe of opium, prisoners will be lined up along the roads, as there won't be room for them in the gaols. The whole thing is absolutely impracticable.[6]

Commissioner Lin at Canton

One man especially stood out in support of the proposal. This was Lin Tse-hsü, the governor-general of the two central provinces of Hupei and Hunan, who had distinguished himself in this post by his zeal in confiscating opium and smoking equipment, and in supplying medicine to those who wished to overcome the addiction. The prescription must have been effective, because we read that whenever he passed through a town, women in the street would kowtow to his sedan-chair in gratitude, calling out that thanks to him their husbands and sons had shaken off the evil habit and were regaining their health. He was now only too eager to let the Emperor hear the voice of experience.

> The sellers of opium are at present protected by the number of smokers in government offices. Consequently, although there is a law providing that a man who keeps an opium-den should be strangled, we never hear that a charge has been brought, let alone that a sentence has been executed. It may indeed seem reasonable to direct all our severity against the dealers and treat smokers with leniency, but the result is that the law as a whole becomes a dead letter.

The words were heeded, and before long Lin was informed that he himself had been chosen as the instrument to carry out the policy he had endorsed. In March 1839 he arrived at Canton as Imperial Commissioner.[7, 8]

He was fifty-four years of age and had never before had any

dealings with foreigners, although he used to boast that as a native of the coastal province of Fukien he had heard all about the wiliness of the barbarians. It was, of course, the British in particular he now had to cope with, and, to complicate matters, five years earlier the monopoly of the East India Company had been terminated and the door opened to private businessmen. In this respect, Britain was now at Canton on the same terms as the Americans, who ever since the War of Independence had built up their commerce with China to impressive proportions. The British merchants were under the general supervision of Captain Charles Elliot who as Inspector of Trade exercised something of the functions of a consul.

A week after his arrival Lin sent a note to the Chinese middlemen and the foreigners, demanding that the latter should surrender all their existing stocks of opium and give a guarantee that for the future they would no longer import the drug to China. Although Lin ended his message by stating that he would never leave his post until the traffic had been stamped out, the foreigners had heard much the same kind of language before and imagined they were being treated to another puppet-show. Their amusement changed to outrage when Lin blockaded the 'factories' in which they were living, so that there was no communication between them and their ships. They had sufficient food on the premises, but as their Chinese servants had been obliged to leave, it was not very entertaining for three hundred and fifty miscellaneous westerners, accustomed to being waited on hand and foot, suddenly to have to empty their own slops. Elliot, seeing that for the time being there was nothing for it but to give way, ordered his countrymen to hand over their stocks of the drug to him against his receipt, and when this transaction had been completed he in turn surrendered the hoard to the Chinese authorities. All told there were more than twenty thousand chests of opium.

Far off in Peking, the Emperor heard the news with delight, and wrote to Lin in the most flattering terms:

Your loyalty to your prince and your love of your country are now revealed for all to see, both within the Empire and in the regions abroad outside the boundaries of civilization.

It was all that was needed to complete the triumph. The opium was thrown into pits, mixed with quicklime, salt and water and then flushed into the sea. The operation took twenty-three days to finish, and was watched throughout by admiring crowds.

Imagining that Lin's mission was accomplished, Peking signified that another governor-generalship was ready and waiting for him, that of Kiangsu, Anhwei and Kiangsi in the Lower Yangtze Valley, in many ways the most desirable appointment of all. But the Commissioner was well aware that the felicitations were premature and that the real trial of strength was yet to come. For Elliot and the British had refused to give an undertaking to discontinue the traffic and had withdrawn to Macao, where they were waiting to see what London would do. The latter half of 1839 and the first half of 1840 were thus taken up with preparations on both sides. Lin closed the approach to Canton by river, and saw to the strengthening of the fortifications. At the same time, he introduced an original element into the proceedings by engaging a number of Chinese, who through contact with the foreigners had become good enough linguists to translate relevant passages from such English books and newspapers as were to be had. Gradually, a premonition of the disparity between Chinese and foreign armaments which was to be revealed in the months that followed began to enter his mind, but he disclosed his thoughts only years later and then in strict privacy to a friend. Publicly he was full of confidence, predicting that Britain, thirsty for tea and costive through lack of rhubarb, would soon come to her senses. Furthermore, a trait which has endeared him to modern Communist historians, he turned for help to the people at large, especially to the fishermen and boat-dwellers who are so numerous on that coast, persuading them not only to stand firm against the seduction of foreign bribes, but also, when the time came, to strike a blow for their country. It is scarcely surprising, considering this activity, that tempers should have become frayed, and as the months passed incidents multiplied.

The War with Britain

In London, at the beginning of April 1840 after the parliamentary debate we have noted in Chapter I, the government by a narrow majority secured approval for military expenditure, and in June a British fleet arrived off the mouth of the Canton River. Its purpose was to demand compensation for the opium destroyed the year before, and for the expense of the present intervention. Impediments on the Chinese side to commerce and diplomatic intercourse were to be swept away. With this larger design in view, the expedition contented itself with instituting a blockade of Canton, and sailed northwards in the direction of the seat of authority. Instructions had been given that, if possible, an island should be occupied, and accordingly, at the beginning of July a landing was effected at Tinghai, the administrative centre of Chusan. As it was practically defenceless the place was soon taken. At the end of the month, the fleet came to the entrance to the Paiho River which leads to Tientsin.

Meanwhile the report of the loss of Tinghai had reached Peking, and the Emperor had already begun to repent of the encouragement he had given to Lin Tse-hsü. No longer did imperial couriers hasten towards Canton with felicitations, but with words of reproach.

When we think of the trouble you have provoked, how can we control our indignation? We are waiting to see in what terms you will dare to answer us.

The immediate responsibility for contriving a way out of the present predicament lay naturally with the governor-general of the metropolitan province, the coast of which the barbarians had now attained, and this was still the same Kishan who less than two years previously had been the strongest opponent of Lin's arguments. He had been overruled then, but today surely he would be listened to. He sent an envoy to call on the strangers, and we can imagine with what satisfaction he transmitted to the Emperor the man's account of what he had seen. The most extraordinary things, beyond a doubt, were the steamships of which there were several with the British fleet:

They can fly across the water, without wind or tide, with the current or against it.

But a close second came the cannon:

These are mounted on stone platforms, which can be turned in any direction.

What a contrast to China, where even at a place as important as Shanhaikwan at the end of the Great Wall the guns were the old

Jesuit relics of the Ming Dynasty, which were being desperately scoured on the chance of being still usable! Then again,

Our military affairs are in the hands of civil officials, who are very likely admirable calligraphists but know nothing of war.[9]

The idea that China could be defeated by these troublesome barbarians certainly never occurred to the Emperor's mind. But Kishan's report confirmed that it would be advisable to take the nuisance seriously. In theory the backbone of the armed forces consisted of the Manchu banners. These represented about two hundred and fifty thousand soldiers, of whom more than half were kept for the defence of the capital itself, while the rest were stationed in the chief provincial cities. Besides the banners, there was a Chinese standing army, maintained throughout the country generally and consisting of six hundred and sixty thousand men. In spite of the stringent laws which aimed at perpetuating the martial qualities of the Manchus, it had become plain a few decades after the conquest that the banners had been spoiled by comfortable living, and in Central Asian campaigns of the eighteenth century it was the Chinese troops who played the principal role. Unfortunately, by the time Tao Kuang came to the throne, even these had lost much of their former virtue, and there had been cases where the government forces had shown themselves so incapable of suppressing local disturbances that volunteers had been recruited to do their duty for them. An attempt had been made, probably with success, to hide this unpleasant fact from the Emperor's notice, so that it was primarily the expense of their equipment and transportation that was agitating Tao Kuang's parsimonious mind, for his treasury was in a fairly depleted state. All the more readily, then, did he listen to the reassuring voice of Kishan, for the latter really seemed to have got to the root of the problem.

As he saw it, one man, and one man alone, was to blame for the whole affair. This much was clear from the communication which the foreigners presented to him for transmission to the throne. What was it, after all, but a petition to the Emperor to redress the grievances inflicted on them by Lin Tse-hsü? And was not this a perfectly reasonable and proper request? He had made it his business to meet the strangers in person, and could vouch for their courteous and even respectful demeanour towards His

Majesty's representative. Put the right man in charge, and the matter could be settled without difficulty at Canton, as it ought to have been in the first place. The British had agreed to return to the south, and, for good measure, had declared their willingness to withdraw their troops from Tinghai. After this what else could Tao Kuang do but appoint Kishan to be Commissioner at Canton, and send the unfortunate Lin to the wilds of Turkestan? Peace was now the order of the day, and the mobilization of the army was countermanded. Nobody on the Chinese side guessed that the British had decided to leave the north simply because the onset of the summer rains had created unfavourable conditions for an offensive in those parts. They had, too, been quite taken by Kishan's affability, for the governor-general had told them in so many words that they had been very ill used, and that Lin Tse-hsü thoroughly deserved any chastisement they cared to administer to him.

The new Commissioner took up his post at Canton in the latter half of November 1840, and it was at once apparent that there was to be a total change of policy. The defence works, on the construction of which his predecessor had spent so much time and energy, were pulled down, and local militia, which Lin had recruited and trained, were disbanded. Kishan's hope was that the restoration of trade, including the traffic in opium, together with the payment of some indemnity, would satisfy the foreigners for the time being, and he was shocked to discover that matters were not to be disposed of so easily. Over and above these conditions, the British demanded the outright cession of the island of Hong Kong, and the opening to their merchants of two ports, Amoy and Foochow, in the neighbouring province of Fukien. It is quite certain that until that moment Kishan had never heard of Hong Kong in his life, but the surrender of Chinese territory, no matter how unimportant, would not sound well in Peking. Surely the British would be content with access to the extra ports? He little knew with whom he was dealing. Early in January 1841, the British captured the forts at the mouth of the Canton River, and on the twenty-fifth of the same month Kishan accepted their terms.[10]

In his report to the throne, he did what he could to minimize the extent of the disaster, but while his excuses were still on the way, news had reached the capital of the reopening of hostilities, and an edict had gone forth proclaiming that the insolent barbarians were to be crushed to the earth. Troops from all over the country were to gather at Canton, and the supreme command was entrusted to the Emperor's cousin, Yishan. It was while Tao Kuang was still in this exalted state of mind that he learned of Kishan's surrender, and on the heels of the courier there followed even darker rumours, emanating from the Commissioner's disgruntled colleagues, which suggested that he had received a huge bribe from the foreigners in return for his services. The annoyance which the Emperor had shown to Lin Tse-hsü was nothing to the fury he now vented on Kishan. Branded as a miscreant unworthy of the favours which had been heaped upon him, the poor wretch was ordered to be carried in chains to Peking and to have all his possessions confiscated. It was a cruel fate, but not untypical of the rapid vicissitudes of fortune experienced by high officials, especially in the Manchu Dynasty, and to brighten the picture it should be added that both Kishan and Lin Tse-hsü were in due course restored to favour and again held important posts.

Meanwhile, hearing the news from Peking, the British had resumed hostilities outside Canton. They had not very much to fear from their new opponents. Yishan in his first dispatches from the city showed that as a near kinsman of the Emperor he had an especially sensitive nose for anything that savoured of anti-Manchu feeling. He believed that domestic treason was a greater danger in those southern ports than foreign aggression, and that the military reinforcements now streaming to the scene of war should be employed quite as much to keep down the local population as to resist the British. In particular he detested the very name of the defence volunteers, disbanded by Kishan, but now coming together again. That government troops, transferred to a new province, should plunder and rape was only to be expected, but in addition they were given a hint that able-bodied civilians found with arms in their hands were in all probability rebels whose throats might be cut without further inquiry.

Towards the British, greater circumspection was employed. It was noticed for instance that Yishan's deputy had placed his artillery at such a distance that the cannon-balls fell short of the foreign ships, whose counter-fire in contrast was lethally accurate. The officer himself had a convincing apology:

Here are our batteries, on good solid earth, while the barbarians' guns are bobbing up and down on the water. Yet they hit us, while we miss them. The only possible explanation is that they are using the sorcery of their evil religion.

It is an old superstition in China that witchcraft can be discomfited by the exhibition of feminine uncleanness and accordingly households in the neighbourhood were ordered to hang out chamberpots used by their women. But even this did not halt the foreigners and before long their artillery, posted on commanding heights, was raining fire on the city itself. Losing all hope, Yishan on 27 May 1841 followed his predecessor and came to terms, ransoming Canton with the sum of six million silver dollars, but warned by Kishan's fate he represented his action as a moral victory and told the Emperor that the British offensive had been brought to a standstill by the apparition of a supernatural being, clad in white and standing on the city wall.[11]

Three days after the armistice, there occurred an event the recollection of which still arouses emotion in Chinese breasts. In spite of suppression by the government forces, local defence organizations continued to exist and were bitterly resentful of what they considered to be a betrayal. At a village called San-yuan-li, a little way north of the city, a group of these enthusiasts inflicted a defeat on a detachment of British soldiers, some of whom were cut off and allowed to escape only at a plea from the prefectural magistrate. To later generations the affair appeared to symbolize the contrast between the patriotism of the masses and the timidity and incompetence of the officials.

London in the meantime was not satisfied with the terms so far extorted, and sent out a fresh plenipotentiary, Sir Henry Pottinger, with instructions to carry the threat of British power closer to the centre of things. In August 1841, the fleet again sailed to the north. Amoy, Tinghai and Ningpo were occupied in quick succession, and in the last place there was a vast plunder both in provisions and money. To face the challenge Tao Kuang chose as commander-in-chief yet another of his cousins, who accepted the post with special alacrity since it would permit him to visit the beauty spots of the Lower Yangtze Valley. Indeed, the singing-girls of Soochow detained him and his entourage so long that a public outcry began to be heard, and even when he was induced to resume his journey and, four months after setting out, arrived on the threatened coast he might just as well have stayed with the ladies for any good he was able to do.

The Treaty of Nanking

In the summer of 1842, the invading fleet entered the Yangtze. Shanghai fell in the middle of June and was followed a month later by Chinkiang where the Grand Canal, the vital line of communication between the capital and the wealthiest provinces of the south, meets the great river. Nanking, the next city to be menaced by the British guns, saw the end of the conflict, for it was there on 29 August 1842, on board a British man-of-war, that Tao Kuang's representatives signed the first of the 'unequal treaties' which imposed on China a century of humiliation.

The cession of Hong Kong to the British crown, agreed to originally by Kishan eighteen months earlier, was now confirmed. Besides Amoy and Foochow, Ningpo and Shanghai were also to be opened to British trade and residence, making with Canton five 'treaty ports'. China was to pay an indemnity of twenty-one million silver dollars, and her customs dues were to be determined by equitable arrangement. The old system of the thirteen 'hongs' was abolished, and British merchants were free to do business directly with their Chinese customers. Oddly enough, the traffic in opium which had been so important in precipitating the conflict was not mentioned.

The war and the treaty which ended it have through the years been abundantly commented on by Chinese writers, and even today the memory of them continues to dominate the Chinese attitude to the outer world. Above all it is the nakedly aggressive aspect of the British intervention and its odious connexion with the trade in narcotics which are recollected most clearly. To be sure, it may be argued that the root cause was not opium but rather the refusal of the old Chinese state to accommodate itself to the changed circumstances of the nineteenth century, but be this as it may the general opinion of mankind has passed judgment on the first Sino-British conflict by the name it has given to it. There are surely no laurels to be won in an Opium War.

Once the fighting had started, was the Chinese defeat inevitable? Few Europeans, bearing in mind the disparity of the contestants in military equipment, will think otherwise, but on the

Chinese side, both at the time and today, many would deny it. They argue that the number of British and Indian troops employed never exceeded fifteen thousand, and that although the superiority of the foreigners in ships and guns enabled them to strike successfully at places on the coast, and to a certain extent along the Yangtze, they could not have ventured far inland. Any Chinese government with the will to resist could have rallied the people behind it in opposition to invaders so detestably alien in race and manners that the mere view of them was sufficient to excite the most violent feeling of hatred and revulsion. In support of this opinion, it must be granted that in Canton, at least, there was a genuine patriotic enthusiasm which if allowed to develop could have inspired a volunteer army, and elsewhere there were many examples of courage both among the civil population and the government troops. The British, too, suffered heavy losses from sickness. Perhaps they could have penetrated as far as Peking, as we shall see they did a few years later, but if the government had retreated further inland, then, in the conditions of 1840, it would have been out of the question for Britain to attempt anything like the Japanese invasion of 1937. Yet even when we have given due weight to these considerations, the fact remains that it would be an anachronism to attribute to the China of Tao Kuang a national consciousness it was to gain from the experiences of the next hundred years. The imperial house, too, was better informed than any outsiders about the circumstances of its own tenure of power. If the Emperor believed that an army of Cantonese volunteers would be just as likely to revolt against the dynasty as to fight the British, his opinion was in all probability based on solid grounds.[12]

CHAPTER IV

THE TAIPING REBELLION

Consequences of the Treaty of Nanking – peasant unrest – Hung Hsiu-ch'uan and the Society of God – the Taiping Rebellion – the capture of Nanking

Consequences of the Treaty of Nanking

THE Treaty of Nanking, in so far as it was imposed on China after defeat in war, was recognized by the country at large to be a humiliation. What were to become the most crippling infringements it imposed on the national sovereignty at the time were strangely enough looked upon as relatively innocuous. By consenting to having her customs dues determined by 'equitable arrangement' China had signed away her right to exercise tariff autonomy. In the following year, the supplementary Treaty of the Bogue filled in the details of the master agreement. The rate stipulated averaged five per cent of the value of goods, and the first reaction of Peking was that it had achieved something of a victory, for previously, no matter how much had been levied by the avarice of local officials at Canton, the rate of four per cent was all that had gone to the treasury. The same supplementary treaty, to the relief of the authorities at the newly opened ports, absolved them from the necessity of administering justice to the aliens by providing that the latter should be subject to their own laws and under the jurisdiction of their consuls. The wise policy, as it was thought, of keeping the foreigners at arm's length was carried a step further in 1845 when the British at Shanghai, who until then had had to rent unsatisfactory accommodation in the old city, prevailed without much difficulty upon the magistrate to allow them to rent in perpetuity a plot of open ground outside the walls for the purpose of building houses and offices for themselves. In this way the two great causes of national resentment for the future, extra-territoriality and foreign settlements, were in their origin almost a welcome relief to the harassed Chinese officials.

That other powers would not be slow in following Britain's example was acknowledged by a 'most-favoured nation' clause in the Treaty of the Bogue which provided that any new benefits granted to such countries would be enjoyed equally by Britain. In fact both the United States and France concluded treaties in 1844, and other states were close behind. Except for the war-indemnity and Hong Kong, these agreements were essentially similar to that of Nanking, but the French, eager to profit from their role of protectors of the Church, introduced a new and important principle by forcing Peking to rescind its anti-Christian decrees of a hundred years earlier. From then on the western religion was to play a capital part in China's foreign relations.

Now the great moment had arrived for which the British industrialists had yearned so long, and the limitless Chinese market representing, or so it was claimed, a third of mankind was thrown open to their manufactures. If every person in China bought no more than a single cotton nightcap a year, said one excited economist, the mills of Britain would have more orders than they could cope with. A Sheffield firm sent a vast shipment of knives and forks. A London maker of musical instruments indulged in an even more daring speculation. There must be, he argued, two hundred million women and girls in China. Surely one in every two hundred of these could be induced to take up the piano? A sample consignment was dispatched and for years disputed the warehouse space of Hong Kong with the arsenal of cutlery which had proved ineffectual against the harmless bamboo chopstick.[1]

If one reason for the initial disappointment of British hopes was that they had been conceived in total ignorance of Chinese social conditions, another lay in the fact that more and more of China's purchasing power was being engrossed by the opium traffic, which now reached vast dimensions. There were five or six hundred shops selling the drug in the city of Canton alone, and the addiction was gaining ground even among the working people whose poverty had formerly exempted them from it. If it had not been for this item of commerce, the balance of trade would again have swung in favour of China, for Europe and

America were demanding her products as never before. In 1843 over seventeen million pounds of tea were exported from Canton. The following year, the figure for Canton and Shanghai was over seventy million pounds, and in 1856, a hundred and thirty million pounds were shipped from Canton, Shanghai and Foochow. The quantity of silk exported increased by more than fourteen times between 1843 and 1850.

This development brought prosperity to certain parts of the country. The silk-producing districts inland from Shanghai benefited especially, and the tea plantations of Wuyi in Fukien, formerly the property of mountain temples, passed into the possession of men of business, dedicated to satisfying the British thirst for 'Bohea'. But not all the results were so advantageous. In the past the tea of Fukien and the silks of the Yangtze Valley intended for export had been carried overland to Canton, and in the course of the years a well-established transportation industry had come into existence, which, now that other ports had been opened nearer to hand, had become redundant. An observer said,

Many thousands of men depended on their work as porters to keep their wives and children. Families which have supported themselves for generations in this way are now demanding what is to become of them.

Illogically enough, the Cantonese, whose warlike spirit had recently been much in evidence, had their xenophobic prejudices reinforced by the diversion of international trade. They were protesting so noisily against the admission of foreigners within the walls of their city that in this particular it was thought wiser to postpone for a while the implementation of the treaty, and restrict the aliens to the suburbs.

Furthermore, although the Chinese market did not live up to British expectations enough foreign goods were imported to deal a blow at native industries. Cottons from Lancashire were the most dangerous of these competitors, and their effect was perceptible not along the coast, but deep in the heart of the country. The ironwork at Fatshan, near Canton, where thousands of men were employed, found they could not hold their ground against the influx of nails and needles from abroad. In the matter of coastal shipping, too, although it was to be another twenty years before regular steamer services were set up the traditional junks were already finding it hard to meet the challenge of the larger western vessels. The result of all this was that increased prosperity in some quarters was counterbalanced by hardship in others, and to make things worse the 1840s witnessed a succession of natural calamities. The Yellow River broke its dykes three times between 1841 and 1843, bringing death to millions. Then in 1849 the Lower Yangtze had its worst flood in a century. Elsewhere, crops were destroyed by drought, insect pests and storms. To the cost of rehabilitation there had to be added the crushing burden of the British indemnity, to raise which extraordinary measures of taxation were applied.

Such times were ripe for unrest, and indeed for decades news of peasant uprisings in various parts of the countryside had been a commonplace. Frequently too these disturbances had been linked with movements of an anti-dynastic sort, the aim of which was to overthrow the Tartar ruling house and set up in its place a native Chinese government. Religion played its part in encouraging these ambitions. In the fourteenth century, the White Lotus Sect, deriving its inspiration from popular Buddhism, had been one of the forces behind the expulsion of the Mongols, and now that China was once more under alien domination the secret confraternity was again recruiting members with the old national slogans. Between 1793 and 1802 there occurred a series of revolts in five provinces of Central and North-West China which cost two hundred million dollars to suppress, and in 1812 the sect had the audacity to attempt a coup within the Forbidden City itself.

The White Lotus flourished especially in the northern half of the country. South of the Yangtze was the domain of a younger organization. The Society of Heaven and Earth had been founded after the Manchu conquest, in 1674, with the purpose of restoring the Ming and from the Buddhist temple deep in the mountains of Fukien where it drew its source, its secret adherents ramified across many provinces between the country watered by the Pearl River of Canton and the upper reaches of the Yangtze. Its first great revolt, which broke out in Formosa in 1786, had been crushed after a year's bitter fighting. Since then in spite of the power of its name, which the Manchus acknowledged by denouncing it in their penal code, its local branches had shown themselves deficient in unity and co-ordination, and had not been able to take advantage of the unrest which economic hardship and the presence of an increased population were provoking throughout the entire south. In the event the vacant leadership was to be seized by another society, also religious in its origins but inspired not by the familiar legends of the Buddhist or Taoist pantheon but by the starker doctrines of Protestant Christianity.

Hung Hsiu-ch'uan and the Society of God

Hung Hsiu-ch'uan, the author of a revolution whose effects are felt and seen in China to this day, was born in 1814 in a village about thirty miles inland from Canton, one of five children of a Hakka farmer. The word 'hakka' means 'stranger' and the people so-called migrated centuries before from Northern and Central China to the southern provinces, from where in turn some of them have gone to Malaya and other countries across the sea. They speak their own dialect, and are noted for their clannishness and aggressive temperament which do not endear them to their neighbours. The Hung family, though not in prosperous circumstances, were still by no means at the foot of the economic ladder, having a water-buffalo or two to help till the land, and keeping pigs, chickens and ducks. The father was, it appears, of some standing in the community. At six years of age, the boy began to go to the village school and study the Confucian classics, in preparation, it was hoped, for an official career. But although he went to Canton on several occasions to present himself at the government examinations, he was never successful. On one of these visits to the provincial capital, while walking in the street between the examination hall and his lodgings he had a book thrust into his hand by a stranger, a convert of the Protestant missionary Robert Morrison, who was taking advantage of the presence in the city of so many educated people to disseminate the still forbidden gospel. It is by no means certain that Hung bothered to read the book, which expounded the elements of the Christian faith; no doubt he glanced at it, but his mind was too much occupied with thoughts of the ordeal from which he had just emerged to have room for anything else. Even so, the Chinese in those days held the printed word in reverence, and instead of throwing the tract away he took it back with him to his home, where it was thrust among other papers and forgotten.

Depressed by his latest failure, he fell ill; an illness which lasted for forty days, and in the course of which he experienced some peculiar hallucinations. It seemed to him that he was transported to a mighty palace, where a venerable old man, sitting in splendour upon a throne, handed him a jewelled sword, with the injunction to go forth and extirpate devils, and to keep his brothers and sisters from harm. There was present another personage of middle age, whom Hung learned to address as 'Elder Brother', who accompanied him when he set out against the demons. At this point the vision was so urgent that Hung rose from his bed in his delirium and jumped round the room striking out right and left at unseen enemies. When at length he recovered, his family began to notice, or so they thought, a remarkable change in his appearance and character. He seemed to gain in height and build, and there was a new air of candour and firmness about him. From being a student, he now became a teacher and set up a school in a village not far off.

It was in that capacity he passed the next six years, unaffected, so far as we know, by the fighting a few miles away. Then in the summer of 1843 a relative who had come to visit him, having the curiosity to rummage among his books, found the Christian tract Hung had brought from Canton. Struck by its oddity he read it through, and teased Hung about his peculiar taste in literature. Only then did Hung read the book for himself, and as he did so the significance of his vision became plain to him. The old man on the throne was surely none other than God the Father, as described in the pages before him, while the man of middle age must have been Jesus Christ. The demons were the idols against whose worship the book inveighed so strongly. Its teaching showed the way to eternal life. In a little while Hung's earnestness convinced the other man too and following the written instructions they mutually administered baptism, each pouring water on the other's head and reciting the words 'Washing away sin we cast off the old and put on the new'. Hung composed a 'poem of repentance' as follows:

The flood of our iniquities drowns the sky,
But we trust in Jesus for our redemption.
Do not put faith in demons, but honour the holy commandments,
And obeying God alone till the field of your heart.
The splendour of Heaven compels our adoration,
While the sombre depths of Hell rouse our pity.
Turn back in time to the right path
Lest your heart be ensnared by worldly desires.[2]

A few of his kinsmen were sufficiently moved by his example to join him in forming a Society of God, but the most important of his followers was a close friend and former school fellow named Feng Yün-shan, whose zeal as a preacher of the new doctrine was scarcely inferior to that of Hung himself. The campaign against idols had one awkward consequence: it extended even to the memorial tablet of Confucius kept in Hung's school. When parents learned that this venerated symbol had been got rid of they soon took their sons away from so unorthodox an academy. Early in 1844, Hung decided to try his fortune elsewhere, and with Feng as his only companion he travelled across country to the adjacent province of Kwangsi, where a relation of his was living. It was while staying in this man's house that Hung perpetrated his first open act of war against traditional Chinese religion by defacing a Taoist shrine in the neighbourhood. It may be that this exploit was not well viewed by his host; at any rate the two lodgers departed in the autumn and for the time being took leave of each other. Hung returned to his native village, while Feng continued his journey into Kwangsi as far as a district called Thistle Mountain, a name destined to be famous in Chinese history.

There is no doubt that the events which followed were to a large extent the result of the special circumstances of the province. For Kwangsi, in addition to the economic and political causes of unrest general to the country as a whole, had its own particular, and endemic, discontents. To begin with, its population was of very mixed origins. There were large numbers of aborigines, the first inhabitants of the land, who had been pushed back to the mountains of the south and west by the irresistible advance of Chinese settlement, and who lived at the best in a state of uneasy truce with their dominant neighbours; a truce which was frequently disturbed by outbreaks of violence and sometimes by full-scale rebellion. The Chinese proper were divided between those who regarded themselves after centuries of occupation as native to the soil, and the Hakkas who had immigrated more recently from Kwangtung, and the two communities were as a rule on the worst possible terms. Such a territory would have set a problem even for an efficient administration, and it was notorious in government circles that Kwangsi was of all the provinces of China the one most carelessly managed. Between 1836 and 1841 the governor had been an elegant dilettante of the old school who regarded his official duties as an infuriating interruption of a gentleman's existence of party-giving and verse-writing, to which the romantic scenery of those parts was particularly conducive. After a while his subordinates learned not to harry him with their worries, and his successor in the post was only too happy to follow what had become an established tradition.

Penetrating into the middle of this anarchy, Feng, who like his friend Hung was of Hakka stock, naturally found a refuge with a community of his fellows, but at the cost of waiving for a while the social pretensions to which his schooling and his attempts to pass the state examinations had encouraged him. For a year or more he earned his living as a common labourer, collecting dung, working on the land, or helping the charcoal burners who were very active on the mountain. During this time he spoke to all who would listen to him of the visions granted to his friend, and of the consolation to be derived from the worship of the universal father. At last his superior attainments were acknowledged by an appointment to teach some of the richer farmers' sons, and, no less gratifying, by the formation of a strong branch of the Society of God.

Meanwhile at home the founder himself was engaged in theological composition, for it was during this period (1844–7) that much of the canonical literature of the movement was written. Already some of Hung's speculations were of a kind that if persevered in were likely to bring him into conflict with the state authorities. Convinced of the fatherhood of God, from whom every creature draws its nourishment, he insisted on the duty of all men, irrespective of their condition, to worship their Maker. He recognized that this was contrary to the traditional Chinese view that only the Emperor had the capacity to offer sacrifice to Heaven, and frankly accepted the challenge. 'God our Heavenly Father is common to all men', he wrote. 'How can any prince arrogate to himself the right to adore Him?' In the world as originally created, men and women without exception were brothers and sisters; the present corruption of society with its injustices and exploitation is the work of demons, whom it was his mission to destroy. Perhaps he could learn more of these mysteries from the people who had first given a hint of the truth in that pamphlet chance had so luckily thrust into his hand years ago. In 1847 he applied for instruction to an American evangelist at Canton, the

Reverend Issachar Roberts. This man was puzzled by Hung's ideas, and dubious of his understanding of the scriptures; it seems, too, that he suspected his sincerity. At all events, when Hung, wishing to insure against the risk that his earlier amateur christening might have been ineffective, applied for baptism in a more professional form, the American refused. The disappointment did not last long. In August of the same year, hearing something of Feng's success, he returned to Thistle Mountain where he was amazed to discover that the Society of God had more than three thousand adherents.

No amount of explanation can make this achievement, and the others that were soon to follow it, less than astonishing. But even if we admit the full magnitude of the obstacles which Hung Hsiuch'uan and Feng Yu-shan had to overcome in order to win converts, we must at the same time bear in mind that these very difficulties, looked at from another angle, could appear advantageous. The two men themselves had been educated in the Confucian classics and as candidates in the state examinations could be expected to have a predisposition against supernatural religion, especially against one which came from abroad. This foreign element would seem as unpalatable to their ignorant listeners, who for all their superstition came from a population notably xenophobic. Yet the Judaeo-Christian theology – and in spite of distortion and vulgarization of every kind this was the ingredient that gave energy to Hung's movement – has appealed to some Chinese hearts precisely because the terrible urgency of its message has sounded so alien in a country where dramatic tension is absent from the common-sense national character. Instances could be multiplied from the history of the Christian missions, but let one example suffice. We are sometimes led to think that the Jesuits in eighteenth-century Peking gained converts by appearing as sophisticated men of the world, ready to effect an urbane compromise between Christianity and Confucianism, but in fact nothing could be further from the truth. The last head of that celebrated community was Father Francois Bourgeois who, on the dissolution of his Order, performed the melancholy duty of handing over the establishment to the Lazarists. In a letter of 1772 this good priest has a very peculiar story to tell. Among his congregation was a Manchu girl named Mary between eleven and twelve years of age and from a family long attached to Christianity.

One day when she had come to make her confession he said to her:

'I believe that by God's mercy you are in a state of grace: but you are young, this country is full of danger and I tremble to think that a time may come when you will offend Him.' 'Don't be afraid,' said Mary, 'I would rather die than offend God.' 'If that is so,' replied the priest, 'I advise you to ask our Lady to obtain for you the grace to die before committing a mortal sin.' Immediately the girl turned to a statue of the Blessed Virgin and kowtowed before it. Then she said, 'You can put your mind at rest, Father. I hope the Holy Mother will grant my prayer.'

'A few days afterwards,' Father Bourgeois continues, 'a slight swelling appeared on her cheek, but there was nothing to suggest it was serious. The child asked her parents for permission to come to the church again. I could not believe that an ailment of the sort would lead to anything worse, but hardly had she got home when the swelling developed into a malignant cancer which in less than twenty days ate away the whole of the cheek, one eye, half of the nose, and half of the mouth and tongue. The sight of her inspired horror. She supported her condition with an angelic constancy and died full of joy and consolation.' In a letter of the following year, he writes: 'The Blessed Virgin is working miracles here. We put all the young people under her protection.'[3]

The notion of a Heavenly Father, much more strongly personified than any of the deities in the native pantheon, had already shown its power to gather followers. What remained now was to equip the Society of God with its own corporate rules and institutions, and this for the next few months occupied most of Hung's and Feng's time. A set of Ten Commandments was promulgated corresponding to those of Moses, and appropriate prayers and rituals were devised for such occasions as the baptism of new members, grace at meals, the burial of the dead and so forth. Meanwhile the feeling of group solidarity which these ceremonies inspired was reinforced by the active hostility aroused in certain of the country gentry by the Society's growing reputation and by its iconoclastic exploits against shrines and temples in the neighbourhood, which looked like an insolent challenge to the established order.

At the end of 1847, the leader of the wealthier landowners, a man who could boast of the academic degree which the evangelists had failed to obtain, led a party of armed volunteers to arrest Feng and one of his companions, and carried them before the nearest magistrate on a charge of disturbing the public with false doctrines. In the event, the situation was saved by the carelessness or incompetence of the official who did not want to worry his superiors by multiplying reports of disorder, and Feng was discharged. But how great his danger had been was shown by the fate of the man charged with him, who died in custody, whether from brutal treatment or neglect we do not know. Curiously enough, Hung at that time was so far from thought of revolt that he hurried to Canton with the idea of saving his friend by invoking the recently promulgated edict of toleration for Christianity which, as we have seen, the French had extorted by treaty. Having no access to persons in authority Hung wasted his time.

For a short while, then, the Society of God was without either of its leaders, and in the general dismay and uncertainty many of its members showed signs of wavering. Help came from an unexpected quarter. A charcoal-burner, Yang Hsiu-ch'ing, suddenly found himself possessed by God the Father, who used him as a mouthpiece to admonish those of faint heart. Not to be outdone, another charcoal-burner, Hsiao Ch'ao-kuei, was inspired by Jesus Christ to utter similar warnings. Today, it is interesting to notice, Communist historians defend Yang and Hsiao against accusations of dishonesty by arguing that they were justified in playing on the superstition of their fellows in order to achieve a revolutionary end. Other critics have been less indulgent, alleging that the whole incident shows the ambition of the two men to gain power for themselves. Whichever school of thought is nearer the truth, from then on both of them, as transmitters of the divine will, stood somewhat higher than Feng in the Society's hierarchy.

With the release of Feng from prison, and Hung's return from Canton, the work of organization went on apace. So far converts had come from the ranks of the poorest labourers, but now men of a different type began to present themselves for baptism. The most remarkable was Wei Ch'ang-hui, a landlord and pawnshop owner from a village called Gold Field. It is probable that his adhesion to the faith was due in a large measure to some racial antipathy between himself and the other rich landed proprietors of the region, for he was of aboriginal stock. With the Society behind him he was able not only to defend himself, but on occasion to carry the war to the enemy, and we hear of raids to plunder his rivals' harvests. His farm became an armed camp, with ditches and palisades, behind which iron was fashioned into swords and spears. Nor was Wei the only man of substance to join the movement. The younger Shih Ta-k'ai was also from a prosperous family. But as a counterbalance, n'er-do-wells and loafers came to enroll and were not turned away. This disparity of classes is much stressed by modern Communist scholars who attempt to explain later developments in terms of the social origins of the principal actors. On the surface, though, the Society appeared to have moved a step nearer towards democratic simplicity by the newly-proclaimed rule that all members must sell their land and houses, and deposit the purchase money in the treasury for the common maintenance. It is doubtful how far this ordinance was applied in such a case as that of Wei, but he might reasonably prefer the power accruing to him as a leader of the Society to that merely derived from wealth.

It is no small proof of the chaotic state of the province that it was not until the winter of 1850 that the Society came into open conflict with the government authorities. The circumstances of the encounter are equally typical of the time and the place. A detachment of the state militia dispatched to the neighbourhood to seize a notorious outlaw took advantage of their commission, in the manner of their kind, to rob the inoffensive inhabitants. They made the error of imagining that a group of charcoal-burners whom they met in the mountains belonged to this harmless category. In fact the workmen were particularly enthusiastic members of the Society of God, and struck back at the aggressors with such fury that the latter fled for their lives. While the passions aroused by this incident were still inflamed, a convert higher in the economic scale chanced to be travelling with his family in the direction of the Society's headquarters and had to pass through a village where there was an outpost of the discomfited militia. Learning who the man was, they decided to avenge themselves by detaining his concubine. (The fact that his household included such an accessory would itself suggest that he was well-to-do.) This outrage, together with the menace of future reprisals which the soldiers had been heard to utter, was the signal for outright war, which was declared from the camp at Gold Field on 11 January 1851.

The Taiping Rebellion

A year elapsed before the rebels crossed the borders of Kwangsi, but by then a dynasty had been proclaimed. This event occurred in October 1851, at a little mountain town called Yungan which had been taken in the course of a successful campaign against the government forces. The name Yungan means 'perpetual peace' and the place was therefore considered an auspicious site for the occasion. The style chosen for the new regime was *T'ai-p'ing T'ien-kuo*, to interpret which requires some explanation. *T'ai-p'ing* is often translated as 'great peace', but it also contains a notion of levelling or equality, and its meaning in this context is best defined in a rebel edict published somewhat later.

The land of the world must be tilled in common by the people of the world. When we have an insufficiency here, the people must be moved there, and vice versa, so that plenty in one place may relieve famine in another. All the world must enjoy the happiness given by God the Heavenly Father, and land, food, clothing and money must be held and used in common, so that there is no inequality anywhere, and nobody lacks food or warmth. For the world is the family of God the Heavenly Father: if men do not hold things in private, but pass them to the Sovereign Lord, then the Lord will use them and everybody everywhere will be equal. This is the edict of salvation especially enjoined by God the Heavenly Father on the True Lord of T'ai-ping.[4]

T'ien-kuo means 'The Kingdom of Heaven' and in a commentary by Hung attached to a translation of St Matthew's Gospel we read:

'The Kingdom of Heaven' refers to what is above in the sky and what is below on earth, for both are the Divine Father's Kingdom of Heaven. Do not be deceived into thinking that the term applies only to the Kingdom of Heaven in the sky. Therefore when the Heavenly Elder Brother (i.e. Jesus Christ) says that 'the Kingdom of Heaven is at hand' he predicts the establishment of the Kingdom of Heaven today by the Heavenly Father and the Heavenly Elder Brother, who have come down among us.

In the Kingdom of Heaven, however, there was to be an aristocracy. The word meaning 'emperor' was applied only to God, and was eschewed in any other sense, but Hung Hsiu-ch'uan was referred to as 'Lord' (an instance may be found in the former of the two passages just cited) and proclaimed to be the 'Heavenly Prince'. There were five other Princes besides: the two charcoal-burners who had so opportunely received the gift of tongues three years earlier, Yang Hsiu-ch'ing and Hsiao Ch'ao-kwei, were declared the Eastern and Western Princes respectively, while Feng Yün-shan was made Southern Prince, and the landlord Wei Ch'ang-hui emerged as Prince of the North. The other man of wealth, Shih Ta-k'ai, became Guardian Prince. An intricate system of minor titles was created at the same time, and, what would seem to offend against the primitive simplicity of the economic programme, respect for these dignities was enforced by the most stringent measures. Whenever the great men went abroad ordinary mortals had either to keep out of their way, or to kneel at the side of the road as they passed, under pain of instant decapitation. The costumes of the Ming Dynasty, or rather what passed as such in the popular theatre, were adopted as court dress, while men cut off their pigtails and ceased to shave the front of their heads in the manner prescribed for two hundred years.[5]

The most remarkable feature of the rebel discipline was no doubt the celibacy maintained within the camp. Women lived apart in strict seclusion, and sexual contact even between married couples was punished by death. The general acquiescence in so unnatural a deprivation is all the more remarkable because the Princes were allowed to maintain seraglios, and pains were taken to devise appropriate titles for their concubines. The harems, though, were staffed by maid-servants instead of eunuchs, and another departure from custom was that the practice of binding girls' feet was abolished.

Meanwhile Peking was concentrating a large force in Kwangsi province, and Yungan was surrounded. However, in February 1852, the Taiping (to adopt a spelling less awkward to western eyes) broke through the encircling lines and marched on towards the provincial capital of Kweilin. Unable after a month's siege to capture the city, they moved out of Kwangsi and into the adjacent province of Hunan. On the way, at the beginning of June, in the course of an engagement, they sustained their first great loss in the death of the Southern Prince, Feng Yün-shan, who in the early years of the Society had played a part almost as important as that of the founder himself. A few weeks later another blow followed when Hsiao Ch'ao-kuei, the Western Prince, was killed beneath the walls of Changsha, the capital of Hunan. Hsiao, it will be remembered, had shared the gift of tongues with his fellow charcoal-burner Yang Hsiu-ch'ing, and had been accepted as the mouthpiece of Jesus Christ. In the three years since that affair he had married the founder's daughter and had risen to second place in the hierarchy.

That position was now beyond dispute occupied by Yang Hsiu-ch'ing himself, not only as the appointed spokesman of God the Father, but as by far the ablest military leader of the movement. Already the faint-hearted were murmuring that too much had been risked, and that only the familiar mountains of Kwangsi could be depended on for safety. Spurning such pusillanimity, Yang declared that no more energy must be wasted on the siege of minor places like Changsha, and that the road into the heart of China lay before them. At the end of November 1852, the Taiping turned their back on the provincial capital and marched northwards towards Hupei and the Yangtze.

By this time a series of proclamations had introduced a new element into the campaign. The Manchus were branded as aliens, and aliens of a peculiar loathsome kind. All the old vituperation against 'stinking Tartars', which had not been heard in public for two centuries, was now revived. Indeed, one would be justified in thinking that the rebel leaders included even their own northern countrymen in their comminations, since one enormity laid to the Manchus' account was the introduction of the Peking accent to the detriment of pure Chinese! A hint of the mental preoccupations of the Taiping leaders may be found in the reference to the sexual activities of their enemies. Tao Kuang had died in 1850 and had been succeeded on the throne by his son Hsien Feng, whom Peking gossip credited with such an inordinate love for small-footed Chinese women that he was said to ignore all dynastic prohibitions of intermarriage and to maintain a small harem of the forbidden beauties in the seclusion of his Summer Palace outside the city walls. It is improbable, however, that by 1852 this rumour had travelled so far to the south, and statements like the following must have issued straight from an inflamed imagination.

Today the Manchu demons collect all our pretty Chinese girls to be their slaves and concubines! Three thousand, with powder and pen-cilled eyebrows, are defiled by dogs! A million rouged faces share pillows with lustful foxes! To speak of such things moves the heart and befouls the tongue! All the women of China are put to shame by them![6]

There were other charges too.

Whenever there is flood or drought, the Manchus just sit and watch us starve, without the slightest compunction. This is because they want to make us Chinese fewer in number. They let loose avaricious and corrupt officials across the whole country, to exploit us to the marrow, so that men and women are weeping at the roadside. This is because they want to make us Chinese poor. If we investigate the origins of these Manchu Tartars, we find their ancestor was born from the copulation of a white fox with a red bitch, a union bound to produce a monster![7]

In December the Taiping army reached the Tungt'ing lake which it crossed in a fleet of captured boats. In the middle of the month the important town of Yochow was taken. A vast accession of recruits joined the triumphant army. Figures are rather conflicting, but the force of ten thousand which had set off from Gold Field had swollen to eighty thousand by Changsha. A multitude of boatmen doubled this number, and provided an armada of river craft, as well as abundant supplies of food. It was as a naval expedition that the rebels came into the Yangtze. They anchored in midstream, severing communications between Wuchang on the south bank, and Hanyang and Hankow on the northern side, which fell on 23 and 29 December respectively. Wuchang, however, was the provincial capital of Hupei. So far the two other provincial capitals encountered on the march, Kweilin in Kwangsi and Changsha in Hunan, had managed to elude capture. For reasons of prestige therefore, as well as because of the city's special geographical importance, the Taiping were determined on this occasion to make good their previous omission. The scale of the operation is convincing evidence of the military skill of the rebel leaders and of the technical assistance they now had at their disposal. A pontoon bridge was constructed across the Yangtze, Wuchang was invested from every side and a government army which had made forced marches from Changsha to raise the siege was attacked and routed. Many of the insurgents had formerly worked as miners, and found themselves unexpectedly set to their old task as a tunnel was excavated up to one of the gates, where on 12 January 1853 a mine was exploded. The city was entered through the breach.

The Capture of Nanking

This was by far the most resounding victory of the Taiping to date, but it put the rebels on the spot. They had to choose one of three courses of action. Should they keep on to the north, against Peking itself? Should they move upstream into the great province of Szechwan, and erect there an impregnable citadel from which they could proceed to the conquest of the whole country? Or should they go down river to the most famous and opulent region of China, the Lower Yangtze Valley, where in the city of Nanking the founder of the Ming dynasty five hundred years before had established his capital after the expulsion of the Mongols? In the light of what followed, it is plain that the first course would have been infinitely the wisest. If the march northwards had persevered, no power on earth could have saved the Manchus from ruin, and by the autumn of 1853 a Chinese Son of Heaven would once again have been sitting on the Dragon Throne, the undoubted ruler of the land. But at the time the thought of the luxury to be enjoyed so near at hand, as well, no doubt, as recollections of history, pre-vailed over all other considerations, and at the beginning of February, the entire army, abandoning the three Wuhan cities, set off eastwards down the river, and on 8 March arrived under the walls of Nanking. Once again the miners started their tunnelling: eleven days later the exploit of Wuchang was repeated and Nanking was in Taiping hands. Exultantly, they named it 'The Heavenly Capital'.

CHAPTER V

THE RISE OF TSENG KUO-FAN

_Tseng Kuo-fan and the Hunan Army – dissension and murder in
the Heavenly Capital_

Tseng Kuo-fan and the Hunan Army

THE rapidity of the rebels' success revealed, even more than the
Opium War, the military weakness of the Manchu government.
True, several of its highest officials had died at their posts – the
Governor of Hupei, for example, who lost his life at Wuchang –
and important cities such as Kweilin and Changsha had repelled
the Taiping assaults, but the general picture was one of cowardice
and incompetence. In those early days, too, the Kingdom of
Heaven had yet to come to terms with reality, and the poor and
dispossessed learned with wonder of the army of liberation which
put oppressive landlords to the sword and destroyed the records
of inequitable transactions. Of course, in the majority of cases
the sentiment inspired a benevolent neutrality, but among the
young and enthusiastic it was strong enough to call them to arms,
a summons which was answered also by the more active members
of the anti-Manchu secret societies. With additions from these
various sources, the Taiping army, at the fall of Nanking, probably
amounted to not less than a million men and women.

In our own day, the Taiping have been criticized for alienating
large sections of the population by their innovations in religion
and morals. It is true that anti-Manchu feeling was latent even
among the most orthodox and respectable of the scholar-gentry.
But to win support in such a quarter would have required an
abandonment of all the ideals which gave the movement its

73

revolutionary vigour. Those aspects of the Taiping Movement drew humbler followers by the thousand, but frightened away the wealthy and the educated, who discovered they had an interest in maintaining the existing order of things. It was to these Chinese subjects that the Manchus owed their salvation.

It happened that the province of Hunan through which the rebels had just passed on their way to the Yangtze, and which forty years later was to give birth to the leader of a revolution far greater than theirs, was the native place of a man whose career, by the early 1850s, could well serve as a proof of the rewards to be won by talent and industry when dedicated to self-advancement. His name was Tseng Kuo-fan, and he was just over forty years old, having been born in 1811 to a landlord family of the middling sort. The examination system which had so frustrated Hung Hsiu-ch'uan had for Tseng been the ideal means to catch the eye of those in authority. In 1852, already holding high metropolitan office, he was recalled home by the death of his mother. Instead of retiring from the world for the statutory mourning he was almost at once invited by the Governor of the province to come to Changsha to assist in organizing a corps of volunteers for defence not so much against the Taiping, who had by then left Hunan behind them, as against the swarms of banditti proliferating in their wake. He obeyed the summons, and scarcely more than twenty-four hours after his arrival he had submitted a scheme of action which demonstrated his complete grasp of the situation. It has always been a curse of China that in military affairs quantity has been esteemed more than quality. Chiang Kai-shek, for instance, on the eve of the Nationalist collapse in 1949 could think of no better way of countering the Communist advance than by enlisting more and more ragamuffins under his colours. But Tseng Kuo-fan, recognizing the uselessness of such a procedure, declared that what he wanted was not a mere crowd of men, but a corps of soldiers, for whose training proper time should be allowed. An essential part of the training would be in Confucian ethics, for this Hunan Army would have a more important role to play than local police work. Soon it would appear as the champion of Chinese civilization against those who would change time-honoured institutions. A proclamation, written by Tseng somewhat later, shows what his opinion had been from the start.

Throughout history the Sages have upheld this doctrine, which expounds the pattern of men's relationships, of prince and subject, father and son, high and low, noble and humble, in an order that may no more be reversed than the position of a cap and shoe. The brigands from Kwangsi have filched the ideas of the foreign barbarians, and honour the religion of the Lord of Heaven [i.e. Catholicism, which to Tseng must have been the most familiar term for Christianity in general]. All of them, from pretended princes and ministers down to common soldiers, call themselves brother, and say Heaven alone is their father, and human parents are no more than brother and sister. Farmers cannot till their own fields and pay tribute, for all land belongs to the Lord of Heaven. Merchants cannot carry on their business for their own profit, for all goods belong to the Lord of Heaven. Scholars cannot recite the classics of Confucius, for they have another work, the New Testament, containing the teachings of the so-called Jesus, while our Chinese Book of Odes and Book of History which for thousands of years have been our guides in manners and morals are used to sweep the floor with. This is a rebellion not merely against the Dynasty but against the doctrine of the Sages ... How can men of education endure to sit with their hands in their sleeves and do nothing?

But the traditions to be defended were not merely Confucian. Buddhism and Taoism had suffered from the iconoclasts even more, and were, when all was said and done, nearer to the hearts of the peasantry who made up the rank and file of the Hunan Army. Another good old custom was being threatened too, 'When women refuse to unbind their feet the rebels cut off their feet and exhibit them as a warning to other women'.[1]

For a start, Tseng had to content himself with suppressing the petty bandits of the countryside, a task which engaged his attention throughout 1853. His severity with prisoners soon became a by-word. On grounds of the gravity of the situation he had a special court constituted in Changsha, where important culprits were put to death with the shortest possible delay, and even lesser ones frequently died of ill-treatment. 'So long as respectable people can live in peace,' he said, 'I don't mind what is thought about my cruelty.' By the autumn of 1853, part of the Hunan Army was emboldened to cross into the province of Kiangsi and try conclusions with a Taiping force there. The defeat it sustained was a valuable lesson that more training and experience were necessary before that particular enemy could be faced with confidence.[2]

The fact that the Taiping army was in Kiangsi at all shows that the rebels, once Nanking had fallen, had no intention of allowing the Manchus to enjoy a respite. The main portion of the troops had stayed, it is true, in the neighbourhood of the Heavenly Capital, but as early as May 1853 two expeditions had set off towards more distant provinces. The first was directed against Peking itself, but it was too small and ill-led for so important a duty. It picked up reinforcements from another group of insurgents, called the Nien, who were active in Anhwei, Honan and Shantung, *en route*. Making a long detour by the north-west, at the end of October it was threatening the outskirts of Tientsin, and had aroused such a panic in Peking that the Emperor Hsien Feng prepared to take refuge on the other side of the Great Wall in Jehol. But the terrible winter of North China was at hand to save the dynasty. The Taiping soldiers, paralysed by cold of a kind they had never encountered, and unable, as good rice-eaters, to digest their unfamiliar rations of millet, began to lose their virtue and early in 1854 fell back in retreat.

It was the first serious reverse the rebels had so far encountered, but the failure was not taken very tragically. The general situation was more than made up for by successes elsewhere. Simultaneously with the departure of the northern expedition another army, for the most part water-borne, had moved up river to recover the cities of Central China which had been captured once before but had been improvidently abandoned in the frantic march on Nanking. Some time was consumed in Kiangsi, where the Hunan army was first encountered and overcome. Early in 1854 Hanyang had been retaken, and Wuchang was surrounded, and was soon to fall. From there the Taiping retraced their original march into Hunan and left Tseng Kuo-fan no alternative but to risk his troops in battle again. At first it seemed that all his plans would be frustrated, but after some initial set-backs of so menacing a kind that Tseng contemplated suicide, the Hunan army achieved what had been thought impossible and in October drove the rebels from Wuchang. Hanyang too was soon restored to government control. By the end of the year the war had been carried down river as far as the port of Kiukiang.

This remarkable success was beyond doubt due to the organizing genius of Tseng Kuo-fan. He had by now recognized the necessity of possessing a naval force if the Taiping mastery of the

Yangtze was to be challenged. It was the river-craft already brought into use which had won the day at Wuchang, where the Taiping vessels had been trapped and set on fire, and Tseng entertained still more ambitious plans for building and equipping a great Yangtze fleet. Whatever he suggested, it was plain, would be listened to favourably in Peking, for the Emperor Hsieng Feng was beside himself with joy at the news, and had written Tseng a letter in his own hand. 'Your report gave Us truly deep consolation' it said. 'Nobody could have anticipated that such a great victory would be won. We implore Heaven speedily to free our people from affliction.' The Taiping, too, acknowledged Tseng's success by decapitating the generals he had routed. The Hunan Army, less than two years old, had shown what it was worth.

But the road ahead was full of pitfalls. The man who confronted Tseng at Kiukiang was the Guardian Prince, Shih Ta-k'ai, who, now that Yang Hsiu-ch'ing was in Nanking, was the most outstanding rebel commander in the field. Part of the Hunan fleet was trapped in a lake and cut off from the main body on the river. Without effective help from the ships, Tseng's land forces were defeated. Then Shih Ta-k'ai resumed the offensive and early in 1855 Wuchang passed for a third time into rebel hands. As the year wore on, the change of fortune seemed to be confirmed and the whole Yangtze Valley, from the Wuhan cities to below Nanking, was firmly under Taiping control, with the Hunan Army cut off to the south. The peasantry of the whole region seemed to think Heaven had unequivocally shown its preference in the matter, and were more and more treating the Taiping soldiers as the representatives of a lawfully established government. All this time, in spite of the victories elsewhere, Nanking itself had had to endure the affront of seeing a Manchu encampment pitched in an almost impregnable position within a short distance of its walls. In May 1856, this eyesore was removed. The place was carried by assault. Yet strangely enough on the heels of this triumph there occurred an event that shook the Taiping regime to its foundations.

Dissension and Murder in the Heavenly Capital

As soon as they had settled in their Heavenly Capital, the rebel leaders, and especially Hung Hsiu-ch'uan and Yang Hsiu-ch'ing, had given their attentions to the development of the new society they flattered themselves they had brought into being. Of the institutions they created, the most ambitious was the system of landholding promulgated in 1853. Its importance is merely theoretical for it was never put into practice. It provided that, as the land was intended by God for the support of all men, it should be divided into lots, estimated according to productivity, and then distributed among households in proportion to the number of their adult members. In the peaceful days to come it was foreseen that the basic social unit would consist of twenty-five households, forming a sort of commune with its own chapel and treasury, and managed by two officers appointed by election. The men of the commune would work in the fields, while the women tended the silk-worms, to feed which mulberry trees were planted outside each house; and did weaving or dress-making. Every family would possess five hens and two sows. Surplus produce would go to the treasury to meet the public need. Disputes would so far as possible be settled by arbitration before the commune officers, and only if this failed would the litigants go to a higher body; for the communes themselves were constituent parts of a system of progressively larger groups.

The spirit inspiring this social pattern may have been communicated to its authors by their reading of the New Testament, but most of its details were drawn from the descriptions in the Confucian canon of the institutions of a vanished golden age. And although the law of land tenure was to be no more than an unattainable ideal, there is evidence to suggest that, at least until this crucial year of 1856, the Taiping armies were faithful to the doctrine of the communal treasuries, and that private retention of loot, whenever discovered, was punished with death. The continuance of the war meant too that among the soldiers the segregation of men from women was maintained.

This Spartan discipline showed up all the more severely in contrast with the luxurious mode of life pursued by the Princes. The old Viceroy's residence was not good enough for Hung Hsiuch'uan, who ordered it to be pulled down, together with other buildings in the neighbourhood. An immense palace was to be erected on the site. Ten thousand workers sweated at the task for six months, only to have the result of their labour destroyed in a fire. The construction was begun afresh and in due course a regular Forbidden City, more than three miles round, was ready for the younger brother of Christ. Its gardens and pavilions, stocked with a plentiful harem, preoccupied the leader, but when he did go out sixty-four bearers staggered under his palanquin.

During the march from Kwangsi, the Eastern Prince, Yang Hsiu-ch'ing, had emerged as the undoubted military genius of the campaign. Now at Nanking, in his capacity as mouthpiece of God the Father, he was scarcely inferior in power or prestige to Hung himself. In proportion as the latter became addicted to domestic enjoyments the practical direction of affairs passed into Yang's hands. The regime as a whole was remarkable for its proliferation of bureaucrats, among whom the staff of the Eastern Prince soon formed a dominant, not to say domineering, clique. As many as three hundred orders a day, of one sort or another, were issued by this formidable organization, and the orders were enforced by sanctions of the direct kind. Gamblers, play-actors, brawlers, drunkards, had on occasion forfeited their heads and might count themselves lucky, for there were still more frightful modes of death, such as being torn asunder by five horses, or being set on fire to form a 'celestial lamp'.

In such circumstances, a clash of personalities was only to be expected. At the end of 1853, Hung Hsiu-ch'uan, already quite the pasha, forgot his dignity so far as to give a violent kick to one of his concubines. It was still early enough for the business to cause a scandal, and the Eastern Prince was inspired by God the Father to demand that Hung should receive forty strokes with a bamboo rod. Amazingly, Hung pretended to receive the divine judgment with meekness, whereupon God, speaking through Yang, graciously remitted the sentence. But after that, it was common knowledge that the two men were on bad terms, and that it was enough for one of them to advocate a certain policy to ensure that the other would oppose it.

It was not only the Heavenly Prince who had grounds for irritation. The Guardian Prince, Shih Ta-k'ai, in spite of his experience in the field, and the urgency of the military situation, found himself unaccountably passed over in the distribution of commands. At the beginning of 1855 the success of the Hunan Army made his presence essential on the western front. The Northern Prince, Wei Ch'ang-hui, the man whose wealth at Gold Field had made him the most powerful supporter of the early movement, found Yang's slights and arrogance even more intolerable, but with greater cunning than Shih he hid his resentment behind a show of complacency. In the spring of 1856, he too left to assume a military command in the countryside. When in May of that year the Manchu camp outside Nanking was taken by assault the credit for the enterprise went to Yang Hsiu-ch'ing alone.

Not long after this victory, Hung Hsiu-ch'uan was informed that God the Father had again descended into the breast of his rival, and was demanding to be heard. On such occasions, it was the rule that Hung must attend at Yang's residence. He did so, to be greeted with a query. 'You and the Eastern Prince,' said the divine voice, 'are both my sons, and now that the Eastern Prince has done this great service why is he still entitled to a salutation of merely Nine Thousand Years?' To understand what this meant we have to bear in mind that in China a ruler was termed 'Lord of Ten Thousand Years', and among the princes Hung alone enjoyed such a style to mark his pre-eminence. Baffled, he was forced to answer: 'As the Eastern Prince's valour has gained the country, it is only right he should be entitled to the salutation of Ten Thousand Years.' But even this was not enough: God the Father would not be content until Hung had agreed that Yang's eldest son should enjoy the same distinction, which was to be transmitted to the eldest son of each future generation of the Yung family. To all intents and purposes Hung was being forced to hand over his leadership, and he resolved not to do so without a struggle. Once back in the privacy of his own palace, he dispatched messengers to recall the Guardian and the Northern Princes to the Heavenly Capital.[3]

Wei Ch'ang-hui being closer at hand received the summons first and without delay set off at the head of picked troops. With these he entered the city during the night of 1 September 1856 and seized control of the main thoroughfares. Then at dawn on 2 September he broke into the residence of Yang Hsiu-ch'ing, and put the Eastern Prince and all his household to the sword. It does not say much for the efficiency of Yang's followers that they allowed him to be taken unawares in this way, but now at any rate they had been given the alarm and there were so many of them that the outcome of the affair seemed far from certain. Wei, however, made no attempt to extend the fighting. Instead, after some delay, a proclamation was made from Hung Hsiu-ch'uan's

palace to announce that Wei himself had been induced to see the
enormity of his conduct, and was to submit to a scourging in
the presence of as many of Yang's adherents who cared to witness
the punishment. At the hour appointed a multitude of onlookers
went to the palace in the expectation of seeing their master re-
venged. Out of respect for the place, they laid down their weapons
at the entrance and crowded inside. The doors were shut and then
at a signal Wei's soldiers appeared from nowhere and slaughtered
every one of them. The rest who had stayed at home were soon
rounded up and dispatched in a similar manner. All told, upwards
of twenty thousand people were massacred.

It did not take Hung long to discover that he had merely exchanged one incubus for another, and of the two Wei Ch'ang-hui
was in many respects the more odious. The memory of Yang's
arrogance began to pass from men's minds as they experienced
the new tyranny. The story was carried by rumour across the
country, and the Manchu partisans heard with delight that the
rebels were cutting one another's throats.

Shih Ta-k'ai, who had been campaigning near the Wuhan cities
when he received the message of recall, did not reach Nanking
until October. The city was enjoying a respite from the bloodshed
of the past month, but Shih saw and heard enough to fill him with
abhorrence. He bitterly denounced Wei's conduct. As a result, he
was warned one night that his own murder was imminent. To
forestall the assassins he took advantage of the darkness and had
himself lowered by a rope from the city wall. His family, whom
he had no time to rescue, were all put to death, but he himself
eluded the pursuers who had been sent after him and made his
way to the nearest encampment of his soldiers. Other troops from
Central China joined him and he marched on Nanking at the head
of forty thousand men with the demand that Wei Ch'ang-hui must
pay for his crimes. Popular sentiment by this time was altogether
on Shih's side, and this nerved Hung Hsiu-ch'uan to take action.
In November, Wei was assassinated but it was considered sufficient
if a mere two hundred of his closest allies were put to death with
him. Shortly afterwards Shih Ta-k'ai entered the capital in triumph;
he was in everyone's eyes the hero who had saved the Heavenly
Kingdom from its enemies.

The latest turn of events obliged Hung Hsiu-ch'uan to reveal
his displeasure and envy by making princes of two of his elder

brothers, whose lack of ability could fairly be inferred from the slowness of their earlier promotion. Talented or not, they could be depended upon to counterbalance Shih's popularity. They were encouraged to assert their new privileges on every occasion that offered itself, in particular by obtruding their authority into the military sphere which, now that Yang was no longer alive, the Guardian Prince might reasonably feel to be his special concern. In June 1857, finding his position intolerable, Shih left Nanking for the war, and when he had reached the safety of his armies, issued a proclamation in which he protested bitterly against the suspicion and intrigue that had been poisoning his life during the past few months. He had no ambitions for himself, he said. When the Manchus had been overthrown, his heart was set on retirement. Until that day he would stay with his troops and do his duty as best he could. And in fact from then on he never again set foot in Nanking.

The rebellion had run only half its course, and for years the Heavenly Kingdom would still inspire men to fight and to die. Yet it is plain now that the events of 1856–7 inflicted a mortal wound on the Taiping cause. The Communist historians of our own day have the satisfaction of finding the whole business a convincing proof of their theory of class contradictions. To Yang Hsiu-ch'ing, the charcoal-burner, everything is pardoned; his pretended inspirations, even his arrogance; for all he did was in the service of the revolution. The mass of Taiping followers must have thought so too, for they venerated Yang as a saint, and kept the anniversary of his murder, the 27th day of the 7th moon in the lunar calendar, as the Feast of the Eastern Prince's Ascension to Heaven. Shih Ta-k'ai, as the son of a comparatively wealthy family, is blamed, in spite of the provocation he had received, for thinking of his personal honour rather than of revolutionary solidarity. But the great villain is Wei Ch'ang-hui, the landlord, whose pursuit of self-interest, concealed for a while, finally turned him into the butcher of his comrades. Here too the Communist verdict was anticipated by the Taiping, and in a way that gives special pleasure to Marxists. In the institutional books of the movement published after 1856, we find no mention whatever of Wei Ch'ang-hui, the Northern Prince. It is as if he had never existed; even the Soviet Encyclopedia itself could not perform a blander job of annihilation.[4]

CHAPTER VI

THE SECOND OPIUM WAR

The Western Powers and the Taiping Rebellion – developments at Shanghai – outbreak of the Second Opium War – Russia returns to the Amur – the Tientsin Treaties – the Anglo-French expedition to Peking

The Western Powers and the Taiping Rebellion

THE irruption of the Taiping forces into Central China and their victorious descent of the Yangtze had of course aroused the greatest curiosity in the foreign residents on the coast, particularly in the missionaries. It was known that the rebels professed a religion based in part on the Bible, and with the establishment of the new government at Nanking there was much speculation that China might pass under the rule of a Christian dynasty.

As befitted the importance of her interest, Britain was first on the scene. As early as the end of April 1853, the Governor of Hong Kong, Sir George Bonham, arrived in Nanking to make contact with the Taiping leaders. He did not succeed in gaining access to the Heavenly Prince, but received a promise in writing that foreigners could come and trade freely, except in opium, since the Taiping were resolute in punishing both dealers and smokers with death. The general impression received was that the new regime recognized its spiritual kinship with the strangers, but was by no means inclined to be subservient to them. Indeed, this was displayed at the outset, for due to some misunderstanding, shots were fired at the vessel carrying the envoy. Later, the Northern Prince, Wei Ch'ang-hui, spoke with great frankness to the English interpreter. 'If you help the Manchus,' he said, 'you will not only be making a great mistake, you will be wasting your time too.'

Wei could not have known it, but the idea of helping the Manchus had already been suggested to Bonham as he had passed through Shanghai. If Britain and France rescued the emperor Hsien Feng, said Mr Alcock, the British Consul, they could in return have the whole country thrown open to their influence. Nor was this merely idle fancy; for if the words were Alcock's, the thought behind them was derived from no less a source than one of Hsien Feng's representatives, who was himself a characteristic product of the place and time.

A frequent expression of abuse among modern Chinese historians is the term *compradore*, applied not only to a class of people but to the type of culture, they are blamed for disseminating. In fact, the Portuguese word came into general use among the foreign traders at Canton in the days before the Opium War to designate the Chinese who acted as agents of western companies. At that time, their role, though important, was comparatively humble, for they were strictly controlled by the licensed Hongs. After the collapse of the Hong system and the opening of other ports by the Treaty of Nanking their position was very much strengthened, for now they were answerable only to their foreign employers, with whom they were on terms of mutual dependence. Shanghai soon became their special theatre of activity, but for many years, whether in Shanghai or the other ports, most of the compradores, or middlemen, who formed the link between the foreigners and their Chinese customers, tended to be Cantonese, who had inherited the craft by family tradition.

It will be readily imagined that even so lowly a occupation as that of houseboy could be very profitable when the master was wealthy and unable to speak or understand a word of Chinese. When it came to negotiating the sale of opium or the purchase of tea and silk there were almost limitless possibilities of self-enrichment. In due course, compradores of substance were not content until they had rounded off their career by acquiring official status for themselves or their sons. One man with such ambitions was Wu Chien-chang, a Cantonese by origin, who having made a fortune out of western trade used part of it to buy his way into the mandarinate and from 1850 onwards was holding the important post of Intendant at Shanghai, where his acquaintance with the foreigners could be used most advantageously. After the fall of Nanking, his superiors in the administration were delighted to have so acceptable a spokesman to help them in their quest for international assistance.

In spite of this pressure upon him, Bonham decided to recommend to London a policy of neutrality. For one thing, Britain would for a while have quite enough on her hands in the Crimea. Apart from opium the rebellion was by no means killing trade. Oddly enough, exports of silk and tea from the areas occupied by the Taiping actually increased. France and the United States, too, dispatched missions to Nanking which reported in much the same sense as Bonham.

Developments at Shanghai

It was in Shanghai that this policy of neutrality encountered its most severe test. Among the Cantonese and Fukienese immigrants who formed a large part of the inhabitants of the foreign settlements already established outside the walls many were enrolled as members of an anti-Manchu organization called the 'Small Sword Society'. This body must have been remarkably circumspect, for it concealed its real nature well enough to have its members accepted by the local authorities into the defence volunteers who, at Shanghai as elsewhere, were being trained for use against the Taiping and other disturbers of the peace. On 8 September 1853, which was the birthday of Confucius, the Society profited from the occasion of a ceremony in the Sage's honour to murder a local magistrate and take prisoner the compradore-mandarin Wu Chien-chang. Wu's foreign contacts stood him in good stead, since he was quickly rescued by a couple of Americans and carried to the safety of the foreign settlements. The insurgents made themselves masters of the Chinese city, and their leader, who assumed the style of 'Marshal of the Ming Kingdom', sent a report of the exploit to the Heavenly Capital.

For a year and a half, the period during which the Small Swords remained in control of the city, the foreign settlements found themselves in the dangerous situation of being directly on the line of march between the rebels and a large force of government troops stationed nearby. Understandably enough, it was felt that the circumstance of the time required some drastic measures to provide for the common safety. Accordingly the consuls of Britain, France and the United States, the three countries with settlements at Shanghai, drew up a new set of Land Regulations in July 1854. To do this, they secured the approval of their good friend Wu Chien-chang in his capacity as representative of the Peking government. This document authorized the election of a Municipal Council to administer the three settlements jointly. Before long, however, the French withdrew their Concession, and from then on managed it for themselves. In 1863, the American and British areas were amalgamated into the International Settlement of famous memory. Meanwhile, by the new Regulations, the Municipal Council was empowered to establish its own police force and to levy rates. The Civil War had driven many Chinese to take refuge under the protection of foreign guns, and the next year the Council advanced a step further and raised contributions from Chinese as well. Residual Chinese sovereignty was acknowledged but for all practical purposes an *imperium in imperio* had been created, which was to remain in existence for ninety years.

One of the duties of Wu Chien-chang before his eviction had been the superintendence of customs, and in order to appease the wrath of the Emperor, from whom he knew he could expect little sympathy for his misadventure, he was anxious that this source of revenue should not be impaired. After much complicated negotiation, the three consuls in June 1854 entered into an agreement with Wu to have the Chinese maritime customs managed by foreigners who would be responsible to the Peking government for the proper collection of dues.

These two consequences made the insurrection of the Small Swords memorable in the history of China. By itself, the rising came to nothing. The Taiping were too heavily committed to the campaign in the central provinces, not to mention the expedition to the north, to have aid to spare for their allies, who were at last reduced to eating the corpses of their dead. As the situation changed, so did the neutrality of the foreigners, especially that of the French whose settlement bordered on the Chinese city. It was a mixed Franco-Manchu force which broke through the walls in February 1855 with a bloody slaughter of the rebels and restored Shanghai to its former obedience.

Local co-operation of this sort was not typical of the general relationship between the Manchus and the Western Powers, which remained profoundly unsatisfactory from the western point of view. There was no diplomatic representation at Peking, North

China was barred to foreign trade and residence, and, what was even more infuriating, access to the city of Canton was still denied in practice a decade after it had been granted in theory. The backbone of the anti-foreign movement in Canton was formed by a society known to be anti-Manchu as well, but even when after 1855 the Imperial Commissioner Yeh Ming-ch'en did his Emperor yeoman service by putting many thousands of the malcontents to the sword, the path towards international understanding was not made any smoother. Yeh, under the existing system, was charged with the responsibility of handling communications between the Western nations and the Court. He not only loathed all foreigners but despised them into the bargain with a megalomaniac arrogance. By 1856, Britain and France were determined to raise the question of treaty revision, only to find that Yeh, alleging the pressure of business, would not even grant their envoys the courtesy of an interview. Then, just at the convenient time, for the Crimean War was now over, fate provided an excuse for bringing matters to a head.

Outbreak of the Second Opium War

In October 1856, police at Canton boarded the sailing vessel *Arrow* and arrested twelve members of her Chinese crew on charges of piracy and smuggling. The ship's owner was Chinese, but she had been registered in Hong Kong, had a British captain and was flying the British flag. True, the registration had expired, but it was decided to pursue the incident to the bitter end. After a few days, Yeh climbed down to the extent of returning the prisoners, but this gesture of appeasement was rejected on the grounds that no mandarin of rank had come to offer apologies. It is possible that the British imagined Yeh's extirpation of the nationalist fanatics had deprived him of popular support in the event of a conflict. At any rate they sent three men-of-war into the Canton River and having occupied the surrounding forts proceeded to shell the city. They then made a token entry within the walls but quickly withdrew to their ships. The Canton mob in retaliation sacked and destroyed the foreign business ghetto. It was clear after this that only a full-scale expedition could accomplish what was desired, and as France too had cause for complaint in the murder of a missionary she signified her readiness to share in the venture.

There were some preliminary difficulties to be overcome. In London, the House of Commons did not support the government's action, but a general election gave Lord Palmerston, then Prime Minister, the majority he needed. Even so, the outbreak of the Great Mutiny in the summer of 1857 made it necessary to divert to India troops intended for the Far East.

In November 1857, the Anglo-French forces assembled in Hong Kong declared the port of Canton under blockade, and the next month an ultimatum was delivered to Commissioner Yeh, demanding the revision of existing treaties, the payment of an indemnity, and access to Canton city. All the reply it elicited was a promise that trade might be resumed. At the end of December operations against the city began. It is scarcely credible, but highly characteristic of the mental befuddlement of the Chinese authorities, that no military preparations whatsoever had been made since the fighting a year earlier. Yeh himself, who was chiefly responsible, happened to be one of those mandarins in whom the aridity of Confucian agnosticism was tempered with a strong dose of superstition, and he was accustomed to seek advice from the spirit world by means of the Chinese equivalent of the ouija board. Among the counsellors summoned up in this way was no less a figure than the most famous of Chinese poets, Li Po of the T'ang dynasty. Total inaction was the course recommended, and the promise given that in fifteen days the nuisance would be over and done with. It might be argued that the prophecy came true; the allies took Canton by storm, sent poor Yeh as a prisoner to Calcutta, where he died in 1859, and accepted the co-operation of the provincial governor in administering the city.[1]

To Britain and France, the seizure of Canton was merely a first step; their main purpose could be achieved only by knocking at the gates of the capital itself. So far there was no sign that the Manchu Court had any idea of the gravity of the situation. The Emperor Hsien Feng had expressed his entire approbation of the policy of Commissioner Yeh, and seemed perfectly indifferent to the hazard of adding alien to domestic enemies. This was all the more surprising because in the meantime, after a hundred and fifty years of respite, the Amur lands were again being invaded.

Russia Returns to the Amur

Russia, who had for years been envious of the maritime trade of her rivals, found her position even more galling after the Opium War, for a new era had now dawned in which the system created by the Treaty of Nerchinsk was plainly an anachronism. The Tsarist government decided, instead of following the British example, to take advantage of the indignation aroused throughout China by the shame of defeat and present itself to the Chinese as an ally against the Western enemy, an ally possessed of all the resources of military science, the lack of which had put the Chinese at such a disadvantage. In the dissemination of their propaganda the Russians enjoyed one privilege for which so far the other nations of Europe had asked in vain, namely a foothold within the walls of Peking itself. For although the Orthodox Mission was established as we have seen to cater for the spiritual needs of the descendants of the Cossack prisoners incorporated in the seventeenth century into the Manchu army, it inevitably fulfilled something of the role of a political delegation. In 1846, in the course of what would nowadays be called a cultural exchange, a collection of Russian books was sent to Peking in return for the gift of a set of Buddhist scriptures. This event seems to have caused quite a stir in intellectual circles and some Chinese men of letters, who were becoming aware of the jealousy the Russian presence in their capital was arousing among other Europeans, went out of their way to compare the solid achievements of Russian learning with 'the boastful narratives of early Western missionaries, anxious only to win converts'.[2]

One reason that had led Russia to acquiesce so long in the frontier delimitation made at Nerchinsk was that the topography of the Amur estuary was still obscure. In particular, it was widely believed that Sakhalin was not an island but was joined to the continent south of where the Amur entered the sea. If such was the case, the value of the river as a waterway would be much decreased, because it would merely give access northwards to the Sea of Okhotsk, and not in the direction of Japan, Korea and China. In 1849, however, a Russian naval officer, Nevelskoi, passed through the narrow Strait of Tartary. The following year he sailed twenty-five miles up the Amur itself and established a camp on the left bank, raising the Russian flag and calling the place Nikolayevsk. In so doing, he exceeded his orders, but the Governor-General of Eastern Siberia, Muravyev, was an ambitious man, still young, who ever since his appointment had been dreaming of glory and aggrandizement. So he supported Nevelskoi at St Petersburg. Tsar Nicholas I declared that the flag, once hoisted, must never be lowered. The Government was forced to acquiesce to the extent of keeping Nikolayevsk as a calling station, and a message was dispatched to notify Peking that foreign ships had been active off the mouth of the Amur and that Russia proposed to assist China in safeguarding the defence of both countries.

The Taiping rebellion diverted the dynasty's attention from these activities, just as two centuries earlier a domestic uprising had compelled the Manchus to allow the first Cossack invasion to go for years almost unchecked. In contrast to the hesitating neutrality of the Western Powers, Russia from the start ostentatiously declared her support for the Manchus. Shortly afterwards Muravyev was able to profit from the occasion of the Crimean War to carry the comedy of joint defence a step further. In May 1854, an expedition of a thousand men on ninety boats and rafts, led by the Governor-General in person, sailed down the River Shilka into the Amur. In June they arrived opposite Aigun, the Chinese administrative centre, where they found a fleet of junks and a garrison about as numerous as themselves, but wretchedly armed, for the most part with bows and arrows. Even so, the officer in charge made a show of questioning the intruders' right of passage, but on Muravyev's informing him they were merely in transit to defend Russian possessions against the British and would create no disturbance in Chinese territory, he thought it wiser not to interfere. On reaching the sea, most of the troops were sent to reinforce the garrison of Petropavlovsk in Kamchatka, just in time to repel an Anglo-French fleet at the end of August. The victory, when contrasted with the defeats suffered in the Crimea, made Muravyev a national hero, and the following year another and larger armada repeated the voyage, with an ominous addition, for the passengers included nearly five hundred colonists with women and children.

By this time Peking was partly aware of what was afoot. Before Muravyev's first expedition, the Russian Government had invited the Chinese to send a commission to delimit the most eastern stretch of the frontier, which the Treaty of Nerchinsk had left vague between the fork of the Stanovoi Mountains. It was no easy matter for the commissioners to catch up with Muravyev and when they did, in September 1855, it was in the surroundings of a new Russian settlement, of more than a hundred buildings, where, to their stupefaction, they were informed that there was no need for them to go mountaineering, as they were already on the most suitable national boundary, namely the Amur itself. To prove the point, as they left for Peking, they were shown a map on which the north bank of the river was coloured as Russian territory.

The following year brought the end of the Crimean War and the death of that patron of imperial expansion, Nicholas I. Muravyev, home on leave, gained the ear of the new Tsar Alexander II with such effect that a province was created on the Amur, with himself as Governor-General at Nikolayevsk. But a fait accompli even more spectacular than this awaited the Chinese. For the naval officer Nevelskoi had surveyed the Manchurian coast down to the Korean border and had urged successfully that this, too, as far inland as the Ussuri River, must be included in the Tsar's dominions. At the southern end, in particular, the town of Haishenwei with its harbour would make a splendid port. As good luck would have it, this maritime region was as sparsely inhabited as the north bank of the Amur had been before Muravyev's arrival. Its colonization would offer few difficulties. Yet how in the world could the Peking Government be induced to consent to so enormous a sacrifice? True, it was in no condition to defend Manchuria by force, but on their side the Russians were determined to do nothing that might topple the hard-pressed dynasty altogether, for a victorious Taiping regime would very likely be under British influence.

This point became all the more important when it was learned in Europe, in the spring of 1857, that Britain and France had determined on a joint military expedition to bring the Chinese to reason. As soon as he got wind of the news, Admiral Count Putyatin, the Russian naval attaché in London, hurried to St Petersburg, where, because of his experience in the Far East, he was appointed Ambassador to China, with the purpose both of settling the Manchurian problem and ensuring that Russia obtained the same privileges as Britain and France. Palladius, one of the resident priests in Peking, was instructed to inform the Chinese Government that the Ambassador was coming to concert plans for meeting the Anglo-French threat. In spite of this, Putyatin was refused permission to enter the country, and finally joined company as an observer with the Anglo-French force off Canton.

If the presence of a barbarian envoy in the capital was regarded with aversion, it was hoped that the Emperor might be spared such an affront to his dignity by having the territorial problem solved on the frontier itself. So a Manchu plenipotentiary met Muravyev at Aigun in May 1858. The conference, if it deserves such a name, lasted for six days, and ended with a mock bombardment by five Russian warships which went on all night and reduced the inhabitants of the town and the wretched commissioner himself to such a state of terror that Muravyev had his terms accepted next morning. The north bank of the Amur went to Russia, and that portion of the south bank between the Ussuri River and the sea became a condominium, thus protecting, as Muravyev put it, the rest of Manchuria from attack by the British. Navigation on the Amur and the Ussuri was to be restricted to Russian and Chinese subjects.

The Tientsin Treaties

While this Treaty of Aigun was being negotiated, if that is the right word to use, other diplomatic transactions were being carried on to the sound of gunfire some hundreds of miles to the south. In February 1858 the main body of the Anglo-French flotilla sailed from Canton northwards up the coast, followed not only by Putyatin but also by an American plenipotentiary, for in the matter of treaty revision the interests of all four countries were equally engaged. During a stop at Shanghai, the allies left a note to be forwarded to Peking in which their chief demands were set out, permission for foreign representatives to reside in the capital, freedom for foreigners to travel in the interior of the country, the opening of more ports for trade, and the readjustment of tariffs. It was clear that nothing would come of this application; the foreigners were simply asked to return and submit a fresh request from Canton; and in April when the fleet reached Taku, at the entrance to the Tientsin River, the commanders had no doubt they must have recourse to arms. Still, as the place was protected by four citadels, equipped with one hundred and fifty guns including thirty large cannon, and garrisoned by nine thousand men, a certain amount of circumspection seemed called for. Accordingly, while taking stock of the situation, the British and French let it be known they were ready to talk only with a fully responsible official. Even the Viceroy of the Metropolitan Province did not measure up to their standard, as they declared he was not a plenipotentiary. Neither the American nor the Russian envoy had such scruples. The American beguiled the Viceroy with his conversation and waited for his friends to strike. Putyatin's role was even more two-faced, for on the one hand he urged his Western colleagues to stern measures, and on the other he wrote to the Chinese authorities to say that, if Russia's claims were met, she would help China to 'destroy the British and French'. Russia, he stated, observed with regret the insufficiency of the Chinese armaments, and would be delighted to supply weapons and instructors.

On the morning of 20 May, the fleet started to bombard the forts, and a landing party went ashore. Resistance was at first vigorous, but by noon the defenders' morale had broken, the Viceroy was seen travelling due west by sedan-chair, and the flags of Britain and France waved over Taku. The river was now open, and on 31 May the invaders reached Tientsin where two imperial commissioners hastened to treat with them.

Of all the foreigners' demands, the one most alarming to the Emperor personally and to those about him was that concerning the residence of diplomats at Peking. The antipathy provoked by the very mention of such a thing may seem strange, particularly when we consider that during the first century and a half of the dynasty's history, Catholic missionaries had been commonly seen at Court and an Orthodox establishment even now flourished under treaty protection. But it must be remembered that what was being proposed was the reception by the sovereign of envoys in whose treatment he would be forced to acknowledge the equal dignity of their masters with himself. Sensing the bitterness of the physic, the French and the Americans were not absolutely insistent that it must be swallowed in one draught, but Lord Elgin for Britain would have nothing less than outright acquiescence. Yet it was known that, even after acceptance, there would have to be a delay while the agreements were being ratified, and in the interval perhaps a way would be found of averting the evil. Such at all events was the hope of the Chinese commissioners as they yielded to the implacable Elgin. The Anglo-Chinese Treaty, signed on 26 June, contained the following main provisions:

1 Diplomatic relations to be conducted on terms of equality, and a British minister to reside at Peking.
2 Ten more ports to be opened to British trade. These ranged from Manchuria to Formosa, and, most important of all, included four towns on the Yangtze as far as Hankow.
3 Freedom of travel and missionary activity.
4 Clarification of extra-territoriality. Disputes between British subjects to be handled by British officials; cases between British and Chinese subjects to be heard by a mixed court formed of a Chinese magistrate and a British consul; while criminal cases were to be dealt with by the country of the accused.
5 British naval vessels to have entry to all treaty ports, and thus to enjoy the right of sailing up the Yangtze to Hankow.
6 Britain to be paid an indemnity of four million dollars.

Treaties concluded with the other powers were in the same general sense. That with Russia was signed in ignorance of what had been done at Aigun a few weeks earlier. Its effect was to put Russia for the first time on the same footing as the maritime powers, with similar access to ports. Future intercourse between the two countries would be managed by the Emperor's Privy Council, in place of the Board of Dependencies. As for Manchuria, there was a vague promise to co-operate in settling the undefined frontier. The offer of Russian technicians was declined, but if arms were sent, China was willing to accept them.

The invaders now retired from Tientsin, on the understanding that they would return next year to ratify the agreements, and with their departure the Manchu Court regained something of its old self-confidence. It had been arranged that Commissioners should go down to Shanghai to discuss the details of tariff readjustments and the Emperor still hoped that by giving the foreigners what they asked on this point, and if necessary by relinquishing custom dues altogether, he could persuade them to waive their recently acquired rights, especially those relating to Peking legations and Yangtze ports.

The atmosphere in Shanghai was not conducive to such a suggestion. The Commissioners had inevitably to rely heavily on local officials, who being accustomed to dealing with foreigners, and, as we have seen, tainted with compradore influence, did not share the Manchu aversion to the barbarians' company. Besides, they recognized that without customs dues the war against the Taiping could not be prosecuted. In the last two or three years, the deficit on land tax because of the rebellion had necessitated the introduction of an additional sort of customs tariff called *likin*. Under this system goods in transit across the countryside were halted at stations erected for that purpose and required to pay dues before they were allowed to continue their journey. The money so raised was devoted to the upkeep of local armies, but the exaction, coming as it did on top of the ordinary duty paid on imports at the port of entry, was unpopular among foreign merchants. The Commissioners, however, seem to have been dissuaded by their Shanghai colleagues from mentioning the bargain that the Emperor had in mind, and it was merely agreed that foreign goods should be exempted from *likin* in consideration of a payment of an extra two and a half per cent tariff besides the import duty. The opium traffic, too, was legalized.

Meanwhile, the defences of Taku were being restored and even reinforced. This was not being done with the express purpose of resisting the unwelcome visitors when they came to ratify their treaties, although it was intended that through the closure of the river the fleet would have to stay behind at the coast while the envoys proceeded in a civilian party to Peking. Word of this activity was carried to Shanghai, and when taken together with some hints that the Peking government had even now not fully acquiesced in the agreements it had been forced to make, led the British to feel they must be on the alert for deceit and evasion. Accordingly the Royal Navy provided a substantial flotilla to escort the British minister northwards. He was Mr Bruce, Lord Elgin's brother, his lordship having left for home at the beginning of 1859. He was accompanied by the French and American representatives, but France had trouble on her hands in Vietnam and was able to spare only two ships for China, while the three American naval vessels belonged to a government which was not committed to the use of force.

The expedition arrived off Taku in the middle of June 1859, to be informed by the Chinese authorities that the river was closed, as indeed they could see for themselves. The waterway was blocked with sunken objects and impeded with chains. They were invited accordingly to disembark at a spot on the coast not far off and from there to proceed overland. The American minister made ready to do so, but Mr Bruce exploded in fury and gave an ultimatum that the river must be cleared. When this demand was not carried out, the British and French ships started to demolish the obstructions, and were soon exchanging fire with the forts while a landing party attempted to repeat the exploit of the year before. It then became evident that against all expectations the Chinese were getting the better of the encounter, and the allies were obliged to withdraw with heavy losses, which would have been even heavier if the American commander had not rallied to their support with the notable phrase 'blood is thicker than water!' The Chinese ignored this breach of neutrality and permitted the American minister, who had disembarked as directed, to accomplish his errand and exchange the instruments of ratification. But he was treated so brusquely and afterwards packed off in such haste that the British and French, who had retired to lick their wounds, said they were glad to have been spared such an insult and contemplated with relish the vengeance they would take before long.

A few months earlier, in March 1859, a Russian envoy named Perofski had reached Peking by the overland route and obtained ratification of the Tientsin agreement on Russian access to ports. But when he turned to Manchuria, and raised the question of the land between the Ussuri and the sea, he was told sharply that the territory was quite outside the sphere of Russian interests and left with no doubt in his mind but that the Aigun treaty had been repudiated. The truth was that the Manchu Court recognized that the north bank of the Amur was irretrievably lost, but the Ussuri country, reaching as it did down to the Korean border, was too close at hand for its cession to be contemplated.

Perofski's place was taken in June 1859 by Major-General Ignatiev who had been chosen not only for his experience in oriental diplomacy, but because as a soldier he seemed well fitted to carry out the proposal, already raised by Putyatin, of bringing the Chinese army under Russian influence. He was accompanied on his journey across Siberia by a group of military instructors, in charge of a large consignment of arms, and a sum of half a million roubles had been appropriated for the scheme. But on the way he was warned of the Chinese change of attitude, and the military mission and equipment were diverted to the Siberian garrisons. As compensation, he made the last stage of the journey with as much splendour as he could. He arrived in Peking at the worst possible moment, a few days, in fact, after the Anglo-French humiliation at Taku. In such circumstances, all Ignatiev's carefully prepared speeches on the necessity of Russian help if China was to resist British aggression fell on deaf ears. The Manchus, as unable to profit from experience as the Bourbons, and in particular the Emperor Hsien Feng, already worn out with debauchery at thirty, were besotted enough to imagine they were now fully a match for the outside world. As for the Ussuri, Ignatiev was rebuked for the intrusion already committed there and reminded of the obligation his country had contracted at Nerchinsk.

Throughout the winter, Ignatiev remained in Peking, wandering unmolested everywhere in the city and encountering restriction only in the matter of his courier, a Cossack of such Herculean dimensions that the Chinese requested the substitution of a man less alarming to the eyes of the country people. Finally, at the end of May 1860, having accomplished nothing, he made his way to the coast, where a Russian ship was waiting to take him to Shanghai.

In that port he found preparations in full swing for another allied expedition to the north, and as one fresh from enemy territory he was naturally very much sought after. Everyone who met him was charmed by his affability and his frankness. It was quite true, he said, that Russia had intended to give military assistance to the Chinese Government in its struggle against the Taiping rebels, but as soon as he learned of the conflict with Britain and France he had cancelled the plan. He now understood that the Manchus respected nothing but force, and would be delighted to put his knowledge of the terrain at his friends' disposal. Both Lord Elgin, the British plenipotentiary, and Baron Gros, his French counterpart, for the original envoys of 1858 had returned to be present at the vindication of their treaties, were ravished by this generosity. Nor did Ignatiev's activities go unnoticed by local Chinese officials, whose urgent warnings to Peking led the Emperor and the Court to surmise erroneously that the Russian was the impelling force behind the assault which everybody now saw to be imminent.

The Anglo-French Expedition to Peking

It was a grandiose armada that arrived off the coast of the Metropolitan Province at the end of July 1860, consisting of over two hundred warships and transports with ten thousand British troops and six thousand French. The Chinese were under the command of a Mongol Prince named Seng-ko-lin-ch'in, whom the British soldiers soon knew as 'Sam Collinson', a veritable fire-eater so far as the suppression of domestic rebels was concerned, but at the moment in a state of confusion because of the self-contradictory nature of his instructions from Peking. These were at any rate specific on one point; he was not to commit his forces to the defence of the coastal ports, and in consequence he permitted the foreigners to land unopposed, and to dispose themselves at their ease for more than ten days. It is not easy to discern what the Emperor and his advisers hoped to accomplish by this passive attitude, but it seems likely they imagined the British and French would be so bemused by their reception that they would be content to have the treaties of 1858 ratified by a small diplomatic party during a brief visit to the capital. The first shock to this complacency was delivered on 12 August when the allies attacked the Chinese position and cut off the Taku ports from the rear. Just at this time, Seng-ko-lin-ch'in received an imperial rescript to certify that 'It would be wasteful to risk your person, on whom Our State relies, in combat with ugly barbarians', and on 21 August when the ports were attacked in strength, he took the advice to heart and escaped precipitately inland, leaving the Viceroy of the Metropolitan Province to manage the surrender of Taku and the peaceful entry of the allies into Tientsin.

There is no need to describe in detail the advance towards Peking, during which Seng-ko-lin-ch'in was routed in several engagements. In the Court itself, opinion was swinging backwards and forwards between peace and war. A meeting was arranged in the middle of September, twelve miles from the city, with an Anglo-French delegation, but when it was learned that the foreigners insisted on entering Peking with at least one thousand men, and demanded besides that Chinese forces should be withdrawn from the neighbourhood of the capital, sentiment all of a sudden hardened in favour of resistance. The unfortunate European spokesmen and their party, who had come to the conference under a flag of truce, were made prisoners and handled with such brutality that less than half of them survived.

Ignatiev, in the quality of a neutral observer, reached Tientsin in the wake of the allied invasion at the end of August, and followed the march on Peking. It is an extraordinary fact that during these hostilities the Chinese did not interfere with the coming and going of priests between the Russian House and Ignatiev in the Anglo-French camp. The foreigners were kept fully acquainted with what was passing in the capital, and where necessary had the use of accurate maps. Meanwhile, Ignatiev continued to send letters to the Chinese proposing his services as a mediator, but it was not until the allies were under the walls of Peking and the Emperor had fled north to Jehol on 22 September, a journey from which he never returned alive, that Prince Kung, the Emperor's brother, who had been left to cope with the enemy, hesitatingly accepted the offer.

By this time the tempers of the Europeans had been roused by the barbarous treatment of their delegates. Lord Elgin was particularly incensed and, to punish the Court for its treachery, he ordered his troops to set fire to the Summer Palace outside the city. This was the place called in Chinese *Yuan Ming Yuan*, or the 'Round Bright Garden', which in the eighteenth century Jesuit artists had collaborated with their Chinese colleagues to make one of the wonders of the world. For this Lord Elgin has to bear the opprobrium of history, kept alive in Chinese minds by the sight of the charred ruins which are left to testify to the atrocity. Of course, all the victors' demands had to be complied with. The provisions agreed to in 1858 were reaffirmed, but the indemnities were increased to eight million dollars for each ally; in addition Tientsin was opened to foreign trade; Chinese labour was permitted to be recruited for work abroad; confiscated Catholic chapels were to be restored, and priests allowed to buy land and build churches in every province; and Kowloon, on the mainland opposite Hong Kong, was ceded to Britain in perpetuity. When treaties to this effect had been signed at the end of October, the one question remaining was, when, if ever, the British and French could be induced to take their troops away?

The fact was that neither ally wished to stay a day more than necessary. Apart from the hardship of a North China winter, the news from Europe hinted at an ominous coolness in London towards Napoleon III's Italian policy, and it would be awkward if the two armies became enemies while on Chinese soil. Ignatiev, on his part, assured Prince Kung that the conclusion of peace was entirely due to his efforts. The Prince was dubious, but when the allied troops still gave the appearance of dallying in the city, he began to think it would be too dangerous to incur the risk of Ignatiev's stirring up further trouble. Consequently, he agreed to Ignatiev's terms, and on 14 November 1860, the Sino-Russian Treaty of Peking was signed. It confirmed the agreements of Aigun and Tientsin, but provided for the outright cession of the Ussuri territory to Russia.

In fact, the allies had postponed their departure simply because of a technical hitch, and both Elgin and Gros were gone by the time Ignatiev had completed his mission. Before following their example, he reminded Prince Kung that Russia was still willing to send military technicians to China, only stipulating that in order to avoid Anglo-French interference they should be employed in remote parts of the country. The Prince listened silently, but in his dispatches to the Emperor he revealed what he thought of the suggestion:

If we think the barbarians are sincere we shall be greatly deceived. They talk of helping us to put down the rebels, but say we must not let the British and French know. In my opinion all the barbarians have the nature of brute beasts. The British are the most unruly, but the Russians are the most cunning. The rebels menace our heart, the Russians our trunk, while the British are merely a threat to our limbs. First of all we must extirpate the rebels: then we must settle accounts with Russia. Britain's turn comes last.[3]

Muravyev had not bothered about diplomatic niceties. Already the year before, Haishenwei had been occupied, given its first Russian inhabitants, and renamed Vladivostok.

CHAPTER VII

THE T'UNG CHIH RESTORATION

The Taiping decline – Yehonala and the T'ung Chih Restoration – the West takes sides – Li Hung-chang and the Huai Army – the end of the Taiping

The Taiping Decline

THE Western Powers had at last got their way, and the Chinese government had agreed that both North China and the Yangtze Valley should be opened to their trade. It was then clearly in their common interest that the regime which had made these concessions should be maintained in its authority, rather than replaced by another dynasty of uncertain policy. Besides, the promise of treaty ports on the Yangtze was of little value while the cities themselves or the country round about them were in the hands of the rebels. Britain and France, it could safely be predicted, would find means of helping the Manchus against the Taiping.

No doubt the calculation was cold-blooded enough, but in any case the Taiping regime in 1860 was totally different from what it had been in 1853. Between these dates there had occurred the two sanguinary *coups d'état* of 1856, in which rebel leaders had slaughtered one another without mercy, to the scandal not only of foreign observers but also of the hero of the Taiping, the Guardian Prince, Shih Ta-k'ai himself, who, sick with disgust and in fear of his own life, had quitted the Heavenly Capital, never more to return to it. The effect of the butchery was almost at once discernible in the shaken confidence of various rebel commanders. Until that time it had been unheard of for any Taiping officers to lead their men into surrender, but within a month or two of the news from Nanking, reports began to arrive of insurgent garrisons in the provinces who returned to Manchu allegiance, and throughout the rest of the war these desertions became ever more frequent. But militarily speaking the great, and immediate, consequence of the feud was the final loss of Wuchang and Wuhan, for when in the summer of 1856 at the time the coup was being planned Shih Ta-k'ai had answered the Heavenly Prince's appeal and had hurried back to Nanking with a sizeable part of his force, these cities found themselves unable to withstand the pressure of the imperial troops and in particular of the Hunan Army, into whose hands they passed at the end of the year. From then on the Manchu side retained the advantage of this base in Central China, from which they were able to extend their operations downstream.

One should not exaggerate the rapidity of the Taiping deterioration, but it seems a fair comment to make that without the Anglo-French war against the Manchus, and the complications arising from the existence of several minor insurrections going on simultaneously in different parts of the country, the Heavenly Kingdom would in all probability not have lasted so long as it did. Yet credit must be given to the rebels for producing during this period of crisis a leader of genius, who even if he cannot be placed as a strategist in the same class as the murdered Yang Hsiu-ch'ing is beyond a doubt among the noblest figures in Chinese history. This was Li Hsiu-ch'eng, born in 1823 of a poor peasant family in the province of Kwangsi, and a recruit to the movement within a few months of the raising of the standard at Gold Field. After the catastrophe of 1856, his merits, though bringing him to high command, seem to have aroused jealousy in the breast of the Heavenly King, who had already given a practical demonstration of his susceptibility to that emotion. All victory and glory must come through himself, the Younger Brother of Christ. True, while meditating upon the divine mysteries in the recesses of his seraglio it was unseemly that he should be disturbed by mundane affairs, but he preferred that these last should be managed by members of his family. In 1859 it seemed that an unforgivable affront had been offered to Li Hsiu-ch'eng when in a distribution of honours he was passed over entirely and a younger rival elevated to the dignity of Prince. One of those Taiping generals who had now transferred their services to the Manchus wrote Li a letter to commiserate with him and to assure him of a cordial welcome in the imperial camp. By chance the message came to the attention of the Heavenly King, who did not doubt for a moment that Li would seize the opportunity to betray him, and for some days he forbade all communication between Nanking and Li's army on the other side of the Yangtze. As time passed, and there was no sign of treason, in a revulsion of feeling he named Li the Loyal Prince, the title by which he will always be remembered by his countrymen, and which he justified by his conduct to the day of his death.

It is depressing to have to note that even in the career of this brave and generous soldier there are certain features which illustrate the degeneration of Taiping manners in the closing phase of the rebellion. In the early days, although the programme of land-reform was from the start an unattainable ideal, the common ownership of goods was strictly practised, and all acquisitions made in the field were taken to the so-called Holy Treasuries, to be put in the common stock. But there is an abundance of proof that this rule was, by 1860 or even earlier, no longer observed, except for such things as foodstuffs or livestock, while money, jewellery, and fine clothing, of which there was such a store to be plundered in the provinces of the Lower Yangtze Valley, became the property of those who had the good luck to set hands on them. In part, the corruption may be blamed on recruits who came to the Taiping armies from plain banditti, and, not receiving the same zealous indoctrination as the original warriors of God, carried old habits with them, and indeed may have joined the movement in the first place in a quest for loot. However that may be, we know from one striking example that the Loyal Prince himself cannot have been immune from the infection. It happened that the Heavenly King appealed for contributions to the war fund and Li Hsiu-ch'eng gave no less than a hundred thousand silver dollars in his own name, a fortune the possession of which cannot be accounted for otherwise than as being the result of plunder.[1]

Meanwhile, as standards of behaviour declined on the Taiping side, the imperialists, by the late eighteen-fifties, were gradually introducing an alleviation of the land-tax in the disputed regions. This reform, coupled with ingrained habits of obedience, and prejudices in favour of the old accepted order of things, were succeeding in winning peasant sympathy from the rebels. The Taiping began to look more and more like the enemies of society that hostile propaganda represented them as being. It is hard to say how far this shift of sympathy had gone before the end of the rebellion. Later on, when the victors had done their best to stifle any favourable recollections of the rising, it was largely true that the inhabitants of the Yangtze provinces ravaged by the war, unlike their countrymen in Kwangtung and Kwangsi, remembered the Taiping without affection. By 1860 there can have been little reason why a peasant community should wish, at the risk of slaughter and pillage, to be set free by liberators who would preserve the old system of taxation and rents, as the Taiping then were doing, when by remaining under existing authority they might well have these burdens lightened.

The Emperor Hsien Feng had acclaimed in 1854 the first great victory of the Hunan Army in Central China. Any hopes of immediate advancement which this commendation may have inspired in the heart of Tseng Kuo-fan were sadly disappointed. The truth was that once the Emperor had time for reflection, he began to brood on the sinister possibilities latent in the situation. Until now, it had been an axiom of the dynasty that its Chinese subjects should be used but kept strictly in their place and it was not realized that in the present crisis the Chinese landowners and gentry might find they had an interest in maintaining Manchu rule against a revolution by less privileged classes of their countrymen. In the spring of 1857 Tseng was obliged by the death of his father to return to his home in Hunan. Before relinquishing his command he addressed a memorial to the Throne in which he complained of his inability to conduct operations successfully so long as he had no control of local officials, and solicited, in terms as frank as could be employed in such circumstances, appointment to the rank of Governor-General. The request was ignored and for a year Tseng remained with his family, ostensibly to observe the requirements of mourning, but all the while longing for a word that would summon him back to the business of pursuing his career. At last there were ominous grumblings from the Hunan Army, which one of Tseng's admirers described as being in the position of a child without its mother, and Peking with none too good a grace condescended to ask Tseng to resume his command.

Yehonala and the T'ung Chih Restoration

In the Court of Peking, there was one voice which consistently supported Tseng's claims, the voice, oddly enough of a young Manchu woman. Yehonala, the Emperor's favourite concubine and the mother of his only surviving son, had spent her early childhood in the Yangtze Valley where her father had been stationed as an official, and any mention of southern people and places was sufficient to arouse her garrulity. This goes some way to explain why she had become an indispensable assistant whenever the Emperor had to handle state papers concerning the Taiping; it was rumoured that dispatches sent to commanders at the front often contained more of her thoughts than of the Emperor's. She was twenty-one years old when in 1856 she produced an heir and thus reinforced her standing at Court. Her husband was only five years her elder but had already lost one consort by death and had the vacancy filled by another spouse, who was therefore his regular Empress and Yehonala's senior in rank.

We have seen that in September 1860 Hsien Feng fled from Peking before the Anglo-French advance, though the fact was not declared so starkly; the public was informed that His Majesty had gone to Jehol, just north of the Great Wall, to enjoy the hunting, leaving his brother Prince Kung to negotiate with the invading barbarians. Until the last moment Yehonala had urged her husband to stand firm, but he was in too much of a panic to listen, and against her will she and her child had to join the exodus. With the party was the Emperor's principal counsellor, Prince Yi, a member of the most rabidly anti-foreign faction, who had distinguished himself a few days earlier by ordering the arrest of the allied peace delegation. In this respect his advice coincided with his master's opinion, for Hsien Feng, in spite of his reluctance to linger in the neighbourhood of the enemy, had his spirits wonderfully enhanced by the journey. Before he reached the shelter of Jehol he was sending orders, as fast as couriers could carry them, that the Western savages were to be extirpated from the face of the earth.

The news of Prince Kung's surrender, and perhaps even more the announcement of the destruction of the Round Bright Garden, set the Emperor into a fury of resentment against his destiny.

Was he seriously expected to return and receive in audience the envoys of the nations who had humiliated him? The idea was unthinkable. Death would be preferable to such an existence, in particular a death achieved through dissipation. So throughout the spring and summer of 1861 the Court remained at Jehol while reports of the imperial debauchery streamed south across the Wall in such profusion that before long the subject was a matter of table-talk even among the foreigners. By August, it was clear that the treatment, coming as it did after years of other excesses, was proving efficacious and that the Dragon Throne would soon be vacant.

There could be no dispute about the succession. Yehonala's son would be the next Emperor. But he was only five years old, and this meant there would be a long regency. The great question therefore was, who would be Regent? The dying Hsien Feng, cut off from his brothers in Peking, seemed to trust only Prince Yi. The confused circumstances of the time offered this last an ideal opportunity, to neglect which, his associates told him, would be unworthy of a man of spirit. These friends were two other Manchus, one an imperial prince like himself; the other a great minister of state. The only obstacle to their plans was Yehonala, the future sovereign's mother, for she was already well used to the management of a court and there could be little doubt that she would know how to make the claims of nature prevail on the boy's mind. By some means, Prince Yi and his fellow conspirators got the Emperor to set his hand to a proclamation creating them Joint Regents, and expressly depriving Yehonala of any control in the upbringing of her son. The next day, 22 August 1861, Hsien Feng died. Shortly afterwards, to placate Yehonala, it was declared that she, as well as the Empress Consort, would be entitled to the style of Dowager.

For the best part of a year, Prince Kung and those around him in Peking, had sustained on their own shoulders nearly the whole burden of government, and the news of such high-handed proceedings was not calculated to give them pleasure. Nor were the foreign diplomats now stationed in the capital any more enthusiastic for they had no faith in the willingness of Prince Yi to abide by the treaties concluded with Prince Kung. But this concern for the future was mild compared with the alarm of Yehonala, who saw correctly that her prospects of reaching middle age were not going to be worth very much at the rate things were going. With some difficulty she succeeded in imparting her fears to the rather lethargic Empress Consort, and with the latter's approval wrote a letter to Prince Kung. A dark mystery surrounds the story at this point. It is generally believed that a young eunuch named An Te-hai, just twenty years old and so far employed in the palace kitchens, offered to risk his life to carry the message to Peking. If the tradition is true it would help to explain the favour which An was later to enjoy, though a considerable intimacy must have existed already for such an offer to be made or accepted. Prince Kung appears to have received the letter before setting out to Jehol to pay his respects to his dead brother, so that he was well aware of what was passing. But whether or not he contrived to have a private interview with either of his sisters-in-law is doubtful. At all events, a course of action was concerted, if not directly then through An or some other intermediary, and Prince Kung returned to Peking to await the arrival of the funeral. It was against etiquette for the widows to travel with the corpse, so they set out ahead, leaving the immense catafalque and its hundred and twenty bearers to struggle for ten days across a landscape already bleak with the approach of winter. This meant that Yehonala would reach Peking well in front of the conspirators whose duty it was to stay with the coffin. The intervening country was wild and mountainous, and the Dowagers' escort was composed of Prince Yi's own men, whose captain had been given orders to ensure that neither of the women should enter the Great Wall alive.

The commander of the late Emperor's bodyguard was a Manchu who according to gossip had been betrothed to Yehonala before her entry into the palace. Some word of what was afoot must have got out, for this man abandoned the funeral train under cover of darkness, taking with him a numerous party, and caught up with Yehonala before any harm had been done. In this way, after an absence of fifteen months, she returned to Peking in safety at the beginning of November 1861, to be welcomed enthusiastically by Prince Kung. A trial of strength was obviously unavoidable, but when it came it proved to be something of an anticlimax. On the arrival of the cortège the conspirators surrendered to an overwhelming show of force; within a few days the two princes among them had by special clemency been allowed to hang themselves, while the minister of state was beheaded.

Even before this happy outcome, at least one distinguished mandarin had had the foresight to suggest that the regency should be exercised jointly by the two Dowagers, and a proclamation to this effect was now issued. The Empress Consort, nominally the senior, was given the dignity of Dowager of the Eastern Palace, while Yehonala as Dowager of the Western Palace, or Western Dowager for short, had in effect, although the phenomenon took some time to be appreciated, emerged at the age of twenty-six as mistress of the Chinese world. Prince Kung was appointed Adviser. The reign of the young Emperor was distinguished by the style of T'ung Chih, or Joint Rule. With the change of management the Dynasty seemed for a while to be enjoying a new lease of life. But this appearance was deceptive; actually it was in process of contracting a debt the repayment of which fifty years later was to bring it to ruin.

The West takes sides

During the years 1860 and 1861, while the attention of the central government was engrossed first by the problems of foreign war and peace and then by the intrigues concerning the regency, Shanghai was again being forced to take affairs into its own hands. In June 1860, a Taiping army under the command of the Loyal Prince seized the famous city of Soochow, only forty miles from Shanghai, and was soon menacing the port itself. Without hesitation, the British and French authorities assumed the defence of the place, and posted a mixed force to guard the suburbs, much to the delight of the local mandarins who were only too anxious to ignore the foreign invasion of North China, then in full preparation, in order to benefit from the protection of the same invaders in the territory under their jurisdiction. Could not the protection be carried a step further? To be sure, the Western Powers, although committed to the defence of Shanghai, were not ready to be drawn more deeply into the suppression of the rebels. But Shanghai was swarming with ne'er-do-wells from every country under the sun whose high spirits could be employed more profitably than in terrorizing the waterfront. The compradore element among the mandarins knew from experience how to deal with such people, and a corps of foreign riflemen came into existence with a New Englander named Ward for leader.

The adventurers soon had a taste of the bitter fighting that lay in store for them. By a surprise assault they succeeded in retaking the town of Sungkiang from the Taiping, but at once the Loyal Prince struck back at them with such vigour that they were driven out with heavy losses in men and equipment. The temper of the Taiping hero was now thoroughly aroused at the discovery that those he had been taught to believe were his brothers in the faith were siding with the infidels, and he sent messages of warning and defiance to the foreign consuls. 'You must know,' he wrote, 'I have over a thousand picked officers, and tens of thousands of brave soldiers. If I should want to capture Shanghai, it would be like taking an object out of a bag.' For a moment it looked as if the Europeans would be in conflict with both Chinese regimes, the Manchu and the Taiping, at one and the same time, but in the event the Loyal Prince was obliged to divert his energies to another battlefield.

The news of the Taiping victories at Soochow and elsewhere had at length forced the Peking government to overcome its suspicion of Tseng Kuo-fan and in August 1860 he was appointed Governor-General of Kiangsu, Anhwei and Kiangsi. It might have been expected that he would thereupon have hurried to the coastal area where the threat seemed most acute, but no such idea entered his head. To him it had always been obvious that the outcome of the war would be determined on the Yangtze above Nanking; if the upper reaches of the river were held, then gradually the rebels would be throttled to death in their Heavenly Capital. Besides, it was essential for him to maintain his communications with the province of Hunan which was the source of his army. For these reasons, instead of going to the rescue of Soochow and the Shanghai hinterland he concentrated his efforts on the recovery of the river-port of Anking, and it was to meet the emergency in that quarter that the Loyal Prince and his men were summoned westward from Shanghai. But the transfer was in vain, and in September 1861 Anking fell to the Hunan Army.

Li Hung-Chang and the Huai Army

The emergence of Yehonala as Co-Regent a couple of months later, as well as the confirmation of Prince Kung's status as adviser ensured that from then on Tseng Kuo-fan could count upon having effective support at the seat of authority. Within a matter of days after the achievement of the *coup d'état* it was announced that in addition to his powers as Governor-General he had been given supreme military control of the four provinces of Kiangsu, Anhwei, Kiangsi and Chekiang. Clearly he was expected to cope with the problems of the coastal area, but even after his success at Anking he was resolved never to move his own command out of the country up-river from the Taiping capital. For the rest, he would have to act through deputies, and here Yehonala had made things easier for him by asking him to recommend two likely men to head the provincial administration of Kiangsu and Chekiang. It was stipulated that the former post required someone capable of dealing with foreigners. As it happened, Tseng had two suitable candidates who were duly appointed: Li Hung-chang to Kiangsu, and Tso Tsung-t'ang to Chekiang. Both names were to become famous, and Li's was to eclipse that of his patron and for most of the next forty years to be synonymous with that of China itself in the councils of the world.

He was born in 1823, the son of a mandarin family of Anhwei province, and thanks to a friendship between his father and Tseng Kuo-fan when he went to Peking in 1845 he was accepted as the latter's pupil. His performance in the official examinations did his teacher credit, but his civilian career was interrupted by the Taiping war. In 1853 he went back to his native province and engaged in the raising of local defence forces of the same type that Tseng himself was organizing into the Hunan Army. For five years he fought against the rebels in Anhwei, with fortunes very different from those of his master, as he was uniformly defeated and on several occasions barely escaped with his life. At last, in the winter of 1858, wearying of his lack of success he presented himself at Tseng's headquarters in the confident expectation of being given a post adequate to his talents, but his hopes were dashed when he found he was to be employed only in secretarial work. He swallowed his pride and did what was asked of him, though at times his dissatisfaction was too painful to conceal, and once, for a period of several months, he quit his clerkship altogether. He returned, however, after the victory at Anking, and made his peace with Tseng so artfully that a few months later he was rewarded by this spectacular promotion.

His first task, in the spring of 1862, was to assemble a force of his own, which he did readily enough in his native place. To be sure, Tseng put some Hunanese soldiers at his disposal too, but the corps thus brought into existence was called, after the name of a local river, the Huai Army. The great problem was how to transport it downstream, through a region where both banks of the Yangtze were occupied by the rebels. The answer to the question came from Shanghai, where a group of wealthy compradores hired eight British cargo ships, on board which, and convoyed by British gunboats, his six thousand odd soldiers made the voyage safely in April 1862.

On his arrival in Shanghai, Li's first concern was to see that his army, which had already received some rudimentary training, should acquire a western formation by direct instruction from foreigners and equipment in modern weapons. Arms were to be bought in the first instance, but for the future it was envisaged they should be manufactured locally, and in addition to European and American drill-teachers, workmen and technicians of various kinds were engaged to meet the requirements of this new industry.

Meanwhile the rebel threat to Shanghai had resumed, but the heaviest fighting was taking place a little to the south in the province of Chekiang. Ward's rifles had undergone an important transformation, Chinese now making up the rank and file, while the foreigners acted as officers. The reorganized brigade was christened 'The Ever-Victorious Army', but its American leader did not survive very long to enjoy his new dignity, for he was killed on the Chekiang front in September 1862, and after his death his followers were recalled to serve in Kiangsu, the original theatre of their exploits. From then on Britain and France agreed between themselves that as the preponderance of Britain's interests in Shanghai gave her the right to have the chief say in any intervention in Kiangsu province, so Chekiang should in compensation be left to France. Accordingly, a Sino-French corps, patterned very closely on the Ever-Victorious Army, soon took the field on behalf of Tso Tsung-t'ang, the newly created Governor of Chekiang. In succession to Ward, after a brief tenure of command by another American, Burgevine, there was appointed in the spring of 1863 a British regular officer, Captain Gordon of the Royal Engineers.

When Europeans are spectators of the affairs of an oriental country, it is only natural that their attention should be captured by any members of their own race who chance to participate in the events they are watching. To the British the striking personality of Gordon, and the tragedy at Khartoum which made him a national hero, have ensured that so far as the story of the Taiping war is known at all, it is remembered only as a background to the deeds of their countryman. Even at the time, there were foreign observers on the spot who assumed without hesitation that it was Gordon, to an incomparably greater extent than anyone else, who deserved the credit for the suppression of the rebellion. Yet if we turn to the Chinese books we are shown a very different, and quite certainly a truer, picture. To begin with, nobody can deny that the quality of Gordon's leadership, and the discipline he imposed on his followers, made the Ever-Victorious Army the spearhead of the imperial forces under Li Hung-chang's command. Without him, the end would undoubtedly have been longer in coming. But Li and Gordon in the Shanghai hinterland, like Tso and his French helpers in Chekiang, sustained what was essentially a subsidiary role in the campaign, of which the supreme direction remained firmly in the hands of Tseng Kuo-fan.

It does not take much knowledge of human nature to understand that a man of Tseng's character would be constantly on the alert for any sign that the subordinates he had advanced might be entertaining ambitions beyond their station, and he had not long to wait before there was a manifestation of the sort from Li Hung-chang. As early as August 1862, a few weeks before Ward's death, Li announced to Tseng that the American was anxious to march against Nanking itself, on condition that if the city should be taken, the Ever-Victorious Army should share equally in the loot with the Manchu forces. Tseng rejected the proposal as an impertinence, but when for a short time in November of the same year, the Hunan Army outside the rebel capital got into difficulties, he toyed with the idea of calling in the freebooters on his own terms. These were that if, providentially, Nanking fell to the besiegers, there should be no indiscriminate looting but that an inventory should be taken of the booty captured, and of this half should be set aside for remittance to Peking, while the other half should be divided among the victors, with the Ever-Victorious Army getting an extra share. A modern Communist historian points out that this arrangement meant that half the spoil, namely that portion earmarked for Peking, would in fact go to Tseng himself, over and above his share of the rest. The suggestion came to nothing, but the whole transaction casts a very clear light on the motives which governed the conduct both of the foreign adventurers and of their Chinese employers.[2]

Although thwarted in its yearning for the wealth of Nanking, the Ever-Victorious Army had before its eyes a scarcely inferior prospect of enrichment to be attained by the recovery from the rebels of Soochow and other towns within the sphere of activity allotted to it. Much of the tension, and, at times, open quarrelling, between Li and his nominal subordinate Gordon which were a constant feature of their alliance can be accounted for only if we bear in mind the steady suspicious watchfulness of Gordon, who was constantly on the look-out to see that in the assignment of duties the men under his command would not be deprived of opportunities of profit which might be to the advantage of Li and his Huai Army. Such an interpretation may cause offence to those accustomed to think of Gordon, and not without a great deal of justice, as the very ideal of a Christian soldier. It is true that he possessed qualities of honour and magnanimity of which such a one as Li Hung-chang hardly understood the meaning, but he had been in Peking in 1860 and had pillaged right and left with the best of his comrades, and now that he was at the head of a brigade of mercenaries it would have been an inconvenient moment for him to develop qualms of conscience.

A curious instance where cupidity and honour joined hands to lead him into open conflict with Li occurred in December 1863, when Soochow, the wealthiest city of the region, was at last recovered from the Taiping. Gordon had contrived to make contact with the commanders of the rebel garrison who agreed to let the place fall provided their lives were spared. With that settled, the great question in the victors' minds was the matter of booty. Li was naturally determined to keep so rich a prize for himself, and Gordon proposed that the Ever-Victorious Army, in consideration of its abstaining from plunder, should receive as gratuity an extra two months' stipend. Li thought this demand excessive and instead offered one month's money, which Gordon refused. Even before the time came to occupy the city, tempers were already wearing thin and when Gordon learned that Li, in defiance of his pledged word, had had the rebel commanders put to death, and as a crowning insult had ordered that the Ever-Victorious Army should be transferred elsewhere, he flew into a rage, cursed Li for an 'Asiatic barbarian', and for a while menaced him with personal violence. Li, seeing that he had gone too far and anxious to retain British goodwill, made extraordinary efforts to pacify his angry colleague. A large donation was given to the freebooters, and no less a personage than Yehonala was induced to present Gordon with ten thousand dollars in recognition of his merits. For a while, the Briton declined to accept the reward, but in the end the pleading of friends who had been sent as intermediaries carried the day and he consented to return to Li's service. As a token of the restoration of friendship, the next town liberated was entrusted to the sole care of the Ever-Victorious.[3]

The End of the Taiping

It would be tedious and unprofitable to relate in detail the remaining transactions of the war. In March 1864, Tso Tsung-t'ang and his French allies on the Chekiang front retook Hangchow, the rival of Soochow for wealth and celebrity. The Heavenly Kingdom was visibly disintegrating, but its ruler, Hung Hsiu-ch'uan, the Younger Brother of Jesus Christ, appeared less concerned with the ruin around him than with schemes for belittling the name of the Loyal Prince, Li Hsiu-ch'eng, whose prestige stood higher than ever among the Taiping soldiers. The only measure Hung's jealousy could suggest to him was a mass creation of princes, and upwards of two thousand men were given the title, many of them Li's subordinates, in the hope that Li's pre-eminence would be swept away in the ludicrous flood of dignity. Then, at the beginning of June 1864, Hung put an end to himself with poison. His son, still a boy, succeeded him on the throne, but reigned scarcely more than a month, for on 19 July, the Hunan Army entered the Heavenly Capital. There was desperate fighting in the streets, and when night fell a body of picked men escorted their young ruler and broke out into the open country. The Loyal Prince was with them, and seeing his sovereign badly mounted, he gave him his own horse. His generosity was fatal to him, for he was soon caught. When he faced his arch-enemy, Tseng Kuo-fan, for a moment even that callous egotist was touched with something of wonder at the confrontation between defeated ideals and the vulgarity of triumph, and treated his prisoner almost courteously.

By rights, so important a captive should have been carried to Peking to be made a show of before his death, but Tseng wrote to the Court that he could not run the risk of transporting this man hundreds of miles through a population which might rise up at the mere sound of his name. The Loyal Prince, therefore, was to end his life in Nanking by the headsman's sword, and he was given a few days' grace in order to write an account of his career.[4]

With the fall of the Heavenly Capital, the history of the Taiping movement proper comes to an end. Its other hero, the Guardian Prince, Shih Ta-k'ai, who had persevered in his resolve never to return to the seat of government which had been disgraced by so much murder and intrigue, and had led his men ever deeper into the country, had been taken and put to death twelve months before in Szechwan. Scattered groups continued to wage guerrilla war in various of the central and southern provinces, sometimes in alliance with local peasant uprisings; but by 1868 these hardy survivors had been hunted down, or had abandoned the struggle. Yet even in its ruin, the Heavenly Kingdom continued to shape men's lives. At the time its most obvious result was the devastation of what had been the wealthiest region of China. To this day a visitor to Nanking, as he stares at the wide uninhabited tracts of land inside the city walls, and wonders vaguely what catastrophe has so drastically reduced the number of inhabitants, is in fact observing the effect of the Hakka schoolmaster's visions. But the Taiping left an even more important legacy behind them, and one which in the long run was to accomplish at least a part of their purpose for them. In order that their revolution might be crushed, forces had been brought into being, which were to lead the country into a new era and in less than half a century to overthrow the Tartar dynasty.

CHAPTER VIII

THE ERA OF ARSENALS

---

*The call for improvement – the forces of reaction – Yehonala and
Prince Kung – rivalry of Hunan and Huai militarists – early
industries*

The Call for Improvement

IN THIS same year of 1864, Li Hung-chang addressed to Prince
Kung in Peking a memorial which can properly claim historical
significance.

In China, our civilian officials are plunged in the elucidation of
classical texts and in the refinements of calligraphy, while our military
men are for the most part ignorant dullards. Our education seems quite
divorced from utility. When we are at peace we despise foreign inven-
tions as worthless, while if trouble comes our way we exclaim that it is
impossible for us to learn how to employ such mysterious contrivances.
In the past Britain and France thought they could do what they liked in
Japan, but the people of that country took courage from their indignation and chose their brightest youths to go abroad to study in work-
shops and arsenals. They also bought machinery for making arms, so
they could manufacture equipment at home. They are now capable of
navigating steamships, and of making artillery. And these, mind you,
are the people the Ming dynasty despised as Dwarf Pirates ... It is my
submission that to turn China into a strong country we must acquire
the use of modern weapons, and for this we must instal machinery
for making these weapons. By learning the foreigners' methods for
ourselves, we shall no longer depend on their services. In order to get
these machines and the experts to use them, we should create a special
branch of the mandarinate, entry to which will be open to candidates
qualified in these technical studies, who will thereafter have their career
assured.[1]

Prince Kung, on receiving the memorial, read it without surprise, for the ideas it contained were already in the air, and, to a limited extent, being put into practice. The importance of the document lies not so much in its originality as in the fact that it states, with greater clarity than had been used hitherto, the policy which was to guide the actions of the Chinese government for the next thirty years, and that the author of it was the man who more than any other was to be responsible for the application of that policy. But however much to the point Li's words were, he took for granted certain basic assumptions on the part of himself and Prince Kung, which will not be present in the minds of a foreign reader today.

The starting-point of it was the recognition that the Confucian theory of state and society was the perfect embodiment of human wisdom. In the passage just quoted, Li's strictures on the weaknesses inherent in classical education may seem to imply the contrary, but to interpret him in that sense would be to misunderstand the emphasis with which he expressed himself. It was simply that the Westerners had perfected certain military techniques which it was incumbent upon any Chinese government to acquire for itself, not least for the sake of preserving peace and order within its own frontiers. In the first instance arms must be bought for immediate use, and arsenals established to ensure a future supply. Yet the aim must be to attain the stage of self-sufficiency as soon as possible, and for this it was necessary that there should be an ample reserve of Chinese technicians. The training of these men would have to extend to the study of certain branches of western science, and the changed circumstances of the last few years meant that the curriculum in some cases would have to include such topics as international law. Of course a good foundation in a foreign language was indispensable, because for years to come the knowledge required would have to be learned from alien teachers, but it was not contemplated that there might be any humanistic or cultural benefit to be derived from the reading of European literature. In that line, China already had enough and to spare.

It was the superior excellence of foreign weapons, which he had tested now for a couple of years in the field, that brought Li to this way of thinking. Prince Kung had been led in the same direction by a rather different experience. True, it could be said that he had stronger reason than Li to acknowledge the power of Western arms. But more even than by the defeat of 1860 he had been impressed by the readiness of the British and French to withdraw from Peking once the allies had obtained his signature to the treaties. It was almost inconceivable that any of the oriental invaders, including the Manchus themselves, with whom the Chinese had grown familiar in the course of their history, would have so readily turned their backs on a capital they had occupied and which was entirely at their mercy. Clearly the rules of international behaviour the Europeans observed must have some efficacy about them. In any case, it was going to be necessary for China to learn them too, now that foreign legations were resident in Peking. A brand new Foreign Office had been established in 1861 to cope with the fresh situation, and it was already showing signs of dwarfing all the other departments of government. Prince Kung was at its head, and his terms of reference extended beyond diplomacy proper to cover military affairs and international trade, while provincial governors were enjoined to keep him posted on all matters of importance within their jurisdiction. For so powerful an institution it was necessary to take special care in providing capable servants, and in 1862 a School of Languages was set up, where it was hoped young Manchu boys might equip themselves to cope with foreigners by learning English, French or Russian, not to mention astronomy and mathematics. In a word, Prince Kung was already of much the same mind as Li Hung-chang, and to silence any critics he pointed out that by calling upon the aid of foreign teachers he was doing no more than following the example of his ancestors who in the seventeenth century had not thought it beneath their dignity to employ Jesuit missionaries in the manufacture of cannon.

The Forces of Reaction

That such a policy should have aroused violent opposition for no other reason than because it introduced a new idea was only to be expected. But with patrons as important as Prince Kung, Tseng Kuo-fan, Li Hung-chang, and Tso Tsung-t'ang, for the last was copying on a smaller scale in Chekiang what Li Hung-chang had began in Kiangsu, one might have predicted that the process of innovation, extending in scope with the passage of time, would have effected transformations not too unlike those of contemporary Japan. In fact, however, the result was wretchedly different.

To begin with, although we can in theory make allowances readily enough for the strength of tradition, it is almost impossible for us today to appreciate the enormous bulk of prejudice against which the Prince and his colleagues had to fight every step of the way, prejudice shared by peasant and mandarin in equal measure. In the case of the mandarin the prejudice was reinforced by considerations of self-interest. Few men who had spent years of drudgery over classical books in order to enter government service would be enthusiastic over the news that others might be given the chance to outstrip them without enduring the same ordeal. Pedagogues who depended for their livelihood on teaching the old learning were indignant to hear that alien schoolmasters would soon be competing for pupils against them. To crown all, there was contempt mixed with resentment, to form an emotion similar to that which might have been felt, not so long ago, by a Regius Professor of Greek who had found himself placed, by government action, in a position of academic and social parity with a demonstrator at a Polytechnic. What complicated the business still further was the fact that the innovators themselves, in their heart of hearts, were not wholly exempt from the same fastidiousness. We shall see later how Li Hung-chang, for instance, did not encourage even his most gifted protégés to imagine that they had acquired in their foreign classrooms anything more than mechanical skills.

It was Prince Kung and his School of Languages that encountered the first serious challenge from the reactionaries. In 1867 the Prince suggested that candidates entering public service by the ordinary examinations might usefully attend courses in such practical subjects as mathematics which were included in the school's curriculum, but the proposal provoked so loud an outcry that it was abandoned. The most vocal of the conservatives declared that true education, on which the theory of government was founded, consisted of the study of the humanities, and had nothing whatsoever to do with technical training.

Beside, do we really suppose that the barbarians will reveal their secrets to us? And even if they do, they will only turn their students into craftsmen. In any case, if it is really necessary to give lessons in astronomy and mathematics, surely we have enough talent in China without calling on the barbarians to teach us.[2]

The reactionaries were to be found without distinction both among the Manchus and among the Chinese. Yet another source of opposition to the new policy sprang from the racial exclusiveness of the former group. For over ten years their status as a ruling caste had been directly menaced by the Taiping, and even the most obstinate of them could not shut his eyes to the fact that the survival of their dynasty was due entirely to Chinese support. In the process of putting down the rebellion it had been necessary to acquiesce in the formation of powerful Chinese military forces, with strong provincial loyalties, and the leaders of these forces, men like Tseng Kuo-fan and Li Hung-chang, had now to be treated with consideration and even with deference as pillars of the Empire. Posts which for two hundred years had been regarded as too important for the security of the Throne to be entrusted to any but bannermen were beginning, as a matter of course, to be occupied by Chinese. In general, this change of attitude was accepted as inevitable by the Manchus at large, especially when the example was set by one as exalted as Prince Kung, but there were some grandees who still hankered after the good old days when the Chinese were made to keep their proper place in the scheme of things, and to these people Tseng and Li were upstarts of the most odious kind, and potentially far worse a threat to the dynasty than all the outer barbarians put together.

On occasion, both the reactionaries and the Tartar chauvinists found an ally in the Palace, for Prince Kung, it must be remembered, was subordinate to the two Co-Regents. Although as far as the former Empress Consort, now called the Eastern Dowager, was concerned this inferiority was merely nominal, since she was a kindly easy-going body, only too happy to see the government in the capable hands of her brother-in-law; the other Regent, Yehonala, or the Western Dowager, soon showed she had claws and knew how to use them.

Prince Kung, who, having put her where she was, thought, reasonably enough, that he could depend upon her friendship, was not long in being undeceived. It was the custom that, when ministers of state reported to the Regents, the Dowagers should be concealed behind a curtain, in front of which the official granted audience would kowtow and then say what he had to say on his knees. Indeed, the Chinese expression for such a female regency means 'to let down the curtain and listen to matters of government'. Prince Kung naturally was the most frequent visitor, and it was reported to Yehonala by the eunuchs in attendance that he used to brush them aside impatiently when they attempted to make him wait in the anteroom for a formal summons. One day he had gone in as usual, when the guards outside heard a loud commotion in the midst of which they could distinguish Yehonala's voice screaming for help. Rushing into the audience chamber they found the Prince in a state of confusion, while from behind the curtain Yehonala ordered them to surround him and escort him from the place. To explain the conundrum the eunuchs later revealed that one of their number, in the service of Yehonala, had peeped round the curtain and had noticed that the Prince, while addressing the Regents, had risen to his feet. The moment this information had been whispered to her, Yehonala had started to shout for help, in the belief, or so she pretended, that some act of violence was about to be perpetrated. The farce was taken seriously enough for a decree to be published announcing the Prince's dismissal from office because of his misbehaviour, and although as a so-called act of clemency he was soon restored to his functions, he never forgot the humiliation, and the private alliance between him and Yehonala was from then on at an end. When a few years later an opportunity presented itself for him to exact revenge, he seized it with both hands.

We have already heard the name of An Te-hai, the eunuch who acted as Yehonala's messenger to Prince Kung during the plotting and counter-plotting that followed the death of Hsien Feng. His loyalty had been well rewarded, for she had carried him with her in her ascent and by the middle of the 1860s he was known as one of the most influential figures in the palace. It was not surprising that now and then attachments of a sentimental kind should come into existence between a widowed empress and a eunuch devoted to her service, and as the Chinese have always delighted in gossip it was only to be expected that the most scandalous interpretation should be put upon such a friendship. In the case of Yehonala and An Te-hai, they had only themselves to blame, for they openly indulged in the most extraordinary familiarities. Yehonala had already shown that delight in amateur theatricals which was to remain with her to the end of her life, and she and her favourite devised masques and spectacles of every kind in which they invariably played the chief romantic parts. There were times even when the eunuch donned the Dragon Robe, and made an imperial cruise on the palace lake with the Dowager at his side. It was rumoured that in fact he had never felt the surgeon's knife at all, and that his mistress could testify that he was as good a man as any in China. All this was unutterably galling to Prince Kung, who had cause of his own to remember An's barely concealed insolence.

The Manchu Dynasty, seeing the ruin brought to the house of Ming by over-powerful eunuchs, had laid down that none of the castrati, under pain of death, should travel in the provinces. For two centuries this ordinance had never been violated, but in 1869, to the general astonishment, An Te-hai and a group of his fellows set off down the Grand Canal in the direction of the Yangtze Valley. The object of the expedition is uncertain, but it was rumoured that Yehonala was dissatisfied with the quality of the silks arriving in Peking, and had decided to send An to select the finest material at its place of origin. Common sense would have recommended that such a mission needed above all things tact and discretion, but instead it was turned into a triumphal progress, to such an extent that shocked reports were soon reaching Prince Kung from the provincial authorities en route. He reacted with a vigour not less than that he had displayed during the crisis of 1861. An Te-hai, he decided, must be made an example of, but a measure so drastic as that which he had in mind needed the concurrence of at least one of the Regents. As luck would have it, Yehonala was consoling herself for her favourite's absence by an orgy of theatricals, and had given out that she was not to be disturbed with business. It was therefore perfectly in order for the Prince to consult with the other Dowager alone, but it says much for his persuasiveness that he was able to talk her into joining his enterprise. For when he left the palace, he carried with him a death-warrant against An and his party in due and proper form, complete with the Regent's seal. The sentence was carried out in Shantung immediately upon the receipt of the fatal document, but somehow a solitary eunuch managed to escape, making his way across country to Peking with the news of the slaughter. Yehonala behaved like a lunatic, storming into the presence of her colleague with curses and threats. Yet the deed could not be undone, and at length she had to acquiesce in defeat, though swearing a solemn oath that one day there would be a settlement of accounts. Meanwhile, as she consolidated her power, Prince Kung's political opponents discovered that her resentment at An Te-hai's death had, sometimes at least, for her temper was not constant, put a useful weapon into their hands.

Rivalry of the Hunan and Huai Militarists

To complicate matters still further, dissension was not long in arising between the innovators themselves. We have already seen a hint of what was to come in the care Tseng Kuo-fan had taken to exclude Li Hang-chang's troops from participation in the capture of Nanking, and now after the suppression of the Taiping the rivalry of the two men emerged into the open. It seems that after the triumphant conclusion of the campaign, Tseng began to feel that the size of his Hunanese Army might provoke the jealousy of Peking, and thus be a stumbling block in the way to future advancement. Besides, he had for some time been aware of a deterioration in quality as numbers increased. Discipline was noticeably becoming slacker, and the men could be depended upon to obey only those officers to whom they had personal or local bonds of attachment. For instance, Tseng's brother was very zealous in gathering recruits. His recruits were so devoted to him that once, in his absence, they refused to accept orders even from Tseng himself, their Commander-in-Chief, who was obliged to send for his brother before the soldiers would return to duty. It seemed wiser, for every reason, to disband the force, leaving intact only a nucleus of three thousand picked men.[3]

But the defeat of the Taiping did not mean the restoration of peace. On the contrary, in various parts of the country, rebellions blazed as fiercely as ever. The most serious of these uprisings has already been mentioned, that of the Nien in the provinces of Shantung, Honan and Anhwei. This movement, which derived its origins from old peasant confraternities, had been given impetus by the initial conquests of the Taiping in the adjacent provinces. Now that the Taiping had been overthrown, some of their leaders, with what troops they could keep together after the disaster, fled northwards to join their neighbours. The magnitude of the Nien rebellion may be gauged from the fact that in 1865, the year following the suppression of the Taiping, the Manchu Court's most trusted military officer, the same Mongol Prince Seng-ko-lin-ch'in who had fought the British and French in North China, was killed by the insurgents and his army routed. To take his place, the dynasty turned to its leading Chinese supporter, Tseng Kuo-fan, who was appointed special Commissioner in charge of the campaign of pacification. No greater sign of confidence could have been shown him, and he accepted the charge gladly. To do so, however, he had to relinquish his post as Governor-General of Kiangsu, Anhwei and Kiangsi, and this splendid vacancy was offered to Li Hung-chang. Here also the Court went out of its way to demonstrate its esteem, for in order to enable Li, who was himself a native of Anhwei, to assume his new functions, the established rule which forbade a man to exercise official powers in his own province had to be waived.

Both of these appointments were due to Yehonala. It was her intention that Li should continue to play a subordinate role to Tseng, and should in particular make sure that Tseng was kept well supplied with all his necessities. But with the greater part of the Hunan Army out of service, Tseng's most urgent requirement was manpower, and here it was anticipated that Li would be of immediate use. His Huai Army now numbered upwards of seventy-thousand soldiers, and whereas the Hunanese had had to make do with Chinese firearms, and not too many of those, Li's troops, thanks to their proximity to Shanghai, were well equipped with foreign weapons. Not anticipating any unwillingness on the part of one whom he had himself helped to achieve honour and dignity, Tseng requested Li to transfer the main strength of his troops to fight the Nien. It was a curious piece of simplicity to imagine that Li would without objection hand over a force on the creation of which he lavished so much care so that another, even if the other was his old patron, should be able to win credit from their efficiency. To Tseng's pained astonishment, he was told that the vital importance of Kiangsu in relation to the great port of Shanghai made it impossible for the coastal area to be denuded of its garrison. Friendly expostulation proving of no avail, he had finally to appeal to Yehonala, and in due course an order came from Peking, peremptorily requiring the dispatch of so many Huai soldiers for employment under Tseng's command. Li Hung-chang submitted with the best grace he could, but he still had a card up his sleeve.

The campaign against the Nien was different altogether from that against the Taiping. The Heavenly Kingdom had been established on a solid territorial basis, the limits of which, though shifting back and forth according to the fortunes of war, could at any one moment be drawn on a map. The Nien, on the other hand, were pure guerrillas, a condition which they were able to maintain thanks to their possession of a vast number of horses. Thus mounted, they swept down out of nowhere to strike at their enemies, and, the blow delivered, vanished from sight the way they had come. Tseng Kuo-fan was not long in discovering that his previous experience was of little use to him in these new circumstances. More vexatious still, the Huai soldiers were proving hopelessly intractable, ignoring his orders and looking still towards Li Hung-chang. Things reached such a pass that Tseng sent his rival an angry letter, insisting that it must be made clear that the men were under his sole command. The remonstrance had no effect, and as the war was rapidly going from bad to worse, Tseng at last abandoned what had become an untenable position and begged Peking to put the burden upon Li's shoulders. The Court was well aware that this was precisely what Li had been scheming to achieve; indeed, he had already submitted a plan for moving the peasants in the zone of operations out of the open country into stockaded forts and thus cutting the Nien off from potential helpers. In November 1866, Tseng and Li exchanged offices, the former returning to the Governor-Generalship he had quitted the year before, while the latter assumed the commission for suppressing the Nien.[4]

There is no need here to enter into details of the fighting. Li's first task was to build up an adequate force of cavalry, which he armed with carbines bought from his foreign associates. Even so, it was a hard struggle before the situation was retrieved, and in the course of it more than one message from Yehonala upbraiding him with his lack of success served to remind him how precarious was the enjoyment of imperial favour. At last, however, his superiority in resources began to tell, and by the autumn of 1868 the Nien had followed the Taiping into defeat, leaving behind them a devastated countryside, where, it was said, every ditch was clogged with bodies.

After that, none could doubt that the pupil had surpassed his master. Already in 1867 he was made Viceroy of Hunan and Hupei, an appointment which when the rebels had been suppressed set the Huai Army astride the middle course of the Yangtze. Other units of the force were dispatched for garrison duty in the north, theoretically to be at the disposition of the local authorities, but in reality taking their orders from Li, and then in 1870 he followed them in person to assume the Viceroyship of the Metropolitan Province. There at Tientsin, he organized what became known as 'the second government of China'.

Tseng Kuo-fan did not long survive his rival's triumph, bequeathing, on his death in 1872, a legacy of ill-feeling to be fostered by his family and adherents. During the next thirty years the feud between the Hunan and the Huai Armies dominated much of China's internal politics. For the Hunanese, though sadly overshadowed, were still very much to be reckoned with; after Tseng's departure from the scene their great champion was that Tso Tsung-t'ang who, while Li Hung-chang was fighting the Taiping with British help in Kiangsu, was making similar use of the French in Chekiang. And, as with Li, another military necessity elsewhere ensured that his talents should be kept in view. The Muslims in the north-western provinces of Shensi and Kansu had seized the opportunity presented by the chaos in central China to revolt on their own, and Tso had the honour of crushing them, an exceedingly bloody procedure which was not accomplished until 1873, and even after that had to be extended to the Turkis of Sinkiang for three years more. Nor were these the only Muslim insurrections; the followers of Islam took to the field in Yunnan, in the far south-west, between 1855 and 1873. Here it is of interest to notice the attitude of the modern Communist historians towards these events. The defeat of the Taiping and the Nien is to them a victory, though of course only a temporary one, of evil over good. The Muslim uprisings are examples of the struggles of minority peoples against a feudal government and as such they are fully justified. Unfortunately, however, the Muslim leaders turned to foreigners for support. The influence of British agents was at work both in Sinkiang and Yunnan, and there were pan-Islamic undertones as well. Consequently, Tso Tsung-t'ang and his colleagues, murderers and reactionaries though they were, performed a function of national utility in restoring the authority of

Peking over territory which might otherwise have been lost to China altogether.

Early Industries

The decade and more of local wars which followed the defeat of the Taiping provided a good argument to Li and his rivals for the development of military industries. Arsenals, already set up in Soochow and Shanghai during the Taiping campaign, were to be seen by the 1870s from Tientsin to Foochow, and some of them included shipyards. The fact that these enterprises were more profitable to their founders than to the nation, and that the armaments they made were employed more effectively against domestic insurgents than against foreign enemies, has led Chinese writers today to underestimate the effort made towards modernisation. For very soon a number of subsidiary industries came into being, and steps were taken in the field of transport and communication. Li himself was strongly in favour of building railways, and submitted plans for the construction of lines between Peking and the chief cities of the country. Conservative opposition by maintaining that the steam engines would destroy the geomantic advantages of the regions they traversed held up the project until the last years of the dynasty; indeed, it is only in our own times that it is being fulfilled in its entirety; but Li did what was in his power by opening in 1881 a few miles of track to a coal-mine he was working not far from Tientsin. The year previously he had inaugurated a telegraph office in the same city, which was soon connected with Shanghai and other places in the Yangtze Valley. Earlier still, in 1872, he had established the China Merchants Shipping Company in Shanghai. By 1877 it owned upwards of thirty vessels, and was competing, though not very successfully, with the British and other foreign vessels along the China coast and the Yangtze. The flag was carried even farther afield, to Singapore, Manila and Japan, and a couple of trial voyages were made to Honolulu and San Francisco, but the last scheme proved too grandiose a venture.

The characteristic of this type of industry was that its management was in official hands throughout, or in other words that Li or whoever was the founder ran it according to his views through men of his own selection. The public at the most were permitted to buy shares, but had no real say in how the business was carried on. Thus the modernization movement on the whole had only a minor effect on the development of native capitalism. In the 1880s some private firms started small paper-mills, match factories, silk works and the like in such places as Shanghai and Hankow, but their growth in comparison with that of foreign or official concerns was slow and precarious.

CHAPTER IX

THE LOSS OF THE SATELLITES

The Loochoo Islands – Ili – Burma – Vietnam and the war with France – Korea – the war with Japan – the Treaty of Shimonoseki

The Loochoo Islands

THE existence of those satellite countries lying on the border of the Chinese Empire proper, which although self-governing paid homage to Peking, apart from being the natural result of China's great size and cultural prestige, was regarded by her rulers as an essential element in national defence. A Minister said in 1881,

> I have heard that the Son of Heaven sets his guard among the barbarians beyond the frontier, which is indeed a far-sighted policy, for if the guard was placed only at the frontier itself, there would be no time to ward off foreign enemies. So in the deserts and seas around our vast Empire we have erected a system of dependencies to keep us from harm – the Loochoo Islands, and Korea, and Vietnam.

One would have thought that the experience of two wars in the space of twenty years, in the course of which Europeans had directly invaded the richest provinces of the country and had dictated peace in the capital itself, would have been enough to refute such reasoning. Not only that; at the time the opinion was being expressed one of the vaunted dependencies, the Loochoos, had already been lost to its old obedience.[1]

As early as 1865, it was obvious to Li Hung-chang that the Japanese would soon be demanding their share of Chinese trade. They should, he said, be admitted like the others, if only to see that the West had a rival. Sure enough in 1870, after the Meiji

Restoration, Tokyo proposed the conclusion of a treaty, and on Li's advice the suggestion was accepted. But almost at once discord came into the relations. For the King of the Loochoos, while rendering homage to the Emperor of China, had also since the early seventeenth century become in some sense a vassal of the feudal chief of Satsuma, in southern Japan, whose rights were now deemed transferred to the Emperor Meiji. When a Japanese envoy came to Peking, he astounded the Chinese by demanding redress for the murder of some Japanese sailors in Formosa. A little inquiry revealed that the mariners in question were natives of Loochoo who had been shipwrecked off the eastern coast of Formosa and had fallen victims to the headhunting aboriginals driven by the pressure of Chinese colonization into that part of the island. 'We don't understand,' said the Chinese officials, 'how Japan can possibly have any interest in what happens to people from our dependency of Loochoo ... In any case,' they added, 'we can't be responsible for the actions of savages living beyond the pale of civilization.' This last remark was unwise, because it encouraged the Japanese to dispatch a punitive expedition themselves, which in April 1874 landed and occupied the eastern part of Formosa outside the area of effective Chinese jurisdiction. This was too much for Peking, and reinforcements were concentrated across the strait in Fukien. In a month or two, the Japanese were in a bad way through sickness, and the moment seemed opportune to drive them into the sea, but Li Hung-chang urged restraint, and a direct collision was avoided. British mediation brought about a settlement in October, under which the Japanese withdrew peacefully, and in the hope of staving off future attempts of the kind Formosa, again at British instigation, was thrown open to international trade.

In 1878, it was discovered that Japan was stopping the King of Loochoo from sending the customary tribute to Peking, and the following year there came a formal announcement that the islands had been reconstituted by the Japanese government into the prefecture of Okinawa. Again there was an outcry, which Li Hung-chang tried to pacify by giving his opinion to the Foreign Office. 'It is of no consequence whether Loochoo sends us tribute or not. We can very well do without such a place.' 'After all,' he wrote to a colleague, 'this dot on the map is closer to Japan than to us. To go to war for the sake of empty prestige would be utterly senseless.' It happened that General Grant, after completing his second term as president of the United States, was passing by the Far East in the course of a world tour, and Li suggested that advantage should be taken of his good offices. At first, Grant tried to please everybody by suggesting that Loochoo should be split in three, the northern part going to Japan and the southern part to China, while the native kingdom enjoyed a minute independence in between, but in the long run he too counselled Peking to waive its claims and acquiesce in the Japanese annexation. The advice was unpalatable, but as chance would have it a more urgent dispute had arisen with Russia and even some of Li's antagonists felt that in the circumstances it would be more politic to seek an alliance with Japan against the common enemy. Loochoo, then, was allowed to go.[2]

Ili

We have already seen how Tso Tsung-t'ang, who during the Taiping war had been with Li Hung-chang a fellow protégé of Tseng Kao-fan, had been put in command of the operations against the Muslim rebels of the north-western provinces, and later had gone on to crush another Muslim rising in Turkestan. Now Tso had retained his connexion with the Hunan Army, and was therefore from every point of view a rival to Li and his Huai force. Those in the know must have smiled to themselves when they heard that Li from the very start was putting obstacles in Tso's way, chiefly by urging upon the Court the worthlessness of Turkestan as a possession, 'hundreds of miles of wilderness', he called it. One reason his protest was overruled was that Yehonala thought it advisable to keep the Hunan Army clique as a counterbalance against him. In 1878, after a campaign of four years, Tso had the pleasure of announcing that resistance had ceased throughout the whole of Sinkiang.[3]

Naturally, Russia, as a next-door neighbour, had observed the rebellion and its suppression with the liveliest curiosity. In 1871 she took a hand in it herself by sending her troops across the border to occupy the region of Ili on the not unreasonable excuse that her commercial interests required the maintenance of order and that as soon as China was in a position to resume her authority Russian troops would be withdrawn. As, in spite of Tso's victory,

Russia showed no sign of keeping her word, a senior Manchu official was sent to St Petersburg in 1879 to negotiate. After months of haggling this man was bamboozled into signing a treaty by which a large part of Ili was ceded to Russia, who also retained the possession of certain passes of great strategic importance, and gained extensive commercial privileges. To add insult to injury China was to pay an indemnity of five million roubles to defray the cost of the military occupation. On his return to Peking in 1880, the wretched envoy was impeached and sentenced to death, a fate from which he was saved only by the intercession of Queen Victoria. Meanwhile, China denounced the treaty and prepared to go to war.

One of the most strenuous advocates of resistance was Tso Tsung-t'ang, and again he, and behind him the Hunan Army group, came into conflict with Li Hung-chang, who now had an extra motive for his animosity. If war did break out it would inevitably be the Huai Army which would have to bear the brunt of the fighting, and Li might well find his military supremacy destroyed for ever. He wrote furiously to Yehonala that Tso 'was putting himself at the head of a rabble of corrupt officials, who were using big words without regard for the national safety'. He urged that the treaty should be honoured; it was signed by a plenipotentiary and although it was a disadvantageous agreement, a breach of it would entail even worse consequences.

All these expostulations were in vain; officialdom generally rallied behind the Hunan group, but war did not come. The Russian fleet demonstrated off the China coast, but the Tsar's advisers knew that their country, so soon after the struggle with Turkey, was in no state for a new adventure. The Manchus, too, understood that the dynasty was unlikely to survive another trial. Diplomatic conversations were resumed, and to emphasize Li's discomfiture, China was represented at St Petersburg by the son of Tseng Kuo-fan, the Marquis Tseng, now Minister to Britain and France. Early in 1881 a new agreement was signed, restoring nearly all the territory, with the passes, to China, and limiting the trading concessions previously granted. Although in revenge the indemnity was increased from five to nine million roubles, the treaty was regarded as a triumph for the Hunan Group, and encouraged the Chinese government into withstanding aggression from states other than Russia.

Burma

This time the menace was directed against the satellite countries to the south. Burma had already since the beginning of the century been twice invaded and had seen portions of her territory annexed by the British, who were now investigating the possibility of trade through Burma with the western provinces of China. Early in 1875, an armed British expedition, entering Yunnan from Burma, met with resistance from the local population, and a man named Margary, an interpreter from the Peking legation, who was accompanying it, was killed. It is true that Margary's journey had been authorized by the Chinese government, but in the circumstances the conduct of the expedition was rather foolhardy and one cannot blame the peasantry for imagining that an attack was being launched against them. Nothing, however, would pacify the British Minister, Thomas Wade, an overbearing bully, famous throughout the Far East for his shouting and his table-thumping, except Chinese acquiescence in his demands. These, as incorporated in the Chefoo Convention made between Wade and Li Hung-chang in September 1876, went altogether beyond the Margary affair, and included the opening of still more ports to foreign trade. In particular, it was agreed that the Indian government should dispatch another expedition to delineate the border between Yunnan and Burma. This in itself was as good as a Chinese admission that Burma was already a British protectorate, and a year or two later the point was made in a conversation between Wade and Li, for according to the latter's notes Wade told him: 'We British like Burma very much: it is a place worth having', to which Li rejoined: 'If you should decide to go to war with Burma, let us know beforehand, so that it will not cause any trouble between us'. The very childishness of Wade's language suggests the record is a true one, and is a verbatim report of the Englishman's Chinese speech. Li is then revealed as perfectly willing to let Burma go.[4]

Vietnam and the War with France

Yet the crisis, when it happened, concerned not Burma but another southern neighbour far more intimately linked to China. Indeed, from the second century BC to the tenth century AD Vietnam, which was then limited to the northern half of its present territory, had formed part of the Chinese dominions, and ever since, though extending its rule gradually southwards to the Mekong River, had been proud to call China its suzerain. Its laws and institutions were closely modelled on those of China, and its official written language was Chinese. But since the seventeenth century, French missionaries had been active there, and converts to Christianity were numerous. On the eve of the French Revolution, a grandee of the country won the throne with the help of French adventurers, and in the middle of the nineteenth century Paris acted towards Vietnam as London did towards Burma. Cochin-China, the southernmost region, became a French protectorate in 1862. The same prospect of trade with Yunnan that led Margary to his death attracted the French into the north of Vietnam, but they were not strong enough to maintain themselves in occupation and were obliged to be contented with a treaty, made in 1874, which gave them trading and extra-territorial rights in the area. One great factor which had frustrated the attempt at conquest had been the intervention of a force of Chinese called the 'Black Flags' under the command of a certain Liu Yung-fu, who in his younger days had fought in the Taiping army and after the collapse of the Heavenly Kingdom had fled with a group of his followers to the Vietnamese border, where the band was allowed to rehabilitate itself in the Chinese service.

It was known that the French looked with displeasure on the Vietnamese practice of sending tribute to Peking, and the Marquis Tseng, who, as we have seen, was Minister both to London and Paris, made such strong representations in Peking concerning China's rights as suzerain that the Vietnamese question began to appear as one of the points of conflict between the Hunan and Huai cliques. It was natural, then, for Li Hung-chang to adopt a point of view diametrically opposite to Tseng's, and when in 1882 another French expedition sent against Hanoi encountered fierce resistance from the 'Black Flags', Li concluded an agreement under which Chinese troops would be withdrawn.

From the start, the arrangement was a dead letter. In 1883 the French government voted a grant of five and a half million francs towards the war. In spite of Li's insistence that China was in no condition to fight a European power, his advice was overruled, but oddly enough he was entrusted with the general conduct of the campaign. On land, the Chinese in northern Vietnam gave so good an account of themselves that the French government, after a spectacular defeat of their troops at Langson, was forced to resign. At sea, however, it was quite another story, and a Chinese fleet, together with the great naval arsenal at Foochow, was destroyed by French bombardment. Meanwhile, the French had occupied the Vietnamese capital of Hue, in the centre of the country, and had imposed a treaty by which Vietnam withdrew from Chinese suzerainty and a French protectorate was established over the whole country. Li, arguing that the Chinese victory at Langson gave a favourable opportunity for making peace, succeeded in having his enemy the Marquis Tseng replaced as Minister to France.

The negotiations in Paris were conducted on behalf of China by a Mr Campbell, a British employee of the Chinese Customs Service. For by now this institution, under its British head, Robert Hart, was exercising a dominant influence on the Chinese government, whose servant it theoretically was. The mere thought of this state of affairs, which, it must be admitted, was sufficiently grotesque, sends the modern Chinese historians into a fury. They argue that the prime duty of the Customs service was to ensure that the debts China had incurred in the form of indemnities, reparations and so forth would have a priority in the allocation of the national revenue, and that Hart and his staff, while acting the pantomime of being Chinese officials, were in reality administering China to suit the interests of the foreign powers. At any rate, the terms arrived at in Paris by Mr Campbell were ratified in a formal treaty signed by Li Hung-chang and the French envoy in June 1885, which acquiesced in the French conquest of Vietnam. In July 1886, a treaty with Britain recognized the latter's occupation of Burma the year before: it is worth remarking that Britain stated her willingness to continue the traditional ten-yearly tribute from Burma to Peking, but the practice was allowed to lapse. For Li personally it was a double triumph; he had carried the day over the war party, and the destruction of the arsenal at Foochow had dealt a crippling blow to his rivals of the Hunan group, to whom it had been one of the great sources of strength. From now on the Huai Army had no serious competitor in the military field.

135

Korea

Of all China's satellites Korea was marked out by geographical propinquity as being of special importance to the security of the Empire. In the year 1592 the point was emphasized when an army of Japanese invaders advanced through Korea and across the Yalu River into Manchuria. A Chinese relief force had repelled the menace, and since then, apart from a brief campaign in the 1630s, when the Koreans were compelled to transfer their allegiance from Ming to the Manchus, the peninsula had slumbered in that profound retirement from the world which had earned it the name of 'The Hermit Kingdom'. Now, in the middle of the nineteenth century, foreigners were again coming uncomfortably near. At first it looked as if the West would break down the unsocial seclusion. In the 1860s France had been angered by the killing of some of her missionaries. Then in 1871 the United States attempted half-heartedly to open the country by force, but an expedition for that purpose returned without effecting anything, and in the end the task fell to the Japanese, who, having just been compelled to admit strangers within their gates, found it particularly galling that the Koreans should persist in a policy which they themselves had followed for more than two hundred years.

In 1875 a party of Japanese surveyors were driven away by Korean coastal defences, and a request by Japan for the conclusion of a treaty was refused, on the grounds that Korea was a Chinese dependency. When Japan took up the matter in Peking, the Chinese government was being driven to distraction by the angry bellows of Thomas Wade over the Margary affair, and had no time to spare for anything else. By an unfortunate choice of words Tokyo was informed that China would not dream of interfering in Korean affairs to the extent of pressing Korea to make a treaty. This certainly gave Japan an excuse for regarding Korea as an independent state, and in 1876 she dispatched a strong naval expedition which forced Korea to conclude an agreement establishing diplomatic relations, opening certain ports, and granting the Japanese extra-territoriality. No protest came from China, but Li Hung-chang privately advised the Koreans to 'counter poison by poison' or in other words to establish relations with the Western powers and thus create rivals for the Japanese, and for the Russians too, whose presence in Vladivostok was making itself felt.

In the event, it proved impossible for China to avoid being involved in the affairs of its vassal. The king of Korea succeeded to the throne, by adoption, while he was still a child and during his minority the government had been in the hands of his father as Regent. Now of full age the young ruler looked with favour on the partisans of modernization who in turn drew their support from Japan. All this was hateful to the ex-Regent and in 1882 he and his ultra-conservative followers attempted a *coup d'état* in the course of which some Japanese military instructors were killed and the Japanese legation set on fire. When the news arrived, Li had returned to his province to attend his mother's funeral, and in his absence the decision was taken to send a contingent of the Huai Army to restore order. With these troops went a young officer destined to play as great a part as Li himself in the history of China. His name was Yuan Shih-k'ai.

The ex-Regent was soon made prisoner and bundled off out of harm's way to Tientsin. Meanwhile the Japanese had sent an expedition too, and although care was taken not to collide with the Chinese, the Korean authorities were compelled to allow Japanese troops to be stationed at Seoul for the protection of their nationals. Encouraged by the presence of these champions, and thinking that China was incapacitated by the war with France over Vietnam, the leader of the progressive party in December 1884 seized the occasion of a state banquet to hold what some foreign wit called 'an oriental general election' by murdering the principal men on the other side and seizing the persons of the king and queen. The Japanese who were in the know from the beginning participated in the transaction to the extent of sending troops to hold the palace.[5]

There was no time to ask Tientsin for instructions. Yuan Shih-k'ai had to make up his mind on the spot. He acted with extraordinary promptness and vigour. Chinese forces together with some Korean detachments they had trained were ordered to break into the palace and take the ruler and his wife into custody. This necessitated an open clash and fighting raged in the palace courtyards until the Japanese acknowledged they had been worsted by abandoning their royal prize to Yuan. With this exploit to his credit Yuan became overnight a hero in the eyes of his countrymen.

His merits were rewarded even by the cautious Li. He was appointed Chinese resident in Seoul.

If a large body of opinion was impatient at the government's finally yielding Vietnam to France, it will easily be understood that the clamour for a strong policy in Korea was even more urgent. Here the enemy was to be merely the despised race of island dwarfs. To some extent, this popular sentiment found a response in Li himself. He had argued all along that the eastern seaboard, and not the frontiers of Turkestan or Tonkin, was the crucial zone of national defence. So far, however, from under-estimating Japanese military power, he had persistently drawn attention to the success of the Meiji reforms, and now he laid emphasis on the need for a stronger navy. The destruction by the French of the southern fleet at Foochow ensured both that funds for shipbuilding would be made available and that Li Hung-chang would be in charge of their administration. Accordingly the main naval bases were transferred to the north, to Port Arthur in Manchuria and Weihaiwei in Shantung.

Yuan Shih-k'ai was in the meantime very active in maintaining his government's rights of overlordship in Seoul, but it was becoming increasingly obvious that an outright clash with Japan could not be avoided much longer. In Korea at large, law and order were breaking down; a semi-religious brotherhood calling itself the *Tonghak*, or 'Eastern Doctrine', in opposition to the 'Western Doctrine' of Christianity rose in revolt in 1893, and soon became the spearhead of peasant dissatisfaction. By May 1894 the rebels had inflicted several major defeats on the government forces, which appealed to China for help. A few weeks earlier a macabre incident had occurred to inflame passions still further. A man murdered in a Japanese hotel in Shanghai had been identified as the leader of Korean progressives who had engineered the abortive *coup* in 1884 and who had since been living under Japanese protection. The Chinese authorities returned both the corpse and the assassin, who was a fellow Korean, to their native country. The criminal was welcomed as a national hero, while the dead body was hacked to bits, and its fragments exhibited ignominiously throughout the kingdom. Naturally enough the Japanese fumed over the insult, and were in no temper to stand aside and watch Korea return altogether into Chinese vassalage. Sensing thunder in the air, Li Hung-chang forestalled an outburst from Tokyo by declaring that the Chinese troops sent in answer to the Korean request would be withdrawn once order had been restored. Meanwhile he would be very glad if the Japanese could themselves spare a couple of gunboats to protect their nationals.

The War with Japan

As things turned out, foreign soldiers were not needed, since the Korean government managed against all expectation to suppress the rebels unaided, but throughout June men poured in from both sides, for Japan was not limiting her intervention to comply with Li's wishes. On his part, Li was pinning his hopes on Russian jealousy of Japan; the Russian Minister in Peking had revealed himself favourable towards a joint Sino-Russian protectorate over Korea. But the Siberian railway was not yet completed, and in St Petersburg, at the prospect of an undertaking of such magnitude, milder counsels prevailed. All that China could look for was the good offices of Russia in talking the Japanese into moderation. But the Japanese were not, it appeared, in a mood to be persuaded. At the end of July 1894 they seized the royal palace and reinstated the Regent, who obligingly asked his new patrons to drive the Chinese from Korea once and for all. War was formally declared on 1 August by both sides, but hostilities had been in progress for some days and already Seoul and the southern half of the country were in Japanese hands.

Chinese forces now poured in across the Yalu but were no match for the Japanese, who demonstrated for the first time in modern war that extraordinary élan which was to carry them in our own day in a matter of weeks to the borders of India and Australia. Pyongyang, the chief town of northern Korea, fell on 16 September, but salvation seemed at hand, for an important squadron of the Chinese fleet had appeared off the mouth of the Yalu River, convoying transports with reinforcements.

Admiral Ting, who was in command of this armada, had not been bred to the sea; he had started his career as a cavalry officer in the Huai Army and had deserved his present eminence by his loyalty towards Li Hung-chang. No doubt of his own capacity seems to have entered his head; he enjoyed to the full every perquisite of his situation, and was celebrated for the magnificence of his entertainments, at which his guests were beguiled by the coquetry of a troop of boy actors who formed part of the admiral's household. It was not, after all, his business to know anything of navigation, gunnery and the like. He had assistants, some of them Europeans, qualified in those branches of science.

When on 17 September units of the Japanese fleet hove into sight, the admiral's jovial self-confidence was unimpaired. He had every reason to feel at ease. True, he lacked any great superiority in numbers, possessing only thirteen ships against the Japanese twelve, but two of these were ironclads of over seven thousand tons while the largest Japanese vessels did not exceed four thousand tons. In firepower too the Chinese were decidedly stronger. From the start, foreign observers had been sure that the Japanese would lose the war and nowhere more signally than at sea. Yet in this encounter things somehow did not go according to plan. The admiral took his place with dignity on the bridge of his flagship, with his British master-gunner by his side, only to discover, what does not seem to have entered his head before, that neither could understand a word of what the other was saying. For a while they tried sign-language, until their ordeal was ended by one of their own shells, which hit the bridge and wounded both of them; the admiral so severely that he was in no condition to observe the rest of the battle. This was a mercy in disguise, for a more convincing demonstration of poltroonery and incompetence could not have been imagined. Even so, the initial advantage of the Chinese enabled them to stay and disembark their troops. But the loss of four ships, and heavy casualties in men, caused Li Hung-chang to issue a strict order that his fleet must never again venture itself in combat. Ting thereupon withdrew to the shelter of Weihaiwei, in the euphemism of Li 'as a tiger to his lair', leaving the southern coast of Manchuria without naval cover.

The precedent of 1592 was repeated. A Japanese army had again crossed the Yalu to Chinese soil, while a sea-borne invasion landed on the Liaotung Peninsula and laid siege to Port Arthur. That fortress fell on 21 November to the accompaniment of an enormous slaughter of its defenders. About the same time Li Hung-chang, with Peking's approval, made the first overtures for peace, in a manner highly characteristic of the period, through the mediation of a German member of the Customs staff armed with a personal letter from Li to the Japanese Prime Minister. But Tokyo, unlike Paris ten years before, refused to treat with a European emissary, and even when Chinese officials were sent in the German's place, their competence was questioned; it was hinted that only Li himself had sufficient standing to be worth talking to. Clearly there was no help for it but to swallow the humiliation, and in the middle of March 1895 Li Hung-chang arrived at the rendezvous in Shimonoseki.[6]

The Treaty of Shimonoseki

From the way the war had been going it was obvious that the enemy's terms would be severe. The month before, even the 'tiger's lair' of Weihaiwei had been stormed, and all that remained of Ting's fleet obliged to surrender, a disgrace which the poor easy-going admiral and some of his officers avoided by suicide. Li then had prepared himself for a shock, but the reality exceeded his gloomiest anticipations. Not even an armistice would be granted he was told, until his own base of Tientsin, and the railway running north of it to the Great Wall, had been handed over. This was out of the question for it would place Peking at the conqueror's mercy.

At this juncture, affairs took an unexpected turn. In going from the conference to his lodgings, Li was shot at by a Japanese fanatic and wounded in the face. Embarrassed by the outrage, his hosts were constrained to be more accommodating, and an armistice was granted forthwith. Yet when the cost of peace came to be reckoned, as it was set out in April 1895 in the Treaty of Shimonoseki, the price was still atrocious. The age-old suzerainty over Korea had, of course, to be abandoned. There was an indemnity of two hundred million dollars, and four inland cities, including Chungking, were to be opened as treaty ports. Worst of all, not only the Liaotung Peninsula in southern Manchuria, but Formosa and the Pescadores were to be ceded to Japan in perpetuity. Indeed, while the negotiations were going forward, Formosa had been invaded, and put beyond the scope of the armistice.

It does not need much imagination to picture the effect of these things on Li's rivals of the Hunan Group. And for a while it looked as if Formosa would provide them with material to upset the hateful agreement he had just concluded. The people of the island, with the Governor at their head, offered it as a protectorate first to Britain and then to France, on condition that China kept residual sovereignty. Failing in this attempt, at the end of May they declared themselves a republic. The government they organized did not last more than a few days, but by a strange coincidence Liu Yung-fu and his Black Flags, who had given so good an account of themselves against the French in Vietnam, had recently been transferred to Formosa, and once again, throughout that summer of 1895, they were the heroes of China as they resisted the Japanese invaders. It was the end of October before Liu was driven to the mainland and Formosa could settle under its new masters. As a crowning degradation, the Hunan group prevailed on the Court to send Li's eldest son as Commissioner to hand over the ceded territory to the victors.

This was certainly the darkest moment of Li Hung-chang's career. His beloved Huai Army was in ruins, and its sister navy no longer existed. Cries for vengeance were heard from one end of the land to the other; respectable mandarins addressed memorials to the Throne in which they declared the satisfaction it would give them to dine upon his flesh; a figure of speech, no doubt, but an uncomfortable thing to have to listen to. How did he manage to survive such a storm? To answer this question it is necessary to turn once again to the scandals and intrigues of the Forbidden City.[7]

CHAPTER X

THE REFORM MOVEMENT

Yehonala again Regent – the Emperor Kuang Hsü – Li Hung-chang and Russia – 'cutting up the melon' – Western political ideas – K'ang Yu-wei and the Reform Movement – the Hundred Days

Yehonala again Regent

WE TOOK our leave of the Western Dowager Yehonala in the year 1869, just at the time when her fellow regent the Eastern Dowager and Prince Kung the Chief Minister had declared open war against her by contriving the destruction of her favourite eunuch An Te-hai. She had had to postpone the pleasures of revenge, and before long anxieties of another sort were engrossing her attention. In 1873, her son the Emperor T'ung Chih entered his eighteenth year and the regency came to an end. It was bitter enough for Yehonala to give up her authority, but to make things worse she was aware that her son had little cause to love her. In his boyhood, any affection he was capable of feeling had gone to the Eastern Dowager, and now, as a married man, for he had taken a bride the year before, he began to act as if his mother did not exist. State papers no longer came her way, and if an heir should be born to the young couple her eclipse would be complete.

It must have been with a certain reassurance that she heard that T'ung Chih, a true son of his father, was already finding the atmosphere of a family too stifling for comfort. Like Hsien Feng before him, he had a craving for Chinese feminity, and when this fit was on him all the beauties of Mongolia and Manchuria together could not serve his purpose. He opened his mind to a pair of his confidants, and was relieved to discover they saw no insuperable difficulty if the Son of Heaven had really set his heart on having an occasional frolic. So the palace sentries became used to seeing these two grandees, with a third and younger man between them, slip out after nightfall and vanish from sight into the town. The year 1874 was not far advanced before those at Court were remarking to one another about the shocking deterioration in the Emperor's appearance. As the months passed it was difficult to conceal that he had become a victim of some painful disorder. Now that it was too late, the sick wretch cursed his folly and turned to the only person from whom he could expect sympathy, the wife he had neglected. For a little while the two of them were all in all to each other, and then Heaven intervened to spare its son further shame. It was announced that His Majesty had been granted the happiness of a visitation of Celestial Flowers or in other words that he had contracted smallpox. On 13 January 1875, the Dragon Throne again lacked an occupant.

In theory, the death of her son should have ended all Yehonala's pretensions to power. During the last few weeks it had become apparent that T'ung Chih's final months of domesticity had given his wife a child. If the baby should prove to be a boy, then it would have an incontestable right to succeed its father and on established precedent it would be hard in such circumstances to deny the widow's claim, as Empress Dowager, to exercise at least the Co-Regency, and this not with Yehonala, whose marital status had never been more than that of a concubine, but with the Eastern Dowager, the only other surviving Empress Consort.

Certain factors, though, were in Yehonala's favour. The same decree that announced T'ung Chih's smallpox declared that the Eastern and Western Dowagers had agreed for the duration of the illness to handle state affairs. Her former authority of Co-Regent had therefore to some extent been restored when her son died, and her native boldness supplied the rest. It was out of the question, she said, that the throne should remain vacant until the sex of the unborn infant was known: an Emperor must be appointed at once.

We have already seen that in private families there was a moral obligation to provide a childless man with a successor by adoption, but that the choice was limited by strict rules. The person adopted had to be a male of the clan, of the same generation as a natural heir would have been, that is to say one generation junior to the adoptive father. Yehonala, however, was not concerned with technicalities. Her younger sister had shared in her good fortune by marrying one of Hsien Feng's brothers and the couple had an infant son. To Yehonala the prospect was decidedly alluring; another long Regency and even after that, the government still in the family. True, the child, being of the same generation as T'ung Chih, could not be his ritual successor. No matter, said Yehonala, let him ascend the throne as son by adoption to Hsien Feng; later when he came to beget sons of his own, one of them could be assigned as heir to T'ung Chih. Yehonala's formidable presence, and the knowledge that she could rely on the support of Li Hung-chang, overawed opposition; the yellow palanquin was despatched to her sister's house, and at dead of night a frightened child of three was hurried into the Palace and made to kowtow before the corpse of his predecessor. The new sovereign was to reign under the style of Kuang Hsü.

An embarrassing possibility still remained, namely that T'ung Chih might have a posthumous son of his own, but here too Yehonala did not shrink from doing what was necessary. 'I feel,' she said, 'that as the Empress is so downcast by the loss of her husband she ought to consider following him'. T'ung Chih's widow took the advice and committed suicide on 27 March 1875.

The transaction was not managed without enormous scandal. It was whispered that the unfeeling mother was not only guilty of a crime against nature by depriving her son of an heir, but that she had deliberately encouraged him in his debaucheries in order to put an end to him and regain the Regency. At least one eminent mandarin killed himself in protest. But the most dangerous potential opponents, the Eastern Dowager and Prince Kung, were disarmed by finding themselves back once more in their seats of authority, as Co-Regent and Chief Minister respectively, and were not courageous or energetic enough to strike a blow for the Confucian proprieties. Meanwhile, Yehonala herself, once she had got her way, relapsed into domestic pleasure, for by this time another favourite eunuch had taken the place of the martyred An Te-hai. This was Li Lien-ying, whose name was to be linked with hers for the rest of her life. No history of the Chinese nineteenth century would be complete without a mention of this enigmatic personage. Steeped in every sort of wickedness, he was also, like his precursor, fanatically addicted to the theatre and an expert contriver of masques and revels.[1]

Yehonala was at no pains to be discreet, and soon all the old stories were being revived. In the spring of 1881, the censorious began to wonder whether perhaps the Eastern Dowager might be persuaded at last to assert her authority on behalf of public morality. She was still only forty-five years old, in spite of her long widowhood and matronly ways, and the boy Emperor was known to have a preference for her over his aunt. There were signs that gave rise to hope. She had certainly uttered a bitter denunciation of the eunuch and, by implication, of his mistress. When one afternoon the news swept round the city that the Eastern Dowager was dead, mandarins who had heard her voice that morning through the audience curtain swore there must have been foul play, but precisely of what sort nobody could tell. Even today opinions are divided as to Yehonala's guilt, but whether in the course of nature or not, she had become sole Regent. Three years later, the war against France gave her an occasion to get rid of her second enemy. Blaming the disasters of the campaign on Prince Kung, she sent him into retirement with a scathing reference to his 'petrified energies'.

The Emperor Kuang Hsü

By rights, the Emperor's minority should have ended in 1887, but the Regency continued until his marriage in 1889. Kuang Hsü, who owed his elevation to the fact that he was the son of Yehonala's sister, found himself called upon to consolidate the circle by receiving to wife the daughter of her brother. The lady was by no means to his taste, but as compensation he was permitted to indulge his own inclinations by taking into concubinage two other girls, who seemed to have caught his sluggish fancy, and once the wedding was over it was with these companions, renamed the Lustrous Concubine and the Pearl Concubine respectively that he spent most of his time. In fact, it was rumoured that the intercession of his father was required before he would so much as go through the form of cohabitation with his consort. Of course, Yehonala was much provoked by her nephew's ostentatious neglect of his duty, and still more by the evidence that the concubines were presuming on their status by accepting bribes for putting in a good word to the Emperor on behalf of ambitious mandarins. On several occasions her own nominees were passed over in favour of candidates enterprising enough to have discovered this alternative road to promotion, and both her vanity and her purse found the affront hard to bear.

For some years her mind had been occupied on a grandiose project, nothing less than the creation of a new Summer Palace hard by the ruins of the Round Bright Garden, that pleasure ground of her young womanhood. The work was now well in hand, and the new domain, christened the Hill of a Myriad Longevities, was being planned to meet her every whim. Such an undertaking needed money in excess of the ordinary revenues of the Court, and it was here that the eunuch Li Lien-ying first revealed his financial genius. After the French war, more was being spent on national defence, and particularly large sums had been allocated to the Navy, with Li Hung-chang as administrator. In 1889, soon after the Emperor's marriage, his father, to encourage the good work, made a tour of the northern ports, including the bases of Port Arthur and Weihaiwei, and to everybody's astonishment the eunuch, undeterred by the fate of An Te-hai, accompanied him on the inspection. The circumstances of the visit were even more extraordinary, for Li Hung-chang, formal and perfunctory towards the Emperor's father, showed himself to the eunuch as the very soul of affability and the pair were constantly in each other's company. From then on it was observed that there was a great air of confidence in the Dowager's entourage which was attributed to the certainty of being permanently in funds, but the Emperor was so thankful to see his aunt engrossed in her building that he did not have the heart to inquire how the toy was being paid for.

It was not until the incapacity of the much-vaunted Navy was made plain to all in 1894–5, that the question was answered. Immense sums of money, exactly how much will never be known, had been diverted by Li Hung-chang to the use of his patroness, and while Weihaiwei and the fleet with it were passing into Japanese hands, it was being recalled throughout the country that one of the treasures of the Dowager's paradise was a marble boat contrived for her entertainment on an artificial lake. So Yehonala and Li Hung-chang shared in the opprobrium. Indeed the war had already drawn them even closer together, for Li's rivals of the Hunan group had gained the ear of Kuang Hsü to form a sort of 'Emperor's party' which advocated the vigorous prosecution of the campaign in opposition to Li and the Dowager who from the start were half-hearted about fighting, and dreaded above all the waste of their assets. Not that the Hunan Army had any reason for complacency; on the contrary, a part of their forces sent to the southern Manchurian front, collapsed disastrously in the face of the enemy. To be sure, they were able to gloat over Li's public humiliation at the terms of peace, but even there they did not have everything their own way. A matter of days after the announcement of what had been agreed at Shimonoseki, Russia, who until then had been unable to do more than offer her good offices, led France and Germany to make a joint approach to Japan, 'advising' the latter to return the Liaotung Peninsula to China. Tokyo thought it prudent to yield to so persuasive a combination, and exchanged the territory for a further thirty million dollars to be added to the indemnity. The appearance on the scene of international champions immeasurably strengthened Li's hand, and with the still formidable influence of the Dowager behind him he emerged from the crisis badly weakened but a man to be reckoned with.

Li Hung-chang and Russia

It was to be surmised that the three rescuers would expect an adequate recompense for their intervention. Russia's purpose was the most obvious. The facts of geography indicated that the Amur lands taken from China in 1858–60 were economically dependent on the rest of Manchuria from which they had been so unnaturally hacked off. Furthermore, during the building of the trans-Siberian railway, then in progress, it had become only too apparent that a line keeping purely to Russian territory would have to make a very tiresome detour in order to reach Vladivostok, to which the easiest and quickest road would lie directly across Manchuria. Furthermore, Vladivostok itself, excellent harbour though it was, became icebound in winter, forming in this respect a tantalizing contrast with Port Arthur and Dairen. That these latter and with them the gateway to Manchuria should pass into Japanese hands was not to be thought of for a moment.

As chance would have it, the year following the Treaty of Shimonoseki saw the coronation of a new Tsar, Nicholas II, and the Manchu Court sent Li Hung-chang to represent it at the ceremony. No opportunity could have been better. Before leaving

Moscow, in June 1896, Li put his signature to a secret Sino-Russian pact providing for joint resistance to any Japanese aggression against either country or against Korea. In this event, China would open her ports to Russian vessels of war. Meanwhile, in preparation for such a contingency Russia would be permitted to build a railway to Vladivostok through the Manchurian provinces of Heilungkiang and Kirin, and to use the line even in peacetime for the transport of troops and military supplies. The construction of this railway, called later the Chinese Eastern Railway, was to be handled by a Sino-Russian bank under the direct control of the Tsarist Ministry of Finance. The contract establishing the railway company, signed shortly afterwards, provided that administrative rights in the railway zone should be vested in the company. Theoretically this was a joint venture; in fact since China did not contribute her share of the capital, it was under Russian domination, and the transaction turned northern Manchuria both economically and politically into a Russian sphere of influence.

It was suspected at the time, but not known for certain until the publication of Tsarist archives by the Soviets, that Li accepted an enormous bribe from the Russian government for his co-operation. With this in his pocket, and the prospect of more to come, he was in quite a holiday mood for the rest of his tour, which carried him round the world by western Europe and the United States, and is remarkable chiefly for the evil stigma it has bequeathed to the reputation of Chinese cuisine. The story goes that Li arrived in an American city late at night, long after the restaurants had shut, and on his complaint of feeling hungry his attendants knocked up a Cantonese eating-house which they persuaded to serve the great man with a makeshift supper. The principal dish consisted of a plate of scraps – in Cantonese, *chop suey* – to which the famished Viceroy did such execution, that from then on Chinatown restaurants catering to foreigners, instead of throwing the day's left-overs in the dustbin, kept them to make a novel item in the menu, looking and tasting like a dog's dinner and totally unknown to genuine Chinese tables.

'Cutting Up the Melon'

The Russian 'alliance' was only one, if the most important, sign that China after her defeat had entered a fresh era. The enormous indemnity exacted by the Japanese was an impossible burden for a government whose combined annual revenue hardly exceeded eighty million dollars, but the good friends who had saved Liaotung were only too ready to oblige in this matter also. In July 1895 came a Franco-Russian loan of four hundred million francs, and this set off the race. Britain lent four million pounds, Germany one million pounds, and then Britain and Germany jointly two sums, of sixteen million pounds each, in 1896 and 1898 respectively. These loans were of course a charge against the foreign-managed Customs, but security of another kind was also sought. In 1895–6 France obtained the cession of territory in Yunnan, on the Indo-Chinese border, trading and mining rights in Yunnan, Kwangsi and Kwangtung, and the right to build a railway from Indo-China into Kwangsi. Germany was not to be left behind, being especially anxious to possess a 'coaling-station' in Shantung for the use of her navy, and when the news came in 1897 that two of her nationals, Catholic priests, had been murdered by bandits in that very province, it seemed that destiny itself was siding with the Kaiser, whose fleet at once steamed into the bay and port of Kiaochow. In 1898, the place was leased to the Germans for ninety-nine years and they acquired besides, rights of railway building and mining in Shantung province.

It will be remembered that Russia, by the terms of the secret pact, was to come to China's assistance in case of aggression by Japan, and China was at such a time to open her ports to Russian warships. No sooner had the German Navy occupied Kiaochow than the Muscovite casuists informed Peking that in the circumstances they felt there was sufficient danger to China from Germany, and very likely from Britain as well, to require them to honour their promise to the extent of sending a fleet to Port Arthur. Li Hung-chang ,who was again the happy recipient of the Tsar's bounty, saw to it that the suggestion was accepted. The only trouble was, when a settlement had been arrived at with Germany, the Russians could not find it in their hearts to say goodbye to their Manchurian harbour. In March 1898, another Sino-Russian treaty leased Port Arthur and Dairen Bay for a renewable term of twenty-five years. In addition, a branch line of the Chinese Eastern Railway was to link Port Arthur to the Russian system of communication.

It must not be thought that Britain was an idle spectator of these events. Early in 1897 an agreement on the boundary between Burma and Yunnan had yielded a sizeable portion of that south-western province, and more river ports in Kwangsi and Kwang-tung had been opened to British commerce. In February 1898, the Peking government was forced to acknowledge the Yangtze area as a British sphere of influence, and once Port Arthur had gone to Russia Britain obtained a similar lease of the Shantung port of Weihaiwei. Finally, not to be outdone by France, which in May 1898 got a lease of the south Kwangtung harbour of Kwang-chowwan for ninety-nine years. Britain the following month entered into possession of the territories inland from Kowloon, the mainland foothold of Hong Kong, on the same terms.

Western Political Ideas

This unexampled series of humiliations, following on the heels of military defeat, was widely understood, both in China and abroad, as being the prelude to something even worse, namely the dis-memberment of the Empire by the foreign powers, who would allot between themselves the severed fragments as colonies. Rage and alarm spread among the intended victims of this anatomiza-tion, though few perceived that any measures more subtle than straightforward resistance were called for on their parts. These few, however, had increased in number in the past two decades; their ideas had outgrown the narrow limits Li Hung-chang and his colleagues had set to the modernization of China. It was all very well to tell bright young men, as they entered upon their western studies that they were expected to confine their learning to the practical domain of military technology. The best of them ignored the warning, and found that the fruit of European litera-ture and philosophy tasted all the sweeter for being put out of bounds.

Yen Fu was one of those who had set out to learn the arts of war only to be diverted into more intellectual paths. He was a boy of thirteen when in 1866 he entered the naval college attached to the unlucky shipyard at Foochow, not because at that age he had any learnings towards such a profession, but induced by the expectation of a modest subsidy which would relieve the poverty of his family. From 1877 to 1879 he spent two years in England. In theory all his time should have been devoted to the needs of his future profession, but somehow he contrived to find enough leisure to investigate such irrelevant phenomena as the English legal system, besides passing his examinations with distinction. On his return to China he attracted the attention of Li Hung-chang, always ready to snatch talent for his own service. In 1880 he moved to Tientsin where he was to work for the next twenty years, most of the time as head of the naval school. Not surprisingly, he felt that he had certain ideas to offer upon topics of wider importance, but he soon discovered that his patron was supremely uninterested in anything he had to say concerning politics and administration, and he suspected that the fact he had opinions on such matters at all, with the implication that he could see something wrong with the present conduct of affairs, was turning Li against him. In his frustration he succumbed to the allurement of opium to which he was ever afterwards an addict.[2]

There was no better vantage point to view the disaster of the Japanese war than Li's headquarters at Tientsin, and the fighting was still in its early stages when Yen Fu decided to carry out an idea which had been at the back of his mind for years, but which the circumstances of the time seemed now to render particularly significant. He began to translate Huxley's *Evolution and Ethics*, and after serialization in a Tientsin journal, the complete version came out in book form in 1898. It was the first time that the theory of evolution had been introduced to the general Chinese reader and the impact of it was all the stronger since the political message, already present in the original text, was developed in the translator's notes. To thoughtful Chinese in the late 1890s the doctrine of natural selection and the 'survival of the fittest' had more than an academic value. Let there be no more boastful talk of Chinese and barbarian, the book seemed to say. The foreign nations by their very success in aggression were proving their superiority, and unless something was done quickly, the Chinese would share the fate of the American Indians and the Australian blackfellows.

It was a shocking prediction, and expressed, as it was, in admirable Chinese, for Yen had the gift of readability, it created nothing less than a literary sensation, the effect of which left some curious memorials behind it. During the first half of this century, no Chinese enjoyed greater esteem in intellectual circles abroad than Dr Hu Shih, the philosopher and man of letters. He was a child when Yen's *Huxley* appeared and his parents, who were of the mandarin class, promptly gave him the name of *Shih*, which means 'The Fit One'. Another boy, destined to grow up into a warlord, was called *Ching-ts'un*, or 'Compete for Survival'.

About the same time that Yen was translating Huxley, he published in the Tientsin press a series of articles in which he suggested what, in his view, should be the steps taken in the emergency. The essential was, he thought, that there should be a reformation in the national ethic which could only be achieved by making the people at large feel they had a part in the administration of the country. There ought to be a central parliament, and local government should be carried on by elected officers. Education must be modernized and provide an adequate place for the study of natural science.

Yen, of course, had the immense advantage of reading a foreign language and of having had personal experience of Europe. But, as was to happen on later occasions also, the most effective agents of political change were men who, understanding no language but their own, had to get their knowledge of the West at second hand, and by their native genius adapt it to Chinese conditions. By these last few years of the nineteenth century there existed, especially in the treaty ports and most of all in Shanghai, an atmosphere conducive to the development of such talent. For almost two generations missionary schools and institutions, particularly Protestant ones, had been disseminating Western knowledge of a general sort, chiefly by translations of suitable text-books. Although the selection and interpretation of the material was in the main done by missionaries lacking the intellectual attainments of men like Yen Fu, yet the total effect was very far from negligible. Furthermore, in Shanghai this publishing industry had since the 1840s brought together a group of cultivated men content to earn a living by acting as amanuenses, whose prime duty it was to impart a polish to the uncouth style of the foreigners. The Taiping Rebellion increased this literary colony with the advent of a swarm of refugees from the Lower Yangtze Valley, for centuries the favourite seat of the arts, and even when Manchu rule was restored, Nanking and the other cities of the region never regained their old prosperity; by the 1870s most of the intellectual prestige they once enjoyed had followed the movement of wealth to Shanghai, where it stayed for the next seventy years.

If one were writing a cultural history of China, it would not be an exaggeration to call the period between the suppression of the Taiping and the establishment of the People's Government 'the Shanghai era', and in certain ways the phenomenon was most strongly marked during the final decades of the nineteenth century. It was the Yangtze provinces which furnished the greater part of the upper civil service, and there was in consequence a perpetual coming and going between central China and the capital. The old overland route via the Grand Canal fell into desuetude during the Taiping war, and steamer services had been introduced on the Yangtze and along the coast. The easiest and quickest method of going from Hankow or Nanking to Peking was to travel by river boat to Shanghai and there change to a coastal vessel to Tientsin. Mandarins in transit became accustomed to dallying in Shanghai where they could entertain and be entertained by their colleagues without the oppressive restrictions to which they were subject in the capital itself. The choicest singing girls flocked from Soochow and Yangchow to meet so nutritious a clientele. Not that a stay in Shanghai need be dedicated exclusively to pleasure. There was serious conversation to be had with the resident men of letters, a number of whom had taken up the profession of journalism, for after thirty years of development there was by 1895 an abundance of Chinese newspapers and magazines. And throughout all this could be felt the influence of Western ideas and Western fashions, varying in degree from the man about town who would treat his mistress to a European dinner washed down with champagne, to the enthusiast who struggled through versions of Adam Smith and Whewell's *International Law*.

K'ang Yu-wei and the Reform Movement

One such visitor in the year 1882 was a Cantonese of twenty-four named K'ang Yu-wei who was glad to break his journey between his native province and Peking, where he was making the first of several attempts to secure a higher degree in the metropolitan examinations. He had already been impressed by the order of Hong Kong, and now, in the intervals of admiring the streets and buildings of the foreign settlements, he bought up all the translations he could lay his hands on, and paid a subscription besides to a missionary newspaper. Today the Communists sneer that the aim of this sort of literature was to 'indianize' China, but its effect on young K'ang was disturbing enough. When he reached home, he resolved to strike a blow for reform by leaving his daughters' feet unbound. This was more easily said than done; a family crisis arose, and indignant kinsmen made his life a misery by complaining of the embarrassment he was bringing on the name of K'ang and commiserating with the poor little girls who could never look for decent husbands. But he persevered, and even found others who shared his views, so that in due course an Anti-Footbinding Society came into existence and the movement spread to Shanghai and Tientsin.

In 1888, he returned to Peking to try his luck, again without success. Since his last visit there the war with France had taken place, and he resolved to address a letter to the Emperor himself. It did not get further than a government ministry, but it was read by some men of influence, and certain prophetic words in it remained in their memories.

With the loss of Loochoo, Vietnam and Burma, our protective plumage is cut off and the next blow will be at our heart. Japan has designs on Korea and Manchuria, Britain is opening Tibet and looking at Szechwan and Yunnan: Russia is pressing on Mukden: France is stirring up rebellion in the South to help her acquire Yunnan, Kwangtung and Kwangsi.

As a remedy for this desperate condition of affairs he urged, in rather vague terms, a reform of laws and institutions and the association of the people with the government.[3]

His failure as an examinee did not prevent him the following year from opening his own school in Canton, with a curriculum which imposed on a Confucian basis such notions of western history and philosophy as he had been able to acquire. He was convinced that Confucius had been an innovator who boldly put his own political ideas in the mouths of heroes of remote antiquity, and that he himself was the real heir to the Confucian spirit. In the same vein, he attempted to discover in the Confucian classics support for his theory that the world was moving stage by stage to an ultimate and inevitable commonwealth of mankind. As to this last, he put his predictions into a book, the title of which may be translated as *Utopia*, and which was considered so shocking that it was not published until more than twenty years later, after the fall of the Empire.

In this happy future, according to K'ang, the states of today will disappear to make way for a world government, to be elected by general suffrage. The family will not survive the nation, for no couple may cohabit for more than a year, after which they will be assigned fresh partners. Children will be wards of the state and on coming of age will be assigned to productive occupation. We shall live in dormitories and eat in mess halls.

Such was the ideal that gladdened the heart of this Confucian scholar; a man who while still cherishing the brave vision was during the latter half of his life – he died in 1927 – the very symbol of traditional China. It is something to ponder over today, when foreigners often express bewilderment at the ease with which Marx and Lenin have taken up quarters in the Forbidden City. A few years ago, while the Commune movement was at its height, some Western newspapers carried a story of a kind to make Christian blood run cold. In China, it was reported, even the bodies of the dead could not evade the duty of production and were being used as manure. The rumour, which it need hardly be said emanated from Hong Kong, was a ridiculous fabrication. But in K'ang's *Utopia* we read that cremation will replace burial, and at the side of each crematorium will be built a fertilizer works.

The trend of events during the next couple of years ensured that K'ang's ideas should attract more and more listeners. He had passed the metropolitan examination in 1895 and had now acquired a group of disciples as fervent as himself. The best known of these was a fellow Cantonese named Liang Ch'i-ch'ao, fifteen years his junior, and preternaturally active in the cause. Liang had already raised the question of foreign support, and had worked as secretary to Timothy Richards, a British missionary better known for his work in secular education, who had assured him that Britain would be whole-heartedly behind any movement of reform. This accorded very well with K'ang's inclinations, for his earliest interest in political matters had been aroused by what he had seen in Hong Kong, and he believed readily enough that Britain and America were comparatively benevolent. Liang himself, in spite of his association with Richards, dreamt of the day when the yellow race would unite against the interference of the white and was all in favour of an alliance with Japan. In any case, both K'ang and Liang agreed that Japan was the immediate model on which the new China ought to pattern itself, and a rapprochement with Britain and Japan had the additional charm of thwarting Li Hung-chang and Yehonala's party generally, for the latter were irrevocably committed to a pact with Russia.

This question of parties was engrossing everybody's attention at Court, where the ill-feeling between the Emperor and the Dowager was rapidly coming to a head. Yehonala made no secret of the fact that she bitterly repented of having chosen the present occupant of the throne and gave broad hints that it might be necessary to correct the mistake. Of course, all she said was duly reported to her nephew, and sometimes he would retort that he would prefer abdication to puppetry. At the moment, though, the temper of the country seemed on his side. In December 1897 K'ang Yu-wei returned to Peking, and addressed another letter to the Emperor. Although it never reached its destination, portions of it were reproduced in the press of Tientsin and Shanghai and aroused intense excitement. K'ang was able to show that what he had predicted was indeed coming to pass. China would be carved up like a melon, unless Kuang Hsü followed the example of Peter the Great and the Emperor Meiji.

The situation was deteriorating so quickly that the appeal could not simply be ignored. In January 1898 K'ang was summoned to a conference at the Foreign Office and questioned at length by Li Hung-chang and other great ministers. The meeting ended inconclusively, but a member of the Emperor's party who was present gave a glowing account of K'ang's opinions to his master, and Prince Kung, whom Kuang Hsü had brought out of his retirement, while cautiously insisting that the Emperor must not do anything so rash as send for K'ang in person, agreed that no harm would be done if instructions were given that from then on all the reformer's communications should be transmitted to the palace without hindrance.

The 'Hundred Days'

As summer drew near, another batch of examination candidates assembled in the capital. In April K'ang called a meeting of his fellow-provincials at the Cantonese Hostel, where a new society, dedicated to the preservation of the national territory, brought itself into being with acclamation. Soon the movement was spreading to form local units for the preservation of Yunnan,

Szechwan, and so forth. Clearly the tide was running strongly in K'ang's favour. And then, unexpectedly, at the end of May, Prince Kung died. The old man had restrained Kuang Hsü from undue eagerness, while throwing all the weight of his seniority among the imperial clan on the Emperor's side against Yehonala. Now that he was no longer there, the choice in front of Kuang Hsü seemed to lie between profiting from the patriotic fervour to consolidate his authority once and for all, or to do nothing and allow Yehonala to plot against his future. Put in this way there was little room for hesitation; on 11 June 1898, an edict was published to announce the inauguration of a programme of reform and on 16 June K'ang himself had his first audience with his sovereign, during which, with his usual exuberance, he assured the Emperor that what it had taken Japan thirty years to accomplish China could easily do in three.

During the weeks that followed a stream of edicts issued from the palace, most of them revealing their authorship by their phraseology, for K'ang's style was decidedly characteristic. Their intention was to introduce some long-needed improvements into the cultural and economic life of the country. The educational system was to be transformed by the substitution of practical topics for the cliché-mongering literary composition which had too long dominated the state examinations to the injury of original thought; all existing schools would have to be reorganized to meet the new requirements; and a university was ordained for Peking. Modernization was to be extended to all branches of the armed forces. The press was to benefit from freedom of publication. Banks and chambers of commerce were to be opened. There were to be special government departments to encourage mining and agriculture.

This was innovation with a vengeance, and many even of those who a few weeks before were joining in the outcry for reform began to have second thoughts. Vested interests of every kind seemed in danger, particularly those of the mandarinate and the teaching profession. But people with a grievance had somewhere to address their complaints. The Dowager, in her new Summer Palace a few miles outside the city, maintained what was to all intents and purposes a rival court, in which by this time it was an article of faith that the one hope of the country lay in the speedy removal of Kuang Hsü. Preparations for this great event were well under way, but the Emperor soon got wind of what was being planned for him. His new advisers, however, were not at a loss. Yuan Shih-k'ai, whose firmness in Korea fourteen years earlier had made him a national hero, after the disaster of 1895 had been delegated the task of building up a new army at Tientsin. Was it not reasonable for Yuan to see that his interest lay in supporting the reformers? At any rate it was worth trying and an emissary was sent to Tientsin to sound him out.

Peking was buzzing with rumours. In the first week of September, the Emperor had proceeded to what was in some ways the most daring measure of all and had dismissed Li Hung-chang from the Foreign Office. Enormous international repercussions were predicted. One moment the British fleet was said to be attacking Vladivostok, while the next it was reported that warships of every country were massing off the entrance to Tientsin river. In the midst of all these alarms, Kuang Hsü was reassured to discover he had no more loyal a subject than Yuan Shih-k'ai, a fact which was confirmed when Yuan came to Court in person. But there was no time to lose. K'ang Yu-wei decided that the proposal must be put to Yuan directly. Would he place himself at the head of his picked troops, confine Yehonala to the Summer Palace, and proclaim the Emperor's authority? Then, perhaps, the capital might be transferred to Shanghai. Yuan agreed enthusiastically but there was something in his voice and manner that did not ring true. K'ang left Peking on 20 September without waiting for the outcome and at first light next morning Yehonala, like an avenging fury, broke into the Emperor's apartments and told him his misrule was at an end. Yuan had betrayed his master. The Era of Reform had lasted just one hundred and three days.

If the Dowager had yielded to her inclinations, we can have no doubt that Kuang Hsü would not have remained in the world much longer. But Britain and Japan, discerning in what had occurred a triumph for the pro-Russian faction, would not stomach so wounding an affront, and through their representatives in Peking warned the Court that the death of the Emperor would be considered a very serious matter indeed. Thanks to this intercession, the poor wretch, who was obliged to proclaim his joy at having with much difficulty persuaded his aunt, for the country's sake, to resume the Regency, dragged out the final ten years of his life in close confinement. There was, of course, a mighty hue and cry for the blood of the innovators. Six of their leaders died on the public execution-ground. K'ang Yu-wei, who had escaped to Tientsin in time, was conveyed under British protection to the safety of Hong Kong. Liang Ch'i-ch'ao succeeded in taking refuge in the Japanese legation and from there was smuggled in disguise to Tokyo, a migration of which, as we shall see, the consequences are observable to this day.

CHAPTER XI

THE BOXER RISING

The origin of the 'Boxers' – the siege of the Legations and the Allied Expedition – the Anglo-Japanese Alliance and the Russo-Japanese War

---

The Origin of the 'Boxers'

OF THE provinces south of the Great Wall, Shantung had during the closing years of the nineteenth century suffered the most from the incursions of the foreigner. The process had started in 1895 with the Japanese assault on Weihaiwei, and no sooner had the people recovered from that invasion than the Germans were scrutinizing the coastline for a suitable harbour for themselves, a search which ended in 1898 with the occupation of Kiachow and the acquisition of railway rights. Then it was the turn of Weihaiwei once more, this time to pass into British hands as a naval base. With all this, it is no wonder that Shantung began to have a reputation for xenophobia, though there were some odd features about the way in which the resentment manifested itself. For centuries, as described in an earlier chapter, the clandestine sect called the *White Lotus* had spread its branches among the peasantry of North China, encouraging them to hope that a day of reckoning would come for oppressive landlords and other evil-doers, and occasionally giving them heart to rise up, not only against local tyrants, but against the alien dynasty itself. By the 1890s, the movement had, in Shantung at any rate, been quiescent for decades, though nobody doubted that it was smouldering somewhere out of sight. When it did return to the notice of the authorities about the year 1896 it had, not surprisingly if we consider the time and place, made a new choice of enemies, and was directed against foreigners in general and missionaries in particular, together with those Chinese who had adopted the Christian religion. What did excite comment, however, was the discovery in 1899 that the most active of all the brotherhoods spawned by the movement – a group which from a ritualistic cultivation of the arts of pugilism and the sword-staff soon acquired the name of 'Boxers' – were apparently willing to forget the bitter memory of the Tartar conquest, kept fresh by generations of conspiracy and persecution, and become loyal subjects of the Empire, for their assemblies met under a banner inscribed 'Support the Manchus, destroy the foreigners'. By chance the Governor of Shantung at that time was one of the most reactionary of the Manchu grandees, and through him Yehonala and the Court were informed that a new sort of enthusiast had arisen, willing to fight for the throne against its enemies. Yehonala did not dispute that Europeans came well into this last category. Not only had some of them stopped her from killing her nephew; they had even prevented her from deposing him. Yet with all their arrogance they backed down when confronted with force; Italy for instance had been demanding the lease of a naval base in Chekiang, but when in March 1899 this had been refused and the province put on a war footing, nothing whatever had happened. Perhaps it was a pity that Russia, Britain and the rest had not been met with the same determination. Li Hung-chang was now Governor-General of Kwangtung and Kwangsi and so was not at hand to remind her that Italy was an antagonist of a somewhat different class from the others. Instead, there came all this intriguing gossip about the mysterious powers of the Boxers. They were said to be immune to bullets, and when in due course they were invited into the Metropolitan Province, the Governor-General reported that he had himself been present when his own soldiers, for a trial, had hacked with their swords at members of the brotherhood without inflicting the slightest injury. We laugh when we remember that this drivel was seriously credited by Yehonala and her advisers, but is it really much more ridiculous than the superstitions about Rasputin current a few years later at the Court of Russia?

So the Boxers flourished, except, strangely enough, in their native province, where at the end of 1899 Yuan Shih-k'ai assumed the office of Governor. Foreseeing where the folly of the Court would lead, he at once put all his energy into the suppression of

the Boxers within his jurisdiction, with such effect that the enthusiasts were driven northwards into the Metropolitan Province.
In consequence a cry of distress rose over hundreds of miles of
northern China from missionaries and their flocks, as churches
and schools were set on fire, and Christians were maltreated and
sometimes killed. In the summer of 1900 there occurred the great
slaughter of the innocent which has left so foul a stain on the
reputation of the country. One can understand easily enough that
a hatred of foreigners was a natural sentiment of a people goaded
beyond endurance by western rapacity and aggression, but to go
so far as some Communist historians and describe the murder of
defenceless women and children as a deed of the most heroic
patriotism is from any civilized point of view both ludicrous and
disgraceful. In fairness it should be pointed out that the admirable
qualities of many of the missionaries, and the benefits they brought
to the Chinese masses in such fields as medicine and education
were too often ruined by the insensitive arrogance with which the
good work was carried out. All the Christian denominations were
equally at fault in this, but the most illuminating examples are to
be found among the Roman Catholics, for only in their case is it
possible to compare the nineteenth century with earlier times.
Before the Opium War, Catholic missionaries were uniformly
respectful and courteous in their attitude to Chinese authority;
evading what they considered unjust laws in their zeal to preach
the gospel, but doing so with marked delicacy and discretion. No
sooner had China suffered military defeat and had been forced to
open her doors, than a new kind of churchman appeared on the
scene in the wake of the foreign gunboats, proud and domineering,
not hesitating to ride roughshod over the feelings of his unwilling
hosts.

What might result from such a policy had been demonstrated
most spectacularly in the Tientsin massacre of June 1870. There
a large temple, occupied by French troops during the campaign
of 1860, was destroyed and a Catholic cathedral erected in its
place. This action very naturally aroused much ill-feeling which
in its turn encouraged belief in the tales which were soon circulating about the devilish practices in the mission hospital. It was
said that young children were abducted and murdered, their eyes
and hearts being used in the making of foreign drugs. The truth
was that the Sisters of Charity, anxious to ensure the spiritual

welfare of the heathen, did pay rewards to those who brought waifs and strays to be baptized and, if viable, maintained in the orphanage. The consequence was that certain criminals began to kidnap infants for profit, and in due course a connexion was alleged between one of these malefactors and a servant of the missionaries. To make things worse, the French consul was exceedingly quick-tempered, a condition not improved by the summer heat, and during an interview with a senior mandarin, in circumstances which have never been properly explained, he ran amuck, firing a pistol, and was lynched on the spot by a crowd of spectators. There was then a concerted attack on the mission, and, to cut a long story short, twenty foreigners, nearly all of them French priests and nuns, were butchered in a manner so atrocious that if it had not been for the intervention of the war with Prussia, France would have sent a punitive expedition against China.

This was merely the bloodiest of a whole series of such outbreaks, but so unready were the church authorities to see any blame in their own conduct that in March 1899, thanks above all to the efforts of the French bishop of Peking, Catholic missionaries succeeded in obtaining from the Chinese government an official status corresponding to the various grades of the mandarinate; bishops were accordingly equivalent to provincial governors or even viceroys. Side by side with this 'triumphalism', the very thought of which makes Catholics today writhe in embarrassment, and to which Communist writers are indebted for some excellent material, there went its inevitable concomitant, a disdain for China and its people which there was no attempt to conceal.

Proud and conceited with his own superiority, he hates Foreigners because their excellence is conspicuous. He is not particularly clean in his person, habits or surroundings and is rather indifferent about smells and noises. He has no lofty ideal of life, and is deficient especially in the higher moral qualities: sense of duty, trustworthiness, sacrifice for the general welfare, public spirit, enthusiasm and active courage in danger.

Such is Chinese man as described by a French Jesuit, L. Richard, in his *Geography of the Chinese Empire*, a work published sixty years ago, to add insult to injury, by the Catholic Mission Press in Shanghai. The good father gives the game away by his reference to courage; he despised the Chinese for their military weakness.[1]

The Siege of the Legations and the Allied Expedition

The Boxers did very little to retrieve the national prestige. Their great feat of arms was the siege of the foreign legations at Peking, one episode in Chinese history that can claim to be known to the world at large. Welcomed to the capital by Yehonala, they had promptly found allies there in another body of fanatics, Muslim soldiers from Kansu in the north-west, who had made themselves notorious by their hatred of Christians. On 20 June 1900 the attack on the Legation Quarter began; it had been preceded by the murder of a Japanese diplomat and of Baron von Ketteler, the German Minister. Three days later an imperial edict, amounting to a declaration of war, commanded the provincial governors to join in the hostilities. And now it was made clear how far the growth of regional forces since the 1860s had weakened the central authority. This order, unquestionably legal and valid, was ignored by Yuan Shih-k'ai as well as by Li Hung-chang in Canton, and the great mandarins of the Yangtze Valley. Instead, Li and his colleagues in central China emerged, almost in the manner of independent princes, to offer their good offices to the foreign powers.

These latter, of course, reacted as might have been predicted. A military expedition was at once set on foot, primarily to save the legations and then to crush the Boxers, whose activity, as has been shown, was confined to the north. The fact that a relief column, reaching Peking on 14 August, found the besieged diplomats still holding out, is sufficient to demonstrate the incompetence and half-heartedness with which the Chinese had conducted operations. In fact some leading members of the government had been against the adventure from the start, and even the Dowager herself wavered from one side to the other. In July, there had even been an armistice with presents of fruit from the Palace to the diplomats.

As the rescuers fought their way into the city, Yehonala fled in the opposite direction, dragging the Emperor with her. Terrified as she was, she still had time before leaving for one final deed of cruelty; she ordered her eunuchs to throw the Pearl Concubine, one of Kuang Hsü's favourites in happier days, to drown in a well. The imperial party headed for the west, and continued its journey as far as Sian, deep in the heart of the country, from where it looked back at the chaos it had left behind.

To the Chinese, the siege of the legations, so famous abroad, is of trivial significance. What matters to them is the aftermath; the occupation of Peking by the allied troops and the vindictive terms of peace imposed on China. The Boxers during their brief time of glory, had, in the manner of their kind, made themselves as obnoxious to their countrymen as to the foreigners, and looting and rape had been part of the day-to-day existence. Now the troops of eight nations had come to exact a reckoning, with even hungrier appetites, convinced that all Chinese and Manchus, without distinction of guilt or innocence were lawful prey. It was not merely shops and warehouses, but the Forbidden City itself which lay open to plunder, while in the matter of women, social rank and respectability served only to stimulate desire. Wherever the foreigners passed, whole families committed suicide to expunge the shame suffered by a wife or daughter. The crusade of civilization had its appropriate Joinville in the person of Pierre Loti, who was sent to report the campaign for the Paris *Figaro*. On 17 October 1900, in the town of Tungchow, twelve miles or so east of Peking, following in the wake of the allies he saw in the house of a family of substance the lower half of a woman's body stuck legs upward in a bucket, while the severed head of the carcass lay under a chair next to a dead cat.[2]

As Germany had the worst grievance in the murder of her Minister, the other powers with varying degrees of willingness acquiesced in the appointment of a German commander-in-chief over the combined expeditionary force. This was Field-Marshal Count Waldersee, head of the Prussian General Staff, whose troops the Kaiser exhorted so to bear themselves that

just as the Huns a thousand years ago, under the leadership of Attila, gained a reputation by virtue of which they still live in historical tradition, so may the name of Germany become known in such a manner in China, that no Chinese will ever again dare to look askance at a German.

Waldersee was at first bent on pursuing the Court as far as Sian, but before long pressure from other countries and the diplomacy of Li Hung-chang, who had been transferred to the governor-generalship of the Metropolitan Province in order to negotiate with the invaders, induced him to be more reasonable. The peace treaty, signed in September 1901, left Yehonala's regime intact, though some of her chief advisers were put to death or told to kill themselves, and others were degraded and exiled. The Dowager's exemption was paid for by the country at large. The new agreement was the most onerous ever imposed. The indemnity was enormous, four hundred and fifty million dollars, secured against the Customs and the Salt Gabelle. The fortifications at Taku and between Peking and the sea were to be razed, and foreign troops to have the right to be stationed along the line from Tientsin to the capital. A properly demarcated legation-quarter was to be opened, garrisoned by foreign troops. Finally, an item of great consequence, the state examinations were to be suspended for five years in those places where outrages against foreigners had been perpetrated. This provision was, of course, intended to punish the educated classes in a manner they would feel most keenly, by barring the road to official and social advancement. In the event, the examinations were never resumed and in 1905 were abolished altogether.

While the peace talks were still going on, it became apparent that the most effective check on the ambitions of any foreign power in China came not from the hapless Chinese government but from the jealousy of other foreigners. This lesson could already be drawn from the declaration of the 'Open Door' policy in September 1899, by the American Secretary of State, John Hay, who requested the powers concerned not to interfere with the rights of third nationals in any 'so-called sphere of interest' which might be created, and to respect the administrative integrity of China. The Communist historians today treat this intervention, which was given all the more weight as the United States had become a Far Eastern power after the acquisition of the Philippines from Spain in 1898, as simply a warning from one burglar to the rest of the gang that he is not to be deprived of his share of the swag. It is possible to argue in this way, but even if we grant that there is an element of truth in the metaphor, it can hardly be denied that in part at least the declaration helped to protect Chinese sovereignty. In 1900, though, tempers flared openly. The first use the Russians had made of the Boxer crisis had been to occupy the whole of Manchuria, and it was learned that, not content with their prize, the Tsar's forces proposed to advance southwards into China proper. At the news British and German soldiers of the allied army hastened to take up position on the Great Wall. The British Yangtze squadron sailed north to Taku, while Japan sent troops to Korea. The gesture achieved its purpose in keeping Russia north of the Wall, but it was not a situation that gave much pleasure to the Japanese, who in 1895 had been obliged by Russia and her friends to disgorge the longed-for foothold in South Manchuria fairly won in war, only to see first the Liaotung Peninsula, and now all three north-eastern provinces fall under Russian control. The great question was, when, if ever, would the Muscovites withdraw? With Li Hung-chang, the Tsar's pensioner, back at the helm there was no telling what might happen.

Li died in November 1901, aged seventy-eight, a millionaire from more than forty years of nutritious public service. Appropriately enough in one answerable for the infamies of chop suey, he was the victim of a surfeit of pastry. His admirers, for he has some, in Taiwan it need scarcely be said, forgive his corruption as being a universal phenomenon in the society of his time, and praise the judgment and foresight which led him further along the road to modernization than most of his countrymen were willing to go. Even his admirers concede that he died at the right moment, for if he had lived many weeks longer he would in all probability have recommended that Manchuria be handed to the Russians, and in that case it would be futile to try and defend his reputation.[3]

The Anglo-Japanese Alliance and the Russo-Japanese War

The Russian threat still remained and in January 1902 it produced a most remarkable result in the shape of the Anglo-Japanese alliance. This recognized the independence of China and Korea and declared that on any step by a third power prejudicial to the interest of the contracting parties the latter would act in concert. If either party went to war with a third power, the other would maintain a benevolent neutrality, and would itself go to war for its ally if a fourth country entered the conflict on the opposite side. The agreement conferred vast prestige on Japan throughout the Far East, and it is worth noting as one of the curiosities of history that the professors of the University of Peking (one of the creations of the reformers which survived the collapse of their movement) petitioned that China too should apply for membership. Confronted by this altered situation the Russians promised to withdraw their forces from Manchuria, but in three stages of six months each, proceeding from north to south. Halfway through they began to make counter-demands, the effect of which would have been to leave the control of Manchuria in their hands. In consequence the relations between Russia and Japan speedily deteriorated. The Russians rejected the suggestion from Tokyo that in return they should at least acquiesce in a similar Japanese domination over Korea, until in February 1904, without waiting for a declaration of war, Admiral Togo launched an attack on the Russian fleet at Port Arthur.[4]

The hostilities which followed showed up, as nothing else could, the anomalous position of China. The Peking government proclaimed its neutrality and informed Japan that no matter what the outcome might be China retained her sovereignty in Manchuria. At the same time, it was obvious that most of the fighting by land would occur on Chinese soil, and, recognizing this fact, all the Chinese authorities could do was to attempt to limit the scope of the operations by announcing that only the Liaotung area was to be used for this purpose. Later, when this restriction was ignored, the boundary was extended.

The details of the conflict do not concern us here. Everywhere things went badly for the Russians, the crowning disaster being the annihilation in May 1905 of the Baltic Fleet, which after sailing from the other side of the world was intercepted by Admiral Togo before it could reach Vladivostok. Yet the Japanese too were beginning to feel the attrition of the Manchurian campaign, in the course of which they had advanced into the interior of the country beyond Mukden. Both parties, then, were glad to avail themselves of the good offices of President Theodore Roosevelt, and negotiate a peace treaty which was signed in September 1905 at Portsmouth, New Hampshire. By it, Japan acquired the rights formerly enjoyed by Russia in Southern Manchuria and took over the lease of the Liaotung Peninsula, with Port Arthur and Dairen, the control of the railway through Mukden up to Changchun and the exploitation of mineral deposits in the area. As regards the northern part of Manchuria, the Russians were to keep their privileges. The southern half of the island of Sakhalin was ceded to Japan, and the paramount nature of Japanese interests in Korea was recognized.

It was then up to China to accept the disposition that had been made of her territory. She did this in an agreement concluded with Japan soon after the Portsmouth treaty; going even further, for it granted Japan the right to hold concessions in Mukden and other Manchurian towns. Japan was thus firmly established on the continent, with access to materials vitally important to her industries, while the victory inflamed the ambitions of her military leaders. Korea, soon declared a protectorate, in 1910 disappeared from the map as a separate country, to be merged into the Japanese Empire, from then on divided from China not by the Yellow Sea but by no more than the width of the Yalu River. The shadow of these coming events already cast a gloom over many Chinese minds in those autumn days of 1905, yet, if they had known, there had just taken place in Tokyo a transaction which was to have even more immediate consequences for their country.

CHAPTER XII

THE FALL OF THE MANCHU DYNASTY

*Sun Yat-sen and the Republican Movement – Japanese influence –
the Three People's Principles – Constitutionalism – the death of
Yehonala – the Regency and the Reformers – the Railway Question –
the Revolution of 1911 – the Emperor abdicates*

Sun Yat-sen and the Republican Movement

IN January 1902, Yehonala, with the Emperor in tow, returned
to Peking from her exile in Sian. That the dynasty had survived
at all was a miracle, but even more surprising was the enthusiasm
with which the foreign diplomats welcomed the woman who
eighteen months before had been longing to see their throats cut.
No doubt the very atmosphere of murder and depravity which
hung over that court fascinated their bourgeois souls. At any rate,
international relations on the personal level had never been friend-
lier, as was shown by numerous palace receptions for legation
wives and daughters. It was understood, too, that in domestic
affairs a new leaf was to be turned. A few years earlier no less a
person than Yehonala's brother-in-law, the Emperor's father, in
a moment of joviality over some Western demand for territorial
concessions had declared that if the Empire had to be given away,
he would rather hand it over to his foreign friends than to his
Chinese slaves. From now on, however, there was to be no more
of this Tartar arrogance, and in token of the change of heart it
was decreed that the old prohibition of intermarriage between
Manchu and Chinese was to be abolished, except so far as concerned the Emperor himself. A grandson of Li Hung-chang caused
a nine-days' wonder by taking to wife the daughter of a bannerman, but otherwise little use was made of the liberty. Indeed, the

government could hardly have failed to be aware that anti-Manchu sentiment was assuming a more dangerous aspect than at any time since the Taiping Rebellion.

One name in particular stood out among the list of political malcontents, and, as was fitting in such a case, it was that of a native of Kwangtung Province. Sun Yat-sen had been born in 1866 in a coastal village forty miles from Canton of a peasant family which boasted links with the Taiping. An elder brother having emigrated to Hawaii, Sun joined him at the age of twelve, and became a pupil at a mission school and later a convert to Protestant Christianity. He then studied medicine at Hong Kong and after qualifying as a doctor practised for a time in Macao. It will be seen from this that his education was almost entirely western, and throughout his life he was never to display much familiarity with the realities of Chinese society. In his early days, this deficiency was scarcely noticeable when placed beside his scientific attainments, and he was convinced that he was eminently fitted to be of use to his country. In 1894, this belief led him to make a trip to Tientsin where he submitted a memorial to Li Hung-chang on the need for qualified men in government service, and on the encouragement they could give to agriculture and commerce. But if Li would not listen to people of the standing of Yen Fu, one can imagine the scorn with which he rebuffed the pushful outsider. After that, any notion Sun had entertained of serving the dynasty went out of his head, and within a few months he had founded a republican secret society from a group of compatriots in Hawaii. The next year the inglorious peace of Shimonoseki saw the disbanding of many units of the Chinese army. In Canton, a substantial number of the men discharged drifted into brigandage, and Sun contrived to use this circumstance to organize an armed attack on the governor's residence. The plot failed and when Sun's part in it came to light, a price was put on his head. In 1896 the reward was very nearly earned, for Sun, again in exile, was walking past the Chinese Legation in London when he was dragged into the building and held a prisoner while arrangements were made to charter a ship for his conveyance to China for decapitation. Fortunately, he persuaded a British servant to take a note to his old Hong Kong medical professor, then living in London, and when the latter had informed the newspapers there was such a public outcry that the Legation was obliged to set Sun at liberty. Of course this adventure gave him huge prestige, especially among the Chinese communities, themselves predominantly of Cantonese stock, in South-east Asia and the United States. Money poured in to help the cause.

Japanese Influence

By the turn of the century, the intellectual centre of the Chinese malcontents was firmly established at Tokyo, as students were increasingly attracted by Japan as a place where western knowledge could be acquired more cheaply and conveniently than by going to Europe or America. After the Japanese triumph over Russia, the stream became a flood. Ideas, the expression of which would be dangerous, even lethal, in China itself were discussed openly and disseminated by means of locally printed Chinese periodicals, which were smuggled across to the Continent by returning travellers and there circulated from hand to hand.

For a while, the acknowledged chief of these expatriates was the reformer Liang Ch'i-ch'ao, who had been living in Tokyo ever since 1898, when he was rescued from the Dowager's anger by the protection of Japanese friends. He had always had a flair for journalism which he was now indulging from a position of security. His opinions, which advocated the reform of the dynasty along constitutional lines, were already too moderate for many of his readers, but in one respect his efforts succeeded brilliantly, and achieved permanent results, not political but literary.

To educated Japanese, the Chinese classics hold the place occupied by Greek and Latin in Europe. When, in the middle of the nineteenth century, there was set afoot the great movement to modernize Japanese institutions the need was felt of contriving standard Japanese equivalents for the huge mass of western technical terms now encountered for the first time, and to do so recourse was had to Chinese, the traditional language of learning. Sometimes an entirely new word was created from Chinese elements, in precisely the same way as European scientists used the Greek lexicon to construct such neologisms as 'telephone'. Often, however, a term existed which was perfectly suitable etymologically, and required only to have a fixed meaning attached to it. In China, where the business of modernization advanced at a more leisured pace, such linguistic equipment was lacking, and it is no wonder that Chinese students, finding the task done for them, should have borrowed freely from Japanese usage. Liang Ch'i-ch'ao both in his own writings and in the journals he edited encouraged this process for all he was worth, with the result that in the space of a few years the Chinese language underwent a radical transformation, and by 1910 or so in spite of opposition by purists was provided with a basic vocabulary for the rendering of modern concepts. An example may be of interest. Today no word in the Chinese dictionary carries such an aura of glory as 'ko-ming' or 'revolution'. The two syllables mean literally 'change of mandate' and in the old classical texts were applied merely to the transition from one dynasty to another, and even so would have been intelligible only to a man of some erudition. The expression was adopted by the Japanese to denote a revolution in the modern European sense, and we read of Sun Yat-sen's astonishment and delight, on coming ashore in Kobe, to find it used by a Japanese newspaper to describe his own activities. From then on he adopted the term himself, and it passed into current Chinese, although we meet in a novel of those days a man who visits a Revolutionary Club without knowing what the word means.[1, 2]

It was natural enough that once away from Manchu jurisdiction students and exiles, besides the Cantonese, should feel anti-dynastic sentiments stirring within them, and by 1905 there were in Tokyo secret societies representing both Central China and the Shanghai area. In the summer of that year, Sun came to Japan again, and succeeded in persuading these other groups to combine with his society into one grand association, called the T'ung-meng-hui, or General League, whose political programme was to be expounded in its own newspaper.

The Three People's Principles

This programme was based on the Three People's Principles, which were at this time only sketched in in outline. In the first place came the principle of Nationality, because the one unquestioned aim of the League was to liberate the Chinese race from the Tartars. But it could hardly be denied that China had other enemies too; for sixty years she had been a prey to Western aggressors, and now to these had been added another imperialism, that of Japan, even more dangerous for being closer to hand. Yet Sun, profoundly influenced by Western ideas, still hoped for support from Europe and America, and had the most sincere admiration for Japan. This latter feeling was shared by many of his countrymen. On the outbreak of the Russo-Japanese War, some Chinese enthusiasts, not only among the students in Tokyo, but also in such places as Shanghai, had organized themselves into corps of volunteers with the rather far-fetched intention of fighting on the Japanese side. Liang Ch'i-ch'ao had for years advocated an alliance of the yellow race against the white. The suggestion was appealing; the one great objection to it was the clearly manifested designs of Japan against the independence of Korea. How agonizing the predicament could be to a sensitive man was shown in December 1905 when a member of Sun's League drowned himself, leaving behind a farewell message which contained these words:

An alliance with Japan today will only take us down the same road as Korea; but if we stay aloof from Japan, it will mean the ruin of Eastern Asia.

It is significant that in 1906 when Sun Yat-sen, again in Tokyo, made a speech to commemorate the first anniversary of the League's newspaper, in touching on nationalism he referred merely to the overthrow of the Manchus, and said not a word of foreign imperialism.[3]

The second of the Three People's Principles concerned the 'People's Authority'. It called for the establishment of a Republic; this, together with the expulsion of the dynasty, was the only clear item on the agenda. In a vague way we are given to understand that the revolution will triumph through armed force, and that for a period China will be ruled by a military government. Then representative institutions will be introduced at a regional level and finally, within six years of the pacification of the country, a constitution will be promulgated and the military government give way to a national one.

The last Principle was that of the People's Livelihood, of which the kernel was the 'equalization of land-ownership', a doctrine borrowed from the American Henry George. This did not envisage the general nationalization of land in its redistribution, but the restriction of unearned profits by private owners whose land, as in certain modern cities, had vastly increased by reason of its situation and the development of industries and communications through the labour of the community. In this manner, Sun hoped that the main evils of capitalism would be avoided.

For most of his life Sun had moved in the atmosphere of secret societies, and the new League conformed closely to the pattern, as the circumstances of the time rendered necessary, for even the Japanese authorities, at the instance of Peking, imposed restrictions upon its activities, and in China it was treason to have anything to do with it. Yet membership grew rapidly; after a year, according to one source, it numbered more than ten thousand adherents. The Chinese students in Japan now included a large body of military cadets, who were as exposed to the new republican virus as the rest, and many of whom were induced to swear their loyalty to Sun's brotherhood. One of these young men was named Chiang Kai-shek; he was twenty-one when he joined the League in 1908.

The Russo-Japanese War contributed a new ingredient to the ideology of the movement. On the collapse of the abortive uprising of 1905, a number of Russian refugees sought asylum in Japan. Among them was a fair sprinkling of Nihilists whose friendship had a stimulating effect on the impressionable young Chinese. Political assassination, though much in use two thousand years earlier in the days of the warring feudal states, had for centuries become out of fashion in China, and during the Manchu dynasty in particular instances of it were exceedingly rare. In Japan, on the contrary, it had very deep roots in the national psychology, and even without the influence of European dynamiters and bomb-throwers, it is likely that the co-operation of Japanese adventurers with the Chinese republicans would have urged the latter into acts of terrorism. As it was, the two traditions of violence came together and from 1905 onwards, with the full approval of Sun Yat-sen, attempts on the life of prominent supporters of the dynasty began to be of common occurrence. At the same time, a series of badly planned local risings achieved nothing beyond providing the cause with a martyrs' roll-of-honour. One at least of the enthusiasts who gave their lives for their ideals was Japanese, not that it was always easy to be certain about the nationality of some of the conspirators. Thus the chief literary ornament of the group was an eccentric Buddhist monk named

Su Man-shu, who not content with his Cantonese father and Japanese mother tried to persuade the world that he was of noble Japanese blood on both sides. But the chief memorial of this Japanese connection is the common Chinese personal name for Sun Yat-sen himself. It is *Chung-shan* which is simply the Chinese pronunciation of the Japanese surname *Nakayama*, first adopted by Sun as a pseudonym, and then regularly used, with the result that today throughout the length and breadth of China there are Chung-shan, or Nakayama, parks, schools and hospitals, named in honour of the Father of the Country.[4, 5]

Constitutionalism

Before 1905, it is probably true to say that Sun's republican views had less following, even among the Chinese communities in South-East Asia, than the Reform Party of K'ang Yu-wei and Liang Ch'i-ch'ao. Although the Russo-Japanese War and the foundation of the General League tilted the balance in Sun's favour, the Reformers' message that a constitutional monarchy was the best solution, was still listened to with respect overseas, while in China even Yehonala herself seemed to be veering round to the same way of thinking. If the effect of a constitution on Japan was to lead her to victory over a European power, then it could be imagined what it would do to China. In the past, senior Japanese statesmen had gone to Europe to study the working of various foreign constitutions before choosing one for themselves. So in July 1905 a party of five leading Chinese, including a prince of the blood, were setting off on a similar mission, when at Peking railway-station their ceremonial departure was enlivened by a bomb hurled by a student. Two of the great men were injured, but the mishap only delayed the journey, and in a report made on their return the following year, they declared that

there is no other way of preventing the danger of revolution than by granting a constitution.

It became clear, however, from some preliminary announcements that the Court's views of constitutional government were rather idiomatic, and when the draft programme was published in the summer of 1908 the worst fears were confirmed. The Emperor's authority was declared sacrosanct. Legislation and judicial powers were united in his hands, with the command of the armed forces. He could summon or dismiss a national assembly at will. Within the limits of the law, the people were to enjoy freedom of speech, assembly, and property, but such freedom could be restricted at any time by imperial ordinance. Even this revised autocracy would have to be waited for until 1917.

The Death of Yehonala

At the beginning of November 1908 Yehonala celebrated her seventy-third birthday. It was a cheerful occasion, for she was in excellent health and spirits, and boasted that she was going to surpass the years of Queen Victoria. The Dalai Lama came from Tibet to pay his respects, and altogether such things as constitutions seemed as remote as they could possibly be. The one touch of gloom was provided by the Emperor's health. For a long time he had been more like a puppet than a living creature, and now his doctors, by petitioning to be replaced, as much as declared that they had given him up for lost. In these circumstances, the succession had to be provided for, and here at least was a task after the Dowager's heart. The Grand Council was summoned as a matter of form, but from start to finish Yehonala dominated the proceedings. A child, P'u Yi, not yet three, the son of the Emperor's brother, was fetched to the palace and introduced to his dying predecessor. The next day, 14 November 1908, Kuang Hsü breathed his last, and the new sovereign was proclaimed. Prince Ch'un, his father, was to be Regent, and Kuang Hsü's widow would now be Empress Dowager, but Yehonala herself as Grand Dowager would most emphatically have the final say in everything. Tired and happy after her exertions, she went to bed and slept soundly. She was busy in conference all the following morning, and had just taken her place at the lunch table when she had a seizure. At three o'clock that afternoon she died, having recovered sufficiently to issue a decree stipulating that in any question of vital importance Prince Ch'un the Regent should act on the instructions of the new Dowager. This at least would ensure that power remained with her family, in the person of her niece. But at the very end, when they pressed her for a last word, she seemed to contradict herself and denounced the rule of women and eunuchs.

The Regency and the Reformers

A grievance rankled in the minds of the Regent and the other Manchu princes who now assumed the management of affairs. The cause of their resentment was the power of the Chinese Yuan Shih-k'ai, now Viceroy of the Metropolitan Province. Everything about him, especially the new army he had created, was an odious testimony of how far a subject could rise above his station. Apart from this jealousy, there was a more honourable reason for dislike. Ten years before, the man had ruined Kuang Hsü by betraying that Emperor's confidence, and the strict Confucian theory enjoined upon the Regent the duty of vendetta against his brother's enemy. In former times the wrong would have been wiped out in blood, but today things were more complicated, and Yuan's life was protected by the loyalty of his Chinese troops. All that could be done was to drive him from office and this was contrived in the most wounding manner imaginable. A decree proclaimed that Yuan Shih-k'ai had a bad leg, which imparted an undignified hobble to his gait and made it unseemly for him to show himself at Court. He was therefore granted leave of absence to go down to his native Honan to recuperate. This insult, in a country whose inhabitants have a keener sense of the ludicrous than any other race of men, was never forgotten and in a few years the leg was again to be mentioned in dispatches.

The dismissal of Yuan, besides being an act of revenge, showed a desire on the part of the central authority to extend its control into fields which for more than thirty years had been cultivated by ambitious individuals largely in their private interests. But the Regent and his colleagues, who now in effect formed a Council of Princes, by carrying out the constitutional programme to which Yehonala had committed them before her death, unwittingly helped to foster the regional and centrifugal tendencies they deplored. In 1909 there came into existence the provincial assemblies which had been promised, and of which the function was merely to advise the governors. Graduates, mandarins and owners of property valued at five thousand dollars or more could on reaching the age of twenty-five elect representatives from their own number. The common people were excluded from all participation. A consultative college met in Peking, but as half of its members were appointed by the Court, and the other half were representatives of the provincial assemblies it was hard for it to agree on anything. Meanwhile, when some of the most progressive elements in the provincial bodies sent a delegation to press for the early formation of a cabinet which would be answerable to a national assembly, they were ordered to leave Peking forthwith, and another agitator to whom this warning was not sufficient, was exiled to Turkestan. But the pressure continued, and the harassed Regent finally conceded at the end of 1910, that cabinet government would be instituted four years earlier than planned, in 1913. Then, in May 1911, the structure of the proposed cabinet was published. Out of thirteen ministers, ten were Manchus, and six of these were imperial princes.

The situation now was markedly different from what it had been at the time of K'ang Yu-wei's fiasco. One consequence of the Treaty of Shimonoseki had been the investment of Japanese capital to create Japanese-owned industrial installations in China, and of course the precedent had been rapidly followed by the other foreign powers. This in turn stimulated the rise of Chinese private industries which the Peking government, after its defeat in the war against Japan, was not strong enough to curb in favour of its own official monopolies. Cotton mills in particular, had sprang up in Shanghai and other cities of the Lower Yangtze Valley before the end of the century. The interval of a decade had witnessed the emergence of a new social class drawn in the main from the old scholar-gentry, but living on its industrial investments. Because of its business and cultural links with the treaty ports this class had a strong leaning towards Western liberalism, as well as a concern to meet foreign competition by the development of Chinese enterprises. It was men of this sort who were now the most vocal in the agitation for government reform, not that they were of one mind regarding the precise nature of the changes they envisaged. No doubt the greater part of them would have agreed with the views of K'ang Yu-wei, for which they were unprepared twelve years earlier. The victory of tiny constitutional Japan over immense unconstitutional Russia was an argument hard to refute, and the abolition of the old state examinations had removed a great block of obstruction out of the road forward.

There were some, however, who felt that talk of representative institutions was still premature. The first need was for a thorough overhaul of law and education, a task which in theory was being undertaken. The chief spokesman of this school of thought was Yen Fu, the translator of Huxley. Since then he had been unremitting in his efforts to bring to China the light of modern knowledge with translations of such authors as Adam Smith, John Stuart Mill and Montesquieu. No one was a more determined opponent of the foreign aggression manifested in such things as extraterritoriality and control of the customs service, but his low estimate of his countrymen's standard of culture led some people to accuse him of despising the Yellow Race and worshipping the White. Thus in a note to his version of *Wealth of Nations* he writes:

> Those in China who urge the establishment of a National Assembly do not bother to ask whether we are sufficiently educated or not. Even if such a step were feasible, what good would be served by ignorant discussions?

To him it seemed that nothing but a long slow process of schooling would prepare the country for democratic institutions. As for the revolutionaries, in his view they were even more mistaken than the constitutionalists.[6]

The Railway Question

These years were remarkable for a great surge of activity in the building of railways, which was not to be repeated in China until after the Communist victory of 1949. Foreign capital had been attracted to the provinces of Szechwan, Hupei, Hunan and Kwangtung where various projects of railroad construction had brought together groups of local gentry as investors. This tendency was viewed by Peking as particularly obnoxious, and with some reason, for it suggested that circumstances might arise when the central government would have less than complete control over what would be the country's most vital system of communications. As to the financial side of the matter, money for the purpose could be raised conveniently by a foreign loan, with the railways as security. This was done through the Four-Power Banking Consortium early in 1911, and it was proclaimed that all main railway lines were to be nationalized, though some branch lines might stay in private hands. The foreign loan itself, with its odious implications, was enough to cause an outcry, but when it was learned that private shareholders were to be bought out on very inequitable conditions, the situation started to take a menacing turn. Not only did the gentry in their provincial assemblies condemn the nationalization decree, but in Szechuan, where feeling was especially strong, the populace terrorized the Governor into taking their side. For this cowardice, he was replaced by a stronger man whose brutal attempts at repression only made things worse. By the autumn of 1911 it was common talk among the soldiers garrisoned at Wuchang on the Yangtze that they might be transferred up river at any moment to put down the disturbance. This was not a prospect to please the younger officers, many of whom either by initiation during cadetship in Japan or by the influence of comrades so initiated were secretly pledged to the anti-dynastic cause.

The Revolution of 1911

At this point, an accident intervened to precipitate the course of events. On 9 October 1911, the attention of the police was aroused by an explosion in a house in the Russian Concession at Hankow, on the bank of the Yangtze opposite to Wuchang. Investigation revealed that the premises were being used as a secret arsenal, and as well as guns and ammunition there was found a list of members of a revolutionary plot, many of them being officers of the garrison. The conspirators of Wuchang thereupon decided there was only one thing to do, and on the night of 10 October – a date still celebrated by the Chinese Nationalists as the *Double Tenth* (the tenth day of the tenth month) – they led their men in revolt. The Manchu viceroy fled, leaving Wuchang in the hands of the rebels, who on the following days crossed the river and occupied Hanyang and Hankow. Simultaneously they conferred with the Provincial Assembly and it was agreed that a Military Government of Hupei should proclaim its independence of Peking. What was of particular significance in the light of future developments was the choice of leaders for the regime. At the head was to be a military commander-in-chief. For this post General Li Yuan-hung was selected, a man lately second-in-charge of the provincial garrison and totally without revolutionary connexions. Having become a prisoner of the rebels, he was persuaded to lend his name and popularity to the adventure. Civil affairs were entrusted to the

President of the Provincial Assembly, who on his part too had no republican affiliation, but on the contrary was known to be a strong constitutionalist.

As the news from Wuchang sped across the country, there followed in its wake a great surge of uprisings of the same type, until by the end of November military governments had been declared in all provinces south of the Great Wall except the Metropolitan Province itself, Honan and Kansu. The pattern of Hupei found much imitation. Revolutionary elements among junior officers would touch off a revolt, which would be given cautious approval by the local provincial assembly, and men of senior standing, here and there even provincial governors, would be induced to head the movement.

The notion of independence asserted by these provincial military governments meant first and foremost that they declared the province in question, with its resources, had been withdrawn from the administration of the Manchu Dynasty, and it was assumed from the start that all the provinces would form constituent parts of a new Chinese State. At Wuchang in the early days there was some talk of another Han Dynasty (the word *Han* having acquired the significance of 'Chinese' as opposed to Manchu), or of a 'Yellow Kingdom' which would date its calendar from the mythical Yellow Emperor of the third millennium BC. But these flights of fancy had not lasted very long, and it was agreed on all sides that a People's Kingdom (*Min Kuo,* or 'Republic') was in process of being born.

From the first report of the revolt at Wuchang, the Manchu Court had entertained few illusions about the magnitude of the crisis. True, its Northern Army was incomparably stronger than anything the rebels could put in the field. But this force had been obliged to acquiesce in the retirement of its old commander Yuan Shih-k'ai, who for more than two years had sulked in outraged dignity on his private estates in Honan. He was closely in touch with what was going on, and they would not fight under the orders of anybody else. The Manchu general appointed to lead it into Central China could do nothing with it, and on 14 October the Regent swallowed the bitter pill and decreed that Yuan Shih-k'ai had been created Viceroy of Hupei and Hunan, the centre of the disturbance, with full charge of military operations in the area. But the great man showed no eagerness to come out of retirement.

His leg was still not up to it, he said, as he pottered about in the lovely autumn weather, wearing a cotton gown and a straw hat, and carrying a fishing-rod. In fact, he was imposing his own terms, which had to be met. The absurd Manchu-dominated Cabinet was dissolved, and Yuan appointed as Prime Minister of a new one which included among its members Liang Ch'i-ch'ao, now amnestied and acclaimed as a pillar of society. There was at the same time a general pardon for all political offenders.

The next step for Yuan was to demonstrate to the world that he was master of the situation. This he did by sending two of his subordinates against the rebels with forces ample enough to guarantee their success. Hanyang and Hankow were retaken without difficulty, but with the northern bank in their hands Yuan's men, instead of continuing their advance south of the river, sent an emissary to Wuchang to establish contact with the republican leaders. The details of the negotiations are obscure. They were carried on through the good offices of the British Consul-General, for by this time Britain and indeed all the foreign powers were looking with approval towards Yuan Shih-k'ai as the one strong man capable of restoring peace in a manner most consonant with their economic and political interests. At the end of November, delegates from all the provincial military regimes met in the British Concession at Hankow. Here, after proposals relating to the formation of a central government had been adopted, it appears to have been decided that if Yuan joined the revolution he would be elected temporary President. On 2 December, Nanking fell to the rebels and the conference transferred itself down river to that more glamorous rendezvous, while Shanghai became the scene of the peace negotiations. On Christmas Day Sun Yat-sen landed in triumph at Shanghai and four days later at Nanking was elected temporary President of the Chinese Republic. He assumed office on New Year's Day 1912 with a characteristic appeal for the prayers of the Christian world, fully realizing from the start that his dignity would be short-lived.

The Emperor Abdicates

Yuan Shih-k'ai was profiting from the delay to transfer, on the pretext of military necessity, as much money as possible from the imperial treasury to his own pocket, but the time had at last arrived for decisive action. He prepared the ground by substituting the palace guards by soldiers loyal to himself. When this was done he intimated to the Regent and the other princes that all things considered perhaps it would be better, in the dynasty's own interests, if a graceful abdication took place. He would make it his business to see that the terms were of unexampled generosity. There would be no expulsion of the ruling house. The boy Emperor would be given an adequate allowance, and all the honours due to a sovereign. He would continue to occupy the Forbidden City, inside which, apart from the business of governing the country, life would remain unchanged. As for the Manchu grandees, they were to be confirmed in the full enjoyment of their possessions. Even so, the idea at first came as a shock, and at least one hothead urged resistance, arguing that if the worst came to the worst the Manchu Empire could survive in Mongolia and Tartary: let the Court once again take refuge north of the Wall, in Jehol. But to men accustomed to the amenities of Peking this summons to the wilderness had little to recommend it. The Emperor, being only five, could not express a preference himself; his predecessor's widow, however, the new Dowager, who stood to him in the role of an adoptive mother, longed above everything else for peace and quiet, and the Regent was no more adventurous. By this time some lessons from European history appear to have been digested; at any rate Yuan thought it worth while to insert, in a confidential memorial to the Dowager on the hopelessness of the situation, a reference to the fate of Louis XVI. The commander of the new palace guards added a warning which it was hard to ignore. The few diehard nobles still calling for war fled to the protection of foreign settlements. On 12 February 1912 the Dowager issued an edict on behalf of the Emperor declaring that, having observed from recent events the inclination of men's minds and the Will of Heaven, she could not endure for the sake of one family to bring misery on an entire people.

I have therefore induced the Emperor to yield his authority to the country as a whole, determining that there should be a constitutional republic. Yuan Shih-k'ai has full powers to organize a provisional republican government to treat with the people's forces on the methods of achieving unity so that the five races, Manchus, Mongols, Chinese, Muslims and Tibetans may continue together in one Chinese Republic with unimpaired territory.

Away in London, *The Times* appraised the situation.

History has witnessed few such surprising revolutions, and perhaps none of equal magnitude which has been carried out in all its later stages with so little bloodshed. Whether the last of those stages has been reached is one of the secrets of the future. Some of those who know China best cannot but doubt whether a form of government so utterly alien to Oriental conceptions and to Oriental traditions as a Republic can be suddenly substituted for a monarchy in a nation of four hundred millions of men, whom Kings with semi-divine attributes have ruled since the first dim twilight of history.

CHAPTER XIII

YUAN SHIH-K'AI

Yuan Shih-k'ai becomes President of the Republic – the murder of Sung Chiao-jen and the 'Second Revolution' – Yuan moves towards the throne – Yuan's failure and death

Yuan Shih-k'ai becomes President of the Republic

THE manner in which the abdication had taken place ought to have struck any republican as thoroughly unsatisfactory. First of all, the Emperor by stressing that he had transferred his authority to the people as an act of grace and for a definite purpose, namely the establishment of an efficient government, left it open for a casuist to argue, as it was to be argued in the future, that he reserved the right, if that purpose should not be fulfilled, to take back what he had given. No doubt such an idea, in those early days, would have seemed too fanciful for consideration, but what was of immediate concern was the fact that the imperial edict, so far from recognizing the newly proclaimed regime at Nanking as the republican government, had empowered Yuan Shih-k'ai to organize a provisional administration of his own. The mandate would likely have prestige enough to be accepted as binding in those northern areas still loyal to Peking. However, negotiations between Yuan and Nanking had already advanced too far for Yuan to see any advantage in premature arrogance. On 13 February 1912, Sun Yat-sen offered his resignation to the Republican Council provided that Yuan came to Nanking to assume the presidency, and two days later a telegram informed Yuan that he had been unanimously elected to office. In the general euphoria of westernization it was thought proper to salute the new head of state as 'the Washington of the Chinese Republic'. Li Yuan-hung, who had allowed himself to be put in command of the Wuchang revolt, was rewarded for his services with the vice-presidency.

In spite of its exultation, the Nanking Council was fully aware of the urgency of getting Yuan away from his private bastion in the North; it had for this reason approved of the stipulation by Sun Yat-sen. On 25 February a delegation arrived at Peking charged with the mission of escorting the President to the South. The party was received with much pomp and circumstance; the noble Front Gate, leading from the Tartar to the Chinese City, was thrown open to give it passage, a thing which, until then, had been done only for an imperial cortege. The President, all smiles and affability, expressed his eagerness to join his government at the first possible opportunity.

On the night of 29 February the delegates were roused from the beds in which they were snoring off the effects of Yuan's hospitality by a mighty clamour mixed with volleys of rifle fire from somewhere in the town. Then a red glow was visible over the Chinese City, whose streets contained the richest shops in the country. Word was not long in coming that there was a mutiny among the troops, who were looting and pillaging after the immemorial fashion of their kind. What was worse, the reason for the tumult was simply that the honest fellows could not bear to say goodbye to their beloved commander – 'the parent who clothes and feeds us', as they called him – and were protesting in the only way they knew. Deciding that it would be foolish to run risks, for there was no telling how far the violence might go, the delegates lost no time in escaping to the shelter of the Legation Quarter, where they engaged rooms at the Grand Hôtel des Wagons Lits. It was in that privileged sanctuary that next day they received a visit from their president elect. The occasion was embarrassing to everybody, most of all it seemed to Yuan himself, but the truth had to be faced, and the truth was, as he declared to them in all frankness, it would be lunacy at such a time for him to absent himself from North China. There was no arguing the question, especially since the discontent had spread among other garrisons in the countryside as far as Tientsin. Early in March Yuan, to the satisfaction of his warriors, assumed the presidential office in his loyal city of Peking.

As if to reassure itself, the Council in Nanking immediately voted a provisional Constitution asserting that sovereign power was vested in the people and its chosen representatives without whose consent the President could not appoint or dismiss civil or military officials, or commit China to war or peace. Having made this gesture, the Council bowed to necessity, and as Yuan would not come to it, it went to him. By the end of April, it was holding its deliberations in Peking, and Yuan organized a Cabinet, taking care that the key ministries of the Army, Navy and Interior, as well as the Premiership, should be occupied by men he could trust.

All these arrangements, however, were no more than temporary expedients, and in August 1912 the Council enacted measures to regulate the election of a Parliament of two Chambers. In theory this was the moment for which the revolutionaries of twelve months earlier had been waiting. But the fact was that a good many of them, especially Sun Yat-sen and his Cantonese followers, revelled in the atmosphere of conspiratorial brotherhoods. They admitted to themselves that they were ill-equipped by temperament and experience for the business of democratic politics, and without much resistance allowed the leadership of their side to fall into other hands.

The Murder of Sung Chiao-jen and the 'Second Revolution'

The province of Hunan, which in the middle of the nineteenth century produced, in the person of Tseng Kuo-fan, the archetype of the warlords, and in its closing years gave birth to Mao Tse-tung, deserves the added credit of having provided China with her first true parliamentarian. Sung Chiao-jen emerged as the one man with the talent to compose a regular political organization out of the welter of clandestine societies. This came into being in August 1912 and was baptized the *Kuomintang*, or in English, the Nationalist Party. Sung Chiao-jen was a pragmatist; principles and doctrines left him cold. The result was that the Kuomintang omitted from its programme anything savouring of the controversial; even the gentle land reforms recommended by Sun Yat-sen were abandoned, as were such theories as the political equality of the sexes. There seemed no reason why there should be any controversy over the mild and inoffensive aspirations for domestic unity and international peace with which Sung proposed to go to the country, but of course the crux lay in something else. Sung was determined that Yuan should be subject to parliamentary control. Yuan therefore bestirred himself to form a rival group. This with unconscious irony was called the Republican Party, and drew its support chiefly from constitutional supporters of the final years of the Manchu dynasty. In 1911 these had, by force of circumstances, attached themselves to the winning side. There was little or no discernible contradiction between the social policies of the two parties, but when in February 1913 the election was held, Sung Chiao-jen's industry was found to have carried the day; the Kuomintang was by far the strongest party in both Chambers, and full of confidence for the future Sung began to act like a man who would soon be forming a government. This was too much to endure, and on 20 March 1913 he was shot dead in the Shanghai railway station. The assassin escaped but a few days later the Shanghai police, acting on information received, arrested two men, one of them being a prominent gangster who it was alleged had hired the other, an ex-soldier, to do the killing. The air was full of rumours. Few doubted that Yuan was the prime mover behind the affair and gossip said that ample documentary proof had been found of his complicity. Then, before the preliminary investigations were completed, it was announced that the ex-soldier had died in his cell, nobody knew how. What was not less significant, the gangster while in confinement was permitted to enjoy such domestic comforts as the use of morphine and opium. Even this easy imprisonment did not last long. In July a cohort of his bullies broke into the gaol and rescued him in time to avoid the worst heat of summer, by retiring in disguise to the seaside at Tsingtao. In October he was confident enough to show himself in Peking, where he solicited Yuan for a decoration and five hundred thousand dollars in cash. He was paid something, but he was so disappointed at the smallness of the amount and at the advice to withdraw from Peking, which was tendered along with the money, that he began to ventilate his grievances to anyone who would listen to him. As could have been predicted, he spent most of his time in a brothel. One night in January 1914, at an hour when normally he would have been at ease with a favourite companion, but at which on this occasion he was by a chance in a thousand somewhere else, a squad of policemen raided the place on the pretext of searching for opium. When he heard the news, he understood what it meant and left at once for the South. As his train passed through Tientsin it was boarded by two men in uniform who shot him dead.[1]

It was a story typical of many that were to be heard throughout China in the thirty-five years that followed, but already before it reached its last act, there had intervened public events so sensational that it had been reduced in importance to a simple *fait divers*. While unfortunate Sung Chiao-jen had been bustling around the country to win support for the Kuomintang, Yuan, not content with organizing his own party, had been negotiating a foreign loan so successfully that in the spring of 1913 an agreement was signed for a sum of twenty-five million pounds sterling to be provided by the Five Power Consortium of Britain, Japan, France, Germany and Russia. The Parliament which was just then assembling, or rather the Kuomintang, as majority party, bitterly resented the fact that the President and his advisers had concluded the contract without the formality of seeking the approval of the people's representatives. On top of Sung Chiao-jen's murder, the transaction provoked a huge outcry, for it was plain to the most obtuse mind that the money would be dedicated to the furtherance of private ambition. Some voices on the Kuomintang side called for armed resistance. This was the view of Sun Yat-sen, expressed at a meeting in Shanghai soon after Sung's murder. But opinion in the anti-Yuan faction was much divided; it was an open secret, for instance, that during Sung's lifetime Sun Yat-sen and some of the other Cantonese had not been, to say the least, boisterously in support of his parliamentary activities. Those who had shared Sung's views were above all anxious that nothing should be done to impair the legality of the parliamentary party he had created.

It was, indeed, precisely the existence of lawful opposition which was proving unendurable to Yuan Shih-k'ai. In June 1913 he took a step clearly designed to weaken the territorial foundations of the Kuomintang by decreeing the replacement of certain military commanders in Central and South China, who were affiliated to that party, by officers of his Northern Army. Even that did not at first provoke the reaction that he probably expected; it looked as if the men concerned would acquiesce in a transfer to other posts. But when units of the Northern Army began to move down towards the Yangtze, the inevitable occurred. From the middle of July, a group of provinces, beginning with Kiangsi, and including Anhwei, Kiangsu, Kwangtung, Szechwan, Fukien and Hunan, followed the precedent of 1911 and declaring their 'independence' of Peking proclaimed a state of war against Yuan. The episode is known to history as the Second Revolution, but the term is a ridiculous misnomer, for in less than two months the uprising had been suppressed or rather had fizzled out. In fact it was scarcely more than a matter of days before certain provinces, whether intimidated by the superior forces from the North, or, as was thought later, corrupted by Yuan's bribes, were already starting to cancel the autonomy they had just asserted. The mass of the population had no stomach for a war which was being fought not on account of any interests of theirs but merely to enhance the importance of politicians. The one grievance which might have been effective, the foreign loan negotiated over the nation's head, was widely interpreted as strengthening Yuan's case. Though the Great Powers, except for America, had not yet extended diplomatic recognition to Yuan's government, they clearly regarded him as properly established in authority. Sun Yat-sen's role in the business was not very heroic. When the fighting began he ostentatiously called on Yuan to retire from office, but very soon afterwards took his own advice and escaped to Japan.

As was fitting, the headquarters of the rebellion were set up in Nanking. It was the citizens of that unfortunate place, which had been ravaged by Tseng Kuo-fan's army on the fall of the Taiping in 1864, and in our own day was to be the stage of countless atrocities on its capture by the Japanese in 1937, who were called upon to pay the price for the enthusiasm of their departed leaders.

The author of this chastisement was named Chang Hsün. From modest origins, he had attracted notice by his exploits in the war with France over Vietnam in 1884 and since then, thanks largely to Yuan's patronage, had risen to the top. The revolution of 1911 found him Commander-in-Chief of the pro-Manchu forces in the Nanking area, and he had never forgiven the republicans for driving him in flight to the North. He displayed his attachment to the old dynasty by wearing the queue himself, and compelling his soldiers to keep to the same fashion. He was by no means alone in this conservatism. The governor of the north-western province of Kansu, for instance, forbade anyone in his jurisdiction to cut off his queue, nor would his colleague of Turkestan lay aside his mandarin's robes. But Chang Hsün gripped the public attention more than any of them, and was called *par excellence* 'The

Pigtailed General'. So far he had acquiesced in the new form of government but was continually embarrassing Yuan with open telegrams, a device that was coming into favour for the dissemination of views, containing reminders of the debt he and his colleagues owed to the Manchu imperial family. Romantic Europeans affected to see in him a paragon of loyalty, but his countrymen knew he was a vile domineering oaf, who liked nothing better than to make life miserable for any gentle or sensitive person who had the misfortune to cross his path. His troops, however, thought the world of him, for he had no compunction in giving them, whenever feasible, a free hand in the matter of loot and women. One can imagine with what relish he re-entered Nanking at the beginning of September 1913. For three days his men were absolutely uncontrolled. Rickshaws were commandeered to pull the loads of booty through the streets, while the corpses of women and girls floating in the river told their own story. Barbers once again found a lively demand for false pigtails, an item of commerce which they had supposed to have gone out for good two years before. The one thing that a Chinese man had to avoid at all costs was to go out dressed in western clothes; even after discipline of a sort had been restored this symbol of innovation made the victors see red, so indiscriminately that they created an international incident by attacking some Japanese civilians, and the Pigtailed General was obliged to swallow his pride and go and apologize at the Mikado's consulate.

Yuan moves towards the Throne

By the end of 1913, the Northern Army was in control, either directly or by means of satellite forces, of all the provinces south of the Yangtze, with the important exception of the western and south-western provinces, Kweichow, Yunnan and Szechwan. Simultaneously with the military action, a political offensive was being launched in Peking. So far, Yuan's tenure of the presidency was in strict theory of an informal nature, since he had been elected by the first republican assembly at Nanking, a body whose enactments, including the provisional constitution of March 1912, were intended to have merely a temporary validity. It was laid down, in fact, that the formal election of a President must be the duty of the proper Parliament. Such a Parliament had now come into existence, and Yuan was all eagerness to have his status regularized. But there was a difficulty. Before proceeding to choose a President, Parliament was obliged first to pass a formal constitution which would regulate the mode of election, and the powers, of the Head of State. This was very irksome, and Yuan began to put it about that the long delay was damaging the country's prestige, and was the chief reason for the hesitation of the nations to grant diplomatic recognition. At the beginning of August 1913, in the full glow of Yuan's triumph on the Yangtze, Parliament received an open telegram from the senior generals in the provinces, urging it to hold the presidential election before dealing with the problem of a constitution. The message initiated what was to become a standard technique. Browbeaten by the news from the South, the Kuomintang delegates allowed the passage of an act to legalize such a procedure. The ballot itself took place on 6 October. When Parliament had assembled at eight in the morning, a crowd of several thousand people of most villainous appearance but carrying placards to show they were the spokesmen of various citizens' organizations, surrounded the building, shouting slogans and declaring:

Not one of you will come out of there until you give us the President we want!

The job took rather longer than had been expected, but at ten o'clock in the evening the famished legislators let Yuan have a sufficient majority, amid roars of exultation from the mob, who hurried off to get paid. On 10 October, the second anniversary of the rising at Wuchang, Yuan was ceremonially installed for a term of five years and anticipated Mao Tse-tung by holding a military review at the Gate of Heavenly Peace. At the same time, by a happy coincidence, came word that Britain, France, Russia, Germany, Austria-Hungary, Italy, Japan, Belgium, Denmark, Portugal, Holland, Norway and Sweden at last recognized the new regime as the *de jure* government of China.

From Yuan's point of view, his success would still be a hollow one so long as his powers even in theory were subordinated to the wish of Parliament. This doctrine was inherent in the basic notions underlying the formal constitution now being drafted. But an excuse was at hand to render Parliament impotent. The majority party was the Kuomintang and it was notorious that these people had been behind the summer revolt in the South. Was it seemly that they should be allowed to impede the affairs of government any longer? The question was put to the provincial military commanders and the reply of the Pigtailed General was typical.

I am only a plain man, but I know this draft constitution is pernicious rubbish. I am for the extirpation of traitors, even if it means giving my life for the country.

Confirmed by such opinions, on 5 November 1913 Yuan issued a decree dissolving the Kuomintang on the grounds of national security and depriving its members of the right to sit in Parliament. A couple of months later, just after New Year 1914, Parliament itself, which was in any case unable to sit for lack of a quorum, was disbanded. So too were the provincial assemblies.

There was now a dictatorship, though an attempt was made to hide its nakedness. Towards the end of 1913 a body called a Political Council was brought into existence and although most of its sixty-nine members were supposed to be sent by the provinces, they were just as much Yuan's choice as were his own official nominees. On the recommendation of these advisers, a Constitutional Council, picked with the same fastidiousness, set about the task of making a state structure that should be in keeping with the President's ideas. Its deliberations resulted on 1 May 1914 in the promulgation of a new Constitution, to replace the temporary one created at Nanking in 1912. It provided that the President should be endowed to all intents and purposes with the privileges that the 'Constitution' of the old Dowager in 1908 had aroused such discontent by reserving to the throne. Yuan could declare war, sign treaties, appoint officials without let or hindrance, and issue emergency decrees having the force of law. Pending the creation of a legislative assembly, a Council of State would serve as an advisory body. As if this was not enough, an addendum promulgated at the end of December 1914 extended the presidency to ten years instead of five, under conditions which allowed an incumbent to renew his term or to nominate his successor. But what spoke more strongly than all this to the minds of his countrymen was the news that during the same month of December on the occasion of the winter solstice Yuan had sacrificed at the Temple of Heaven. After that nobody could doubt where things were tending.

It is hard to credit that from the autumn of 1911 onwards the idea of founding a new dynasty had not been constantly present in Yuan's thoughts, for every lesson of Chinese history would have put it there. As evidence, we can point to an open telegram he sent to the Vice-President and the various provincial commanders as early as June 1912 in which he specifically denies having such an intention.

Ignorant people are fabricating rumours to delude the masses, with alarming reminders of the story of Napoleon 1.

But two years had passed since then, and the time seemed as ripe for the project as it ever would be. The first moves were fairly discreet. Yuan had a number of foreign advisers who quite sincerely discerned in him the strong man that China needed. One of these was the famous *Times* correspondent Dr Morrison. A figure of even greater prestige was the American Professor Goodnow, who in the summer of 1915 wrote a study on the form of government best adapted to China and in the course of it arrived at some very striking conclusions. He had no difficulty in showing that republicanism was not a plant which could flourish in such a soil. If persevered in, it would inevitably bring China to the condition of Portugal and Mexico. Only the elegant simplicity of a monarchy offered any prospect of stability. This opinion, coming as it did from a citizen of the greatest of republics, was not to be taken lightly; the reference to Mexico was especially apposite at a time when America had found it necessary to dispatch a military expedition across the Rio Grande. The professor's essay was translated into Chinese, and published in a Peking newspaper, with the result that less than a week later, in the middle of August 1915, a group of six public-spirited men all of intellectual pretensions formed themselves into a Committee of Public Safety to investigate the claims of various political philosophies. Some preliminary fruits of their researches reached the newspapers and gave a broad hint that they were coming down on the side of monarchy, whereupon other activists both at Peking and in the provinces, not to be outdone, whipped up enthusiasm even in those strata of society one would have least imagined to be interested in such problems. As a result delegations of singsong girls, rickshaw pullers, and beggars were emboldened to add their voices to the chorus. So urgent a demand was hardly to be resisted, but still Yuan's in-grained modesty forbade him to yield. The country would have to express itself in a more formal manner. A Convention of Citizens' Representatives was summoned by provinces to choose between monarchy and a republic. In all, one thousand nine hundred and ninety-three votes were cast and every one of them was for monarchy. Not only that; going beyond their terms of reference, the representatives in each province insisted on adding a recommendation which curiously enough was identical word for word in every case, to the effect that,

in accordance with the will of the people, we respectfully propose President Yuan Shih-k'ai to be Emperor of China, and to him as Emperor we offer the supreme authority in the state, to be transmitted for ten thousand generations.

After the first shocked refusals required by decency, Yuan was at length induced to acquiesce in the general will so unequivocally manifested, and announced in December 1915 that the New Year would usher in a Chinese Empire.

The news of these transactions provoked no excitement among the mass of the people, to whom, in so far as they knew of what was happening, Yuan's designs seemed no more than what was to be expected of a man in his situation. Sun Yat-sen, after the col-lapse of the so-called Second Revolution, had followed the dictates of prudence and remained in Japan, where the familiar atmosphere of conspiracy, quite like old times, induced him in the summer of 1914 to found the Revolutionary Party of China by means of which he hoped to revive the spirit of the secret brotherhoods from the debilitating effects of parliamentarianism and, not less important, to regain control of the movement. The Chinese com-munities in South-East Asia and elsewhere abroad could be relied on for money, and until the time came for a general uprising on the mainland it was proposed to revert to the policy of assassina-tion. In 1915, the murder of a garrison commander at Shanghai was hailed as a triumph, but the exultation was brief, for in the matter of terrorism Yuan could give his enemies points and a beating. Soon new names were being inscribed on the martyr-ology, while here and there stray adventures spluttered out like damp squibs.

Yuan's Failure and Death

Ruthless as Yuan's ambition was, he had too much intelligence not to understand that if the new dynasty he was meditating was to have any chance of success it must sponsor a programme of social and economic modernization. For this reason, there was no lack of enlightened men who at the beginning were well content to attach themselves to his cause and to support him against the Kuomintang. True, the name 'republican' as applied to his party was never very apt, but the later title of 'progressive', which it sported in the final days of the parliament, was by no means ridiculous. One of its leaders, for instance, was Liang Ch'i-ch'ao, whom Yuan had wooed on first coming to power and who proved very amenable to approaches from a destined leader of the country. Yet in the long run, and indeed by the end of 1913, Liang Ch'i-ch'ao was thoroughly disillusioned. If he could have believed in the possibility of Yuan's becoming a constitutional sovereign in any real sense of the word he might well have stood by him, but the treatment accorded to parliament demonstrated the folly of entertaining such a notion. Then there was the scarcely concealed use of terror and intimidation, not to mention the impudent contrivance of a referendum. Spurning the offer of a huge bribe, Liang somewhat rashly put his trust in the fact that he had a house within the security of the Italian Concession at Tientsin and published a manifesto in favour of the republic.

Even more remarkable was the case of Yen Fu. As we have seen, this great evangelist of Western ideas stated openly, on the eve of the Revolution of 1911, that China was not yet ready for parliamentary government, let alone republicanism. He had always been a support of Yuan, ever since the latter, after the war with Japan, had been given the task of constructing a new national army. He had stayed loyal even during his hero's temporary eclipse in the last three years of Manchu rule. In 1912 his faithfulness had been rewarded with the presidency of Peking University, a post he soon quitted at his own request to become Yuan's trusted adviser on foreign affairs. What more natural than that such a man should be one of the six eminent persons who in August 1915 under the style of the Committee of Public Safety launched the imperial movement on its whirlwind career? Yet it is almost certain that Yen Fu's name was used without his consent and that although the fear of reprisals kept him from openly dissociating himself from the Committee he never attended any meetings. A few months earlier, noticing which way the wind was blowing, he remarked in a letter to a friend:

Of course the President is an outstanding man, but even at his best his ability is only that of a provincial governor under the Empire. He really does not have the knowledge and experience of the world to be able to cope on equal terms with the leaders of the foreign powers. His obstinacy and wrong choice of subordinates cause much dissatisfaction. To expect him to change society and to lay the foundations of a stable regime is totally out of the question.[2]

But in the last resort, the success or failure of Yuan's projected empire would depend on the generals of his Northern Army, and it needed little acquaintance with human nature to understand that although these men had acquiesced in the elevation of a senior and patron to the office of president, it would be a different matter altogether when it came to bestowing a throne in perpetuity on himself and his descendants. Yuan had, it is true, been at pains, in his relations with his subordinates, to maintain something of military comradeship, but from the middle of 1914 it was becoming clear that his policy was aimed at controlling them more strictly. Meanwhile, the ill humour was inflamed further by the extraordinary behaviour of Yuan's eldest son who omitted no opportunity of flaunting an arrogance which would have been considered insufferable in a proper dynastic occupant of the Dragon Throne, let alone in an upstart from nowhere at all.

In December 1915 the provincial authorities of Yunnan sent a telegram to Yuan demanding that the proposed creation of an empire should be abandoned. As the request was ignored, Yunnan in January 1916 declared its independence of Peking. Kweichow at once followed suit, and a so-called Army of National Protection set out from the south-west to overthrow the usurper. When it was too late, Yuan discovered that his folly of the last two years had left him without a friend worth the name. Like the Manchus in 1911, in theory he commanded an army capable of crushing the revolt to the earth, but he knew only too well that none of his officers would lift a finger to help him. In a desperate bid to temporize, he declared at the end of February that the new empire was postponed, but the only reply was the news that Kwangsi too had announced its independence. Then came the bitterest pill of all. A group of his most senior commanders, including the Pig-tailed General, urged him to annul his dynasty altogether. With death in his soul, on 22 March he issued a proclamation to inform his countrymen that he willingly vacated the throne which their importunity had forced upon him, and would again govern them as President. Even this was not enough. Nothing, it seemed, would pacify the South but his total withdrawal from public life. Kwangtung, Chekiang, Szechwan, Hunan, one after the other the greatest provinces of China were seceding, and grouping themselves to form an alternative regime. Liang Ch'i-ch'ao in person had gone down to head the political side of the movement. Meanwhile the cruellest turn of fate was that Yuan was being exposed to the world not as a tyrant but as a buffoon. The teahouses of Peking every few hours of the day had some fresh tale to snigger at. Even his seraglio, it was rumoured, had been resounding with disputes on the comparative precedence of its inmates. Cartoons were passed surreptitiously from hand to hand showing Yuan draping his unwieldy bulk in ceremonial robes of an unknown cut. It was too much to bear; between rage and frustration he broke down completely. His last words, uttered shortly before his death on 6 June 1916, were 'He has destroyed me'. The phrase was supposed to be applied to his eldest son, whose autocratic manners had certainly played their part in the fiasco. But at least that unpleasant young man and his numerous brothers and sisters could console themselves with the reflection that they were well provided for, as their father, like Li Hung-chang before him, died a millionaire.

CHAPTER XIV

THE WARLORDS

---

*The fall into chaos – the attempted Manchu Restoration – Peking
and Canton – the Literary Renaissance*

The Fall into Chaos

PITIFUL and even ludicrous as the end of Yuan Shih-k'ai was, he
had towered over his fellows and until the last months of his life
he had managed to impose the authority of his central government. There could be no better testimony to the force of his personality than the chaos into which the country began to drift soon
after his death, and which lasted for the next ten years. This was
the warlord period properly so called. It is important that its main
characteristics should be understood for it was a decade which saw
the birth of the Chinese Communist Party and the alliance between
the Communists and the Kuomintang. It ended with the victory
– a counterfeit victory as some would say – of the Nationalist
Revolution so long dreamt of.

For sixty years, since the days when the armies of Tseng Kuo-
fan and Li Hung-chang fought against the Taiping, the stage was
being got ready for the spectacle now at last on display. The
essence of warlordism was already contained, for those with the
wit to discern it, in the relationship between Tseng Kuo-fan and
even more so his heirs on the one hand and Li Hung-chang on
the other: a steady implacable jealousy of all rivals for power and
wealth, an awareness that the ultimate threat to such power and
wealth came from the people of China, and in consequence an
instinctive dependence upon the foreigner for help against this
common enemy. But men such as Li Hung-chang, corrupt and
unscrupulous as they were, still retained habits of deference to a

system of social morality and were, besides, servants of a government which claimed to be based on that system. A residue of this deference, lingering in the mind of Yuan Shih-k'ai, compelled even that power-hungry tyrant at least to make a show of incorporating his personal ambitions into a grand design for national prosperity. But no considerations of public welfare, however tenuous, deterred those who succeeded him from the pursuit of self-interest.

This meant, in the first place, the ruthless exploitation of the peasantry within the territory of each local satrap. Taxes were exacted for many years into the future. Warlords on occasion printed their own paper-money which, when the day came, as it generally did, for them to be deposed by a victorious rival, was declared worthless by the incumbent warlord. The knowledge that their tenure of power was precarious was itself sufficient to cause them to regard any long-term investments as a waste of time, for a warlord could not hope to found a local dynasty. Once and once only, in Manchuria in 1928, did a son step into the shoes of his dead father, and to do so he had first to carry out a wholesale massacre of the latter's subordinates before these could mete out the same fate to him.

Whether to guard his dominion against attack or to extend it by victory over others, a warlord looked first and foremost to his troops. In spite of the training in military science many of them had received, their attitude in this matter was usually that of the bronze age, and they estimated an army's value almost wholly by a counting of heads. To have as many soldiers as possible was their great aim, and the harassed condition of the countryside made sure that there would always be plenty of wretches desperate enough to enter their service. The number of men under arms continued to increase. In 1914 there were 457,000 of them; in 1920, 900,000; in 1925, 1,470,000. Their commanders intrigued and made alliances among themselves, and huge armies marched and countermarched across the land.[1]

In all the chaos there was a certain pattern which remained constant. A government enjoying international recognition was seated in Peking, and was controlled by the Northern Army. True, the recognition was of a derisory kind and was accorded only as a matter of convenience, but it carried with it some material advantages, notably the right to receive such items of national revenue as the income from the Customs, or rather what was left of it after the sums earmarked for foreign creditors had been sub-tracted. This was a prize worth contending for, and the emulation it created, especially when any serious competitor was justified in hoping for patronage from abroad, proved to be too much for the feeble *esprit de corps* which survived from Yuan's time. The northern militarists, then, split into two great parties, formed from perpetually shifting elements and relying on support from Japan and from the Anglo-Saxon powers respectively. For ten years the control of the Peking government was decided by the result of the campaigns fought by these two groups against each other. Meanwhile, ever since 1911 the provinces of the south-west, Yunnan, Kweichow, and Kwangsi, had been under commanders drawn from outside the Northern Army. This factor was decisive in leading to the revolt of 1915–16 against Yuan's empire, and although the military regime set up by the rebels as a rival to Peking lost its reason for existence after Yuan's death, the prece-dent it had established had an important consequence. In 1917, as we shall see, the remnants of the old parliament under Sun Yat-sen's leadership migrated southwards to Canton, which had fallen under the south-western aegis, and met together in a body which claimed to be the National Government. To be sure, this claim was never accepted by the world at large, and indeed the 'government' in question was a creature even more lamentable than its counterpart in Peking, being obliged, on several occasions, to abandon its capital city at the local warlord's change of whim and scatter for safety to Hong Kong or the foreign settlements of Shanghai. Nevertheless, the time came when this abject puppet-show was transformed, as if by a miracle, into the heart and brain of the national revolution. Such was the general pattern, as far as the warlords were concerned, of this strange and confused period. Let us now take a look, very briefly, at some of its salient events and meet a few personalities whose names should be heard.

On the death of Yuan Shih-k'ai in June 1916, he was succeeded by his Vice-President, that amiable nonentity Li Yuan-hung who owed his elevation entirely to the accident of finding himself nominal leader of the original mutineers at Wuchang in 1911. After the disastrous attempt to reintroduce monarchy, there was a great show of returning to republican legality as typified by the Nanking constitution of 1912. The southern revolt came to a halt and the parliament dispersed by Yuan more than two years previously again assembled in Peking. Power was once more vested, not in the President, but in the Cabinet, whose Premier was the most important of Yuan's subordinates, the Commander-in-Chief of his armies, Tuan Ch'i-jui, a premier by no means oblivious of the fact that his brother generals would acquiesce in his present authority only so long as he championed their privileges.

The course of China's foreign relations during this period will be dealt with in the next chapter. Here we must content ourselves with noting that China was being pressed in some quarters to enter the World War on the allied side. The question became more acute after the declaration of war on Germany by the United States in February 1917. Tuan Ch'i-jui emphatically approved of China's joining the Allies, but it was known that he did so in order to strengthen his own hand with loans from Japan, whose patronage he was in process of gaining, and that in this and other machinations he was not inclined to submit to the will of parliament. In consequence there arose a bitter quarrel between himself and the President, behind whom stood, for what they were worth, the elected representatives of the nation. In May 1917 Li Yuan-hung, with extraordinary rashness, it must be confessed, dismissed Tuan from office, whereupon the latter called upon his comrades of the Northern Army to rally to his side. Once more the telegraph wires hummed with proclamations of independence, this time not from the distant south-west but from the provinces of the centre and north, including the Metropolitan Province itself, and the word came that a military expedition was being assembled to march on the capital and topple the President and the Parliament together. Thunderstruck at the result of his handiwork, Li Yuan-hung looked around desperately for some means of retrieving the situation. The only hope he could discern anywhere lay in the Pigtailed General, Chang Hsün, who although reckoned one of the northern generals kept himself rather aloof from his colleagues. Chang did not reject the call for help, but made it clear that he could do nothing so long as those nuisances the parliamentarians were permitted to meddle in public affairs. Bowing to necessity, Li Yuan-hung on 12 June 1917 disbanded the Assembly, and at the same time Chang entered Peking with a substantial detachment of his troops. His moment of triumph,

he imagined, was now at hand; the folly of the republican government had presented him with what he was longing for, the chance
to restore the Manchu Dynasty.

The Attempted Manchu Restoration

For five years, P'u Yi the boy Emperor had continued to reside in
the Forbidden City, supervised by an ageing group of imperial
widows and waited upon by a swarm of eunuchs. He was still
only eleven years old, but he was fully aware, from the persistent
reminders of his foster mothers and his tutors that the good old
cause still had its supporters in the country and that in particular
there was a whole army which, from its general downwards,
sported the pigtail as a token of its allegiance. The news that
Peking was now to all intents and purposes in the hands of these
warriors sent the imperial family into a frenzy of anticipation.
They were not in suspense for long. On the morning of 1 July
1917, the citizens of Peking awoke to find the Dragon Flag of
the Manchus once again flying in the streets after five years disuse.
Shortly afterwards in a special edition of the newspapers the
Emperor informed them by an edict that he had been persuaded to
return to the throne. The document was drafted by none other than
the veteran reformer K'ang Yu-wei, who had been only too willing
to return to the scene of his former exploits and try and resume
under fresh auspices the career blighted so abruptly in 1898. But
already on this first day of the restoration he can have had few
illusions left. At a distance, Chang Hsün might seem an appealing
example of fidelity, but on closer acquaintance his clipped barking
speech and his military brusqueness of manner did not conceal
his contempt for ineffectual dreamers and intellectuals. The proclamation, too, which K'ang had been obliged to compose, was
as he knew packed with lies. It asserted for instance that the
President, in his distress at the condition to which the Republic
had sunk, had of his own accord begged the Emperor to resume
control. In fact Li Yuang-hung, who had been offered a dukedom
as the price of submission, rejected all such approaches with disdain, and only when there seemed a danger to his life did he flee
for safety to the Japanese Legation, having first sent a message
to Tuan Ch'i-jui in Tientsin reinstating Tuan as Premier and
commanding him to crush the revolt of the pigtails.[2]

Tuan did not stand in need of any such orders, for the expedition his colleagues were preparing to launch against the President and the Parliament was transformed overnight into an Army for the Suppression of Treason, with Tuan at its head. Nowhere outside the walls of Peking did anyone rally to the dynasty, while within the city the population as a whole cursed in their hearts Chang Hsün and all his works, for the Pigtailed Army was already showing what it was made of. Women and girls with any pretensions to good looks went out on the street at their own risk. If a shopkeeper asked the soldiers to pay for what they took, it was proof positive he must be a republican and he was knocked on the head. It was quite like the Boxer times, people said. As a precaution there was a brisk demand at the barbers' for false queues, but after the first couple of days nobody doubted that the restoration was a failure; the one hope was that it would be suppressed without bloodshed.

The best guarantee of a peaceful solution lay in the presence of the foreign legations, and republican emissaries were soon using the good offices of the diplomats to try and bring Chang Hsün to reason. Even he knew the game was up. On 7 July a republican plane flew over the capital and dropped three bombs on the Forbidden City. Fortunately only one exploded and the damage was trivial, but China had her first taste of aerial bombardment, and next day Tuan's army was positively outside the city. Yet Chang persisted in bargaining, until during the night of 11 July the besiegers succeeded in forcing three of the gates and at dawn on 12 July attacked the three thousand pigtailed soldiers who were holding the Temple of Heaven. After a token resistance most of these surrendered and Chang found sanctuary in the Dutch Legation. Those of his followers still at large lost no time in cutting off their most distinctive feature; all that was left of the twelve days of Manchu restoration was this trail of severed plaits which in places covered the ground like matting. From beginning to end fewer than a hundred men had lost their lives.

Chang Hsün stayed in his diplomatic asylum till, the year after, he benefited from an amnesty. His military power was gone, but the fortune he had extorted from the people during his satrapy remained undisturbed, and he bought a fine house in the British Concession at Tientsin where he passed the rest of his life in that peculiarly brutal debauchery his nature craved. At his death in

1923, P'u Yi conferred on him the posthumous title of 'Loyal and Brave'. His funeral procession was four miles long and cost over one hundred thousand dollars. It was reported in the newspapers that he had bequeathed a large sum to encourage the cultivation of the pigtail.

As a matter of policy, the republican authorities laid the entire responsibility for the episode on the shoulders of Chang Hsün alone, and absolved the Emperor and the Court from any blame. P'u Yi resumed his life of seclusion inside the palace, but with his hopes of being restored one day to the throne of his ancestors scarcely dimmed by the fiasco. Nor was such an expectation totally absurd. Chang Hsün had overreached himself in his eagerness to seize an advantage over his fellows and become the chief minister of the revived dynasty. The other warlords were even less inclined to play second fiddle to one of themselves than they had been in the case of Yuan Shih-k'ai, who after all was their senior and patron. Having the power to crush the attempt, they did so without hesitation. Yet none of them had any invincible reluctance to acknowledge P'u Yi as sovereign. There were occasions during the next few years when an observer, judging from surface appearances, and ignorant, as nearly all observers were, of the latent trends and developments of the nation, would have rated quite highly the young Emperor's chances of being accepted by way of compromise between the chief satraps. Some speculation of the sort must have been in the mind of the British government when in 1919 it allowed the secondment of a distinguished member of the Colonial Service, Reginald Fleming Johnston, to become P'u Yi's English tutor.

Peking and Canton

The collapse of Chang Hsün's putsch seemed to have placed Tuan Ch'i-jui back in control more firmly than ever, for the President, whose obstinacy had provoked all the trouble, was induced to step down in favour of the Vice-President. On 14 August 1917, war was declared on the Central Powers. Of course it was never contemplated that China should take any military part in Europe, but a labour force of Shantung peasants was enrolled to work on the Western front, while Austrian concessions were recovered at Hankow and Tientsin, enemy property was commandeered and debts under such headings as the Boxer indemnity were cancelled. Still more important, Tuan was able to negotiate a very reassuring loan from Japan.

From the parliamentary point of view all these proceedings were tainted with illegality. Neither the replacement of the President, nor the declaration of war had been ratified by the people's representatives. To make matters worse Tuan announced his intention of having an entirely new parliament elected. Abandoning hope of a change of heart in that quarter, the offended politicians, or the majority of them who adhered to the Kuomintang, made their way to Canton, where Sun Yat-sen had preceded them, and in August 1917 a new military government was created in that city by the union of Sun and his followers with the south-western militarists. The appointment of Sun as leader, with the title of Marshal, together with the regime's announced opposition to the men of Peking, who were selling their country's interests to the highest foreign bidder, conferred upon it a certain aura of nationalism which later Kuomintang historians have sometimes exaggerated. The truth was that Sun Yat-sen by now was moved above all by resentment at his exclusion from the councils of Peking, and was willing to go to almost any lengths to force his way back on the stage. If Tuan Ch'i-jui could get loans, why should a true patriot not enjoy the same benefit? The idea appeared so reasonable, that with all the dignity of his new office behind him, he was soon hawking round economic concessions in the hope of finding a Japanese or American buyer, but in neither country were men of affairs so naïve as to imagine that he had anything of value to sell.

The great object of Sun Yat-sen's criticism was of course Tuan Ch'i-jui for his juggling with the constitution and his clandestine negotiations with Japan. As it happened, the protests from Canton aroused an echo in the breasts of many of Tuan's colleagues of the Northern Army, whom jealousy and resentment were bringing together into an opposition party. Before long Tuan's insistence that the southern secession must be put down by military force gave these dissenters a chance to make a bid for power under the popular slogan of 'Unity through Peace'. From that time on, the two groups competed for the control of the Peking government. Tuan and his adherents were called the Anhwei Party; their opponents took their name from Chihli as the Metropolitan Province was then styled.

At first the Anhwei Party retained their mastery of the situation by summoning to their aid one of their nominal colleagues from across the Great Wall. This was the notorious Chang Tso-lin, a Manchurian bandit who had attached himself to the Japanese during their war with Russia in 1904–5 and with these patrons, had raised himself to be warlord of the North-East. At the beginning of 1918 the intervention of this savage ensured that Tuan Ch'i-jui carried the day over the Chihli Party, and Tuan and his friends signalized their triumph by organizing an administration which stands out by its corruption even in the history of the warlords. The leaders of this regime are known as the Anfu clique, from the name of a street in Peking where they held their private meetings, and as such we shall encounter them in our next chapter when we come to describe the development of the national revolution. Their ill fame derives especially from their conduct of foreign affairs, for Tuan's main target in domestic policy, namely the achievement of unity by force, proved impossible to attain. Peking reasserted its authority over Hunan, the nearest to hand of the seceding provinces, but that was all.

To add to Tuan's difficulty general opinion was against his design of conquest, not only among his own countrymen, whose views he might ignore, but in foreign governments as well. In December 1918 the diplomatic corps urged a peaceful settlement, and a couple of months later delegates from North and South met in conference. Sun Yat-sen was not represented; in the summer of 1918 his patrons, the southern warlords, had outraged his pride by forcing him to share his powers as commander-in-chief with six colleagues, and he had resigned in order to devote himself,in the safety of the French Concession at Shanghai, to the theory of statecraft. His optimism was justified; in two years his services were to be demanded again. In spite of Sun's withdrawal, the southern leaders were intransigent in their opposition to Tuan's subservience to Japan and it is most likely that the peace conference would have broken down. Before things came to such a pass, however, the month of May 1919 had arrived and with it the great tide of national indignation which swept through the whole country and which, as will be shown in the next chapter, obliged Tuan to yield on many of the points stipulated by the regime of Canton. The war between North and South was therefore not resumed.

Tuan's government was so violently buffeted by that May storm that it is a wonder his authority survived at all. As it was, he clung to power for another year, while his rivals in the Northern Army took advantage of his discomfiture to prepare the ground for themselves. The prime movers in the business were, of course, the Chihli group, whose ablest member was emerging in the person of Wu P'ei-fu. In spite of the title of his party, this man's territorial domain lay in Central China, and as such he was admirably placed to advance Anglo-American interests, a consideration which London and Washington duly bore in mind. But even so, Wu and the Chihli group needed an ally on the spot and they found one in the Anhwei camp itself, for the Manchurian Chang Tso-lin was eager to play a leading role south of the Great Wall, and saw little chance of doing this so long as he remained in subordination to Tuan Ch'i-jui. Yet the question was complicated by the fact that both Chang and Tuan were pensioners of Japan. Of the two, though, the former, as satrap of Manchuria, was of more immediate importance to Tokyo, and for this reason his paymasters connived at his personal ambitions. A plot was hatched between Chang and the Chihli group, and in July 1920 they took the field. By August they had entered Peking under a triumphal arch put up by the citizens in their honour, and Tuan had gone into retirement.

That year, the dissident southern provinces witnessed a phenomenon of a different kind. Ever since the Reform Movement of 1898, voices had been raised advocating provincial self-government, and the establishment of a Chinese Federation on the lines of the United States. The idea was now revived in Hunan and the south-east, and there was much talk of provincial constitutions and the like. But in Kwangtung province in particular the notion appealed so much to the local commander Ch'en Chiung-ming that proclaiming the watchword of 'Canton for the Cantonese' he shook off the control of his superior warlords and invited Sun Yat-sen to return from exile. In December 1920 a new Canton Military Government was formed, with Sun bearing the style of President in direct opposition to the Head of State in Peking.

There was from the start an obvious contradiction between the cause of local autonomy espoused by Ch'en Chiung-ming and the aims of Sun Yat-sen, who was as keen as ever to see a great nationalist army marching northwards to put an end once and for all to the puppet-show in Peking. It was a splendid ideal, but in the circumstances of the time few people would credit it with much chance of success, and nobody was better aware than Sun that the most he could accomplish would be to attach himself to a hopeful contender for the northern supremacy. The man obviously cast for this part was the Manchurian Chang Tso-lin, who by the end of 1921, had already discovered that his friendship with Wu P'ei-fu was turning sour in face of Wu's increasing sense of importance. It looked, in fact, as though Wu and the Chihli group felt themselves to be the successors of Tuan's old mission of national unification, and at the very least this would mean Chang's exclusion from affairs south of the Wall, a diminution of grandeur not to be endured without a struggle. Fortunately allies were ready and waiting, Tuan Ch'i-jui himself in the first place, only too glad to combine with one enemy against another, and, less predictably, Sun Yat-sen, who sent his right-hand man up north to assure Chang of his good intentions. In the background, Japan too smiled on the enterprise, for both her protégés, Chang and Tuan, were to unite against that pawn of the Anglo-Saxons, Wu P'ei-fu.

The auspices could hardly have been brighter, but when the blow was struck, in April 1922, everything went wrong, and Chang's forces were routed so disastrously that he was forced, on 16 June, to buy peace at the price of undertaking to stay for the future beyond the Wall. The day before the conclusion of this humiliating treaty an even more remarkable event had occurred. Down in Canton, Sun Yat-sen's warlord supporter Ch'en Chiung-ming, who had on the quiet been in correspondence with Wu P'ei-fu, suddenly contrived a *coup-d'état* and overthrew the government. Sun, deposed from the presidency, hastened to take the now familiar road to the French Concession in Shanghai.

In the middle of 1922 the scene was a depressing one. China seemed doomed to be perpetually a prey to the rapacity of these cut-throats, encouraged in their greed by the machinations of foreign powers. The revolution with its hopes of national regeneration had only served to drag the country into a more abject posture, its leader, any ideals he once had long since abandoned, seeking as a favour to be admitted on subordinate terms to the thieves' kitchen.

The Literary Renaissance

Whatever one might have supposed, China then, as at any other time, was never short of talent and many of the officials who staffed the offices of the derisory administration in Peking would have done credit to the public life of any nation. The tragedy was that they were operating in a vacuum. It was little use, for instance, having diplomats as accomplished as Dr Wellington Koo, to mention but one figure whose name is familiar in the West and who at the present time (1966) is a judge of the International Court, if the foreign powers with whom they treated found it almost too much for their patience to acknowledge China as a sovereign state at all. Again, to take a domestic example, the Supreme Court of Peking, itself a product of the theoretical deference paid to modernization during this time, was diligently attending to the task of law reform by the creation of a corpus of decisions upon which it was hoped a new system of codes would in due course be erected. Nor was such an activity so ludicrous as at first sight it might appear. After all, fifteen hundred years earlier in the West, the jurisconsults brought Roman law to perfection at the very time when the ancient world was most anarchical. Nobody could have foreseen that the work of the Supreme Court was in the long run to have little or no relevance to actual behaviour throughout the country as a whole.

Yet if government policy was almost negligible as a force of change, these years of chaos were fruitful in social and intellectual development, which followed inland from the treaty ports in general and from Shanghai in particular. From the turn of the century onwards the Chinese had discovered the European literature of imagination. In this field one name stands out preeminently, that of Lin Shu, like Yen Fu a native of Fukien province, but differing from Yen in that he had never set foot outside China and knew no foreign language. His method of working was to listen while an assistant read an extempore version of the original text and then to compose his own rendering of it into literary Chinese of which he was a master. In this way he is said to have translated some one hundred and seventy works of European literature, chiefly English and French novels. Supplied by Lin and other less celebrated writers, magazines appeared devoted almost entirely to the translation of western fiction and accomplished something which the missionaries themselves had found impossible. The strangeness of the supernatural and theological background had proved a serious, almost an insuperable, barrier to the propagation of the gospel, but now, through the art of Charles Dickens and Victor Hugo, sentiments, if not formally Christian at least deeply tinged with Christianity, found a response in breasts to which they could never have been communicated by religious means. In a lighter vein, such characters as Sherlock Holmes were almost as famous among the reading public of the treaty-ports as they were at home, and were soon paid the honour of being counterfeited. Holmes in particular, under the style of *Fu-erh-mo-ssu*, is the hero of a whole set of apocryphal adventures, many of which are supposed to take place during visits made to China by himself and Dr Watson.

In the same way that the example of the West had inspired the various schools of political reform, the history of European literature provided the model for another sort of revolution. In the course of two thousand years and more, written Chinese had become markedly divergent in vocabulary and grammar from the spoken language, to such an extent that an official proclamation, for instance, might be to all intents and purposes unintelligible to the ear when read aloud. All serious literature, or rather what was acknowledged as such, both prose and verse, was composed in this highly cultivated idiom, but its use was far wider than this, for it was the vehicle of ordinary daily correspondence. Yet over the centuries another sort of literature had come into being based on the colloquial tongue; this consisted of plays, for obvious reasons, and novels, which by convention were written in the form of storytellers' narratives, as if for recitation. Nobody acquainted with the Chinese people needs to be told that works of this description delighted all classes of society impartially, but by a curious kind of hypocrisy scholars, although reading them avidly in private, pretended to despise them in public.

There was an obvious parallel between this situation and the role of Latin in Europe up to the end of the Middle Ages and beyond; and the points of resemblance may be multiplied. Literary Chinese differs from the colloquial by a certain lapidary terseness not unlike the quality of Latin, and like Latin it served throughout the ages as an international language, by means of which Chinese,

Vietnamese, Koreans and Japanese could communicate with one another in writing. Many Chinese students had read the story of the European Renaissance and knew that one feature of it was the cultivation of vernacular literatures in opposition to Latin. Could there not be a revival of Chinese letters on a similar pattern? Was it not true already that many of the finest works in Chinese literature were in the language that pedants affected to disdain? By any valid criterion, what other book written during the whole of the Manchu Dynasty was worthy to be mentioned in the same breath as the great eighteenth-century novel *The Dream of the Red Chamber*?

The honour of being the first to compare literary development in China and Europe belongs to a teacher and man of letters named Ch'en Tu-hsiu who in 1915 founded a magazine called *La Jeunesse*. Still more pragmatic advice came from another scholar then in America, but destined to be equally famous in China, Hu Shih. As from 1918 *La Jeunesse*, edited by a group of professors of Peking University including by that time both Ch'en and Hu, came out entirely in colloquial Chinese. The innovation aroused violent passions, whose strongest expression, curiously enough, came from the very same man, Lin Shu, who had done most to naturalize European literature in China. Yet in a couple of years the reformers had carried the day sufficiently for the Ministry of Education to recommend the use of the colloquial in teaching. Even so, the literary language continued to be much used, and until the Communist victory in 1949, its superior brevity caused it to be preferred by the daily press for the news columns, while editorial comment and articles were written in the more diffuse vernacular.

The literary renaissance, as it was termed by its supporters, soon acquired political overtones, and even before this happened its opponents discerned in it an iconoclastic attack on the traditional social order. The severe blow that had been dealt to the Confucian system by the abolition in 1905 of the old state examinations, a measure which encouraged foreign-type education at the expense of the native claims, had already by the beginning of the Republic rallied a number of stalwarts to the defence of the Sages. The unseemly spectacle of the European War dismayed some enthusiastic westernizers into revising their opinions and recognizing the superior wisdom of their ancestors. Yen Fu, who in 1913 had

1 (*above*) A girl marries her dead fiancé. The bride is kneeling beside the corpse (19th century).
2 (*below*) An unfilial son is drowned in well by his clan (19th century).

3 The Opium War: British forces in action near Canton (1841).

4 The curse of opium: a crazy addict threatens his wife and mother (early 20th century).

林文忠公燒燬鴉片

道光十九年林文忠公督兩廣比至，即查洋商所藏之鴉片，查得二萬二百八十三箱盡燒之于海口。後有泊舟外洋暗中輸入者，公乘月黑潮退時，出奇兵以搜之，復燬其船二十三艘于長沙灣。遂以此釀成交涉鴉片之進口日多。今則英國政府已樂贊成烟毒，由今思昔，有令人轉戚為欣者。

5 Commissioner Lin (seated) superintends the destruction of opium (1839).

曾文正練
水師平賊

咸同間洪逆倡亂蹂躪皖吳
越各省湘鄉曾文正奉詔討賊
以東南形勢多阻水欲勦賊非
水師不可乃奏請在衡州荊造
戰艦南中匠卒不知辦此公研
精覃思博採眾議得之遂成大
小戰艦二百四十艘募水陸萬
人訓練成軍後恃此以平賊

6 Tseng Kuo-fan trains river squadron for use against Taipings (1854).

曾文
正創
設製
造局

曾文正公在兩江總
督兼南洋通商大臣
時。中外和議初成公
陰有爭雄海上之志
因設內軍械所又在
安慶仿造小火輪船
一艘試之江可用乃
設局于上海用西法
製造鎗礮中國機器
之興自此始

7　Tseng Kuo-fan inspecting arsenal at Shanghai (*c.* 1870).

8 Travelling by wheelbarrow near Shanghai in the 1880s.

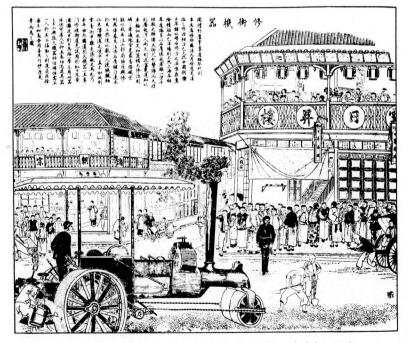

9 Repairing a road in the International Settlement, Shanghai (c. 1880). Notice the Sikh policeman.

10 Shanghai ladies at the sewing machine (*c.* 1885).

11 A Shanghai rickshaw in the 1880s.

12 Yehonala in 1903, with ladies of the Court: on extreme right Empress
Lung Yü.
13 Li Hung-chang during his visit to England 1896.

14 A woman barber (cleaning a customer's ear) was a rarity in 1908.

15 Men forced to do public penance for having cut off their pigtails (1908).

國喪後之狎妓者

太原函云。

晉垣自開設妓院以來。其政學各界。頗染狎妓陋習。自遭國喪。猶復冶遊自若。當有某學堂教務長吳某暨某學堂體操教員莘等。經巡警查見其赴妓院。旋又有人據即稟知志廉訪。此情形告于學司。錫宗師大怒爰于本月初二日懸牌嚴禁。

16 Students defy law by visiting singing girls during state mourning for Emperor Kuang Hsü and Empress Dowager (1908).

17 A singing girl in Shantung (early 20th century).

乘脚踏車之危險

蘇垣護龍街某少年。日前乘脚踏車赴閶門間游。比至穿珠巷因踏走過速。衝入亂磚堆內車即倒翻。並傷及脚骨。呻吟痛楚。面如死灰。後經路人。扶掖以去。是誠咎由自取也。

18 A cycling accident (1909).

19 (*left*) Yuan Shih-k'ai.

20 (*below*) Sun Yat-sen and Soong Ch'ing-Ling after their marriage in 1914.

21 The Long March (1934–5). 'Crossing the Snow-capped Mountains' (oil painting by Ai Chung-hsin).

22 A Chinese army on the march (1923).

23 Triumphal entry of Japanese army into Nanking (December 1937).

24 Mao Tse-tung (*left*) and Chu Teh at Yenan in 1937.

25 Chinese girls walk past Japanese propaganda posters in occupied Hankow (October 1939).

26 Chinese women soldiers write letters for wounded (1938).

27 Chiang Kai-shek addresses welcoming crowd on his victorious return
to Shanghai (February 1946). On his right, Mme. Chiang, on his left
General Wedemeyer.

28 Communist troops attack Nationalist-held town in Manchuria (1948).

29 Peasants in 'Liberated Area' transport food to Communist troops in front line (1948).

30 Nationalist soldiers, wounded fighting Communists in central China, are flown back to Nanking (1948).

31 Peking shop celebrates its take-over as a joint state and private enterprise.

32 'Children report on their work to Chairman Mao': an example of contemporary Chinese art.

33 Workers demonstrate machine of their own invention for processing rubber washers (1959).

34 Health institute of a commune in Kwangtung Province (1962).

35 A policewoman directs traffic in Peking (1959).

36 Street in Commune near Canton (1962).

37 View of living quarters of state-run farm for returned overseas Chinese in Kwangtung Province with junior members (1962).

38 Girl in Canton City, carrying baby brother (1962).

39 Chinese building road in disputed territory near Indian frontier (1962).

joined such men as Liu Shu and Liang Ch'i-ch'ao to launch a Confucian Association, wrote to a friend five years later:

When I look at the bloody struggle in Europe, I feel that the progress made by those nations during the last three centuries has only brought them to the slaughterhouse. Today even western thinkers acknowledge the merits of our Confucius.

True enough, but then and for years afterwards, the connexion between Confucianism and reaction disgusted many people who were otherwise not unsympathetic towards their own cultural heritage. Thus K'ang Yu-wei, who was among the most advanced of Confucianists, hurried to participate in the attempted restoration of 1917, which, if it had succeeded, would have made the boy Emperor a pawn of one of the most brutish and ignorant of all the warlords. Yen Fu, for that matter, who had previously thought Chang Hsün pretty much a savage, found the *coup* 'something any loyal man with blood in his veins would be proud of'. What was more nauseating still, in 1923 a Chief of State, who had openly bought his office for money, solemnly pledged the Republic of China to honour Confucius and his doctrines. No wonder, when confronted with scenes like this, the most serious-minded of the younger generation did not allow even the spectre of the European War to deter them from calling for a root and branch westernization of their country.[3, 4]

CHAPTER XV

THE COMING OF MARXISM

---

*Japan's Twenty-One Demands – China enters the First World War –
the impact of the Russian Revolution – the Fourth of May – the
Washington Conference*

Japan's Twenty-One Demands

THE two decades since the Sino-Japanese war of 1894–5 had
witnessed a marked increase in Japanese exports to China. On the
other hand Japanese industries, in the year 1914, had still only a
limited access to the raw material of the mainland, thorough exploitation being limited to the southern portion of Manchuria.
The outbreak of the European War at once provided Tokyo with
an opportunity of changing this situation to its own advantage.
First of all, it was clear that the European powers for some time
to come would have too much on their hands at home to concern
themselves with what was passing at the other side of the world,
while the attention of the United States would be concentrated
on the struggle in the West. In the second place, her alliance with
Britain gave Japan an ideal excuse for intervention of a peculiarly
satisfying kind. The Shantung peninsula, reaching out into the
East China Sea towards the southernmost promontory of Manchuria, had long since beckoned to the geopolitically conscious
of the Mikado's generals. Although a Japanese landing on that
coast had in 1895 contributed in large measure to bringing China
to her knees, the advantage could not then be followed up. In the
event it was Germany who, as we have seen, entrenched herself
on Shantung soil in 1898 by the lease of Tsingtao and Kiaochow
Bay, together with the railway and mineral rights in the hinterland.
Now, after sixteen years, the Kaiser was to be supplanted.

Significantly enough, the British, who themselves had a foot-hold in Shantung by the lease of the naval station of Weihaiwei, showed little enthusiasm at their allies' readiness to observe their obligations. None the less Japan transmitted to the Germans an ultimatum requiring the surrender of the territory and when this was ignored, declared war on 23 August 1914. The government of Peking, which had already proclaimed its neutrality, attempted to limit the scope of hostilities by following the precedent employed in 1904 in Manchuria on the occasion of the Russo-Japanese campaign, and designating a certain specified area in the vicinity of Kiaochow Bay as a battle-zone. The Japanese, alleging their intention to see that the territory was ultimately returned to its original owner, had not bothered to consult China in the first place. Japan paid not the slightest regard to this assertion of sovereignty, and not content with wresting the leased districts proper from the hands of the Germans, occupied the whole stretch of the railway between Kiachow and Tsinan, as well as the adjacent mining regions, and replaced Chinese personnel by Japanese.

This was merely a prelude. In January 1915 the Japanese Minister submitted directly to Yuan Shih-k'ai, without going through the Peking Foreign Office, what have become known as the Twenty-One Demands. These required, notably, that China should cede to Japan all German rights in Shantung and more besides; that over and above the existing lease of Port Arthur and Dairen, Japanese nationals should have right of residence, land-holding, and mineral exploitation throughout South Manchuria as far as Inner Mongolia; that the great Hanyehp'ing Iron Company in Hupei should be turned into a joint Sino-Japanese enterprise; that China would undertake not to grant leases of coastal harbours or islands to any third country; and, most far-reaching of all, that the policing of important places in China should be a joint Sino-Japanese responsibility; that Japan should supply the Chinese army with weapons and advisers; that Japan should construct railways in Central China south of the Yangtze; and that Japan should have the first option of developing railways, mines and harbours in the province of Fukien.

It is no exaggeration to say that the acceptance of these conditions would make China a Japanese protectorate. Yuan had been advised, at the time the demands were served on him, to keep the matter quiet, but some word of it got abroad, and the Western

Powers asked Japan for information. In reply, Tokyo thought it expedient to omit any mention of its proposals about police and army, as well as of its designs upon Central China and Fukien. Even so, the American government was startled into proposing to Britain, France and Russia a joint remonstrance to Japan. The three European nations refused to intervene, and in the end Washington alone sent identical notes to Peking and Tokyo declaring that it would not recognize any agreements the pair of them might conclude to the detriment of American rights or Chinese sovereignty. Meanwhile a wave of anti-Japanese feeling swept across China. Japanese goods were boycotted everywhere, and at one place, Hankow, Japanese shops were sacked. This in its turn gave Japan the excuse for a display of force; naval units loomed menacingly off Chinese ports from Amoy to Taku, and there were substantial movements of troops in South Manchuria. Recognizing that China was in no state to resist, and without doubt hoping that compliance would bring a reward in the shape of assistance with his personal ambitions, Yuan Shih-k'ai, in May 1916, accepted the demands, except for the ones relating to police and military co-operation and the railways in Central China, which were shelved for further consideration.

China Enters the First World War

So far China had maintained an attitude of neutrality to the European War. In the circumstances this was only to be expected, as she had if anything, less cause to be hostile towards Germany than towards the Allies. Britain and France, however, had from the start urged Chinese participation, though the one good argument in favour of such a step, namely that the German possessions in Shantung could thereby be recovered directly by the Chinese, was almost at once rendered void by the rapid Japanese action. In the beginning of 1917 the pressure was renewed and this time with greater effect because it came from America, which of all the powers seemed to have the most honest motives, and was itself about to enter the war. If China joined the allied camp, said Washington, she would automatically qualify for a seat at the eventual peace conference and would be able to defend her interests against Japan or anyone else. On the other side, to be sure, the mere fact that the step was to be taken by the warlord regime of Peking was enough to dispose Sun Yat-sen against it, and there were in addition some Jeremiahs, among them K'ang Yu-wei, who predicted that a victorious Germany would one day call China to account. None the less, the Chinese government, having broken off diplomatic relations with the Central Powers in March 1917, declared war in August of the same year.

The man most active in putting China in the war was Tuan Ch'i-jui, who was known to be the dedicated servant of Japanese imperialism. As it was in no way to Tokyo's advantage that China's opinion should have any weight in a peace settlement this development may seem paradoxical. In fact, Japan had recognized that it might well in the long run prove difficult to stop China from following the American advice and had resolved, instead of fighting against the inevitable, to forestall any harmful consequences and even to profit from the occasion. With this in view, behind America's back she approached Britain, France, Russia and Italy and persuaded all of them to promise for the future that they would support her claim to the former German rights in Shantung. In other words, before China entered the war, any hope that by so doing she was improving her own bargaining position was already condemned to failure. Furthermore, Japan now had a fresh reason for reviving the proposal for military co-operation which she had had to drop from the Twenty-One Demands a couple of years earlier. The Russian Revolution had broken out, and the idea of allied intervention in Siberia was in the air. In such a case the troops of the Western Powers would be coming uncomfortably close to a part of the world which Japan regarded as peculiarly her own concern. Of course such a cause for alarm could not be frankly admitted, and the blame was put on the German and Austrian penetration of the Russian line on the west. In March 1918, the marionettes of Peking signed two agreements for joint Sino-Japanese defence against what was termed

the advance of enemy power into Russian territory which seems likely to threaten the peace and security of the Far East.

China acknowledged Japan's privileged role in Manchuria and Inner Mongolia and accepted a large number of Japanese officers on secondment to the Chinese armed forces. Prudently, Tuan Ch'i-jui saw to it that the details were not disclosed until in the following year circumstances made further secrecy impossible.

The Impact of the Russian Revolution

It is hardly necessary to say that the events taking place in Russia, above all the October Revolution and its sequel, aroused the liveliest interest in those Chinese who read newspapers. There was every reason why it should attract their attention, for the position of Russia was strikingly similar to that of China. Both countries were large and backward when compared to the industrialized West. Both had endured the humiliation of being defeated by the pigmy Japan. Chinese intellectuals anxious to put their own house to rights were intrigued to see how the Russians would set about the same task. When it became apparent that the very powers, Japan, Britain, France and even the United States, whose greed and ambition had plunged China into chaos, were to intervene against the Russians, the initial interest warmed into friendliness, which in its turn, after the defeat of the intervention, became enthusiastic admiration. This still lay a little distance in the future, but already by the beginning of 1918 the news from Russia had drawn some enquiring minds into an investigation of the doctrines of the Bolsheviks. It was then, for the first time, that China heard the name of Karl Marx.

That this discovery came so late goes to show how essentially practical, even in the most academic circles, was Chinese interest in European political and economic thought. Mere theoretical speculation hardly aroused curiosity. In the seventy years since its publication nobody had bothered to translate the Communist Manifesto until it was adopted by a government as a working programme. But once Marx and Engels had been discovered, the effect of their teachings was immediate. To be sure, it is a far cry from the agnosticism of Confucius to the atheism of Marx, but it was an eye-opener to scholars brought up in the Confucian tradition. Western institutions had usually been presented in China through missionary influence in the context of Christianity. They turned with relief to a system which claimed to define the whole duty of man without reference to the supernatural. Lenin's additions to the Marxist canon, when they in their turn became known, were equally acceptable. His theory of imperialism, in particular, seemed to offer a convincing explanation of the reasons for China's present condition. How naïve, by contrast, was poor Sun Yat-sen's expectation in 1912, that the Christian and liberal West would welcome the advent of a modernized Chinese Republic into the comity of nations!

The first notable converts to the new gospel were members of the staff of Peking University, especially the Dean of the Faculty of Literature, Ch'en Tu-hsiu, one of the advocates of the colloquial movement. Li Ta-chao, the Librarian, was a solid dependable northerner of peasant origins whose thirst for knowledge had just led him to the works of Bergson, of all unlikely authors, when the Muscovite revelation burst upon him. His enthusiasm was communicated to all around him, and very particularly to a twenty-five-year-old library assistant from Hunan by the name of Mao Tse-tung. Before long a study group had been formed among teachers and undergraduates in order to digest Marxist theory, but without waiting for scholarly perfection Ch'en Tu-hsiu's magazine opened its columns to the good tidings. The titles of articles by Li Ta-chao such as 'The Victory of the Common People' and 'The Victory of Bolshevism', both published in *La Jeunesse* in October 1918, tell their own story. Two fresh magazines appeared, also under Ch'en's editorship. It was for a time a straightforward battle between reaction and progress. At first even liberal westernizers like Hu Shih made common cause with Li Ta-chao and his friends under the banner of 'Democracy and Science' or, as they were personified by Chinese mouths *Mr Te and Mr Sai*. A powerful recruit to the enemies of reaction was the writer known by the pen-name of Lu Hsün who in this year of 1918 began his exposures of traditional Chinese society. The world he described was cannibalistic, and not only in the metaphorical sense that man preyed ceaselessly on man; sometimes the actual flesh and blood of the victims was demanded. In one tale, for example, *The Medicine*, set in the last days of the Manchu Dynasty, the father of a boy dying of consumption tries to cure his son by going to the public execution-ground and bribing the headsman for permission to steep a loaf of bread in the blood of a revolutionary, so that he can give it to the invalid to eat. Opinion in the local teahouse, while deciding that the decapitated man must be a lunatic for proclaiming 'the country belongs to the people', admires the common sense of the father in taking advantage of the situation for his son's benefit. After all, does not the most celebrated of Chinese pharmacopoeias stress the medicinal properties of human flesh?[1]

The old order of things, so bitterly attacked by Lu Hsün, was scarcely less odious to the bourgeoisie which in the last two decades had sprung up, especially in the treaty-ports, in the wake of modern industry and commerce. The European War had given Chinese capitalism a precious opportunity for development, although Japanese aggression prevented full use of it. Light industries, the chief of them being cotton-spinning, were developed, followed by such manufactures as flour, matches and electric equipment. The so-called 'national capitalists' were resentful of the unfair privileges enjoyed by their foreign competitors and of the eternal struggles of the warlords which destroyed all hope of industrializing the country. Another factor in the situation was the corresponding growth of an urban proletariat, though the importance of this last lay more in the political and military adventures which its existence was later to provoke than to its actual size, which in 1919 was reckoned at almost three million (compared with less than one million in 1914) out of a total population of five hundred million.

The Fourth of May

These various forces now combined to give notice that beneath the chaos a new China was in process of coming into being. Throughout the latter half of 1918 university teachers and students were venturing more and more to express their dissatisfaction with the state of the country. There were demonstrations in Peking and elsewhere, and besides writing for the magazines Li Ta-chao and his friends began to address public meetings. At one such gathering, assembled at the very spot by the Gate of Heavenly Peace where today the great parades march past the Communist chieftains, the President of Peking University spoke on 'the Sanctity of Labour'. But by January 1919 attention was concentrated on the Peace Conference at Versailles. Nowhere was Woodrow Wilson's doctrine of national self-determination heard with more enthusiasm than in China. Agitation on the subject of the Japanese demands was so troublesome that the government was obliged to instruct its delegation to make a vigorous plea for the return to China of former German bases in Shantung and, such was the optimism of the season, to press for the abolition of extraterritoriality and of the stationing of foreign troops on Chinese soil.

At the beginning of April 1919, newspaper circles in Shanghai received a telegram from one of the Chinese delegates at Versailles complaining that the efforts of himself and his colleagues were being stultified by treachery.

Certain of our countrymen have given way to the Japanese in order to enrich themselves. We now hope that public opinion at home will rise up against these traitors so that we here at Versailles may have a chance of negotiating for the annulment of the Japanese demands.

It was understood that the alleged 'treachery' referred to the action of three men in particular, namely the Minister of Communications, the Chinese Minister in Tokyo, and the Director of the Peking Mint who the year before, in concluding an agreement with the Japanese on a loan, ostensibly for railway construction, had gone on record as 'consenting with pleasure' to the Japanese aggression in Shantung. By the middle of April the cry had been taken up in the press, and in Peking protests began to be organized not only among students, but among shopkeepers and even, it was said, some sections of the army. On 3 May, at a meeting in Peking University, it was decided that a great demonstration should be held next morning at the Gate of Heavenly Peace to demand that China should refuse to sign the Versailles Treaty. At the height of the excitement one young man initiated what during the weeks that followed was to become a fashion. He tore a strip from his dress, and biting his finger wrote in blood on the piece of cloth the words: 'Give us back Tsingtao!'

First thing in the morning, upwards of three thousand demonstrators assembled at the appointed place, and began to make their way into the Diplomatic Quarter towards the Japanese Legation. Here there occurred an incident whose significance is much dwelt upon by Chinese historians today. It was necessary for the procession to pass in front of the American Legation, but the road was barred by the Legation guards who refused to let the students proceed. Two hours were wasted in angry recriminations, after which the crowd, abandoning its original goal, set off towards the house of the principal Chinese culprit, the Minister of Communications, where they found the gate locked and guarded by policemen. While some of the students treated the police to a harangue on their patriotic duties, others managed to crawl through the window of the porter's lodge and unbarred the gate. The mob rushed inside where they nearly had the satisfaction of finding all three of their enemies at once, the Minister of Communications, the Minister to Tokyo, and the Director of the Mint, who had had the unlucky idea of choosing that day for a conference. As it was, the chief criminal had the presence of mind to take to his heels at the first alarm and the patriots had to make do with the others who, with a Japanese journalist for good measure, were trapped in the reception room. The diplomat and the journalist who tried to protect him, were savagely manhandled and would probably not have survived to tell the story if it had not been for the arrival on the scene of the military, who put the crowd to flight, not however before the house had been sacked and set on fire. Thirty-two of the rioters were carried away to gaol.

It was soon known that there was disagreement in government circles about the best policy to pursue. Tuan Ch'i-jui himself, who had little contact with, or sympathy for, intellectuals, could not be brought to see that students were in a different class from any-body else and was all for repression and exemplary punishment. Orders were given to the police to that effect, and official con-dolences were offered to the victims of the assault. But from one end of the country to the other came messages of support for the disturbers of the peace. That Sun Yat-sen should have kind words for the students was only to be expected; the surprising thing was that even K'ang Yu-wei, by now considered an arch-reactionary, declared that the turbulence was fully justified in view of the gravity of the situation. As the agitation, so far from lessening, was gaining momentum and spreading to the provinces, those members of the government who were comparatively sensitive to public opinion, or at any rate to that of the educated classes, prevailed upon their colleagues to have the arrested students set at liberty on 7 May.

Instead of showing gratitude for this leniency, the universities and even the middle schools were more obstreperous than before. Lessons were to all intents and purposes at a standstill, while delegations went from city to city. In Tientsin the Student Associ-ation put out its own news-sheet, with a young man called Chou En-lai as its editor. The most significant development occurred in Shanghai, for there, on 3 June, a mass meeting called for a nation-wide strike in support of the students, in addition to the boycott of Japanese goods. The summons was answered, and between then and the middle of the month in most towns and cities workers had downed tools and shops had shut their doors for three or four days. Of course this did not pass off without violence; there were innumerable clashes with the army and the police, and in Peking alone during the first three days of June three thousand students were arrested and as the gaols were overflowing university buildings were turned into detention centres.

It was financial circles who were the quickest to recognize that the game was up. On 9 June a group of Chinese bankers told the government plainly that unless the popular demands were met the country would be faced with economic collapse. The next day it was announced that the Finance Minister and the other two culprits had been relieved of their posts. Still the crowds of students, sometimes as many as ten thousand, continued to swarm around the principal offices of the government until on 28 June word came that the Chinese delegation had been instructed to leave Versailles without signing the Peace Treaty.

Such was the celebrated Fourth of May which may fairly be said to have opened a new chapter in Chinese history. Many of the features of this new phase show some resemblance to the landscape of earlier times. The students and their teachers who had constituted themselves the spokesmen of the nation had always been recognized as the élite of traditional Chinese society. The governing authority had tried, as far as possible, to treat them with indulgence. Their humblest members were linked by a certain *esprit-de-corps* with the greatest ministers of the Empire. The disintegration of the old state structure, symbolized by the abolition of the classical examinations in 1904, had deprived them not merely of their privileges but of their entire significance as a group, and the events of that summer of 1919 meant to them first and foremost their reinstatement both in their own esteem and in the respect of their countrymen. For the next thirty years the students claimed to be the guardians of the national spirit and it would be ungenerous to deny that in most cases the boast was justified. Yet often, too, their self-appointed mission degenerated into a petulant rejection of discipline. Anyone familiar with Chinese universities can tell stories of how teachers were cowed into submission by fear of unpopularity. Apart from blackmail of this sort, holding meetings and marching in processions were to many young people a more agreeable mode of passing the time than the acquisition of knowledge, and academic standards suffered accordingly. Since 1949, of course, the universities have lost this censorial function and the only extra-mural role they are permitted to sustain is that of providing a claque to applaud whatever policy may seem good to the Communist party.

Over and above its political importance, the Fourth of May marked a decisive cultural victory for the anti-traditionalists. From then on the triumph of the colloquial school of literature was assured. But almost at once it was evident that there was dissension among the champions of the Renaissance. Men such as Hu Shih, who had stood shoulder to shoulder with Ch'en Tu-hsiu and Lu Hsün so long as the fight was simply for Democracy and Science against the forces of reaction, now shrank away with alarm from the path their allies were beginning to follow. 'Good government,' said Hu Shih, was all he wanted; the less talk of ideologies the better. Change must come 'a drop at a time'. A democratic revolution to unify the country was out of the question. Let there be a federation of autonomous provinces: after all that was the American system, and what Chinese in his right mind could ask for a better? The truth was that in those few weeks of turmoil Hu Shih had caught a glimpse of something he did not like. For a moment a demon had been conjured up, at the sight of which even the corruption and idiocy of past and present misrule seemed by contrast comfortable and reassuring. Indeed, as time went by one or two of the wizards themselves came to dread the potency of their new magic and, having recanted, turned into the most zealous upholders of established order. But for the young and high-spirited, both of that generation and the next, nothing could match the seduction of the gospel from Russia.[2]

The Washington Conference

A word remains to be said about the problem of Shantung, which had touched off the explosion of the Fourth of May. For a couple of years it lay in abeyance. At the end of 1921 an attempt was made by the Washington Conference to create a new balance of power in the Pacific, acceptable to all the nations with interests in the Far East, except of course Soviet Russia which was manifestly beyond the pale. For some time Britain, pressed by Canada and Australia, had been unenthusiastic about the alliance with

Japan, which might drag her into collision with the United States, and was glad to have it terminated. In return, Japan's hegemony in Eastern Asia and the Western Pacific was confirmed by an arrangement fixing the ratio of Japanese, American and British naval strengths at three: five: five respectively. As for China, who was a party to the Conference, the traditional American principles of the Open Door and respect for territorial integrity were accepted with varying degrees of willingness by the other countries. In February 1922 Japan concluded a bilateral agreement with China to return the Shantung territories to Chinese control. Britain on her part declared her perfect readiness to give up Weihaiwei, although the surrender was not effected until 1930. Another sop to Chinese national sentiment was a concession on tariffs, which, while retaining foreign control of the customs, resulted in a substantial increase of the revenue received by China. Furthermore there were some pious resolutions promising to look into the question of extra-territoriality and the possibility of withdrawing foreign troops from Peking and elsewhere. In the event these and other provisions of the 'unequal treaties' stayed under discussion until they were swept away once and for all by the Pacific War twenty years later. On the whole, it was this obvious reluctance of the Western Powers and of Japan to abandon their special privileges, rather than the grudging concessions wrung out of them, that impressed the Chinese and led more and more of them to believe that their true friends were to be found elsewhere.

CHAPTER XVI

THE NATIONALIST-COMMUNIST ALLIANCE

Foundation of the Chinese Communist Party – Moscow turns to Sun Yat-sen – Chiang Kai-shek – Kuomintang reorganization – the Christian General's Coup – Death of Sun Yat-sen – the Thirtieth of May and its sequel – Factions inside the Kuomintang – Chiang gains control

---

Foundation of the Chinese Communist Party

As early as the summer of 1918 the Soviet government notified the Peking authorities that Russia, in contrast to the other powers, freely abandoned the privileges extorted from China by Tsarist regimes in the past, and looked forward to enjoying friendly relations on terms of equality. In furtherance of these aims Russian envoys duly made an appearance in Peking, first of all from the short-lived creation known as the Far Eastern Republic, which had been established in Siberia to confront the White Russians and the allied interventionists, and then in 1922 directly from Moscow itself. The Russians certainly meant what they said as regards their right of extra-territoriality, and their voluntary repudiation of this most humiliating insult to China's sovereignty did not fail to win them golden opinions. But when it came to the awkward question of Russian control of the Chinese Eastern Railway, the short cut across Manchuria to Vladivostok, it was obvious that Moscow felt the privilege had been fairly earned by Russian money and Russian enterprise. As for the north bank of the Amur and the Maritime Province, wrested from China in 1858–60, nobody seems to have had the temerity to mention them. In any case, even the railway fell within the competence rather of the Manchurian warlord Chang Tso-lin than of Peking, since in 1922 Chang had been driven back north of the Wall by the victory of Wu P'ei-fu. The Russians on that account offended Wu by treating separately with Chang. Wu's Anglo-Saxon patrons, in any case, frowned upon his coming to an understanding with the Bolsheviks. Diplomatic relations between the two countries were, therefore, not resumed until 1924. In fact, however, these transactions were only of the faintest significance in comparison with the true Sino-Russian entente which had come into existence during those years.

The Comintern after its foundation in March 1919 lost little time in making contact with Chinese Marxist students. Early in 1920 Gregory Voitinsky, head of its Far Eastern section, was sent out to supervise the organization of a Chinese Communist Party. His first stop was naturally at Peking where he met Li Ta-chao, but he soon continued his journey to Shanghai. That industrial city was the obvious choice for a headquarters. He also wished to make the acquaintance of Ch'en Tu-hsiu who having at last fallen foul of the Peking authorities had in the time-honoured manner beaten a retreat to the French Concession. In May, a nucleus of sympathizers had come together in Shanghai and later in the year similar groups were formed in Peking and the provinces. The founder of the Hunan cell was Mao Tse-tung. As may be imagined some of those recruited lacked the energy or the conviction to persevere, but all things considered the movement gained ground so encouragingly that in July 1921 the Communist Party of China was able to hold its first general meeting. Twelve delegates arrived from the various cells, including a representative of Chinese students in Japan and Voitinsky himself and the Dutchman Maring to speak for the Comintern. It was estimated that the Party contained at that time slightly over fifty members. Mao Tse-tung made his way from Hunan, but neither of the spiritual fathers, Li Ta-chao and Ch'en Tu-hsiu, was able to attend. Ch'en, who was working in Canton in the Education Department of Sun Yat-sen's government made up for his absence by submitting a draft programme. He was rewarded by being elected Secretary General. Needless to say all this was carried on in the most entire secrecy; even so the proceedings were interrupted half-way through by the apparition of a spy in the vicinity and the meeting just managed to withdraw to safety before the French police arrived on the scene.

Ch'en Tu-hsiu promptly returned to Shanghai to take up his new post and at once began centralizing the Party's activities in a Labour Union secretariat with its office in Shanghai. Communist historians today reckon that between January 1922 and February 1923 more than a hundred strikes were organized by the newly formed party in the mining, railway and shipping industries, beginning with the large-scale and successful campaign of the Hong Kong seamen for increased pay.

The Party held its Second General Meeting in Shanghai again the following year. This time twelve delegates represented upwards of a hundred and twenty members, and some far-reaching decisions were taken. It was resolved, for instance, that steps should be taken to join the Communist International. A Manifesto was voted which included the declaration that one of the fundamental tasks of the Party was to promote a democratic revolution, side by side with workers, peasants and petit-bourgeois, against imperialism and 'feudalism'. Immediately afterwards, in July 1922, the Central Committee adjourned to the more pleasant surroundings of the lake resort of Hangchow and at the instance of Comrade Maring gave its attention to practical measures of putting the policy into effect. When the Dutchman urged that Communists ought to join the Kuomintang as individuals and make use of the Nationalist organization to advance the Marxist cause, Ch'en Tuhsiu, according to his own account, at first was for rejecting this advice as harmful to the Party's independence, and yielded only when the authority of the Communist International was invoked. But an event early the following year seemed to prove Moscow's good sense. In February 1923 a strike fomented by the Communists among the workers in the Peking-Hankow railway was ruthlessly stamped out by the ruling warlord Wu P'ei-fu. This débâcle was interpreted as convincing evidence of the need to find allies outside the Party.

In spite of this set-back membership increased steadily and by the date of the Third General Meeting in June 1923, amounted to four hundred and thirty-two persons. This time, significantly, the delegates assembled at Canton and formally agreed, though not without the expression of some dissident opinions, that individual members should be free to join the Kuomintang. Ch'en Tu-hsiu pointed out, with some justification, that the aims of Sun Yat-sen and his followers were confused in the extreme. They had fostered the erroneous expectation that the Western Powers would help the Chinese Revolution, and had concentrated all their efforts on military activities, thereby forfeiting their political leadership. However, according to Maring, the Kuomintang, though rather an amorphous body, was emphatically not the party of one economic class. Communists could enter it with a clear conscience, and with them as leaven there would spring to life a new and formidable alliance of national bourgeois, petit-bourgeois, workers and peasants, united to a man against the imperialists and the warlords.

Moscow turns to Sun Yat-sen

As a matter of fact, to be strictly truthful the Russians had once, though only for a very brief moment, toyed with the notion of coming to terms with another Chinese force altogether. In 1921, Maring had actually interviewed Wu P'ei-fu, but immediately reported to his employers that the warlord might well control the strongest army in the country, but was totally lacking in political value. With Wu ruled out, Sun Yat-sen seemed to Moscow the only possible champion of the New China they envisaged. In spite of the lamentable state of the Kuomintang the Russians were far-sighted enough to discern that something could be done with it. Both Voitinsky and Maring had been very favourably impressed by Sun. From the start he had expressed his admiration of the Soviet government, and by the end of 1922 the utter failure of his attempts to erect a 'national government' in Canton on the basis of warlord support made him more than ready to listen to suggestions that he ought to seek allies elsewhere. In January 1923, during one of his periodic spells of exile in the French Concession at Shanghai, he received yet another Russian emissary, Adolf Joffe. The ensuing conversations ended with the publication of a joint statement, to the effect that Moscow appreciated that Chinese conditions did not require a Soviet system, but first and foremost independence and national unity. From the Nationalist side, then, there appeared to be no serious obstacle in the way of co-operation, and it was well known that among Sun's adherents there was a group of markedly left-wing sympathizers. With such people in the Nationalist ranks, the Communists might be assured of a welcome. Soon a stream of candidates, headed by Li Ta-chao, presented themselves for admission while retaining intact their allegiance to their mother party. Among Sun's left wing adherents the one whose name was to become most famous, though in a tragic context, was a Cantonese called Wang Ching-wei, a man distinguished by great good looks and charm of manner. He had joined Sun's clandestine organization while a student in Japan, and in 1910 had been carried on a wave of revolutionary enthusiasm to Peking to assassinate the Prince Regent. He had instead fallen into the hands of the police, but even the Manchu authorities had not the heart to put this charming youth to death. Set free after the rising of 1911, he had spent some years in France, and now close to forty, cultured and urbane, he was Sun Yat-sen's right-hand man.

Chiang Kai-shek

In the summer of 1923, the wheel of fortune carried Sun Yat-sen back once more to his 'capital' of Canton, but this time he had resolved to profit from his new alliance to free himself from his humiliating dependence on the whims of the local warlords. With Russian help he would create an army loyal to himself, and he knew the very man to carry out the assignment. Though Sun relied more and more in political matters on the highly literate Wang Ching-wei he felt he needed someone of a more aggressive type to lead the army, a post where intellectual cultivation was less important than a ruthless will to command. We have already met, very briefly, Chiang Kai-shek as a military cadet who in 1907 was sworn into Sun's revolutionary brotherhood in Tokyo, but now in 1923 at the age of thirty-six, he makes his first effective entry upon the political scene. There is some mystery about his origins. The approved version of his career states that he was born in 1887, the son of a prosperous salt-factor of Chekiang province, but his mother was his father's second wife and as Chiang in adult life restricted his filial piety almost exclusively to the memory of his mother, it has been surmised that she too may well have been married before and borne Chiang to her original husband. She had been left a widow while he was still a child, and the absence of a father may have made it easier for him to embark on the adventure of a military life. During his student days he made some useful acquaintances in Japanese army circles. His immediate patron was not at first Sun Yat-sen himself but a man named Ch'en Ch'i-mei, prominent in the secret societies of Shanghai, who had seen a prospect of power in the republican movement. On his return from Japan Chiang took part in the rising of 1911 under Ch'en's leadership. Subsequently he had been involved with him in the rather ineffectual attempts to dislodge Yuan Shih-k'ai's henchmen from their control of the Shanghai area. Ch'en Ch'i-mei had been murdered by an unknown assassin in 1915. Apart from an occasional trip to Canton to maintain a foothold in Sun Yat-sen's camp, Chiang seems to have spent most of his time there-after at Shanghai in and around the Stock Exchange where his links with the secret societies proved beneficial. Chiang was ap-pointed Head of the new loyal army, and as a sign that the appointment was to be taken seriously, he was sent to Russia in the summer of 1923 to take a few months' refresher course in military science. In the long run, this experience had an effect contrary to what had been intended; it is said that Chiang took great exception to the critical attitude adopted towards him by Chinese students in Moscow. One can well imagine that to young people from a Marxist seminary the accents of the Shanghai ad-venturer, imperceptible to foreigners, must have sounded gro-tesquely out of place in one cast for the part of a revolutionary commander.[1]

Kuomintang Reorganization

Meanwhile, in Canton, preparations were going on apace. In October 1923, there arrived the man who was to become the most influential of all the Soviet advisers, Michael Borodin. A veteran of the class struggle both in Britain and America and fresh out of a Glasgow gaol, Borodin at once set to work on a massive plan of reorganization. First of all the Nationalist Party itself, the Kuomintang, had to be revitalized, and the model chosen, natur-ally enough, was the Communist Party of Russia. The old brother-hood disappeared to make way for an intricate structure of cells contrived in the shape of a pyramid, within which, in theory that is to say, for the ideal was never achieved in practice, power was derived in stages from the base upwards. Allowance had none the less to be made for Sun's historic eminence. He was appointed President for life with the final control of policy-making machinery. This constitution is believed to have been first drafted by Borodin himself in English. Its Chinese text was adopted with enthusiasm at the first Congress of the renovated party, which was held in

January 1924. The left wing, reinforced by the influx of Communist recruits, including Mao Tse-tung, was very much in the ascendant in the revitalized party organization.

The reconstruction of the Kuomintang was emphasized by the Congress' approval of another document from Borodin's pen. This was a Manifesto to the effect that the Revolution recognized as its enemies the warlords and the imperialist powers associated with them; that support would be given to workers and peasants; and that the Kuomintang would join with all revolutionary forces to form a united front. While the Congress was in session, the news of Lenin's death provided Sun with an opportunity to send a message of solidarity to Moscow.

The old doctrine of the Three People's Principles was shortly afterwards published in a revised version. The principle of Nationalism which originally demanded the liberation of China from Manchu rule, was now confronted with a new bugbear, foreign imperialism, in face of which the Chinese people needed to cement themselves together into a strong modern state. The principle of the People's Rights would thus deprive all counter-revolutionary groups and individuals of their rights, and even the innocent mass of the population would only gradually become competent to enjoy them. In the beginning there would have to be a military government, which would be replaced in due course by a period of Kuomintang tutelage, during which the Party would handle affairs, until little by little from the local to the national level the people, without distinction of wealth or class, would be allowed to elect the organs of the state, which besides a Legislature, an Executive and a Judiciary, as in the West, would include offices to fulfill the traditional Chinese functions of Examination and Censorship. The content of the third principle, that of the People's Livelihood, was considerably amplified. The keystone of it, the policy on land, continued to show, by its vagueness, that Sun was still not at his ease with the problems of the peasantry. The goal remained that of the equalization of land ownership according to value, but it was now declared that landless peasants would be given land by the state. Large industrial enterprises were to be publicly controlled, and labour laws would be enacted to protect the workers.

It was assumed from the start that the realization of such a programme depended in the first instance on military victory, and accordingly very special attention was paid to the creation of an efficient army. Chiang Kai-shek, his reputation enhanced by his studies in Moscow, assumed the post of Commander-in-Chief. Hardly less important at the time, he became President of the Whampoa Military Academy in the suburbs of Canton. Arms and equipment were imported by sea direct from Vladivostok and there were Russian instructors at Chiang's disposal, the best known of these being General Galen, whose real name was Vassily Blucher. The education of the cadets was not confined to military science; political indoctrination was regarded as equally essential, and was entrusted to the capable hands of Chou En-lai. Since we last met him at Tientsin during the riots of 1919, Chou had been a student in France where he had joined the Communist Party.

The embryo army was soon blooded in circumstances which corroborated what it had been taught about imperialist machinations. A group of local gentry and businessmen, tired of being pestered by the riffraff of the warlord troops, had followed precedent by organizing their own Volunteer Defence Corps of mercenaries. In the beginning, Sun had not objected to this, and relations between the Kuomintang and the merchants had been relatively cordial. Alarmed at Sun's championship of workers and peasants the merchants began to wonder whether in the end the Nationalists might not constitute more of a threat to men of property than the warlords ever had done. They were encouraged in this state of mind by the British authorities in Hong Kong, with whom they were in the closest contact through a Chinese compradore of the Hong Kong and Shanghai Banking Corporation. Some word of what was being meditated must have come to Sun's ears. He seized a consignment of weapons intended for the merchants, and when in October 1924 the Volunteers attempted to overawe him he promptly ordered his Whampoa cadets to suppress and disband them, a task they accomplished with commendable rapidity.

The Christian General's Coup

Just at the same time as this first exploit of the new Nationalism, there occurred in the North events of far-seeing significance for the warlord regime. Wu P'ei-fu, who had driven his predecessor Tuan Ch'i-jui from Peking in 1920 by means of an alliance with the Manchurian Chang Tso-lin, had some two years later freed himself from dependence by expelling Chang north of the Great Wall. Now in the autumn of 1924 war flared up once more, and Wu marched off to invade Chang's own domain of Manchuria. His way there lay through the gateway of Shanhaikwan, where the Wall comes down to meet the sea, but before setting out on this punitive expedition he took the precaution of guarding his flank by having the other passes towards the West garrisoned by one of his subordinate commanders. The commander he chose was General Feng Yü-hsiang who though reared to the life of a soldier – his father had fought against the Turkestan rebels in the 1870s – was distinguished from his fellows by some interesting traits of character. He had, for example, become a convert to Protestant Christianity but his religious ideas seemed to owe more to the Old Testament than to the New and his zeal could be displayed in a rather bizarre fashion. He was said to have forcibly baptized whole regiments at one go with a hosepipe. The austerity of his private life in the midst of carnal temptations of every sort was a sufficient proof of his faith. Latterly, however, the pride felt by missionary circles at such a paragon had been marred by stories that the hero was flirting with Communism, an aberration which would be all the more dangerous as his territorial fief lay in the north-west in convenient access from the Soviet Union. Actually, in his more reflective moments the Christian General, as he was called, had feelings of remorse at the condition to which years of anarchy had reduced the country, anarchy which he and his fellows were perpetuating. Visitors to his headquarters noticed that side by side with biblical pictures there was in every room a map showing the territories lost to China during the last century; these included, significantly, both Korea and Vietnam.

Lately there had been rumours that everything was not well between Feng and his overlord Wu P'ei-fu. Wu, like most of his kind, was a very heavy drinker and on his birthday Feng had had the impertinence to send him a bottle of water as a present. By all accounts Wu had used some pretty vigorous language on that occasion, and now, in spite of the exigencies of war, he was treating Feng and his troops very churlishly in the matter of supplies. This proved to be a mistake, for in the second half of October 1924 Feng profited from Wu's absence at the front to move his troops from the Great Wall and occupy Peking. He appealed to the nation thereupon to stop the senseless war. This blow at once put an end to the invasion of Manchuria, for Wu P'ei-fu was obliged to abandon North China and withdraw his army by sea down to the Yangtze Valley, where he entrenched himself in his former domains. The perennial veteran Tuan Ch'i-jui and, of course, the chief beneficiary of the coup, Chang Tso-lin, hastened to fill the seats of power in Peking, acknowledging that things could not be allowed to continue as before. There was much talk of a Ministry of All The Talents, and in the general glow of enthusiasm Sun Yat-sen was invited to come to Peking.

The Death of Sun Yat-sen

Sun's ready acceptance of the invitation may appear surprising, so soon after the universal denunciation of all warlords contained in the new Kuomintang manifesto, but it must be remembered that only two years earlier he had been an ally of Tuan and Chang against Wu P'ei-fu, who still loomed in his mind as the chief villain of the piece. However, any idea he might have entertained of participating in a coalition was quickly frustrated, for he had hardly set foot in North China when he was laid low with an illness which medical examination showed to be an advanced stage of cancer. Nor for that matter did Tuan Ch'i-jui or Chang Tso-lin take kindly to his proposal that a provisional Assembly should be convened, including representatives of workers' and peasants' unions and of the students and professors. Yet his journey had not been in vain. The students in particular gave him a triumphal reception, and when three months later, in March 1925, he died in Peking it was with all the acclaim of a national hero. Conscious of the solemnity of the occasion he addressed a valediction to the Soviet government to confirm that he was enjoining upon his party the absolute necessity of continuing to collaborate with Russia. He took leave of his own countrymen with a testament which together with his doctrine of the Three Principles was to become the Bible of the Nationalists and to ensure that in death his influence far exceeded what it had been during his life.

The Thirtieth of May and its Sequel

The friendship with Moscow abroad and Chinese Communism

at home, which Sun had bequeathed to his followers in such affecting circumstances, was made all the more cordial a couple of months after his death. In the middle of May 1925, a dispute at a Japanese-owned cotton-mill in Shanghai resulted in the killing of the labour representative by the Japanese. He had been a member of the Communist Party. On 30 May students held anti-Japanese demonstrations in the International Settlement, and the police were misguided enough to arrest several hundred of them. The news brought an immense multitude of sympathizers, estimated by some at nearly ten thousand, to the street outside the police-station in order to demand the release of their comrades. Faced with such a tumult a British police officer ordered his men to fire on the crowd, ten of whom were killed. This was the celebrated incident of the Thirtieth of May, which at once aroused a storm of fury throughout the country. In Shanghai itself, the Communists formed an Action Committee. The very next day a Workers General Union of two hundred thousand members was set up. On 1 June a strike, supported by shopkeepers and students, testified to the efficacy of the arrangement. But the most enduring consequence was felt in the South. In Hong Kong in the middle of June more than two thousand workers came out in a strike which was to last for sixteen months. The name Hong Kong means 'Fragrant Harbour', but even after a few days visitors to the place remarked that without coolies to attend to the menial tasks the atmosphere was redolent more of stinks than of perfumes. Many of the strikers went to Canton, and the movement spread to the British Concession there. This in its turn led to another shooting incident. A crowd demonstrating against the foreign concessions was fired on by British, French and Portuguese police and gunboats. Altogether two hundred people were killed or injured. But the workers had still one weapon up their sleeve. They organized a blockade of all goods coming from Hong Kong, and established their own tribunals to punish transgressors.

Factions inside the Kuomintang

The National Government which Sun Yat-sen had planned to create from his reformed Kuomintang made their tasks easier. Founded in Canton in July 1925, the government consisted of a committee of sixteen senior Party members under the chairmanship of Wang Ching-wei. There was a report that Sun Yat-sen himself had named Wang as his successor, and although the story was doubted in some quarters it seemed likely enough in view of the intimacy which had existed between the two men. Everything conspired to consolidate the leftist control of the Kuomintang. Yet under the surface the Party was racked with internal tensions which now and then broke into the open. Even in 1923, when Sun had first proposed the Communist alliance, a few of his old followers had found the suggestion too much for them, and had withdrawn from their obedience. At the first meeting of the remodelled Party, in January 1924, voices had been raised against that passage in the Manifesto which denounced the warlords in general. What folly, cried certain cautious people, to offend Chang Tso-lin and Tuan Ch'i-jui when the only enemy was Wu P'ei-fu! Sun himself, as we have seen, was not altogether immune to such ideas, and in the last months of his life snatched eagerly at what he fancied was a chance of combining forces with Chang and Tuan. When Sun's death removed his unifying influence and the violence of the labour troubles began to alarm more timid spirits, it is not surprising that attempts were made to divert the Kuomintang. What was more ominous, methods hitherto used only against the common enemy were now employed towards party brothers. In August 1925, a member of the two-month-old National Government, Liao Chung-k'ai, who had made himself prominent by his left-wing opinions, was assassinated in circumstances which pointed to the complicity of one of his colleagues, Hu Han-min. The matter was judged too delicate to admit of public investigation. None the less Mr Hu was induced to see the advisability of temporarily retiring from the scene. The place chosen for him to retire to was Moscow, where he made speeches extolling proletarian solidarity.

It was intended that Sun Yat-sen, as befitted the Father of the Republic, should enjoy a spectacular funeral in his old capital of Nanking. Meanwhile, in accordance with a common Chinese practice, his remains were deposited in the Green Cloud Monastery, one of the many Buddhist shrines which embellish the Western Hills a few miles outside Peking. At this place, in November 1925, there assembled a group of Kuomintang dissidents, later known as the 'Western Hills Group', who in the presence of their dead leader's coffin passed a series of resolutions to demand the expulsion of Communists from the Nationalist Party and the dismissal of Borodin.

Chiang gains Control

So far the only signs of unrest had come from these outright opponents of the Communist alliance. But there was another school of thought, apparently unsuspected at the time, whose principal adherent was Chiang Kai-shek himself. This held that co-operation with the Communists, at this stage and within strict limits, was indispensable for a Nationalist victory. Seen from this point of view, the policy advocated by the Western Hills Group was utterly disastrous since it would prevent the Kuomintang from ever coming to power. Chiang Kai-shek, in fact, presented so thoroughly trustworthy an aspect that in the tightening of organization which followed the murder of Liao Chung-k'ai, he was advanced on Borodin's recommendation into a position where he shared the chief responsibility of the regime with Wang Ching-wei. This confidence seemed to be justified when in November 1925, about the time the expulsion of the Communists was being voted in the Green Cloud Monastery, the troops under his command defeated the local warlord and reduced the whole province of Kwangtung to Nationalist allegiance. The Party General Meeting held in January 1926 could hardly fail to result in an overwhelming triumph for the left wing. Some of the Western Hills Group forfeited their membership; others were humiliatingly reprimanded. When the assembly dispersed, Borodin, in the best of moods, set off to visit the Christian General, whose friendship was considered eminently worth cultivating.

The Russian's absence gave Chiang Kai-shek the opportunity to make his first open move against the Communists. In the circles in which he had influence, especially in his Military Academy, there had been a great deal of tacit encouragement for what was ostensibly nothing more than the study of the late Dr Sun's political theories, but which on closer inspection turned out to be an exposition of the Three People's Principles very much on the lines of traditional Confucianism, purged of all Marxist accretions. The angle of these interpretations was that any doctrine of a class war was totally alien to the dead leader's purpose, which aimed at promoting the National welfare by fostering such mutual confidence between the different sections of the community that the workers would find their living conditions improving simply through the benevolence of their employers.

The excuse for Chiang's intervention was that the captain of a Nationalist gunboat had suddenly transferred his vessel from her proper station to the vicinity of the Whampoa Military Academy with a view to starting a revolt. The Communist historians suggest that Chiang himself directed the ship to move. At all events, on 20 March 1925 Chiang ordered the gunboat to be seized and at the same time surrounded the headquarters of the Canton-Hong Kong strikers and disarmed the volunteer corps which had been formed there. Communist political workers attached to the Military Academy and to units under Chiang's command were detained and the Russian military advisers put under house arrest, and then sent home.

Chiang was now clearly the master of Canton and in circumstances which rendered untenable the position of Wang Ching-wei, who promptly treated himself to a holiday in France. Moscow, of course, was much perplexed but Borodin on his return from the North decided that all things considered it was the Communists who had brought the trouble on their own heads by their indiscretion and impatience. The strikers' committee, for instance, had been behaving almost like an independent government. The alliance itself did not appear to be in question; Chiang was quite emphatic on that point when he addressed a meeting of the Kuomintang Central Committee in May 1926. He declared:

For us to kill Communists would be just plain suicide.

Elsewhere he expressed the opinion that the Communist Party as a whole had not been behind the attempted revolt in March. Nevertheless, the Central Committee had assembled. The long-awaited expedition against the northern warlords could be approved and with this in prospect there was no room for disunity of command. It was agreed that no Communist should head a department and that not more than one-third of the members of the Central Committee should be Communists. Among those eliminated by this rule was Mao Tse-tung. Simultaneously Chiang assumed supreme control of all the armed forces and of the civil and financial administration and of all territories under the Nationalist Government. Borodin watched in silence, confident that there would be changes in plenty before long.[2]

CHAPTER XVII

THE NATIONALIST VICTORY

The Northern Expedition – the Wuhan regime – Chiang's blow at the Communists – the Nationalist-Communist split – the Nanking Government – the murder of Chang Tso-lin – Chiang and his rivals

The Northern Expedition

SUN YAT-SEN had long cherished the dream that one day the Chinese Revolution would march in arms from its home in Canton and sweep invincibly northwards to rid the land of the warlords and their foreign masters. He had not lived to see his dream fulfilled, but it remained as the fundamental ambition of Nationalists and Communists alike. Yet now that the hour had come the prospect failed to arouse universal enthusiasm. During that early summer of 1926 the Chinese Communist leadership, as represented by Ch'en Tu-hsiu, and the Russian observers, agreed that the adventure was premature and that in all probability within a few months the Army of Liberation would be ingloriously back at base.

The Nationalist left did not agree. They were in favour of launching an expedition without further delay, and were prevented from having second thoughts by the fact that Chiang Kai-shek was determined to act at once. The decision to take the risk that summer was essentially his, and reveals an appreciation of the political and military situation that fully justifies Sun's selection of him to be head of the army. At first glance things were by no means reassuring. Chang Tso-lin, who had emerged by now as the puppet-master of the Peking regime, had broken with the Christian General, for General Feng had connived at a revolt among Chang's subordinates in Manchuria, and had instead come to an understanding with his arch-enemy of two years before, Wu P'ei-fu, now firmly established in his old domain in Central China. A combination of Wu and Chang was something to shudder at, and those conservative prophets of disaster who had denounced the folly of taking on all the warlords at once had the consolation of finding that some of their Marxist opponents now shared their forebodings.

Chiang Kai-shek, however, took a different, and as it soon proved, more accurate view. To him the league and covenant which bound the northern warlords together meant no more than any of their previous pacts of mutual support and loyalty. Chiang's only real worry was the possibility that Japan or the Western Powers might be induced to intervene massively in order to prop up the counter-revolutionary government, and the more time elapsed the greater this chance became. The wave of labour unrest since the spring of 1925 had been an ominous sign of what was likely to happen to foreign interests in the event of a victory for the Canton regime, and so far Chiang Kai-shek's action against the Communists had not mitigated the gloom of foreign investors in China. Meanwhile, Chang and Wu were doing everything in their power to represent Chiang as a howling Bolshevik. The warlord manifestos of those days are identical word for word, except for the names of the villains they hold up to execration, with the denunciations which Chiang himself would shortly be hurling at his Communist allies.

It was in June 1926 that the Canton government finally conferred on Chiang Kai-shek plenary authority as commander of the Northern Expedition. With the departure from the city on 9 July Chiang issued a proclamation which makes interesting reading.

The bandit Wu P'ei-fu has for his slogan 'Put down the Reds!' This is the watchword of the Imperialists against the oppressed peoples of the world and is aimed at destroying the united revolutionary front. What does 'red' mean? It means the Red Party and the Red Army of Soviet Russia, who use the Red Flag as a symbol of the red blood of the revolutionary masses, shed as the price of their national independence and freedom. It means the release of mankind from misery, the guarantee of human rights, opposition to international imperialism, the abrogation of unequal treaties and the liberation of two thousand and fifty million people over the whole earth. If a government is a government of the masses, and its army is an army of the masses why should it fear to be called 'red'?[1]

The army, consisting of upwards of fifty thousand men, advanced in three main columns. One marched due north to the great base of Wu P'ei-fu's power, the Wuhan cities. It was Wu, astride the Yangtze in Central China, who was the most formidable of the nearer enemies as can be seen from Chiang's proclamation. Chang Tso-lin, entrenched in the North, would not be encountered until later. It had been anticipated that the first serious resistance would be met as the revolutionary forces entered Hunan, the next province to Kwangtung in the line of march. But here the ground had been well prepared, for Mao Tse-tung's propaganda had been supplemented by the efforts of a group of special agents who preceded the army proper. The result was to surpass all expectations. Everywhere the peasantry rallied to the invaders, while Wu's soldiers were impeded by strikes and revolts. The provincial capital of Changsha was occupied with little trouble on 12 August, and as the victors pressed on towards the Yangtze their numbers were increased by a constant flow of enemy deserters. Wuchang, across the river from Wu P'ei-fu's headquarters of Hankow, fell on 10 October, and Wu fled northwards to the temporary safety of Honan.

In comparison, the progress of the two other columns was considerably less spectacular. The easterly expedition along the coast into Fukien did not reach Foochow till 2 December. The central force, led by Chiang Kai-shek himself, moved in a northeasterly direction through the important province of Kiangsi with Shanghai as its ultimate goal. In spite of the presence of the Commander-in-Chief, the advance proceeded rather slowly, either because the resistance was more serious or because little attempt was made to win over the peasantry. Nanchang, the provincial capital, passed into Nationalist hands on 8 November, and Chiang decided to halt there for the winter.

The Wuhan Regime

The central administration had of course been left behind in Canton. The news of Mao Tse-tung's phenomenal success in rallying the peasants of Hunan had been received with mixed feelings by Ch'en Tu-hsiu and some other Communist leaders. The Russians, ever dubious of the timing of the expedition, were now terrified of alienating the bourgeoisie by agrarian reform.

But inevitably the general atmosphere of triumph was conducive to a revival of self-confidence among the Nationalist left wing in Canton, which had for months acquiesced in Chiang Kai-shek's monopoly of power.

When the Central Committee of the Kuomintang met in September, however, it became clear that Chiang's dictatorship would no longer go unresisted. The first sign of discord was seen in the argument about the removal of the government from Canton to the interior of China. The obvious choice for a new seat of authority was Hankow, the great city on the Yangtze. But Chiang bitterly opposed the idea. If the government moved anywhere, he insisted, it must be to the place where the Commander-in-Chief had his headquarters; that is to say, to Nanchang. The now dominant left wing and their Communist allies ignored the demand and deliberately went ahead with their plans for transferring to Hankow. The transference was completed by New Year's Day 1927, and three days later the Wuhan government was ushered into power by an extraordinary event. On 3 January a crowd of workers, driving out the foreign police, occupied the British concession at Hankow. The exploit was directed by Liu Shao-ch'i, who thirty years later was destined to succeed Mao Tse-tung as Head of State. This achievement was striking enough, but its sequel was even more remarkable, for shortly afterwards Britain, recognizing the practical impossibility of maintaining so invidious a privilege deep in the heart of a hostile country, agreed to relinquish her concession not only at Hankow but also at the other Yangtze port of Kiukiang, half-way down river towards Nanking. This was indeed a significant reversal of a policy which had begun with the Treaty of Nanking.

Chiang's Blow at the Communists

Chiang Kai-shek, nursing his indignation at Nanchang, was by no means the man to sit moping in his tent. The snubbing he had just received at the hands of his comrades was more than compensated for by the deference that was beginning to be paid to him in other and perhaps ultimately more useful circles. A little Court had gathered round him in his winter quarters. Leaders of the powerful secret societies, and representatives of the banking world thought it worth their while to make the journey from Shanghai in order to pay their respects to the leader at their gates. It was rumoured that they did not come empty-handed.

In Shanghai itself, the foreign Settlements were haunted by the spectre of Chinese insubordination. Every mile covered by the revolutionary armies seemed to bring nearer the day of reckoning. True, the home governments were solidly committed to upholding the interests of their nationals. Britain, for instance, had bowed to necessity at Hankow, but regarded any appeasement in Shanghai as out of the question. Reinforcements poured in from every side to swell the international garrison. But for the large numbers of Japanese, one would have said it was a crusade for Christian civilization. Such concord and unanimity had not been witnessed since the Boxer year. At the same time, it was thought only reasonable to seek allies among the natives. Chinese people of substance were flattered to find themselves honoured guests at tables to which none of their race had ever previously been admitted and where they listened in bewilderment to eulogies of their ancient and splendid culture now prey to the Bolshevik hordes.

The less privileged classes of Shanghai had been for months the special target of Communist propaganda; Chou En-lai himself was now in their midst, and the extent and timing of labour action revealed the touch of the master. The easterly Nationalist column that had been marching through Fukien entered Chekiang and on 19 February took Hangchow, a bare hundred and fifty miles away. In response, on the same day a general strike paralysed Shanghai, and an anticipatory rising took place in the Chinese City. But unaccountably the deliverance did not come. In the days which followed freshly severed heads, exhibited in the market places and thoroughfares, warned the people that the warlords were still in control of the situation. Then as the Nationalist soldiers were almost on the doorstep, the forces of labour, armed and determined, rose again. This time, they succeeded. On 22 March 1927 they were masters of the Chinese City, and a revolutionary municipal administration came into being, to welcome the liberators. Chiang Kai-shek travelled the last stage down river in the comfort of a gunboat, landing in Shanghai on 26 March.

His triumph was marred by some disquieting news. A few days earlier the Kuomintang Central Executive, assembled at Hankow, had resolved that the concentration of command in Chiang's hands should come to an end and that henceforward he should merely be one member of a committee on which left wing and Communist influence was to predominate. What was still more ominous, during the Nationalist entry into Nanking on 24 March, several foreigners had been killed and foreign naval vessels had shelled the city in retaliation. There was no doubt that the troops responsible were led by Communist officers. Was Chiang to see the patient preparation of months ruined after all?

At this juncture, an old acquaintance reappeared on the scene. Wang Ching-wei, who had withdrawn to France on Chiang's emergence as virtual dictator of the Kuomintang the year before, had been summoned back from exile by his left-wing friends in the Wuhan government. He reached Shanghai on 1 April en route for Central China. During his short visit to Shanghai he conferred with Chiang, but the meeting, predictably, was not very cordial. On the eve of his departure for Hankow he published a joint statement with Ch'en Tu-hsiu denouncing as a malicious fabrication the rumour that there was discord between the Kuomintang and the Communists. The Communists, said the statement, had never for one moment contemplated organizing the workers into making armed attacks on the foreign settlements, since this would have the disastrous effect of involving the National Revolution as a whole in a war with the imperialist powers. Nor did the Kuomintang leaders have any intention of expelling the Communists or of suppressing the workers' armed volunteers. The military authorities at Shanghai, in this as in everything else, would obey the National Government at Hankow.

Two days after Wang had left, however, the very event that he and Ch'en had been at such pains to deny took place. On 12 April 1927, a date now marked as infamous in the calendar of the People's China, Chiang Kai-shek struck the blow he had for so long been meditating. The Workers' General Union was surrounded and the volunteers disarmed, after which most of those active in the movement were shot out of hand. Gunmen belonging to the secret societies whose leaders had gone to Nanchang during the winter to pay court to Chiang raided the lodgings of known Communists and carried them off to execution, while a crowd which attempted to demonstrate outside Chiang's headquarters was dispersed with copious bloodshed. Within a few hours the revolutionary municipal administration had been disbanded. Three days later a similar coup was effected in Canton. Then, on 18

April, to render the significance of these transactions quite un-mistakable there was proclaimed the establishment of a new National Government with its seat at Nanking, another city from which in the last few days Communist influence had been purged. There were now in existence three self-styled Chinese govern-ments. The warlord regime in Peking still enjoyed international recognition. The National Government at Hankow, managed by the left-wing Kuomintang, and the Communists, controlled the provinces of Hupei, Hunan and Kwangsi. The territory subser-vient to Chiang and therefore to Nanking was more extensive, consisting of the southern half of Kiangsu together with Chekiang, Anhwei, Fukien and Kwangtung.

The Nationalist-Communist Split

The Hankow administration made a show of accepting the chal-lenge; it declared that Chiang was deprived of all his powers and ordered his arrest. But during the three months that remained to it, its morale showed increasing evidence of decline. Cut off by economic blockade from the provinces further down river as well as from the original base at Canton, Wang Ching-wei and his friends were becoming increasingly aware that certain military leaders, who had formerly intended to become pillars of a Nationalist China, were suddenly having second thoughts. The prospect of an alliance in which they would be partners of the Communists, and no doubt junior partners at that, and take up arms against their former comrades and Commander-in-Chief was a daunting one. The news from Hunan, where Mao was busily proceeding with the organization of the peasantry, had already alarmed certain officers who were joining with landowners in preventive action. Most important of all, the Christian General, who had now openly espoused the Nationalist cause and from whom great things were expected when the final drive against Peking should get under way, plainly showed that notwithstanding a recent trip to Russia he was in no mood to support Hankow unconditionally.

The leadership of the Chinese Communist Party, in so far as Ch'en Tu-hiu represented it, still followed the policy of Borodin in regarding the role of the Kuomintang as essential to the success of the present stage of the revolution. Mao Tse-tung's unseasonable advocacy of what looked like a jacquerie there and then was a source of considerable embarrassment. Stalin himself seems to have been of the opinion that the effective military forces on the revolutionary side were mercenaries depending for maintenance upon the national bourgeoisie, whom it would therefore be folly to offend at this stage. A plenary meeting of the Comintern Executive in November–December 1926 upheld the thesis that the Chinese Communists must strive to develop the Kuomintang into a real people's party by supporting the left wing while at the same time demoralizing the forces of reaction by arming the peasants. Soon afterwards the Indian Communist M. N. Roy, who had played a major part in inducing Stalin to acquiesce in this proposition, was sent to Hankow as a special delegate from the Comintern. He arrived at the beginning of April 1927, a few days before Chiang's sanguinary coup took place in Shanghai, and at once manifested his disagreement with the cautious advice of Borodin. Apparently Roy was convinced that Wang Ching-wei and his friends would cling to the Communist alliance in order to preserve their authority intact from the machinations of Chiang. In this belief, he went so far, in the middle of June, as to show Wang a confidential telegram he had just received from Moscow in which Stalin signified his general approval of Roy's attitude and recommended that the Kuomintang leadership should be galvanized by the introduction of peasant and working-class elements. This indiscretion is generally believed to have frightened Wang into breaking with the Communists. Even more impressive to Wang and his associates must have been the growth of anti-Communist sentiment among the Nationalist officers. At the end of June this reached to the seat of government itself, when the garrison commander of the Wuhan cities disarmed the volunteer brigade of the local Federation of Unions. Added to this there came news from the world outside which helped to fan suspicion of Russian motives. Two raids had recently been carried out, one by the British police against the Arcos establishment in London, the other by Chang Tso-lin on the premises of the Soviet Legation in Peking. Both exploits were alleged to have uncovered conclusive proof of Moscow's aggressive designs against China. The Peking raid, for good measure, resulted also in the arrest and execution of Li Ta-chao, the former university librarian who had guided Mao Tse-tung along the path to Marxism; today, appropriately enough, the gallows on which Li was hanged is exposed for the veneration of pilgrims.[2]

The cumulative effect of these events was to turn Wang and most of the other left-wing Kuomintang irrevocably against the Communists. True, there were one or two notable exceptions; Sun Yat-sen's widow, for instance, was vehemently opposed to any rift, and on the Communist side Borodin and Ch'en Tu-hsiu made desperate promises of loyalty to the Kuomintang leadership. But it was too late. On 15 July 1927, the Communists were expelled from the Kuomintang, the Wuhan National Government and the National Revolutionary Army and on 28 July the total separation of the two parties was proclaimed. By then, Roy, Borodin and Madame Sun were all on their way to Russia.

The Nanking Government

Relations with their former Communist allies apart, the Nationalists' achievement of the immediate goal of the revolution to overthrow the warlord regime in Peking was yet to be fulfilled. While the administration at Hankow had been engrossed in its domestic problems, Chiang Kai-shek had already resumed the march to the North. The campaign had not, it must be admitted, gone very well; there had, in fact, been something of a setback. But now, like a wise man, Chiang was able to turn the mischance to good account. It was clear that with the Communists expelled, the reunification of the Kuomintang must be given precedence over everything else. Wang Ching-wei and his colleagues, conscious of their own theoretical seniority, could not be expected to come cap in hand and plead to be admitted as Chiang's subordinates. About three weeks after the Hankow purge, a group of officers at Nanking made the first open gesture of reconciliation by sending a telegram to Wang urging the amalgamation of the two regimes. Wang, as had been foreseen, demanded Chiang's retirement as a prior condition; Chiang, on 13 August 1927, divested himself of his authority and announced in the classic terms of Confucian piety, that he was returning to his birthplace to tend his mother's grave. It was an excuse of which he was to make use on several occasions in his later career, and always with the same purpose, namely at the proper moment to reappear on the scene like a giant refreshed. This time the holiday was especially rewarding; a brief sojourn in the country to satisfy the conventions, and he was off to Japan.

There, as well as his reunion with military and political acquaintances of twenty years standing, romance was waiting for him in the person of Miss Meiling Soong, the elegant American-educated daughter of a compradore family of Shanghai. The Soong family specialized in the production of *femmes fatales*, for their middle daughter Soong Chingling had, as far back as 1914, charmed Dr Sun Yat-sen into repudiating the wife of his youth in order to be free to take her as his bride. Madame Sun it was whose leftist sympathies had just carried her from Hankow to Moscow. The eldest of the Soong girls, Eling, married Dr H. H. Kung, eminent under two heads, as a descendant of Confucius and, what was more to the purpose, as the scion of a famous house of bankers. A son, T. V. Soong, was an old friend of Chiang's from his stockjobbing days, and was now active in promoting an understanding between his future brother-in-law and the financial circles of Shanghai. Clearly such a marriage would set the seal on Chiang's bourgeois respectability, while for the Soongs it would mean an alliance with a man whom they were astute enough to recognize as the coming leader of the nation. There was, however, one obstacle in the way; Chiang already had a wife, mother of two sons. The Soongs were convinced Christians. Soong *père*, now dead, had in his humble beginnings been a colporteur of bibles, and had bitterly opposed his daughter's marriage to Sun Yat-sen. But Mrs Chiang had been discreetly pensioned off, and Chiang swore that he wanted nothing better than to be instructed in the Christian faith. Besides, Miss Soong was thirty-four and had made up her own mind to marry him. The suitor pursued her and her mother to a Japanese holiday resort, and his offer was accepted. The wedding took place in Shanghai in December 1927 and in due course the bridegroom was baptized into the Methodist Church.

While Chiang was conducting his courtship, his absence from the political stage gave the various factions of the Kuomintang an opportunity for reconciliation. Early in September 1927, the Wuhan government was amalgamated with its rival to form a new national administration at Nanking, a combination to which those conservatives who had abandoned the Party rather than accept the Communist alliance, found it possible to adhere. Yet old suspicions and antipathies could not be eradicated all at once. A military group based on the Wuhan area believed correctly that Chiang behind the scenes was scheming to retain control of the army and rose in resistance. The movement was suppressed by Nanking forces in November. Its leaders had been avowed partisans of Wang Ching-wei, who now withdrew to the more congenial climate of Canton, where he assumed the chairmanship of a regional political committee. As ill luck would have it, the following month, December 1927, saw an unsuccessful attempt to establish a Canton commune. Its suppression was a bloody affair – the episode will be described later – and Wang Ching-wei, seeing that Nanking attached some blame to him for the business, decided it was high time he was off again on his travels. Accordingly, only nine months after his return from France he set out once more for that agreeable country, which by now had become in his eyes a real home from home. On 7 January 1928 Chiang Kai-shek, called back from his honeymoon, announced in a telegram to the world at large that he had resumed supreme command of the revolutionary armies.

The Murder of Chang Tso-lin

The Northern Expedition, in abeyance for some months, was again put in motion at the beginning of April. The Nationalists were in good heart. The tide was running in their favour. Their one great antagonist, Chang Tso-lin, was already more or less conceding them the victory and was waiting in Peking only in the hope of being given lenient terms. Two powerful militarists, the Christian General and Yen Hsi-shan, satrap of the province of Shansi, were in the field as allies of Chiang, and it was not thought necessary for the revolution to stoop to bargaining. Then, suddenly collision with Japan began to threaten.

A few months earlier, while Chiang had been in Tokyo, he had profited from the occasion to pay his respects to the Japanese Prime Minister, Baron Tanaka, an army general and a vigorous advocate of a strong policy towards China. His name has become celebrated because of the so-called *Tanaka Memorial*, a document, to say the least, of the most dubious authenticity, in which he was alleged to have predicted that the conquest of China would start Japan on the road to the mastery of the world. Of course the story was ideally suited for the purposes of Chinese propaganda and full use was made of it. Tanaka felt it was vital to Japan to have a dominating influence in Manchuria and Mongolia, and there is some evidence that Chiang had offered to acknowledge Tokyo's special interests north of the Wall in return for recognition of the Nanking regime. But the problem at present lay nearer to hand, in Shantung, through which Chiang had to march on his way north. He was following the railway line from Nanking to Tientsin. Japanese troops had been sent to Shantung during the previous year to protect their countrymen's lives and property. As was generally the rule, the immediate circumstances of the clash are obscure. Nationalist troops entered the provincial capital, Tsinan, on 3 May 1928 and it is quite likely that some Japanese shops were ransacked in the general exuberance. The outrage, if it occurred, was punished handsomely, for within a few days the Japanese, though massively outnumbered, had driven the Chinese headlong out of the city. Once again an anti-Japanese boycott swept through the land. The affair detained Chiang in Shantung and though the matter was settled by diplomatic means the year afterwards, it deprived Chiang of the glory of capturing Peking in person.

It was his ally Yen Hsi-shan who marched into the old capital on 8 June 1928. The splendour of the exploit was somewhat overshadowed by an event still more spectacular. Yielding to the inevitable, Chang Tso-lin had quitted the place five days earlier for the security of his Manchurian fastness. On his way to his lair the train on which he was travelling was blown up by a mine on the outskirts of Mukden and he perished in the explosion. It was later ascertained that the business had been managed by the Japanese garrison in South Manchuria; the *Kwantung Army* as it was called, from a geographical name meaning 'East of the Pass' which described the situation of the area to the gateway in the Great Wall at Shanhaikwan. The truth was that Chang, who had grown so mighty thanks to Japanese benevolence had lately been showing a marked disposition to forget what he owed to his patrons, and with nationalism apparently triumphant in China proper it was felt that Manchuria at least must be kept safe for Tokyo. For a few days the satrapy lay vacant, while subordinate commanders canvassed eagerly for their masters' favour. Then the dispute was settled in a manner as brisk as it was unexpected. Never yet had a warlord's domain passed to an heir and in this case the eventuality was peculiarly unlikely, for the dead ruffian's eldest son, enslaved by opium and actresses, seemed to exist for the sole purpose of demonstrating how a family could pass directly from barbarism to decadence without dillydallying in any intervening stage of civilization.

In this crisis, however, Chang Hsüeh-liang revealed himself as a true son of his father. Suddenly and with no hint of warning he dispatched the claimants to join their leader in the shades. As the noise of the shooting died away there was a shocked silence, and then all Manchuria acclaimed the genius of the Young Marshal. The Japanese, as astonished as the rest, accepted the *fait accompli*. The Nationalists for their part made no attempt to penetrate through the Wall, beyond which the five-barred flag of the old warlord regime, hauled down elsewhere to make room for Nanking's 'white sun in a blue sky', continued to flutter in the northern air.

Save for Manchuria, the Nationalists could fairly claim to have accomplished their first task; China was no longer ruled by a Peking government. In token of its change of fortune the name of the city, which means 'Northern Capital', was altered to Peip'ing or 'The North Pacified', a style which it was to retain until the Communists made it the seat of the People's Government in 1949, but which for the sake of simplicity we shall ignore in this book.

On 6 July 1928 Chiang Kai-shek, at last able to leave Tsinan behind him, led his generals to the Green Cloud Temple, where after more than three years the coffin of Sun Yat-sen still awaited burial, and solemnly announced to the Father of the Nation that his most cherished wish had come to pass. In due course the august remains were transferred to a tomb worthy of their dignity in the Purple Mountain outside Nanking.

Dr Sun, it may be remembered, had taught that the revolution would begin with an armed seizure of power, to effect which a brief period of military government would be required. This seizure of power now having been achieved, it was possible to proceed to the next stage of the founder's plans, namely the Period of Tutelage, during which the affairs of the country would be handled by the Party. Accordingly, from the first week of August 1928, a plenary meeting of the Kuomintang Central Executive Committee was convened to discuss the creation of an administrative structure for this purpose. In October the necessary laws were promulgated. These provided in effect for a Party dictatorship, which, it was estimated, would last until 1935. Sun's notion of having separate Yuan or departments to exercise functions of examination and control, in addition to the legislative, executive and judicial powers, was carefully adhered to. The presidents and vice-presidents of the five Yuan so constituted, were chosen by the Party's standing committee, and formed a State Council. Chiang Kai-shek became Chairman, and, in consequence, first Head of State. This State Council together with the Party's Central Executive made up a Central Political Council which ensured the control of the government by the Party.

Chiang and his Rivals

The three years which followed the appearance of this tutelary government were, paradoxically enough, the most confused in the entire history of the Republic. Without considering the activities of the Communists in China at the time, and it must be borne in mind that already a Soviet territory was being consolidated in southern China, the defunct Peking regime, even subject to warlord manipulation, went through fewer upheavals than its successor at Nanking had to endure in its first months of life. It would be tedious even to attempt to describe the chaos in detail. But it will be readily understood that at its inception the new administration was dependent on the continued support of those military commanders who had thrown in their lot with Chiang Kai-shek. The most important of these were Li Tsung-jen and Pai Chung-hsi, warlords from the south-western province of Kwangsi, who had accompanied the Northern Expedition from its origins in 1926. Then there were the Christian General and Yen Hsi-shan, the satrap of Shansi province in the north-west, who had lent their aid in the final drive against Peking itself. All of them had been rewarded by posts and honours but their appetite for power was insatiable and it soon became clear that they were not going to acquiesce in orders from Nanking without a struggle. Besides the warlords, whose jealousy was understandable, political factions within the Kuomintang were still at variance. The principal malcontent was Wang Ching-wei, who from his exile in France continued to exert a strong influence on his old followers. He had formed a group called 'the Association for Reorganization of the Kuomintang' with the purpose of curbing Chiang's growing power. Wang and his disciples were reckoned on the left of the Party. On the right, Chiang was opposed by a section of Cantonese members, headed by Hu Han-min.

The Kwangsi generals were the first to show open signs of revolt. They had been left in control of the Wuhan area, which, like some other key districts, was administered by a political sub-council of its own. Nanking's instructions were to dissolve this council, but Li Tsung-jen and Pai Chung-hsi refused to accept the order. Issuing an anti-Chiang manifesto, they proceeded to take over the province of Hunan. In March 1929, Nanking launched a punitive expedition which in the space of a few weeks dislodged the Kwangsi men from Central China and drove them back to their home territory.

During these events the Christian General, who occupied the post of Minister of War, co-operated with Chiang Kai-shek, but very soon afterwards he too went into the wilderness, outraged by what he considered to be an intolerable affront. The foreign powers were adjusting themselves to face the new order of things in China. The United States accorded *de jure* recognition to the Nanking Government in November 1928 and Britain and France followed suit in December. Japan too decided to come to terms and after extending recognition went on in March 1929 to settle the quarrel which had been outstanding between the two countries since the clash at Tsinan the year before; Tokyo agreed to withdraw its forces from Shantung in return for a Chinese guarantee of the protection of Japanese interests. This decision raised the question of who was to undertake the garrison of the province, and the Christian General felt he had incomparably the best claim to the privilege. His disgust at the discovery that he had been passed over in favour of one of Chiang's subordinates will be readily imagined, and when in May 1929 a group of his loyal officers invited him to take command of an Army of National Salvation they had assembled in the north-west, he hurried to join them. The rising miscarried and the Christian General, now branded by Chiang as a traitor and with a warrant out for his arrest, had to wait another year before he could show what he was made of.

By that time Wang Ching-wei had returned from France and had added his voice to the clamour, while prudently keeping out of Chiang's reach in Hong Kong and elsewhere. The substance of the charge he brought against his successful rival was that Chiang was simply a tyrant of the same stamp as Wu P'ei-fu and the other enemies of the people whom the Kuomintang was pledged to exterminate. Wang himself was very probably sincere, but to a neutral observer his case was irremediably spoiled by the nature of his supporters. Among these the Kwangsi generals were at first the most considerable, but it was the warlord of Shansi, Yen Hsi-shan, who brought Wang back on the national stage. In February 1930 Yen issued a statement calling for Chiang's resignation, and in the weeks that ensued a most remarkable alliance, military and political, directed against the dictator of Nanking, began to take shape in the northern provinces. The backbone of it consisted of Yen and the Christian General, but all kinds of Kuomintang dissidents came to lend a hand, from the extreme right-wing 'Western Hills' Group down to the leftist adherents of Wang Ching-wei. Even old Tuan Ch'i-jui and his Anfu clique emerged from their obscurity, and behind these could be discerned Japan herself, for Tokyo saw a chance of providing a counter-weight to the Anglo-Saxon favourite Chiang Kai-shek. From Kwangsi, too, came messages of solidarity. A conference of the Kuomintang was convoked to meet in Peking, Wang Ching-wei travelled up from Hong Kong and in September 1930 a new National Government was proclaimed, with Wang, the Christian General, and Li Tsung-jen of Kwangsi occupying the leading posts, and Yen Hsi-shen as Chairman. The feudal rule of Chiang Kai-shek, it was declared, was to be swept utterly from the land.

Another notability had been summoned to Peking for the occasion, but he had not replied to the invitation. Chang Hsüeh-liang at the end of 1928 had defied the Japanese by putting himself and his domain of Manchuria under the Nanking government. It is said that persuasion from Washington, anxious as always to out-manoeuvre Tokyo, had counted for a great deal in this decision. Chang had of course been confirmed in his satrapy, and now the infant regime of Peking saw that its continued existence depended at the very least upon his benevolent neutrality, for his armies just over the Wall vastly outnumbered any forces Yen or the Christian general could put in the field. But Chiang Kai-shek was able to offer a more tempting reward for loyalty. If the Manchurian troops came down through the Wall and suppressed the revolt, Chang Hsüeh-liang was given to understand that he would be allowed to take back the control of North China that his father had enjoyed during the last years of his life. In such circumstances there was little room for hesitation. Less than three weeks after the birth of the new 'government', on 18 September, Chang's soldiers entered the Wall, while the armies of Nanking pressed on the rebels from the South. The coalition disintegrated almost without resistance. Yen Hsi-shan resigned and took refuge with the Japanese in Dairen; Wang found asylum once again in Hong Kong.

In theory at any rate the authority of Nanking was now undisputed from the Yangtze to the Amur. But the southern half of the country was far from pacified. There were the Communists, masters of a sizeable territory, and beyond them the Kwangsi warlords, still as active as ever and giving encouragement to fresh troublemakers, this time from the Cantonese section of the Kuomintang. The head of the last group, Hu Han-min had been, for the sake of conciliation, created an important Minister at Nanking but in spite of this was chafing at Chiang Kai-shek's ever-growing power. By March 1931, he had become such a nuisance that he was put under house-arrest. This was the signal for an exodus of his followers to their native Canton, where they were joined by other dissatisfied politicians. The political opinions of the dissidents were highly varied, but they were unanimous in their detestation of Chiang Kai-shek. In May 1931, the bewildered country was informed that yet another brand-new National Government, presided over by Wang Ching-wei, claimed the allegiance of the Chinese people. And Canton, casting round for international backing, like Peking the year before, found it most natural to turn eastwards. After all, had not Sun Yat-sen himself had dreams at one time of a Sino-Japanese alliance under the banner of Greater Asia? With this in mind, Wang Ching-wei as Dr Sun's heir sent his 'Foreign Minister' to Tokyo. The emissary received a courteous hearing, but discerned that Tokyo was moving in a direction where no self-respecting Chinese could follow, in a word towards the colonization of Manchuria. Sure enough, in the autumn of 1931 the first shots were fired of a conflict which was to lead to the Second World War, to destroy the British, French and Dutch empires in Asia, and to guarantee the victory of Communism in China. For the moment, however, the Japanese aggression silenced the quarrels within the Kuomintang and brought the angry factions together into some degree of unity.

CHAPTER XVIII

THE HEYDAY OF NATIONALIST CHINA

Japan seizes Manchuria – the Fighting at Shanghai – Manchukuo – the heyday of Nationalist China

Japan seizes Manchuria

CHANG HSÜEH-LIANG's decision, at the end of 1928, to rally to the Nationalist Government was to Tokyo both an affront in itself and a warning that from then on Manchuria, for a generation the seat of so many vital Japanese interests, was no longer administered by marionettes. One sign of the changed situation was that all matters arising between the north-eastern provinces and any foreign power, including Japan, had now to be referred to the Chinese Foreign Office at Nanking, instead of, as before, being handled on the spot at Mukden. But the most ominous development, which had indeed been going on for a long time but was lately proceeding at a greatly accelerated pace, was the influx of Chinese immigration north of the Wall. By 1930, the population of Manchuria was estimated at about twenty-nine millions, of whom no more than two hundred and fifty thousand were native Japanese, with eight hundred thousand Koreans, reckoned as Japanese subjects. The rest, apart from a hundred thousand Russians and a small number of Tungus and Mongols, were Chinese. At this rate, dreams of Japanese settlement on the land seemed to be quite futile. As for the possession of Dairen and Port Arthur, which, in addition to the South Manchurian Railway, was designed to ensure Japanese control, it was common knowledge that the Chinese were determined to divert traffic to other harbours, served by independent railway lines. What made this harder to bear was the fact that the very government at Nanking which was showing such a parade of sovereignty over Manchuria was itself torn asunder by dissension. Little wonder, then, that the Japanese armed forces were beginning to be restive. The world-wide economic crisis, which had begun in 1929, had created in their homeland conditions very favourable to the establishment of a militaristic regime with an adventurous foreign policy. Japanese intervention, in these circumstances, seemed highly predictable.

There was first of all a prelude, as encouraging as it was unexpected. Japan was not the only foreign power with special interests in Manchuria. Soviet Russia while denouncing imperialism had shown a marked disposition to profit from some rights acquired by the Tsars, notably in the matter of the Chinese Eastern Railway, which provided the shortest route to Vladivostok. Control of this railway had been reserved by Moscow in a treaty concluded with the old satrap Chang Tso-lin in 1924. It would have been inopportune for the Nationalists to denounce this transaction at the time, for they were depending on Russian help in their own revolution. But in December 1927, some months after the split between the Communists and the Kuomintang, the Russians were involved in the abortive attempt to establish a Commune in Canton, and in consequence Nanking severed diplomatic relations with the Soviet Government. At the best, Chang Hsüeh-liang's recognition of Nanking would have made the matter of the Chinese Eastern Railway extraordinarily delicate. As it was, Chang, backed up by Chiang Kai-shek and, it was rumoured, by the latter's Anglo-Saxon patrons, resolved that this Muscovite intrusion on Chinese soil must be repelled without further delay. Accordingly, on 27 May 1929, the Soviet Consulate in Harbin, and the offices of the railway were surrounded and searched by Chinese police, who alleged that the Russian organizations were centres of subversive propaganda. On 7 July it was announced that the railway had been compulsorily taken over. The declaration provoked an answer that nobody on the Chinese side had bargained for. That the Russians should copy the Chinese in severing diplomatic relations was neither here nor there, but that an armed Soviet attack should be made in November against the frontier town of Manchuli, and then against Harbin, was altogether a different matter. In December the Chinese were glad to come to terms and to acknowledge the Russian *status quo* on the railway.

Moscow was, of course, Tokyo's great enemy in Manchuria, but on this occasion the Japanese looked on with complacency at their rivals' victory, which seemed an excellent augury for their own designs. Meanwhile there was no shortage of the kind of incidents required by the makers of propaganda as material to inflame national hatreds. Two of these in particular, following each other in rapid succession, helped to set the stage for the drama proper. First came the business of the Korean settlers, who in their capacity as Japanese citizens were regarded by Tokyo, if not by themselves, as pioneers in the Mikado's service. Ill feeling between these aliens and the Chinese was inevitable, and in the province of Kirin the latter had a genuine grievance in the damage done to their fields by Korean irrigation work. There were clashes between the two communities and in July 1931 a party of gendarmes, sent to the troubled area by the Japanese consular authorities for the protection of their nationals, fired on a Chinese crowd and inflicted casualties. The excitement spread to Korea, where there were anti-Chinese riots in the main cities. Then, while emotions were at their height, it was reported that Captain Nakamura, an intelligence officer of the Kwantung Army, had been arrested by the Chinese as he made a tour of the countryside and shot out of hand. True, the captain had only himself to thank for the disaster since it appeared that he was travelling disguised as a peddler of narcotics, but even so the killing of an officer of the most arrogant corps in the Japanese Army, fanatically conscious of its imperial mission, was by any standard of judgment an enormity. Nanking hastily ordered an inquiry into the story, which was regarded in some quarters with scepticism. But before the investigation could get under way, Captain Nakamura's comrades settled accounts in their own characteristic style.

During the evening of 18 September 1931 a bomb exploded on the track of the South Manchurian Railway, just outside Mukden. Little damage was done to the line, but the Japanese forces reacted with a promptness that could not have been surpassed if they had been waiting for a signal. Few impartial observers doubted what was later proved to be the case, that the Kwantung Army had itself contrived the affair. Mukden and the other cities of South Manchuria passed at once, almost without loss of life, into Japanese hands. As it happened, the Young Marshal was away in Peking undergoing a cure for opium addiction, and no doubt his absence partially explains his subordinate's lack of resolution. But it is asserted by left-wing historians, though denied by Nationalist writers, that Chiang Kai-shek himself had sent instructions that the aggression should not be resisted for fear that the war might spread. However this may have been, it is certain that Nanking decided to place its hopes in the League of Nations. On 30 September the League Council resolved that the Japanese troops should withdraw to their original zone of garrison. But the invaders, so far from obeying, were set upon extending their control over the whole of Manchuria. From one end of China to the other there was an outcry over the government's pusillanimity. There were student demonstrations, strikes, and, of course, an intensification of the boycott of Japanese goods.

The Fighting at Shanghai

The centre of the enthusiasm was Shanghai, where there was a large Japanese population. The northern portion of the International Settlement was guarded by Japanese forces. A delicate situation was thus created, which the Japanese commanders on the spot omitted no opportunity of fostering, since they foresaw with pleasure that given any luck at all they would enjoy an equal chance of glory with their colleagues in the North. At last the inevitable happened. A Japanese Buddhist friar was killed in a brawl, and in a matter of days a Japanese flotilla, including an aircraft carrier, was at anchor off the Shanghai waterfront. Yet it did not look as if the armada would be put to use, for the Chinese Mayor, understanding that he could not expect any support from his government, promised to comply with all the Japanese demands for indemnities, apologies, punishment of the culprits, and, though this last was an impossibility, the dissolution of all anti-Japanese organizations. The Mayor's humility did not protect Shanghai from an atrocious act of vengeance. Much light may be shed on foreign attitudes towards the Chinese by a study of the circumstances leading to these reprisals.

Japanese menaces brought refugees flocking into the safety of the foreign areas, haunted by the chronic nightmare of seeing pride and privilege swept away in a flood of Chinese humanity. It was decided by the governing body of the International Settlement that the boundaries must be manned without delay. Each nation took responsibility for its own sector. An inspection of the map revealed that the defence of the northern part of the Settlement, known as Hongkew, would be made easier if a salient were established inside the neighbouring Chinese district, called Chapei. Hongkew was garrisoned by Japan, and the effect of the decision, in the words of Professor Arnold Toynbee was that

authorized by a body representing all the powers with interests at Shanghai the Japanese troops would go outside the boundaries of the International Settlement and occupy a portion of Chinese administered territory which formed part of an area that was believed to be held by a strong force of Chinese troops.

If indeed security demanded that such a measure should be taken, one might surely have expected that a warning would be given to the Chinese authorities. Yet by acknowledging this we only reveal how alien our mental processes are to the way of thinking habitual to the International Settlement. No idea of the sort entered anybody's head. The plain truth is that not a soul could be bothered to inform the Chinese of the disposition that had been made of their territory. The first the Chinese knew of the matter was when during the night of 28 January 1932 the Japanese started to force their way into Chapei. Thinking the war had begun, the defenders resisted and the fighting spread. Infuriated by this unexpected stubbornness, the Japanese commander-in-chief gave orders that Chapei was to be bombed, and within a few hours the obnoxious district was one vast bonfire.

This bombing of a crowded area, without warning, was bound to cause great loss of life and damage, and it struck terror into the hearts of the hundreds of thousands of civilians whose homes were in Chapei. It was this feature of the Japanese operations which made the most painful impression upon international public opinion. (Toynbee.)

Today the name of Chapei has been driven from our memory by later events, but the story is worth meditating upon by anyone who wishes to understand the foreign policy of the present government in Peking.[1]

Helpless in the face of the Japanese Air Force, the Chinese troops around Shanghai continued to put up a stiff resistance, rather, one imagines, to the annoyance of their government which at that moment would have given almost anything to avoid a war. The Western Powers, too, were appalled at the prospect so brutally opened to view and tried at all costs to bring about an armistice.

But the Japanese would not listen to any proposals until they had inflicted an undeniable defeat on their opponents. Nanking itself was shelled from the Yangtze, the government being driven for refuge to Loyang, deep in Central China. Then, when Tokyo judged that a lesson of adequate severity had been administered, it consented to a cease-fire at Shanghai.

Manchukuo

While attention had been diverted to the Yangtze Valley, Japan had been proceeding imperturbably with her main task, the subjugation of Manchuria. By early February 1931 Harbin fell. Of course, large areas of the countryside were hard to digest, but otherwise the task of the Japanese Army was more or less completed. A few years later the Japanese were to be confronted with the same problem south of the Wall, and Manchuria, with its secular tradition of banditry, and its great tracts of mountain and forest, offered peculiar difficulties, especially now that the brigands were reinforced by swarms of the Young Marshal's troops in flight from the invaders. By no means all of the former Manchurian army had taken to the greenwood; a sizeable part of it had transferred its allegiance and was willing to serve under Japanese officers.

The towns and lines of communication were readily controllable, and the conquerors were finding that they could persuade or terrorize Chinese of local standing into accepting the role of puppet administrators. Reputable scholars were discovered in the Japanese universities to prove from the dynastic histories that Manchuria had never, by any proper title, been Chinese territory. On the contrary for nearly three centuries China had been ruled by the Manchus, and what could be more appropriate than that the heir of that illustrious race should return to lead the land of his ancestors into glorious independence? The last Emperor of China, P'u Yi, expelled from his residence in the Forbidden City by the Christian General's *coup d'état* in 1924, had for seven years been living in the Japanese Concession at Tientsin awaiting just such an opportunity as this. On 9 March 1932 he was formally declared Chief Executive of the Republic of Manchukuo, as the new state was christened; the word *kuo* means 'country'. It was made clear at the outset that there was to be no question of any restoration of the Dragon Throne. Manchukuo was to be a modern creation entirely separate from China. But in due course it was to be transformed from a Republic into an Empire with P'u Yi as Emperor, a metamorphosis which was effected in 1934. From the start the Head of State received a good stipend and his principal adherents were given jobs to maintain them. This prospect of financial security reconciled P'u Yi to becoming an instrument of Japanese policy, for he was well aware that neither he nor anybody else in Manchuria would be able to lift a finger without the approval of the Kwantung Army. But such as it was, he played his part with fidelity until the end of the Pacific War, when the realm of Manchukuo vanished from the face of the earth.

The League of Nations could not but take cognizance of what was happening and decided to send a Commission under the chairmanship of Lord Lytton to inquire into the situation at first hand. The Commissioners seemed in no great hurry; when they at last reached Manchuria P'u Yi was comfortably installed in his seat of government, the city of Changchun, renamed Hsinking or 'New Capital'. The Commission was received with appropriate ceremony. The elaborate facade did not impose upon them so much as was hoped, and although their report, published in October 1932, was noticeably mild – it recommended a large measure of autonomy for Manchuria under Chinese sovereignty – it made it clear that the Republic of Manchukuo was purely of Japanese manufacture.

As had been anticipated, there was never any serious probability of action by the Western Powers to stop the aggression. Even Washington, whose Secretary of State, Henry L. Stimson, in January 1932 proclaimed the refusal of his government to recognize any change brought about by armed force, could not be altogether displeased to see a formidable Japanese military base being created on the Russian frontier. This sentiment was heartily endorsed in London and Paris. If only the Japanese generals would point their guns northwards for the future! But events soon took an ominous turn. The Chinese governor of Jehol whose province had been declared an integral part of Manchukuo, had, at the end of 1932, a change of heart and returned to his old loyalty. This was something the Japanese could not ignore, and in February 1933 they began to invade Jehol. The mountainous country was greatly in favour of the Chinese and Chiang Kai-shek ordered the Young Marshal to hold the province. Yet to their own astonishment the Japanese in a week or two had put the defenders to flight, and in April entered the Great Wall to threaten Peking itself. Bitter as the pill was to swallow, the Chinese, faced with complete disaster, had no choice but to seek an armistice on Japanese terms. Not only had Jehol to be abandoned; the victors insisted that an area south of the Wall no less than five thousand square miles in extent must be demilitarized. China, by acquiescing in these conditions on 31 May 1933, acknowledged Japan's special position in North China, and as good as accepted the loss of Manchuria. In Geneva, however, the remorseless continuance of aggression at last provoked a condemnation, at which in March 1933 Japan, comparing her treatment to that of Our Saviour on Mount Calvary, strode out of the League in dudgeon.

The Heyday of Nationalist China

Japan was tempted into the Manchurian adventure by the internal conflicts in China, within the Nationalist camp, as well as between the Nationalists and the Communists. In the event, the Chinese government decided that the war against the Communists must be given priority over resistance to foreign invasion. On the other hand the Japanese action brought about a certain measure of reconciliation among the Nationalist groups. In October and November 1931 a Conference for Peace and Unity was held in Shanghai. Both Nanking and Canton sent representatives. It was necessary for Chiang Kai-shek to make concessions to his opponents and he agreed to yield his post as Head of State to an elderly right-winger named Lin Sen, who from then on was President of the Republic until his death in 1943. To emphasize the new equilibrium, it was decided that power should be put in the hands of a triumvirate consisting of Hu Han-min, the leader of the Cantonese right, Wang Ching-wei and Chiang Kai-shek. From the start Hu took a back seat and the financial dependence of the regime on the bankers of Kiangsu and Chekiang provinces made the Cantonese share of authority in the Nanking Government largely nominal. The continuance and intensification of the anti-Communist struggle enhanced the importance of Chiang Kai-shek as Commander-in-Chief and weakened the influence of Wang Chang-wei, who, nevertheless, between 1932 and 1935, was head of the Executive Yuan, a position equivalent to that of Prime Minister.

And although Chiang was mostly absent from the capital to conduct operations in the field, his brothers-in-law T. V. Soong and H. H. Kung were keeping a sharp eye on Wang's activities in Nanking.

Yet in spite of everything, during these years of the early and middle 1930s, down to 1937, much was accomplished by the National Government. It was in effective control only of the Lower Yangtze Valley, but although today Nationalist China has become a synonym for corruption and ineptitude, to foreign observers at the time it was a truism that the provinces ruled by Nanking were the heart of an emerging modern state which was attracting the loyalty of more and more Chinese.

One would have expected that the essential characteristics of this new China would have been contained in the legal codes, criminal, civil and administrative, which began to be promulgated from 1928 onwards. Superficially, this legislation was a most impressive achievement; foreign lawyers, some of whom had participated in the task, were not niggardly in their praise; but a closer inspection reveals that the actual social impact of the codes in question was of the slightest. The overwhelming mass of the population, even in the territories administered directly from Nanking, continued to be regulated in day-to-day transactions by the traditional customary law, which lacked little of its former binding force throughout the peasantry in spite of the disappearance of the old Chinese state. When, as sometimes happened, the text of the codes was reflected in the conduct of a section of the public, this was due not to governmental efficacy but to the spread of modern ideas through extra-legal influence. One hears it said quite often by those who ought to know better that concubinage was 'abolished' by the Nationalist Civil Code. It was certainly the intention of the government to recognize only monogamous unions, which in any event were the rule in the overwhelming majority of cases, and adultery by either spouse gave the other partner grounds for divorce, but the best opinion maintains that concubines, if accepted by the wife, were by the Code indirectly granted rights as members of the husband's family. It is true that in sophisticated and intellectual circles old-fashioned concubinage was becoming infrequent in the twenties and thirties, but the reason for this had nothing to do with any legal policy, being simply a consequence of the westernization of those particular classes of society. Among the more conservative elements, concubinage was still common whenever financial circumstances allowed, and it was rare for a wife to resent it to the point of suing for divorce.

Today Nationalist historians looking back from their refuge in Taiwan at the achievements of that time remind us that much was done to meet the most urgent of all the country's needs, which were beyond doubt in the field of communications. As regards railways, nobody could claim that anything spectacular was accomplished, at least south of the Wall, for in this respect Manchuria formed a category of its own. The great epoch of railway construction had been the last decade of the Empire, continued here and there into the first years of the Republic. The line from Peking up to Shanhaikwan on the Wall had been finished earlier, by 1888. The train journey from Shanghai to Peking, with a break to cross the Yangtze at Nanking, could be accomplished from 1912. The Peking-Hankow line was working by 1906, and a connection onwards from Wuchang to Canton and thence to Hong Kong was in operation by 1918 except for a hiatus half-way, the linking of which in 1936 is reckoned one of the Nanking government's major feats of railway building. The same year saw the opening of a line from Hangchow, joined to Shanghai since 1914, south-westwards into the province of Kiangsi. But all told, the problem of railways was bequeathed by the Manchu Dynasty to the People's Government with comparatively few contributions from intervening regimes.

In the matter of motor roads, the Kuomintang had something to show for its efforts, and its accomplishments were all the more noteworthy for being to a large extent situated outside those provinces under the immediate control of Nanking. From Sian one road ran north-west to Lanchow and onwards into Sinkiang, while another led south into Hupei. A highway from Shensi reached Chengtu and Chungking in Szechuan. In the south-west another system of roads radiated from Kweiyang, the capital of Kweichow Province, to Yunnan, Kwangsi, Szechuan and Hunan respectively. It will be readily imagined how vital a role these various motorways played during the Sino-Japanese war of 1937–1945. In civil aviation, too, the Nanking government as early as 1930 concluded an agreement with the United States for the establishment of a Chinese National Airways Corporation with a capital of ten million dollars. Forty-five per cent of the shares were held by America, who was to supply material, pilots and instructors.

The first routes flown were between Shanghai and Hankow, Shanghai and Peking, Shanghai and Canton, and from Chungking to Chengtu. In that same year of 1930 a contract was signed with Germany for the creation of Eurasian Airways, to link Shanghai to Lanchow and Lanchow to Urumchi in Sinkiang.

In July 1931, a couple of months before the Japanese attack on Manchuria, floods in the Yangtze Valley covered an area of seventy thousand square miles and drowned more than one hundred thousand people. A government-sponsored Relief Committee employed the multitude of refugees to build dykes along the river-banks. In the space of six months from December 1931 to June 1932 altogether more than two thousand miles of dykes had been erected, from western Hupei to Yangchow in Kiangsu Province. Meanwhile, the north-west was plagued with a curse of another sort, drought, and an important irrigation project was completed in Shensi.

But what contemporaries regarded as the outstanding success of the Kuomintang regime was its reform of the currency, something which had been advocated constantly since the last days of the Empire, but never tackled seriously. In the 1930s together with the world economic crisis there had come a great outflow of silver from China because of the high price the metal fetched abroad. Various attempts by the Western Powers to organize loans through international banking consortia floundered against Japanese opposition. Finally in November 1935 the Nanking Ministry of Finance was forced to abandon the silver standard, and launch a paper currency with notes issued by three government-controlled banks. Silver was nationalized and private transactions in it, if discovered, led to confiscation and severe penalties. In May 1936, the United States agreed to buy silver in return for gold, which latter was put into a stabilization fund. In spite of the obstacles created by the amputation of Manchuria, as well as a hundred other difficulties arising from the limitations on the Nanking Government's power, the measure was for a while more successful than could have been hoped, until the memory of its early promise died away in the inflation of the 1940s.

The revolution which had brought the Nanking government to power had as one of its first objectives the abolition of the unequal treaties and the general advancement of China's international standing, and in this domain, too, the achievements of the

Kuomintang have today been largely forgotten. Down to 1927 the arch-enemies of Chinese nationalism had been Japan and Britain. It was a British police officer whose trigger-happiness led to the bloody incident at Shanghai in May 1925, and of the labour troubles which ensued the most serious were directed against Hong Kong. Even so, there were soon signs that the British government, unlike its citizens in China, was alive to the necessity of coming to terms with the situation created by the Northern Expedition. Proof of this change of heart was demonstrated by an event which, before it took place, would have seemed almost unthinkable, namely London's calm acquiescence in the Chinese seizure of the British concession at Hankow, and subsequent ratification of the transfer of authority. Nor was Washington less accommodating. The outrages against foreigners during the entry of the revolutionary forces into Nanking in March 1927 seemed for a moment likely to cause a setback, but Chiang Kai-shek's denunciation of the crimes and still more his purge of Communists were accepted as corroboration of his good faith.

One grievance of the Nationalists which the foreign powers found relatively easy to rectify was the loss of China's tariff autonomy, which the Manchu authorities had signed away in the 1840s. In 1928 a series of agreements with America and the leading countries of Europe provided that from the following year China would be free to regulate her own customs charges; Japan, too, though with rather a bad grace, let it be known that she would accept this Chinese victory. In return, the local transit duty called *likin*, which had been raised since the Taiping War more than seventy years earlier and was an irksome fetter on commerce, was abolished in 1931.

But the really stubborn problem was that of extra-territoriality. Serious breaches had been made in the system when the Central Powers were deprived of the privilege upon China's participation in the Great War, and when Russia had voluntarily abandoned it as a relic of imperialism. A number of minor states, such as Belgium, in negotiating fresh treaties had expressed a willingness to follow suit provided that the other nations agreed. But the matter aroused the most frantic opposition among those foreign communities whose size and importance compelled their home governments to pay regard to their views. The doubts of the old China hands were not without some foundation. In spite of the efforts made by Nanking to reform legal institutions, the Codes were still ineffectual over most of the country, so, although London, Washington, Paris and even Tokyo expressed a general willingness to see the change come gradually, they were less than enthusiastic about giving practical effect to the proposal, and in the event the unequal treaties had to wait until the Pacific War to be abolished.

Another irritant to national pride scarcely less odious than extra-territoriality itself was the continued existence of foreign settlements on Chinese soil, and on this matter also the Nanking government could point to some progress. Britain took the lead in conciliating Chinese sentiment, and between 1927 and 1930 handed back her concessions at Hankow, Kiukiang and Chinkiang on the Yangtze and at the seaport of Amoy in Fukien, beside her leased naval-base at Weihaiwei in Shantung. Yet even when Belgium, too, returned her concession at Tientsin in 1932 there were still thirteen foreign areas remaining, of which incomparably the most important was the International Settlement at Shanghai, with a population of forty thousand aliens and over a million Chinese. Until 1928 the latter had no say in the administration, which was in the hands of a Municipal Council elected solely by the foreign ratepayers. Of course this state of affairs made the Settlement the great target of nationalist claims, but these won the barest minimum of satisfaction. By 1930 a total of five seats on the Municipal Council were allotted to the Chinese. As in the case of extra-territoriality, the Pacific War was necessary to induce the outright rendition of the Settlement, with all other foreign concessions throughout the country, into Chinese hands.

Chiang Kai-shek's determination to postpone the reckoning with Japan until the Communist rebellion had been suppressed ensured that, as far as Nanking was concerned, the problem of Manchuria was in effect placed in the lap of the League of Nations. This passive attitude was encouraged by the Chinese tendency, itself not without some justification, to blame the country's troubles on the outside world generally and to regard it as the prime duty of the foreign powers to come to China's assistance. To be sure, the League soon revealed its impotence, but the apparent weakness of Nanking, and the flagrant nature of the Japanese aggression, coupled no doubt with guilty recollections of the Opium War and other crimes of the not too distant past, firmly established China in the eyes of the West as a martyr of international peace. During the 1930s a mythical Cathay was created by the propagandists, a country whose inhabitants were distinguished from other races of men by their profound aversion to violence. Now and then, it must have occurred to someone to wonder, civil war apart, how such a nation had contrived to extend its empire half-way across Asia, but the embarrassing question was not asked very loudly and the fiction was not exposed until the Korean campaign of twenty years later.

Nevertheless, even in the 1930s, a closer inspection of the Nanking government revealed certain disquieting features, symptoms of diseases which proved ultimately beyond cure. Even allowing for the exigencies of the time and the necessity for firm leadership, Chiang Kai-shek's autocratic desires seemed inordinate. As an instrument of his ambition he had since his headship of the Whampoa Military Academy in 1924-6 taken care to build up an élite corps of young officers devotedly loyal to his person. His agents in this task were especially the two brothers Ch'en Li-fu and Ch'en Kuo-fu, nephews of the political adventurer Ch'en Ch'i-mei whose acquaintance we have made earlier as Chiang's patron at the outset of his career. By the summer of 1927 so many adherents had been recruited to what seemed a decidedly promising cause that the *C. C. Clique*, as it became known from the name of its two organizers, was already making its presence felt. Its programme called for unconditional obedience to the orders of Chiang as Supreme Leader of the Party and the Government, and for opposition to Communism and all other ideologies incompatible with Sun Yat-sen's Three Principles. Significantly, it advocated a return to the ancient Confucian morality. The history of the past century furnished an ideal model in the person of Tseng Kuo-Fan. At the end of 1931 a *Blue Shirt Society* came into existence, of a more overtly fascist type, demanding the liquidation of all opponents of the State, the Party and the Leader and the suppression of all political groups other than the Kuomintang. The people who were attracted by the Society were not of the most delicate turn of mind, and to gain their ends were perfectly willing to employ terrorism and, should the necessity arise, murder.

Of course the doctrine of Party dictatorship, though conceived of as only temporary, was the official theory of the Nationalist Government. Those Chinese and American financiers who supported Chiang watched complacently as he assumed the part of the 'strong man', dedicated to the immediate extirpation of Communism and in the future, if his luck held, likely to thwart Japanese designs. But the appetite of Chiang and his friends was not limited to political power. Their gaze was also fixed on a great financial empire. From the beginning Chiang and the Ch'ens were familiar with the world of the Shanghai speculators. They had added to this foundation the alliances contracted through the leader's second marriage, especially the connexion, mutually beneficial, with T. V. Soong, and with the other brother-in-law H. H. Kung. These constituted the celebrated *Four Families* in whose private interests, so the Communists allege, the economy of Nationalist China was administered. Even if we discount most of what is said against them by their enemies, it seems true that in public affairs – they controlled, for instance, the banks authorized to issue the new currency of 1935 – the Four Families found a highway to great fortunes. Their virtual monopoly of large-scale industrial enterprises during the last years of Kuomintang rule were to alienate many capitalists and merchants, and to prepare the ground for the Communist victory.

Yet the picture of Nationalist China drawn in the Communist history books, a country terrorized by fascist thugs where all freedom of thought and expression was mercilessly crushed, is a grotesque caricature of the truth. Admittedly there were those at Nanking to whom such a state of affairs would not have been unwelcome, but on the whole the Party dictatorship, whatever the theory, was in practise very ineptly applied. Compared with the People's Government, the Kuomintang had not the slightest idea what totalitarianism meant. Of course, militant Communists were hunted down and every effort was made to keep the labour movement purged of disaffected elements. Yet the writer Lu Hsün, now acclaimed as a 'revolutionary', dominated the literature of the period. Lu Hsün lived and worked in Shanghai, unmolested save for minor inconveniences, some of them of his own making, until his death of illness in 1936, openly meeting such foreign visitors as George Bernard Shaw. It is superfluous to inquire what would be the fate of an anti-Communist author in Shanghai today.

It was not that the Kuomintang in general or Chiang and his followers in particular underestimated the importance of propaganda and censorship. Both weapons were employed not only as regards the press, but also in the more recently developed channels of films and the radio. Films had first been introduced to China in 1903, and ten years later, after some false starts, the Chinese film-making industry was established in Shanghai. Its early history was undistinguished but in 1925–6 it yielded to the excitement of the time and produced a number of films in support of the anti-foreign labour agitation then sweeping the country. The events of 1927 cooled the enthusiasm for this theme, and from then until 1931 the Chinese film-makers concentrated, in the phrase of one critic, on 'putting Douglas Fairbanks into Chinese dress', or in other words on the manufacture of costume romances, with little or no discernible social content. But the Japanese attack on Manchuria, which occurred a year after the appearance of Chinese talking-films, and still more the fighting at Shanghai in 1932, galvanized the studios with fresh energy. Patriotic films were the order of the day, to an extent that cannot have been pleasing to Chiang, who was anxious that anti-Japanese fervour should be kept within manageable bounds pending the destruction of the Communists. Then gradually certain producers ventured to cast a glance at the rural scene, and by 1935–7 a few films of merit showed the lives of peasants and fishermen. Before then, film stars had acquired a following of devotees among the urban populations from which audiences were formed, and in the Shanghai newspapers photographs of old-fashioned singing-girls were giving way to pictures of Miss Butterfly Woo and other reigning beauties of the screen.[2]

The experience of the cinema demonstrates, in a simpler form, the tendencies revealed in literature and the press. Censorship prevented open Communist propaganda, nor was there among the reading public at large any great appetite for it. But anti-Japanese feeling was universal and inevitably led many people to ask why Chinese should be fighting Chinese instead of combining against the foreign invader. In due course, as we shall see, this sentiment, skilfully fanned by Communist policy-makers, became irresistible. Meanwhile, a new field of literature was being exploited for political ends in the 'spoken drama', the western-style plays so-called in contrast to the traditional Chinese theatre. This form of entertainment was so alien to native taste that it was very slow in gaining general acceptance and indeed even now cannot rival, say, the Peking opera in popularity. Its first halting attempts were contrived by Chinese students in Tokyo, and in 1908 a version of *Uncle Tom's Cabin* was put on the stage in Shanghai as a novelty. From the start the movement had close links with the universities and during the ferment of 1925-7 was in the forefront of the revolutionary struggle. Between 1927 and 1931 its progress was hamstrung by Kuomintang interference, but the Japanese aggression gave it a new lease of life and in Shanghai acting groups were organized not merely among students but also among factory workers. As their performances were dedicated to the relief of refugees and similar charities, and in consideration of the public temper, the censorship, though always obnoxious, could hardly fail to be somewhat relaxed. Radio on the other hand, apart from foreign broadcasting, in the Settlements, was firmly in government hands and the Nanking station, established in 1931 and claiming to be the most powerful in the Far East, was a vehicle of Kuomintang doctrine – unheard by the great mass of the rural population and even in the towns listened to more in public places than in private homes.

But when all is said and done the spirit of that heyday of Nationalist China is expressed most perfectly by a product of a very different kind. Apart from the loss of the queue, the dress of the peasantry of both sexes had changed little since the fall of the Empire. Men of the middle and upper classes generally wore the long gown, often with the addition of leather shoes and trilby hats, though western clothes were common enough among urban businessmen and intellectuals. Government officials affected a uniform, adapted by Sun Yat-sen from the attire of Japanese students and called after him, which gives the wearer the appearance of a ticket-collector. Fashionable women, during the early Republic, had been disfigured by a succession of lumpish modes, until about the year 1926 a dressmaker of genius, needless to say in Shanghai, hit upon the idea of transforming the Manchu bannerman's robe into the 'split skirt'. This garment, in the eyes of the world the symbol *par excellence* of Chinese femininity, is therefore coeval with the Nationalist regime and, significantly, on the Mainland is now generally eschewed as out of harmony with Communist ideas. So many harsh words have been said against the poor discredited exiles in Taiwan that it is only fair to give credit where credit is due and to put on record that their days of power in one respect at least can be remembered with pleasure.

CHAPTER XIX

THE RISE OF MAO TSE-TUNG

Obscurity of Communist Party history – Chu Teh and the origins of the Chinese Red Army – Chingkangshan and the spread of Communist bases – the Party leadership and Mao Tse-tung – the Chinese Soviet Republic – the Nationalist offensives – the collapse of the Kiangsi Soviet – the Long March and the hegemony of Mao – the call for a United Front – the mutiny at Sian – a truce in the Civil War

------

The Obscurity of Communist Party History

THE last two chapters have been concerned with the origins and early progress of the Nationalist Government. It is now time to turn to the vicissitudes of the Communist Party. This story, as regards contemporary China is of even greater importance, for the years 1927–37 saw the emergence of Mao Tse-tung as leader of a Chinese soviet state. Yet while the proceedings of the Kuomintang are as a rule open to all to see, the Chinese Communists and their transactions are to a large extent shrouded in mystery. There are many reasons why this should be so. In the first place, the Communist Party itself during this period was, in the eyes of the Nationalist authorities, an illegal organization, to be stamped out ruthlessly wherever encountered. The only references that could be made in the press to the soviet areas consisted of highly coloured accounts of the atrocities of the 'red brigands' written to please the Nanking censors. To be sure, there was a certain amount of forbidden literature in circulation, principally among students, but it is true to say that most Chinese readers, even of leftist sympathies, were profoundly ignorant of the career and achievements of Mao Tse-tung and his colleagues until the publication in 1937 of *Red Star Over China*, by the American journalist

Edgar Snow, a work based on personal experience of the Communist areas and conversations with the men concerned, which the truce then existing between Nationalists and Communists permitted to be distributed in the Chinese version, and which to this day remains our chief source of information on the early life of Mao. Even so there are formidable gaps in our knowledge which may never be supplemented. Many of the Communist records were destroyed during the civil wars. In China since 1949 only a hagiographer may write of Mao Tse-tung, though if the example of Stalin is anything to go by we may be confident that sooner or later even in Peking some dirty linen will be washed in public. Indeed one or two disgruntled veterans of early days, exiled in Hong Kong and elsewhere, have already been induced to set themselves up as laundrymen in order to give the Free World its money's worth.

The expulsion of the Communists from the Wuhan Government in July 1927 marked the failure of that policy of appeasement which for some months had led Ch'en Tu-hsiu to attempt to placate the Kuomintang by curbing the revolutionary organization of the peasantry, the effectiveness of which Mao Tse-tung had demonstrated so convincingly in the countryside of his native Hunan. From now on the way seemed clear for the adoption of a root and branch programme. This, however, required fresh leadership. Borodin and his colleagues, whom an unbiased observer might have thought equally to blame with Ch'en Tu-hsiu for the fiasco, had conveniently left for Russia and had been replaced by two new agents, Besso Lominadze, a Georgian of twenty-nine, high in the confidence of his fellow-countryman Stalin, and Heinz Neumann, a Berliner of twenty-six. These men summoned an emergency meeting of Communist leaders for 7 August 1927; typically, it is not clear whether the venue was the Japanese Concession at Hankow, or further down the Yangtze at Kiukiang. A violent attack was launched against the unhappy Ch'en Tu-hsiu who was ousted from his post as General Secretary.

A temporary political committee of seven members, which included Chou En-lai and Liu Shao-ch'i, was nominated with, at its head in Ch'en's old position, the young Russian-speaking Ch'ü Ch'iu-pai, ravaged with tuberculosis but enjoying the prestige of intimate acquaintance with the great men of Moscow. It was decreed that the peasants must be armed in the cause of revolution, and preparations were made for an agrarian uprising on as large a scale as possible timed to coincide with the autumn harvest, then close at hand. The estates of the great and middling landlords were to be confiscated and redistributed. Small landlords would merely be compelled to reduce rents. Local magnates and gentry, with other counter-revolutionaries, would be liquidated and usurious debts and harsh contracts of tenancy would be annulled. Village government would be put into the hands of armed associations of peasants. Similarly, workers in the towns would be armed and given military training.

Chu Teh and the Origins of the Chinese Red Army

The conference was still by no means convinced that it was useless to look for allies among the left-wing Kuomintang, and this optimistic view had already a few days earlier encouraged some adventurous spirits to try and retrieve the situation by creating a revolutionary regime at Nanchang, the capital of Kiangsi province. The officer in charge of the policing of the city was Chu Teh, a career soldier from Yunnan who had joined the Communist Party some years before while studying in Berlin; his appointment is no doubt to be attributed to the fact that he had returned to China only in 1926 and his political views may not have been generally known. As he was concurrently head of the local military academy he had considerable influence among the garrison, and with a few other like-minded officers he seized the city during the night of 31 July 1927 and proclaimed the establishment of a Revolutionary Committee. This included several left-wing Nationalists whose names had been used without the formality of consulting them in advance. One of these was the general commanding the largest army in the neighbourhood, and he showed how little he appreciated the honour done to him by marching in at once to suppress the mutiny. On 5 August 1927, the rebels abandoned Nanchang and retreated to the South. Nothing, it seemed, could have been more futile than the exploit which had just ended so ingloriously, but in reality a new force had come into existence which was to change the face of the world. The Nanchang rising marks the birth of the Chinese Red Army.

At first, contemporary observers might have been pardoned for not being aware of the significance of the event. One section of the rebels found its way into Kwangtung Province and late in September 1927 occupied the seaport of Swatow, to be promptly driven out by Kuomintang forces. Continuing their retreat, the fugitives wintered in an area near the coast where they ostentatiously established a 'Soviet', only to be dispersed again in February of 1928. Meanwhile, an even heavier disaster had been sustained in the city of Canton. In December 1927 the Comintern agent Neumann had engineered a putsch which gained the Communists possession of the city for forty-eight hours at the cost of five thousand men, slaughtered in reprisal by the Nationalists on their victorious re-entry.

Chingkanshan and the Spread of Communist Bases

Meanwhile Mao Tse-tung had been sent back to his native Hunan with the mission of directing the 'harvest uprising' which was scheduled to occur in that province, as well as in Hupei, Kiangsi and Kwangtung. In Hunan the peasantry were already well organized. Mao succeeded in swelling their ranks with a detachment of Nationalist soldiers, as well as a substantial following of miners. It was imagined that the capture of Changsha, the provincial capital, would be a task easily within his capacity. Instead in September 1927 Mao was routed as ignominiously as were his comrades in the neighbouring provinces, and two months later he was glad to take refuge in the mountain called Chingkangshan, on the border between Hunan and Kiangsi. He was joined in this asylum in the spring of 1928 by Chu Teh together with the remnant of the force from Nanchang remaining under Chu Teh's command. From then on the destinies of these two men, Mao and Chu, were to be inseparably linked; Communist China had already found its true creators.

In those early days the combination was known as Chu-Mao, for of the two the soldier appeared to be of the most immediate importance. Clearly the movement had no future without an army, and it was equally obvious that Chu was bound to be the commander-in-chief. But the soldier, apparently from the start, recognized the superior genius of Mao Tse-tung, and was content to place his own talents, and the army he controlled, at the service of Mao's political career.

The first task of the Kuomintang after the purge of 1927 had been the completion of the Northern Expedition by the overthrow of the warlord regime in Peking. Even when this had been accomplished the National Government was almost at once menaced by the mutual intrigues of the Christian General, the Kwangsi militarists and Wang Ching-wei. This unedifying story is meaningful today only because it explains why Chiang Kai-shek, with all his determination to destroy the Communists, found it impossible to undertake any large-scale campaign against them until the end of 1930. In other words, Mao, Chu and their companions had three years of comparative respite in which to consolidate their position. And as Mao had already noticed, those very conditions which in the last few decades had favoured the growth of regional militarism, poor communications and economic self-sufficiency, were just as propitious to the establishment of local soviets. This advantage was reinforced by the topographical choice of bases; Mao was quick to profit from the lessons of history. The first refuge, Chingkangshan, was an old brigand stronghold. This was due not only to its mountainous inaccessibility but also to its situation on the border between two provinces, Hunan and Kiangsi. The authorities of either province tended to leave any nuisance for the neighbouring administration to deal with. Other suitable areas were taken over by the Communists, astride the borders between Kiangsi and Fukien, between Hunan and Hupei, and between Kiangsi and Anhwei, but they did not restrict their activities entirely to border regions. There were other localities too, whose remoteness and special conditions made them attractive. By 1930 Communist strongholds were found in eleven provinces, from Kwangtung in the South to Szechwan and Honan in the West and North respectively; of these by far the largest was in Kiangsi.

The Marxist gospel was carried to these territories by units of the Red Army, which were gradually fanning out from the headquarters in Kiangsi not merely to spread the faith but also to provide a larger area from which to forage for food. As they went they acquired recruits of the same origins as themselves, that is to say mostly from the peasantry, but with a plentiful admixture of deserters from the government forces and of ex-bandits. All were subjected to the same training in guerrilla warfare and, what was not less important, the same political indoctrination which had welded together the confused mass of defeated fugitives at Chingkangshan into an efficient body of soldiers. For, if Chu Teh was commander-in-chief, Mao Tse-tung was the political commissar whose ideas were making themselves felt throughout the length and breadth of the rural soviets. What had been urged in vain on Ch'en Tu-hsiu and the other faint-hearts was now exuberantly coming to pass. The richer landlords and moneylenders were mercilessly expropriated and often enough lynched into the bargain, while the liberated peasants were encouraged in the village assemblies to behave as the new masters and shown how to fight for their rights.

The Party Leadership and Mao Tse-tung

All this was happening in the depths of the countryside. The central direction of the Party, as was only proper, had seized the first opportunity of transferring itself to Shanghai, where it could more easily maintain contact with Russia, and at the same time breathe the atmosphere of an urban proletariat. Here the leaders listened with pleasure to the reports of what Mao was doing; so far were they from seeking to impose any restraint on his activities that they urged him to even more radical measures. Thus, while the emergency conference in August 1927 had specifically protected the smaller landlords from expropriation, a plenary meeting of the Party Central Committee in November declared that the whole landlord class without exception was to be liquidated, an injunction which Mao thought it prudent for the time being to ignore. Yet the encouragement the rural soviets derived from the approval of their superiors was much weakened by the realization that, to the master minds in Shanghai, Chingkangshan and the other border areas seemed to play a minor role in the scheme of things. Certainly the revolutionary ardour of the peasants was admirable, and Mao Tse-tung deserved the fullest credit for his percipience in unleashing it, yet when all was said and done a socialist state could not be erected on such foundations. In the last resort it was through the proletariat that victory would be achieved. The great secret was how to co-ordinate the revolution in town and country, and how to gauge the precise moment for action. One thing was clear; no blame for mistakes would attach to Moscow. The Chinese Party alone would be responsible.

Ch'en Tu-hsiu had already been taught this bitter lesson, and in no time at all his successor Ch'ü Ch'iu-pai was called upon to swallow the same medicine. Of course Ch'ü and the other Party leaders had been enthusiastically behind the disastrous attempt to establish a Canton Commune in December 1927, but not more so than Moscow or the Comintern representatives in China. It was impossible to gloss over the enormity of the failure, which was one of the main items on the agenda of the Sixth Congress of the Chinese Communist Party, held at Moscow in July 1928. Ch'ü Ch'iu-pai, who had literary inclinations, incurred a scathing rebuke from the Russians for having, as they put it, staged the Chinese Revolution as though it were a play, and was told to remain behind in Moscow for rehabilitation. The effective leadership of the Party was assumed by his colleague Li Li-san, like Mao Tse-tung a native of Hunan, but with a totally different background of revolutionary activity. In 1923, as a student in Paris, he had been inducted into a Young Communist Group, at the same time as Chou En-lai, and ever since had devoted himself exclusively to the organization of the urban proletariat. In 1925 as President of the Shanghai Labour Union he had directed the famous general strike. With experience of this kind it was easy to predict that he would intensify the policy of giving priority to town over country. It made no impression on Li that the proletariat in any rational sense of the word formed an insignificant minority of the Chinese population, and that even in Shanghai, the one city where a proletariat of any dimensions might be said to exist, control of the industrial unions, after Chiang's purge of 1927, was exercised by Kuomintang agents. Indeed the theory of the indispensability of proletarian leadership, in spite of its initial refutation by the experiences of Mao Tse-tung, has never to this day been openly abjured by the Chinese Communists. Further, the prestige lent to the Party chieftains in Shanghai by the presence of Russian advisers, and the acknowledgment of their status by Moscow, were not without an effect on Mao, who in that period of 1928–30 continued a show of subservience to higher policy.

What that policy was, however, was something of a conundrum. Following the financial panic of 1929, Moscow was convinced that the day of crisis was near; the rival imperialisms would go to war with one another, or they would unite to attack the Workers' Fatherland. In either case, the proletariat of China, like its brothers throughout the world, would arise in its wrath. But from a proper revolutionary point of view, too hasty a rising, such as that of the

Canton Commune, was every bit as reprehensible as not rising at the right moment. On the question of timing, Moscow's utterances were cryptic, to say the least. Li Li-san had sufficient contact with reality to perceive that China, unlike the industrial countries of the West, lacked a single nerve-centre from which the whole country could be controlled. He advocated that the liberation should begin with one province, or perhaps a group of provinces. Clearly Hunan and Kiangsi, thanks to Mao and his followers, offered the best opportunity, though Li Li-san was sure that the decisive part would be played by the workers of the two provincial capitals, Changsha and Nanchang, while the peasant soldiery would launch a strictly co-ordinated offensive in their support. In the summer of 1930 Mao acquiesced in the venture, no doubt against his better judgment. Neither at Nanchang nor at Changsha did the proletariat make its presence felt, but the Red Army abandoning the attempt to take Nanchang, managed on 27 July to occupy Changsha. For ten days the capital of Hunan was the seat of a Soviet Government, with Li Li-san as its chairman. Legislation was promulgated concerning land and labour. And then, on 5 August, Changsha was recaptured by nationalist units.

The Central Executive of the Chinese Communist Party was at that time anything but a band of brothers. Li Li-san's post was as eagerly coveted and intrigued for as if he had been a British Prime Minister or an American President. A group of young men just back from finishing their training in Moscow had in the past few months been especially obnoxious in their criticisms, and now after the débâcle, when stock had to be taken of the situation, the same odious upstarts made it clear they would not be satisfied until Li had been deprived of his authority. In spite of all his talk about the proletariat, they said, he had totally neglected to prepare the working class for the uprising. In November 1930, Li was expelled from the Political Committee and was packed off to Russia for a refresher course, which was destined to last until after the Pacific War. The direction of the Party, with the approval of the Comintern, passed into the hands of the 'returned students', who were even more fanatically dedicated to the proletarian thesis than Li had been. One of the old brigade, however, survived the storm; Chou En-lai, politically speaking, had a charmed life and dexterously contrived a niche for himself in the changed administration.

The Chinese Soviet Republic

The defeat at Changsha, fatal to Li Li-san, only served to reinforce Mao Tse-tung in his rural predilections. We have some reason to think that his journey to power was not accomplished without the overthrow, and indeed the physical destruction, of opponents within the Party. One thing is self-evident; if Mao had not been utterly ruthless he could never have reached where he is today. In general his ruthlessness was directed at the class enemy; but it would take a bold man to assert that the same quality was not employed on occasion against comrades who had become rivals. He was, however, lucky to have at his side one constant ally. Chu Teh's loyalty was all the more precious because of the spectacular development of the Red Army which by the beginning of 1931 contained more than three hundred thousand men. Of these only about one-tenth belonged to the first army group which was directly under Chu's control, but his influence and prestige counted heavily almost everywhere in the scattered soviet regions. The total area administered by the Communists amounted to more than three hundred counties with a total of roughly fifty million inhabitants. Already in May 1930 a preliminary meeting of representatives from these districts was held at Shanghai, but the first General Assembly was summoned to the town of Juichin in Kiangsi in November 1931, and formally announced the creation of a Chinese Soviet Republic. A Central Executive Committee of Provisional Government was chosen, with Mao Tse-tung as chairman.

Today, when we hear so much about the Two Chinas, it is useful to remember that we were confronted with the same phenomenon thirty-five years ago, though, to be sure, the new state did not find any foreign recognition. Nevertheless, it was in many respects a forerunner of the People's China and as such deserves our attention. In contradistinction to the Nanking regime, its constitution guaranteed the 'democratic dictatorship' of the proletariat and peasantry, which it vowed to extend to the whole country. Men and women over sixteen had the capacity to vote and to be elected to the Assembly, always excepting anti-revolutionaries. The scope of this exception had been enlarged, for landlords of every category, and even well-to-do peasants, were now branded as reactionaries to be expropriated. Much attention was given to the development of industrial co-operatives and, when circumstances allowed, to trade with surrounding non-soviet areas. A vigorous campaign was launched against illiteracy; it is claimed, with what degree of truth it is hard to say, that sixty per cent of the children received primary education. Finally, in spite of the complete lack of diplomatic relations, there was a People's Committee of Foreign Affairs. In this field the most remarkable accomplishment was a declaration of war against the Japanese Empire, for although no practical results ensued the gesture by itself aroused sympathy in many breasts.

The Nationalist Offensives

In November 1930, Chiang Kai-shek at last found it possible to undertake what he considered the great task of his government; the extirpation of the Communists. The assault was directed against the central 'red area' in Kiangsi, and the preliminary offensive lasted for two months, until January 1931. It was the first time that the Communists could give effect on a large scale to Mao's theory of guerrilla war:

when the enemy advances we retreat, when he retreats we advance; when he stops we harass him, when he is tired we attack him

and the effect surpassed all anticipations. The Nationalists, foiled in their first attempt to come to grips with so elusive an enemy, embarked on a second offensive, and then between July and September 1931 on a third, which was halted by the news of the Japanese invasion of Manchuria. The respite was short; in June 1932 a fourth campaign began on a wider front and with some initial victories for the government troops, who reoccupied certain outlying soviets in Hupei and elsewhere. But when it came to the main objective in Kiangsi, disaster struck again. By the end of the offensive in March 1933, three of Chiang's divisions had been destroyed with the loss of ten thousand rifles to the Communists; two divisional commanders had been taken prisoner.

Meanwhile, the position of the Party headquarters in Shanghai had become more and more precarious, thanks to the zeal of the Settlement Authorities who were co-operating with the Kuomintang in hunting down the enemies of mankind. One especially successful round-up, in the course of which a group of Communist leaders was seized by the British authorities and handed over to the Nationalists for execution, has been attributed, with what truth is uncertain, to a deliberate leakage of information by certain comrades who adopted this method of eliminating their rivals. At all events the time came, late in 1932 or early in 1933, when the Shanghai organization had to be dispersed, the Secretary going to Moscow, and his colleagues, who included Chou En-lai, taking refuge in the Kiangsi Soviet. The two years that followed form the most obscure chapter in the history of the Party. The problem is, what precisely was the relationship of Mao Tse-tung to the new arrivals? Was his local status so firmly established that his power was not diminished? Or did he out of Party loyalty defer to authority, properly constituted and stamped with the seal of Russian approval? The official Communist historians insist that the latter account is the correct one, but as they are thereby enabled to absolve Mao of any blame for the disaster which followed, it is not surprising that their testimony does not convince everybody.[1]

Before the Shanghai leaders had reached Kiangsi, or in any case before they had asserted their influence, in January 1933 the Soviet Republic called for an end to civil war and the alliance of the armed forces of the whole country to resist the Japanese aggression. In a few months such an offer was spurned. Trouble began brewing on the Nationalist side. The Nineteenth Route Army had distinguished itself in the fighting at Shanghai in the spring of 1932 to such a degree that it was whispered Chiang Kai-shek was not too well pleased; at any rate, the heroes to their disgust were soon transferred from Shanghai to garrison duty in Fukien. Here, in November 1933, they raised the banner of revolt for patriotic and anti-Japanese motives. In answer to the signal a miscellaneous collection of politicians met at the port of Foochow and proclaimed the foundation of a People's Revolutionary Government. There were some rightists among them, inspired by a personal antipathy towards Chiang Kai-shek, but the dominant group were socialists. Madame Sun Yat-sen and others whose views had led them out of the Kuomintang supported the adventure, which was believed, besides, to have the sympathy of the Kwangsi warlords and of the Christian General. A preliminary statement of policy called for a redistribution of land, the nationalization of such resources as mines and forests, the encouragement of 'national capitalists' and the unity of all revolutionary forces opposed to foreign imperialism and the Nanking regime. As a practical token of friendship, stocks of salt, in short supply in the Communist area as were arms and medical necessities, were dispatched to Kiangsi.

In October 1933, a few weeks before the uprising in Fukien, Chiang Kai-shek had launched the fifth and, as it proved, the last offensive against the Kiangsi Soviet. It was by far the largest operation of the kind yet undertaken, with a million troops and two hundred planes. As Fukien province was adjacent to Kiangsi, part of this huge force could be conveniently diverted against the Nineteenth Route Army, and as the latter numbered only fifty thousand men, the future of the Revolutionary Government at Foochow did not, from the start, seem very promising. In fact, by the end of January 1934 the rising had collapsed. It may be that the Party leadership in Kiangsi discerned the impotence of their would-be allies and that this explains the contempt with which they received their approaches as

no more than idle words and propaganda. They are simply another bunch of politicians out to trick the people. They could never overthrow the imperialists or the landed bourgeoisie. On the contrary they would be an impediment in the way to national liberation.[2]

The Collapse of the Kiangsi Soviet

This arrogance was not only out of harmony with the appeal for a united front at the beginning of 1933; it was uttered at a time when the Kiangsi Soviet itself was finally confronted with the prospect of annihilation. Chiang's fifth offensive was the strongest in manpower and had been prepared far more carefully than its predecessors. The Nationalists had at their disposal a group of German advisers headed by General Von Seeckt, who was later to command the Nazi army of occupation in Belgium. Lines of communication had been laid down and a system of blockhouses, erected at frequent intervals along the periphery of the Communist area, facilitated the maintenance of a blockade, for Von Seeckt appreciated that in the long run the mere deprivation of salt would suffice to bring the Soviet Republic down in ruins. In addition, we read in what has now become the official Chinese version of history that not content with rejecting the proffered alliance from Foochow, the refugee dogmatists from Shanghai exerted enough authority to have the tried and proved guerrilla techniques of Mao Tse-tung replaced by less cautious methods. There is probably no need for such an explanation to account for the increasing success of Chiang's well-armed and carefully organized attack. By the summer of 1934 it was plain that Kiangsi and the other Soviet areas in Central China would have to be abandoned; on 15 July it was proclaimed at Juichin, the capital, that

the Chinese Red Army of workers and peasants would march North to resist the Japanese.

In October, the main body of troops set out from Juichin on the Long March, soon to become one of the legends of the New China. The following month, Chiang's soldiers entered the Communist capital, and everywhere in the recovered territory the administrators from Nanking set about their task of restoring, as far as was possible, the confiscated estates to the former landlords or survivors of their families. Ch'ü Ch'iu-pai, who since his return from Russia had devoted himself chiefly to literary work, was in too advanced a state of tuberculosis to make the journey, and was left behind to find his way to the anonymity of Shanghai; en route he fell into Nationalist hands and was shot in June 1935. It would be hard to substantiate the rumour that he was deliberately sacrificed by Mao as a potential competitor.[3]

The Long March and the Hegemony of Mao

Under whose auspices the Long March was decided upon is unknown. The word may have come from Moscow, which maintained radio communications with the Communist capital of Juichin. There was a Soviet area in the north-west, and if a withdrawal from Kiangsi was becoming inevitable this would afford a temporary refuge in a remote part of the country, with a further escape route into Russian territory through Outer Mongolia conveniently to hand. But the interpretation of the removal as an advance against the Japanese has all the look of a Chinese idea. If indeed the Red Army could, from a northern base, come to blows with the invaders, even Chiang Kai-shek might well flinch from the scandal of making common cause with the foreign devils against his own countrymen.

The March itself at the time was recognized to be an unmitigated calamity. A well-established domain in the heart of the country was being abandoned for the most barren portion of a poverty-stricken province, merely to reach which needed a year's journey through difficult terrain, harassed nearly all the way by the pursuing enemy. In fact, of one hundred thousand Communist troops at departure less than thirty thousand arrived safely in October 1935 in the Soviet zone of North Shensi.

The route from Kiangsi led though Hunan, Kweichow, Yunnan, Sikang and Szechwan, and with detours and zigzags has been estimated to be about eight thousand miles in length. There is no room here to give details; it is enough to mention the two crises of the adventure, in the course of which Mao Tse-tung emerged as the undoubted leader, not merely of a rural soviet administration, but of the Chinese Communist Party itself.

The first of these incidents occurred in January 1935 during a halt at the town of Tsunyi in Kweichow. At a meeting of the Central Political Committee we learn that Mao Tse-tung launched a vigorous attack on the left-wing extremists, whose impracticable theories he blamed for the mistakes of the last fifteen months, namely the disuse of the guerrilla methods of war and the rejection of the alliance from Fukien. There must have been general resentment against the bright young men from Shanghai, for the denunciation was effective in driving them and their doctrines into the background.

The second crisis arose over a point of immediate importance, the destination of the journey in progress. Besides the main Kiangsi base, other Communist areas in Central China had been given up, especially that lying on the borders of Hupei, Honan and Anhwei, whose very sizeable Red Army was under Chang Kuo-t'ao, a man sufficiently important to have been appointed Vice-Chairman of the Chinese Soviet Republic in 1931. Following a separate route, Chang and his troops finally caught up with the Mao contingent in June 1935 at a rendezvous in the west of Szechwan, and it soon became clear that there was a serious divergence of opinion between the two commanders. The difficulties so far encountered had convinced Chang that it would be folly to persevere in the struggle northwards; instead, he proposed to turn towards the

West, where in the province of Sikang they might be left in peace for a while and from where they could make contact with Russia through Turkestan. No doubt some pique over Mao's ascendancy reinforced Chang in his opinion and, when his arguments had failed to move the others, provoked him into going his own way. But in a short time, finding the Sikang project unfeasible, he was glad to take his forces to rejoin Mao in Shensi, and what might have become a most damaging split in the Red Army was mended with little harm. For this result, Mao owed a debt above all to the unshakeable loyalty of Chu Teh. Chang Kuo-t'ao's personal animosity, however, was unappeased; in 1938 he was expelled from the Communist Party altogether and went over to the Kuomintang. Today he lives in Hong Kong nursing his memories.

When in October 1935 the survivors of the Long March reached Shensi, they were coming, as has been mentioned, to a region where a Soviet administration was already functioning, and this circumstance was the cause eighteen years later of the first acknowledged scandal of the People's Government. The local Communist chieftain was a man named Kao Kang, who because of the remoteness of the place had inevitably turned into what the Chinese call 'a local emperor'. With the coming of Mao and his companions, this isolated dignity was completely submerged and Kao had to be content with a subordinate, though important, role. We may guess what his feelings were, but he concealed them successfully and on the Communist triumph in 1949 he was appointed chairman of the Manchurian region. There, in his north-eastern satrapy, did old resentments and grievances, suppressed for years, come to life again? We may fairly suppose so, for in 1953 he was suddenly deprived of his authority and taken in custody to Peking to face a charge of having entertained separatist ambitions. A timely suicide was interpreted as a confession of guilt.

Even with the assurance of his newly confirmed status Mao Tse-tung can hardly have foreseen that in the space of two or three years the parched countryside over which he now ruled, and in particular the city of Yenan, to which he moved his headquarters in 1936, would become to millions a kind of Holy Land where those with resolution to make the pilgrimage could hear the gospel of Marx and Lenin from the lips of a Chinese apostle. The general opinion in the country at large was that the Communists in all likelihood would be forced within a few months to continue their flight as far as Russian territory itself. Meanwhile their retreat across China had conferred an extra advantage on the Nationalists in that the warlords of the western provinces, customarily jealous of their privileges, had been compelled to accept the help of the central government against the Red Army, and in consequence the influence of Nanking now extended to regions it had been unable to touch before. No wonder, then, Chiang Kai-shek found it richly amusing that his enemy, at that moment of all moments, should have the effrontery to offer him an alliance.

The Call for a United Front

The proposal was made in stages. The first intimation of it came in an Appeal to the Nation, issued on 1 August 1935, when Mao and his companions were still on their march, in the name of the executive of the Chinese Communist Party and the Chinese Soviet Government. This called on patriots of all parties, including the Kuomintang and even the Blue Shirts, to combine with the Communists to form a Government of National Defence. Both then and in a Communist resolution of December 1935, Chiang himself was referred to as a 'bandit' and a 'traitor'. In May 1936, however, an open telegram from the Red Army to the Military Affairs Committee of the National Government hoped that

Chiang Kai-shek and the patriotic soldiers under his command

would even at this late hour see where their true duty lay and agree to end the civil war.

From the start Russia approved of the venture, and as it coincided very happily with the Kremlin's attempt to counterbalance Nazi Germany and Japan by the encouragement of 'national fronts', especially in France and China, and as the Japanese attack in Manchuria had led Moscow and Nanking to re-establish diplomatic relations, some people have surmised that the idea may have originated from the Comintern, which already in August 1935 had been able to resume radio communication with Mao's headquarters. Yet the evidence suggests that the Chinese Communists themselves were responsible for the initiative; this in itself would be a striking example of Mao's ascendancy in the Party councils, for the young leftists from Shanghai would have cried horror on any bargain with the Kuomintang, still more with Chiang in person.[4]

No matter whose plan it was, the acknowledgment of Chiang's importance as the leader of a National Front came from a shrewd assessment of the realities of the situation. In spite of the widespread resentment over the perpetual concessions to Japan and the unpopularity of the civil war, Chiang's prestige had oddly enough shown no sign of flagging. He had somehow established himself as the symbol of a revitalized modern China gradually rising to confront the Japanese enemy. The public seemed willing to distinguish between his personality as leader and the deplorable, not to say treasonable, activities of some of his colleagues. The fact was that after the humiliation in North China in 1933, when as we have seen an area south of the Great Wall had had to be demilitarized at Japanese direction, a number of people in government circles were asking themselves whether after all it might not be in China's best interests, seeing that no effective help had been forthcoming from the West, to abandon a futile resistance and submit to the necessity of becoming a junior partner of Japan. Although the invasion of Manchuria had obliged Wang Ching-wei temporarily to discontinue his overtures to Tokyo, he had by no means lost hope of finding in Japan sponsors to outweigh the Anglo-Saxon patrons of his rival. His pro-Japanese tendencies were so well known that he was given the major share of the blame for the policy of surrender. One patriot tried to murder him at Nanking in November 1935, inflicting injuries which forced Wang to convalesce in Europe for more than a year, and from the remote consequences of which he died in 1944.[5]

Some others of Chiang's personal adherents were believed to have been seduced by Japanese propaganda. These included the Minister of War, Ho Ying-ch'in and certain members of the C.C. Clique. Chiang's brother-in-law, the Finance Minister T. V. Soong, remained firmly committed to his Anglo-Saxon patrons, but even he and his associates were convinced of the necessity of appeasement. Tokyo began to pin its hopes on a genuine Sino-Japanese entente, in which Nanking would abandon once and for all any irredentist hankerings after Manchuria. But the Japanese best acquainted with the realities of the Chinese situation, in particular the high command of the Kwantung Army, had no such illusions. Chiang himself and the central kernel of the Nanking government were, they said, merely biding their time. Tokyo ought to support anti-Chiang factions such as the Kwangsi militarists and above all to wrest North China completely out of Nanking's hands.

In 1935, this drastic school of thought carried the day. In May of that year the Japanese alleged that Nanking had infringed the agreement of 1933 by supplying assistance to Chinese guerrillas in the demilitarized zone south of the Great Wall. They demanded that the Kuomintang party organization should be withdrawn from Hopei Province, including the cities of Peking and Tientsin, that military forces of the Central Government should quit the province, and that the provincial governor, together with the mayors of Peking and Tientsin, should be transferred. Once again, Nanking swallowed its pride and in June Ho Ying-ch'in met the commander of the Japanese garrison at Tientsin and concluded the so-called *Ho-Umezu Agreement* on these terms. In the same month, similar concessions were made regarding the neighbouring province of Chahar. But the Japanese appetite came with eating. In November 1935, with almost unbelievable impudence, a new political entity was ushered into the world, the *East Hopei Anti-Communist Autonomous Government*, staffed by renegade Chinese, and ruling a population of seven million souls, entirely in the Japanese interest. The 'capital' of this peculiar regime was the city of Tungchow, a bare twelve miles to the east of Peking, and as the domain reached to the seacoast it afforded a splendid base for all kinds of smuggling. In particular, heroin was conveyed from there throughout the cities of North China. Nobody living in Peking at the time will easily forget the ravages of this terrible traffic, carried on with impunity by the Korean jackals who followed in the wake of the Japanese army.

It does not need a strong imagination to picture the effect of these transactions on the Chinese public, especially on the students and the intellectuals. Yet in spite of all the uproar, Chiang remained imperturbable. His own views had been confirmed by his German military advisers; armed resistance to Japan was out of the question for years to come, whereas the Communists could be defeated, indeed quite clearly were being defeated, there and then. It is hard for a foreign spectator not to feel a certain admiration at the firmness with which Chiang maintained his stand, though one cannot help wondering if his speeches had to be phrased in the way they were. For instance, at a plenary conference of

Kuomintang representatives in November 1935, at which it was resolved that

positive action would be taken to prepare the armed forces for the duty of mopping up the remnants of the Red bandits,

Chiang declared that, as regards Japan,

so long as hope of peace is not altogether lost, we shall never abandon peace. We are determined to make even the ultimate sacrifice in our efforts for peace.

To show these were not idle words, anti-Japanese demonstrations were everywhere sternly suppressed.

The Mutiny at Sian

But if the opinion of students and civilians was not worth taking into consideration, soldiers fell into another category. Towards the end of 1936 Chiang became more and more aware that the very troops on whom he was depending for the final campaign against the Communists were themselves heavily infected with the anti-Japanese virus. In their case the reason was self-evident. A large proportion of them consisted of the Manchurian battalions of Chang Hsüeh-liang. They had been driven across the Great Wall by the invaders, and then been prudently transferred even further south by Chiang Kai-shek, in order to remove them from the temptation of committing a breach of the peace to which the proximity of their hated enemy would expose them. They were now stationed with their Young Marshal at their head, at the ancient city of Sian in Shensi, and consequently in the front line against the Communists. Their lack of relish for the task assigned to them was plain from their half-hearted performance in the field; it was reported that they had in places reached a tacit armistice with their opponents. Chiang Kai-shek therefore went to Sian in person, confident that the awe of his presence would cow them into obedience. He was soon undeceived; on 12 December 1936 the troops revolted, and Chiang and his staff found themselves prisoners.

There are few events in modern history so important as this famous mutiny. The war between China and Japan, the destruction of the British, French and Dutch empires in South-east Asia, even, if we remember that America came into the western conflict only when Hitler declared war on her after Pearl Harbour, the liberation of Europe from the Nazis, all of these we owe in some measure to the transactions of those December days in Sian. Yet much of what happened is still obscure. At first it was generally assumed that Chiang would be put to death out of hand; and it is very likely that such would have been his fate if it had not been for the intercession of the Communists, for at the news of what had happened Chou En-lai hurried to Sian to lend his counsel to the mutineers. He convinced them of Chiang's potential value as a figurehead. Even so, the Generalissimo's survival was touch and go for a few days. Certain of his colleagues at Nanking, Ho Ying-ch'in being prominent among them, demanded a military expedition against Sian and proclaimed their intention of bombing the rebels into allegiance. Whatever its motive, any action of the kind would inevitably have been lethal for Chiang, but fortunately more moderate advice prevailed. Meanwhile Chiang listened to the demands of his captors; these were, in brief, that the civil war should be stopped, and political prisoners released, that patriotic movements should be tolerated, and freedom of political association granted. No formal treaty was made, but when Chiang was set at liberty on Christmas Day it was known that he had in principle agreed to the terms. It was a double triumph for the Communists; not only had the civil war come to an end, but Chiang had been preserved to play a role which only he could sustain. The wave of hysterical enthusiasm that swept across the country at the word that the Generalissimo was safe and sound must have reassured Mao and his friends that they had been right in their assessment of his value. It showed too, and the point is worth remembering to Chiang's credit, that the Chinese people, infuriated as they so often were by his policy of appeasement, knew, as the Japanese military knew, that he had endured the unendurable solely in the desperate hope of buying time, until a modernized, united, non-Communist China could emerge to take her proper place among the nations.

A Truce in the Civil War

In February 1937 the Kuomintang in a plenary conference voted to approve the truce and the formation of a national front. On their part the Communists, only too eager to clinch the bargain, cheerfully acknowledged the supremacy of the National Government and restyled their own soviet regime as the regional administration of the 'Special Areas'. Similarly the Red Army became part of the national forces under the Military Commission at Nanking. In the so-called 'Special Areas' themselves, the confiscation of landlords' estates was to cease, and the doctrine of the class war was to be replaced by propaganda in favour of national solidarity. A few buoyant Kuomintang members pretended to see the whole business as a great surrender by the Communists. In fact, as Mao Tse-tung well understood, the eventuality most dreaded by Chiang Kai-shek, a full-scale war with Japan long before China was in a condition to fight it, had now become to all intents and purposes inevitable: at long last the Communists would have the chance they had been waiting for.

But the Young Marshal, unaware of what he had contrived, knew only that honour demanded he must atone for his insubordination. He went to Nanking and surrendered for punishment, little imagining what lay in store for him. His quixotic punctiliousness was rewarded by no less than twenty-seven years of confinement, the latter part of it in Formosa, where in 1963 he celebrated his release on parole by marrying in a Christian church the faithful concubine who shared his captivity. Chiang Kai-shek has some admirable qualities, but magnanimity is not one of them.

CHAPTER XX

THE SINO-JAPANESE WAR AND THE RUIN OF THE KUOMINTANG

Japan strikes – the defection of Wang Ching-wei – the breakdown of the Nationalist-Communist alliance – international relations – the Pacific War – Western disillusionment with Chiang – the gospel from Yenan – China among the Allies – the 'liberated areas' – the Japanese surrender – the Civil War resumes – the Communist triumph

Japan Strikes

THE prospect of national solidarity which began to appear in the spring and early summer of 1937 was welcomed rapturously by those sections of the Chinese people who had an understanding of public affairs. It would be a mistake, however, to suppose that the talk of a united front implied any willingness in the country at large to undertake a war in the foreseeable future for the purpose of liberating Manchuria. That sooner or later a regenerated China would recover her north-eastern provinces was an article of faith. For the time being the utmost that was expected was that a halt would be called to the insidious erosion of North China. It was also hoped that perhaps Tokyo might be induced to abandon its unsavoury puppet-show of the East Hopei Autonomous Regime. To be sure, if the Japanese persisted in enlarging the scope of their aggression, then China would resist, but this was a possibility that one did not care to contemplate. The students, who were most vocal in their demands for firmness, had not the faintest notion what the consequences of resistance would be.

It is sometimes remarked that the dates of great Chinese events have a happy knack of being easily remembered. As the *Double Tenth* (10 October 1911) saw the dawn of the Republic, so the *Double Seventh* (7 July 1937) ushered in the Second World War.

The opening shots were fired on that day at Marco Polo Bridge, a few miles outside Peking. The circumstances of the incident are obscure, but it was in itself a trifling affair and although it was undoubtedly due in the first place to the provocative manoeuvres of Japanese troops in the area, the Chinese authorities both on the spot and in Nanking desired nothing better than that the dispute should be settled peacefully. Negotiations dragged on until the end of July when the Japanese launched an attack in force and compelled the Chinese to withdraw from Peking and Tientsin which then, except for the foreign concessions in the latter city, fell altogether into the hands of the invaders.

It is an open question whether, if the Japanese had been content with the local victory, Chiang might not, in spite of what had passed at Sian and afterwards, have found it possible to acquiesce. At any rate he might have tried to do so. In fact the problem never arose, for it was clear at once that Tokyo contemplated no less than the occupation of the whole of North China as far as the Yellow River. This was, of course, something which even the most determined appeaser could not accept. To remove all doubts, the Japanese repeated the example of 1932. In the middle of August they attacked Shanghai with the obvious intention of forcing the Nanking Government to its knees. The war so long dreaded by Chiang Kai-shek had begun.

It was to last for eight years, and may be conveniently divided into three periods. The first, down to October 1938, was taken up with the military invasion and the establishment of the basic geographical pattern of Japanese occupation. In the second, ending with the attack on Pearl Harbour in December 1941, political activity overshadowed the fighting. During the final period China was to become one of the theatres of the Pacific War.

From the start the enormous superiority of the Japanese in equipment and training was crushingly evident, particularly on the northern front. It took the invaders only a little over three months to reach Taiyuan in Shansi. At Shanghai, as had been the case five years earlier, an unexpectedly stiff opposition was encountered, and it was not till early in November that the defenders began to retreat, having inflicted heavy casualties. The next objective of the Japanese was Nanking, but this was no longer the seat of authority, for already in October the government had moved fifteen hundred miles inland to Chungking, a port on the

Yangtze in the province of Szechwan. Some departments, however, remained nearer to the scene of operations in Hankow, which was the Chinese headquarters for the next twelve months.

The invaders entered Nanking on 13 December 1937, and proceeded to signalize their triumph by an orgy of rape and murder. As the memory of this beastliness has, with good cause, befouled the honour of Japan ever since, it is only fair in mentioning it to recall another horrible business which had taken place a few months earlier. At the end of July, wild rumours of Chinese victories, created, it is said, by over-confident broadcasts from Nanking, swept across the countryside of North China. We have seen that the Japanese had erected an East Hopei Autonomous Regime just outside Peking; they had moreover recruited a miscellaneous rabble from the dregs of the Chinese population into a puppet 'army'. These cut-throats, in a panic at the thought of what would happen to collaborators, made a desperate bid to redeem themselves by revolting at the 'capital' of Tungchow and slaughtering as many Japanese as they could lay their hands on. Women and children were put to death with an atrocity rivalling the best efforts of the Boxers. Moreover the outrages perpetrated in reprisal by the Japanese at Nanking were no worse than those carried out in North China by the soldiers of western nations in 1900. This is not said by way of excuse. The massacre at Tungchow, like those of the Boxers, was provoked by foreign aggression, and the victims had forced their presence on a people who did not want them; at Tungchow, the criminals had in the first instance been employed for the express purpose of terrorizing their fellow Chinese. And the reprisals, both at Nanking and in the North in 1900, far exceeded the original misdeeds. The most that can be argued is that it would be unjust on the facts to impute to the Japanese nation a unique talent for savagery.

After the event, one may be inclined to think that the Japanese made a serious error in not pressing home their advantage and driving on immediately from Nanking towards Hankow. Instead, they decided to consolidate their position by linking their armies. To do this they began simultaneously to move from north and south along the railway which connects Tientsin with Pukow on the north bank of the Yangtze opposite Nanking. Their goal was the important junction of Hsuchow, from which another railway ran across the country from east to west and intersected the

Peking-Hankow line. At first all went well; they crossed the Yellow River in December 1937 and seized Tsinan, the capital of Shantung. Further south, however, they over-reached themselves and in March 1938 suffered a heavy defeat at Taierchuang, a place too unimportant to find admission to the geography books but deserving mention as the scene of the greatest nationalist victory of the war. Although the success merely gained the Chinese a brief respite, for the enemy, bringing up reinforcements, reached their goal at Hsuchow in March, it stiffened the morale of the nationalist troops. By the end of October 1938 when the Wuhan cities had to be abandoned, the defenders had withdrawn in good order into the mountains guarding the approaches to Szechuan. A few days earlier, a new front had been opened in the south. So far, the Japanese had hesitated to disturb the neighbourhood of Hong Kong, but after pondering the lesson of the Munich Conference in September, they landed on the coast of Kwangtung and on 21 October 1938 marched into Canton.

The shape of 'occupied China' could now be discerned. The deepest penetration inland was north of the Yellow River, where the invaders had pushed some distance westwards of Taiyuan. From Chengchow to Hankow their westward limit did not extend much further than the line of the Peking-Hankow railway. The Yangtze itself was controlled from both banks from the Wuhan area to the sea. Across the Yangtze, the Japanese held the northern end of the Wuchang-Canton railway as far as the north of Hunan, and their occupation of Canton ensured that the line could not be used for the carriage of materials from Hong Kong and abroad.

It will be seen that the occupation was much denser north of the Yangtze where it had been facilitated by the existence of two north-to-south railways and several east-to-west branch lines. This meant that most cities of importance, as well as lines of communication, were in Japanese hands. South of the Yangtze it was not until the last year of the war that the Japanese held the length of the Wuchang-Canton line and sealed off the south-eastern provinces. Even north of the Yangtze, large areas between the cities and main routes of communication never saw Japanese soldiers. In some of these regions the writ of the Central Government was still enforced by nationalist troops, but in others Communist-controlled guerrillas were already setting up bases in their old manner. But for the time being this did not unduly worry Chiang

Kai-shek; in fact, relations between Nationalists and Communists were still relatively cordial. Immediately after the outbreak of hostilities the Communists had taken steps to carry out their promises. Their political and military institutions were placed under the control of the Nationalist Government, and although the subordination was entirely theoretical there was no doubt that their policies, especially concerning the expropriation of landlords, had been drastically reshaped so as not to offend bourgeois susceptibilities.

Meanwhile, Chiang Kai-shek's own status had been considerably enhanced by the national emergency. Apart from his role as Commander-in-Chief, which had naturally become vastly more important, his pre-eminence in the Kuomintang was in the spring of 1938 formally recognized by his appointment to the specially created post of Leader, which he has held ever since. Another political innovation was the summoning in July 1938 of a People's Political Council; its members (numbering two hundred in the beginning and three hundred and sixty-two in the Council's last session in 1947-8) although in great majority belonging to the Kuomintang included people from other parties, and for the first three years or so Communists too. The presence of these last, in a body designed to advise the government on policy, was yet another sign of fraternal warmth.

Over and above the domestic entente, the government had nothing to complain of from International Communism either. In August 1937 China had signed a treaty of non-aggression with Russia. Moscow was alarmed at the German-Japanese Anti-Comintern Pact concluded in 1936 and was now furnishing far more abundant assistance in war materials than any other nation. Indirectly, too, Russia helped China by keeping a massive Japanese army tied down in Manchuria; there were Russo-Japanese frontier clashes on a considerable scale both in 1938 and 1939.

The Defection of Wang Ching-wei

Very soon after the outbreak of the war, the Japanese government had been sounding out Chiang's readiness to come to terms. The first explorations had been conducted through the German Embassies in the two countries, but had proved so unfruitful that in January 1938 Prince Konoye, the Japanese Prime Minister, had declared loftily that he would no longer treat with the Chiang regime. In the summer of the same year, Germany was persuaded, rather belatedly, one may judge, to withdraw the military mission which had rendered Chiang Kai-shek such outstanding service. Then on 3 November 1938, immediately after the capture of Canton and Hankow, Prince Konoye proclaimed the creation of a 'New Order in East Asia' which envisaged the emergence of a political and economic bloc, formed for a start by Japan, Manchuria and China, under the leadership of the first and dedicated to the exclusion of Communism from the area. So long as the Chinese government persisted in its co-operation with the Communists, the war against it would be maintained. If, however, it had a change of heart, and would, besides, reconstruct itself in the matter of personnel, then it could be received into the Grand Alliance.

There were of course some people in Chungking in whose hearts the message aroused a response. The loss of territory during the last fifteen months had, after all, been enormous. Nor did the international situation show any sign of turning to China's advantage. The League of Nations was impotent. The United States rejected the idea of a New Order and granted China a credit of twenty-five million dollars. Britain lent nearly half a million pounds for the acquisition of trucks to transport supplies along the freshly opened Burma Road to Yunnan. But the Munich agreement certainly did not encourage undue confidence in the resolution of the western democracies to support their friends.

The man who listened most eagerly to Prince Konoye's words was, as may well be imagined, Wang Ching-wei, who had returned from Europe at the beginning of 1937 and resumed his uneasy deputyship to his more forceful rival. At last he made up his mind and on 21 December 1938 fled to Hanoi in what was then French Indo-China. A week later he revealed his defection to the world by the time-honoured means of an open telegram, in which he urged Chiang Kai-shek to cease resistance to Japan. As was to be expected, the appeal was treated with contempt. The French amenities of Hanoi were all the more welcome in contrast to the rigours of China at war, and Wang continued his stay there for the next three months. During this period, although he met representatives from Tokyo, it seems likely that his plan was to retire once again to France and wait there in comfort until Chiang Kai-shek was ruined by inevitable defeat and he himself could return to guide his countrymen into the New Order. Then on 21 March 1939 a group of Chungking agents broke into his house and tried to shoot him. They killed instead an old friend who was his confidential secretary. The shock of this outrage drove Wang to take the irrevocable step of putting himself under Japanese protection. He left for Shanghai.[1]

From the first months of the war, Japan had recognized the necessity of ruling the occupied areas by means of Chinese puppets. In December 1937 a Peking Provisional Government was established to administer the northern provinces, and in March 1938 a *Reformed Government of the Chinese Republic* came into being at Nanking to play a similar role in the Yangtze Valley. This arrangement was unsatisfactory in a number of ways. First of all, and what was the most serious, hardly any Chinese of standing could be found to participate, and the Japanese had to fall back upon derelict politicians who, especially in the Peking group, had been pensioners of Tokyo for years. Desperate attempts were made, for instance, to recruit the veteran warlord Wu P'ei-fu, who was living in retirement at Peking, but he turned a deaf ear to all suggestions. Then again, although it is easy to see why the existence of separate military commands in Northern and Central China should have led to the creation of two local regimes, the spectacle was not reassuring, even when in September 1938 a liaison committee was set up between the rival marionettes.

In these circumstances the advent of Wang Ching-wei was nothing short of a godsend. To have any semblance of authenticity, a Chinese government, it was felt, needed some kind of spiritual descent from Sun Yat-sen, and who better qualified than Wang Ching-wei, the beloved disciple and political heir of the Great Father of the Nation, to confer this stamp of respectability? Besides, Wang would bring with him a train of followers who included some of the most capable men in Chinese public life. Yet precisely because of his origins and background Wang could not be managed so unceremoniously as the poor renegades already to hand, and much time was consumed in deliberation until in March 1940 Wang Ching-wei announced to the shades of Sun Yat-sen that the National Government of China had returned to its rightful capital of Nanking, leaving behind in Chungking Chiang Kai-shek and his bunch of defectors. This fiction was maintained with the utmost care, and the collaborating regime was in structure the twin of the resisting one. Yet even then, Tokyo still cast longing glances towards Chungking and did not extend formal recognition to the Wang government till November 1940. Soon afterwards the example was followed by Germany and Italy, as well as by such Axis sympathizers as Spain.

A treaty concluded at the same time between Nanking and Tokyo interpreted the war as a rebellion by Chiang Kai-shek and his partisans which Japan was helping the lawful Chinese authorities to suppress. Japanese troops would be withdrawn from China within two years after peace had been restored, except for certain areas of North China where the exigencies of joint defence against Communism required their presence. Wang acknowledged the independence of Manchuria and the autonomous administration Japan had by this time established in Inner Mongolia, but, with these exceptions, claimed jurisdiction over all China; he had, however, reluctantly, we may be sure, to acquiesce in effective Japanese military control in any matters of importance so long as the war lasted. Yet for all that, and in spite of the odium which both Chiang and the Communists attached to his name, it cannot fairly be said that Wang Ching-wei was hated by the mass of the people in occupied China. On the contrary, to a large extent he and his followers were looked upon as benefactors who stood between the conquered population and the alien soldiery and were able in a hundred ways to make life more endurable for their fellow countrymen. In Wang's favour, too, were his great personal amiability and sweetness of manner, in contrast with the forbidding ruthlessness and aridity of Chiang Kai-shek. But no lack of charm could obscure the fact that Chiang was continuing to fight the Japanese, and this alone was sufficient to ensure that in the eyes of his countrymen behind the Japanese lines the Generalissimo would appear as a national hero. It should be noted that until the outbreak of the Pacific War in December 1941 the foreign settlements in the coastal ports, especially at Shanghai, were controlled for the most part by countries who continued to recognize the Chungking regime and although the settlement authorities, in order to avoid provoking the Japanese unduly, exercised a measure of censorship, they permitted the publication of journals favourable to the cause of resistance.

A visitor to wartime China was soon struck by one or two

anomalous features of the situation. Until the very end of the conflict the Chinese post office was able to maintain its services between the free and the occupied parts of the country, and mail sent from Chungking reached Shanghai about a month later. Travellers came and went between the two areas with little difficulty, taking care to choose routes which gave the battle-zones a miss. A fair quantity of Japanese manufactured goods seeped into the western provinces.

The Breakdown of the Nationalist-Communist Alliance

The defection of Wang Ching-wei, which we can see today as having inflicted a mortal wound upon Nationalist China, from Chiang's point of view at the time appeared by no means an unmixed evil. More disquieting was the steady deterioration of the Communist-Nationalist alliance which began to be visible during the second period of the war. We have already noticed that large areas of what was theoretically 'occupied' country remained in Chinese hands. It was to be expected that such districts would soon become centres of guerrilla activity, and the guerrillas were in a great majority Communist partisans. By the end of 1940, such 'resistance bases' were found across the whole of occupied China, from Hopei in the North to Hainan Island in the South. In the first days of the war the Nationalists seemed to watch this development with equanimity. They approved of the incorporation of the residual Communist forces in Central China, left behind from the Long March, into what was styled the New Fourth Army. So extensive were the guerrilla territories in North China that early in 1939 a so-called Shansi-Chahar-Hopei Border Government was established to administer them, and in spite of its being heavily under Communist domination the regime, the first of several 'border governments', was officially blessed by Chungking. Yet alarm and jealousy were not long in making their presence felt, and before the year 1939 was out, clashes between Nationalist and Communist troops had been reported from the North. There were rumours of what later was to assume the dimensions of an international scandal, namely that Nationalist troops were being diverted from the duty of fighting the Japanese to institute a blockade of the main Communist areas in the North-west. It was left to the New Fourth Army to bring the feud fully into the light of day.

In January 1941 that Communist force, which had been stationed in the southern part of Anhwei Province, was attacked and dispersed by a Nationalist general, whether to prevent it from enlarging its sphere of influence in the Lower Yangtze Valley or simply as a penalty for its disregard of Chungking's orders is uncertain. Casualties were heavy and as the decree of the New Fourth Army's disbandment was published in Chungking the affair made a great stir. From then on the Communists started to boycott the meetings of the People's Political Council, and one would be justified in saying that the united front had in fact come to an end.

At the same time, the war with Japan was going badly. In the field, an enemy advance towards Changsha, the capital of Hunan, was twice frustrated, but in the air the overwhelming superiority of the Japanese enabled them to bomb the main cities of Free China almost at will. From May 1939 Chungking was subjected to massive raids which for a while, until even greater horrors were perpetrated elsewhere, shocked the conscience of the world.

International Relations

In the midst of these difficulties, Chiang Kai-shek was sustained by one belief. He was convinced that sooner or later the struggle in which he was engaged would become a part of a wider conflict, in fact of a Pacific, not to speak of a World, War, when Japan would be crushed by the irresistible might of America, and China would emerge on the winning side. Seen in this way, even Japanese successes could be recognized as merely stepping-stones towards the grand *dénouement*. Thus when in February 1939 the Japanese invaded the island of Hainan, off the southern coast, 'this', said Chiang to some of his intimates, 'is the 18 September (the day in 1931 when the Japanese began their attack on Manchuria) of the Pacific War'. Many of his followers found it impossible to share his optimism. To them it was in the order of nature that America should be far more interested in Europe than in China, and when Washington in 1940 turned a deaf ear to the French appeal for help, these people asked one another what had they themselves to look for in the face of such determined neutrality. The events of 1940 had other consequences too. In June, following the armistice with Germany, the Vichy Government debarred material for China from using the route through Indo-China, and later went still further and permitted Japan to station troops in Indo-Chinese airfields for raids against Chinese territory. As for Britain, not long since so proud and overbearing in the Far East, her conduct was hardly more glorious. In April 1939 a Chinese collaborator was murdered in the British Concession at Tientsin and the Japanese demanded that the alleged assassins, all Chinese subjects, should be handed over for trial to their local military authorities. This the British declined to do, on the grounds that the men, whom they had taken into custody, should be tried by a court of what London recognized as the legal government of China, that is to say of the Chungking regime. The Japanese thereupon sealed off the Concession and obliged all British sub-jects entering and leaving it to undergo a most humiliating search of their persons. The British Ambassador to China made a point of visiting the accused men in their cells and telling them to be of good heart, for His Majesty's Government would never yield to such blackmail. Yet as the months passed, and the news from Europe grew worse, other counsels prevailed. The British Ambassador in Tokyo held talks with the Japanese government and in June 1940 succeeded in achieving what neutral observers did not hesitate to call 'a Far Eastern Munich'. As the first fruits of this agreement, the prisoners were escorted by British soldiers to the boundary of the Concession and there solemnly handed over to a fate from which it is probably wiser to avert the attention. What was less spectacular but to the Japanese of more solid im-portance, the banks in the Concession accepted the currency of the local puppet regime for purposes of foreign exchange. For good measure, British subjects in occupied China were enjoined to do nothing prejudicial to Japanese interests. Then, as if all this was not enough, London agreed to shut the Burma Road for three months to war supplies destined for Free China.[2]

At this same dark time, discouragement came from yet another quarter. After the Russo-German pact of August 1939, there was much uncertainty about relations between Japan and the Soviet Union. In September 1940 the existing anti-Comintern Pact be-tween Japan, Germany and Italy was transformed into a military alliance, which was directed more at America than Russia, for Washington was given warning that undue assistance to Britain in the West, or to China in the East might result in a war on two fronts. Nevertheless the problem of Russia weighed heavily on the minds of the statesmen in Tokyo. In April 1941 it was resolved by a pact between the two powers which not only stipulated that each would observe neutrality if the other should be at war with a third party, but in addition included what was in effect a Russian acknowledgment of Manchukuo as a separate state.

Against all this, however, there was the undoubted fact that President Roosevelt and the American Government, if not the American people as a whole, were now reassured of Britain's determination to resist the Axis powers, and were straining the doctrine of neutrality to its limits in order to help the British; a process which must ultimately lead to the global conflagration which Chiang was waiting for. Sympathy, for whatever it was worth, was even stronger, among the Americans at large, for China than for Britain, and by the summer of 1941 was being manifested in a most practical form by the arrival in Free China of American volunteer airmen, the famous 'Flying Tigers' of General Chennault. True, sympathy had no part in the conduct of Big Business; the great western oil companies, for instance, were happy to sell the Japanese all the fuel they needed for their conquest of China, and their Shanghai offices were specially staffed with Japanese speakers to facilitate the transactions. But then, on the other hand, even hard-pressed Britain now recognized the fact that her own interests were largely identical with those of China, and having bought time by shutting the Burma Road opened it again when the agreed three months had expired towards the end of 1940.

The Pacific War

One effect of the Japanese pact with Russia was to remove the danger of an attack from the rear if Japan should decide to strike southwards, and a considerable strengthening of Japanese forces in Indo-China in the summer of 1941 suggested that the Tokyo government had committed itself to such a course. The Americans had succeeded in breaking a Japanese code and the highest circles at Washington were aware of the aggression that was being planned against Malaya and the Dutch East Indies. In July 1941 by decree of the American government all Japanese assets in the United

States were frozen and when the British and Dutch followed suit an effective embargo on the supply of war materials to Japan had at last been instituted. Probably this step made the Pacific War inevitable, but conversations between Japan and America dragged on. There were those in China who wondered whether Roosevelt could persuade his countrymen to go to the aid of the colonial empires of Britain and Holland. Then on 8 December 1941 the question was settled in the most decisive manner. By their attack on Pearl Harbour the Japanese ensured that the enormous power of the United States should be dedicated to their destruction.

That must, one imagines, have been the happiest moment of Chiang Kai-shek's life. For him the war against Japan was to all intents and purposes at an end. To be sure, victory would not come overnight, and the allied reverses at the beginning suggested that it would be a slower business than had been anticipated. But of the result he never for an instant entertained the slightest doubt. No country or combination of countries could withstand America. When the great day came, not only would Chiang be at America's side as a fellow-victor, but his most persistent rival would not be there to contend with him for the glory. By throwing in his lot with the Japanese Wang Ching-wei had committed political suicide.

Meanwhile, however, there was China's new position to be considered. Curiously enough it was only now that she formally declared war on Japan; at the same time by extending the proclamation of hostilities to Germany and Italy she became a full ally of America and Britain, though her role in the European struggle was merely nominal. It was accepted from the start that the war in the West would enjoy priority, but neither Chiang nor anybody else foresaw the British disaster in Burma which in the spring of 1942 cut China's great lifeline, the Burma Road. For the next three years, communications with the allies were maintained by the air route from India to Yunnan, over the Himalayan 'hump' but although this service was steadily augmented until by January 1945 it was carrying more than forty thousand tons a month, there were many vital war supplies which were not transportable by air. By this circumstance the Chinese potential was weakened far more than could be accounted for simply by the higher priority given to other areas.

Western Disillusionment with Chiang

It was the Burma campaign which provided the first new military development for the Chinese army, since within China itself the outbreak of the Pacific War brought for a while some respite from the Japanese offensive. Chiang Kai-shek had been declared Supreme Allied Commander of the China theatre, which was understood to include Indo-China and Siam, and he was given a senior American officer, General J. W. Stilwell, as his chief of staff. When the serious nature of the Japanese threat to Burma became apparent, the British, who had at first been reluctant to accept such assistance, agreed that the Chinese should participate in the defence of a region which was, after all, of peculiar importance to their own security. Accordingly a Chinese expeditionary force entered Burma from Yunnan early in 1942, and centred on Mandalay fought a delaying action against the invaders. But before long, it was routed, part of it falling back towards the Chinese border, the rest sharing the British retreat towards India.

It was General Stilwell who had been in charge of this operation and the defeat rankled in his mind. To him the re-opening of the Burma Road appeared as a prime necessity, and he had little patience with anyone who did not at once fall in with his views. Added to this, he was the kind of American congenitally anti-pathetic towards the allies destiny had given him. That he should have loathed such quintessential 'limies' as Lord Mountbatten was only to be expected. What was far more serious was his attitude towards the government to which he was accredited and to Chiang Kai-shek in particular; Nationalist China had other western critics, but none whose opinions were likely to carry so much weight.

And there was in fact more than enough to criticize, for the long attrition of the war had only too obviously sapped the virtue of the Chungking regime. For five years the Nationalist Party, or rather that section of it which had persevered in the struggle, had been separated from the Lower Yangtze Valley and the coastal cities, in other words from the most culturally advanced area of China where it had always derived its material and intellectual nutriment. Instead of the industrialists and merchants of the eastern provinces, it was surrounded by a more traditional society, in which the men of substance, whose support had to be canvassed, tended to be landowners of a markedly reactionary type. For these remote inland provinces were still relatively untouched by industrialization, and when the requirements of the time urgently demanded industrial development, it was only natural that the process should be largely set in motion under government auspices. This in turn vastly increased the opportunity for official corruption. By the outbreak of the Pacific War, the growing wealth of the so-called Four Great Families was a frequent topic of conversation throughout Free China; at least between trusted friends, for careless talk could have unpleasant consequences and it was rumoured, not without due grounds, that here and there in the countryside were concentration camps where unseasonable commentators could brood over their indiscretion.

A host of refugees had flocked westward out of occupied China; among them students and intellectuals were strongly represented, for the great national universities had migrated *en masse*. Teachers, whose status was so important in the Chinese world, were for the most part in a wretched condition, for inflation was now in full swing. A growing and influential body of discontent was in this way created, and there were those who looked longingly towards Mao Tse-tung's north-west, where life was hard but had a purpose. In contrast, Nationalist China seemed a morass where nothing could be accomplished beyond waiting till the issue of the war should be settled elsewhere by the hands of others. Nor was that the worst; Chiang Kai-shek, it was said, had intensified the blockade of the Communist zone and had even concerted his action with the troops of the pro-Japanese puppet government to expel guerrillas from the territory they controlled.

It was certainly true that Chiang was content to leave the burden of defeating the Japanese to the Americans who were infinitely better equipped for the business than a China worn out already by years of resistance. Among the Americans themselves there was a school of thought which maintained that the essential function of China was to provide airbases for raids on Japanese land and sea communications. This school was represented notably by General Chennault whose 'Flying Tigers' were now incorporated in the American forces. As to the blockade of the Communist zone, Chiang was convinced that from the beginning the Communists had been manipulating events with the sole purpose of bringing the entire country under their control. For the moment Soviet

Russia was precluded by her life and death struggle in Europe from taking any part in the Pacific War, but when Hitler had been defeated, as in due course he would be, Stalin would certainly have designs in East Asia. It was the merest common sense therefore, unless one wanted to see the Communists masters of China, to seize the present opportunity of restricting their territorial gains. There may well have been collusion on this matter with certain commanders of Wang Ching-wei's puppet forces, for it is true that some of Wang's followers retained links with their old comrades. Many an allied airman, brought down over occupied China, had reason to bless this state of affairs when he found himself safely conveyed by puppet functionaries through the Japanese lines. Be that as it may, it was put about by the Communists in the summer of 1942 that they had been driven by treachery from a sizeable extent of the so-called 'liberated areas' in the North, and that the fighting effective of their main force, the Eighth Route Army, had been reduced by losses from four hundred thousand to three hundred thousand men.

Stilwell was driven to fury by news of this kind. There was an element of personal pique in his resentment, for with the loss of the Burma lifeline, the importance of General Chennault and his airmen increased at the expense of his own. Besides, he was genuinely unable to see that Chiang could have anything but the basest motives in erecting a *cordon sanitaire* round the Communists, who to his way of thinking presented no conceivable threat either to Nationalist China or to the allies. He was confirmed in this view by a solid body of American experts in Chinese affairs, both in government service and in the academic world. It is easy to understand why professional soldiers, and even diplomats for that matter, should have wanted to benefit from the enthusiasm which the Communists would bring to the fight against the Japanese. But one finds it harder to account for the fundamental misinterpretation of the goal and purpose of Mao Tse-tung and his followers which at this time came into fashion. According to this theory, the very title of the Chinese Communist Party was a ludicrous misnomer, for there was nothing faintly reminiscent of bolshevism about it. The heroes of the Long March were simply Agrarian Reformers whose doctrines, when subjected to unbiased analysis, proved to be, in terms of western democracy, somewhat to right of centre. This theory, even if not wholly accepted by the

American and other western governments, nevertheless formed part of the background of their political planning.

No doubt a variety of causes led to this surprising assumption. Soviet Russia was showing herself a valiant ally against Hitler, and the dissolution of the Comintern helped to lull fears of her intentions. Even more to the point, the Chinese Communists, from the inception of the united front, were no longer, in the territories under their control, 'liquidating' the landlord class, as they had done in the old Kiangsi Soviet, but were contenting themselves with the reduction of unreasonably high rents and usurious rates of interest. But they never for one moment pretended that this moderation was anything but a temporary policy of expediency. For anybody with eyes to see, during those wartime days of the 1940s, Mao Tse-tung was rising to full eminence as a theoretician and teacher, and a great deal of the master plan for the People's China of today was being formulated and rehearsed in the north-western 'liberated areas'.

The Gospel from Yenan

In January 1940 Mao published what was to be the most fruitful of his many essays, a discussion on *The New Democracy*. The Chinese revolution, he declared, was now an important part of the world revolution. After 1917, the notion of a bourgeois republic was out of date, but on the other hand the pattern of a socialist republic, as exhibited in Russia, was not for the time being feasible in those countries, of which China was one, emerging from a colonial or semi-colonial state. For these, a new type of structure must be adopted, a dictatorship not simply of the proletariat as in Russia, but of all revolutionary classes; though naturally with the proletariat (i.e. the Communist Party) in a position of leadership. In China specifically this meant that the Communists would

persist in a long term co-operation with all those classes, strata, political parties and groups and individuals who are willing to fight Japan to the end.

The aim must be the establishment of a new democratic republic. In this republic big banks and big industrial and commercial enterprises would be state-owned, but this was no more than the goal set by the Kuomintang itself during the first period of Nationalist-Communist co-operation. Apart from this, the new democracy would not interfere with other forms of capitalist private property or restrict capitalist production. As to the farmers, the slogan of Dr Sun Yat-sen himself, 'land to the tillers', would become official policy in so far as the estates of greater landlords would be confiscated and distributed among the landless, but the economic activities of rich peasants would be tolerated, and for the time being socialist agriculture would not be generally intro- duced. This New Democracy would be the first stage of the revolution. The second stage would be socialism. But Mao was careful to point out that

the first stage will take quite a long time and cannot be accomplished overnight. We are not Utopians, and we cannot depart from the actual conditions confronting us.

The *New Democracy*, having been written just after the Russo- German pact of 1939, made no distinction between the govern- ments of America, Britain and France on the one hand and the Axis on the other. All were the imperialist enemies of the Chinese people, whose steadfast friend was the Soviet Union.[3]

Another development, no less important though overlooked at the time by the outside world, was the movement called in Chinese *Cheng Feng*, a phrase of which the nearest English render- ing is 'rectification of conduct'. This was inaugurated by Mao Tse-tung in February 1942 as a campaign to turn out large num- bers of correct party members equipped with a new system of ethics. Study groups were formed to master selected texts, chiefly from the works of Stalin and Mao himself, on which they were examined. But mere book-learning was not enough; the student was called upon to criticize his own shortcomings in the light of the Marxist-Leninist creed, and to persevere until Party interests had replaced his individual purpose. In one year, it was claimed, thirty thousand people were successfully subjected to this process of 'brain-washing'.

As it took place in the remote fastnesses of north-western China, thought-control, even on this enormous scale, did not arouse inter- national attention. It was not so with a piece of ineptitude com- mitted about the same time in Chungking. In March 1943 there was published a volume entitled *China's Destiny*, bearing Chiang Kai-shek's name and stating his views, though written in fact by one of his friends. Tracing the record of the country's misfortunes during the past century, the book represented western imperialism as the chief villain of the piece. This of course is, quite naturally, the opinion of every Chinese, but its expression just then distressed the western allies. It was felt, not only by foreigners but by many progressive Chinese as well, that the picture the author painted of a paternalistic system of society regulated on neo-Confucian principles, did not offer much encouragement to liberal and democratic forces in a future China.

China among the Allies

In 1944 the Japanese, whose sea communications with South-East Asia were being effectively curtailed by American submarines, decided to try and open an overland route through China. With this purpose they launched an offensive along the Wuchang-Canton railway, and moved into Kwangsi Province, occupying the provincial capital of Kweilin. General Stilwell's demands that he should be given more effective control over the Nationalist forces were now difficult to resist. Pressed by Washington, Chiang yielded the point, but stipulated in return that Stilwell should be replaced by another American officer. This was done in September 1944; the new incumbent was General Wedemeyer, who was free from Stilwell's animosity. Things took a turn for the better. The Japanese offensive in the south-west wore itself out, and further South still communications by road through Burma were resumed. But relations between Nationalist China and the allies had, at a personal level, gone sour. Three or four years before, when Chennault's 'Flying Tigers' had arrived, they had been the heroes of the hour. Now in 1945 there were seventy thousand American servicemen in China, half of them concentrated at Kunming in Yunnan which had become one of the busiest airports in the world. For three years all supplies had had to be brought in by plane. Many things which in other theatres of war American soldiers considered as daily necessities had been banned as articles of luxury. This deprivation was not calculated to put them in a good humour. The Chinese amenities surrounding them demanded a sophistication of taste which few of them possessed, and while the diet of their messes astonished their hosts by its gross abundance, and their living quarters were by local standards well appointed, the soldiers were sickened by the pre-industrial sanitation and by the multitudes of rats which, until the People's Government arrived to destroy them, were the great secular pest of the western provinces. Bad temper frequently vented itself on Chinese near to hand. A special cause of offence was the free-and-easy American attitude to women which shocked Chinese notions of propriety. Anybody who lived in Chungking in 1944–5 will remember the perpetual 'jeep-girl' incidents of those days. In a word, by the end of the Pacific War the Americans were unpopular among a large section of the inhabitants of Free China, nor were matters made any better by the obvious fact that the credit for the victory over Japan was almost exclusively due to America.

At the time this seemed of small account. China had acquired enormous international stature from the war. In October 1942, both America and Britain had finally, after a century, abandoned the detested 'unequal treaties' and at the beginning of the following year had concluded new agreements on a footing of parity. Extra-territoriality and the concessions had both been swept away. Then, in November 1943, Chiang had met Roosevelt and Churchill at the Cairo Conference and the allies had declared that Japan would be forced to disgorge all the territories she had acquired since 1895; not only Manchuria but also Formosa would return to China, while Korea would regain her independence. As a crowning glory, China was officially given the rank of Great Power when the United Nations Organization came into being in the spring of 1945 by being appointed one of the five permanent members of the Security Council.

Behind the scenes, however, things wore a rather different aspect. It was certainly not at the wish of the allies in general that China had received her promotion. Churchill, for instance, did not conceal his exasperation at what he considered a piece of tomfoolery. But America insisted, and had her way. Undoubtedly generous, even sentimental, motives influenced Washington. It was also possible for cynics to argue that America was seeking to ensure that she would have one of the seats of power occupied in perpetuity by a creature of her own. An event in the last months of the war suggested that the Americans did in fact treat China as a puppet. At the Yalta Conference between Stalin, Roosevelt and Churchill, terms were fixed for Russia's entry into the Pacific War after the defeat of Germany. It was agreed that as a reward for her participation she should regain

former rights violated by the treacherous attack of Japan in 1904.

Some of these concerned Chinese territory; thus Dairen was to be leased to Russia as a naval base, while the two chief railways in Manchuria would be operated by a joint Sino-Soviet company recognizing the 'pre-eminent interests' of Russia. In addition the question of Outer Mongolia was raised. On the fall of the Manchu Dynasty, this portion of the Chinese Empire had asserted its independence, and the government of Yuan Shih-k'ai in a pact with Russia had conceded its autonomy under residual Chinese suzerainty. After the Russian Revolution, a People's Republic had been established in Outer Mongolia under Soviet patronage, and Stalin now insisted that the full independence of the country should be recognized. It was decided that to protect the secrecy of these arrangements, to which America and Britain agreed without question, China for the time being should not be informed of the way her territory was to be disposed of, but America undertook to secure her acceptance in due course. And indeed China did as she was bidden in a Sino-Soviet treaty 'of friendship and alliance' in August 1945. So much for her standing as a Great Power.

The 'Liberated Areas'

In 1945, as the Pacific War drew towards its close, the Japanese front in Southern China began to crumble and the Nationalist forces were able to recover a considerable extent of territory, particularly in Kwangsi. However, this counted for very little when compared with the massive expansion of the 'liberated areas', for after the grave setbacks of three years earlier, when between the Japanese and the Nationalists their domains had shrunk alarmingly, the Communists were pulsating with new energy. In March 1945 it was estimated that of nine hundred and fourteen counties theoretically under Japanese occupation, six hundred and seventy-eight were controlled by the Communists. In July of the same year the Communist *Liberation Daily* announced that the nineteen separate 'liberated areas' contained between them upwards of a hundred million inhabitants. The Red Armies had kept pace with this growth. Figures varied, but a moderate calculation at the end of 1944 reckoned that the main force, the Eighth Route Army, had a strength of three hundred and twenty-eight thousand men, while in Central China, the New Fourth Army, reorganized after the disaster of 1941, consisted of over a hundred and fifty thousand. Even in the South there were twenty-seven thousand men in the field.

The Liberated Areas were experiencing the New Democracy, which was being applied in a form known as the *Three Three System*. The administration was of the familiar pyramidical soviet pattern, with its base in the publicly elected village councils, whose members chose representatives from their number to form higher bodies, and so on up the scale. But the Communists ensured that one-third of the people elected at any level should be members of the Party, and that this third should have the complete direction of affairs. Steps were taken to see that another third were what we should term 'fellow-travellers', that is to say people who though technically outside the Party were indistinguishable in their views from Party members. The remaining third were described as 'middle of the road' types. With the limited means available every effort was made to indoctrinate the peasantry in Mao's teachings. The *joint dictatorship* was beginning to be exercised, too, against a domestic enemy, for in the North as territory was 'liberated' it was not difficult to find rich landlords and others of note who could be accused of collaboration. Dragged before People's Courts, they were lucky if they escaped with their lives. It was a foretaste of what was to happen on a larger scale six years later.

The Japanese Surrender

The Japanese surrender caught both the Americans and the Nationalists by surprise. It had been half-expected that the enemy might make a desperate last stand on the continent, which was why America and Britain were so anxious to have Russian participation. In the event this proved to be superfluous. Nevertheless, if Russian intervention did come before the end of the war Russian troops would be in occupation in territory in the north adjacent to that held by Communist guerrillas. To prevent a fatal division of the country Washington was consequently already anxious in 1944 to bring Mao Tse-tung and Chiang Kai-shek into one

mutually agreed government. Mao's reply was simple. The Kuomintang should abjure its one-party rule and a real National
Government of all 'democratic' parties, including the Communists,
should be formed. To such a government it would be possible to
entrust the supreme direction of the Red Army, but not to the
Chungking regime as it then was.

Looking back today we can readily appreciate the part that the
Communists intended to play in such a coalition. At the time,
though, the foreign allies thought the suggestion reasonable
enough. There was some resentment over Chiang Kai-shek's
noticeable lack of enthusiasm at the idea. The utmost concession
he was prepared to make was to permit some minor representation
of Communists and others in the government. He would listen to
recommendations of a joint commission, including a Communist
and an American officer, concerning supplies for the Red Armies,
provided the Communists and their forces had previously pledged
loyalty to what would still be a Kuomintang-dominated regime.
So matters dragged on until the capitulation of Japan in August
1945.

That occurrence at once raised an urgent problem, namely,
who was to accept the surrender of the various Japanese armies
stationed in China? In the northern provinces, it was in most cases
the Communists who were closer to hand. A continuous belt of
'liberated country' ran from Shensi to the coast of Shantung,
completely severing Peking and Tientsin from the south. In
Manchuria, the Russians had attacked Japan as she was on the
point of collapse, and overrun the whole territory in a matter of
days. Elsewhere Chiang insisted that the surrender must be made
only to the forces of the Nationalist Government, and this stipulation was accepted by the Americans who felt obliged in consequence to put means of transportation, both planes and ships,
at Chiang's disposal. However this appeared to Washington, it
was interpreted, at once by the Communists and later by many
others, as a direct involvement in the Civil War and an act of
aggression against the 'liberated areas'.

Even so, the Americans continued to make valiant efforts to
bring the two sides together. At the end of August 1945 the US
Ambassador escorted Mao Tse-tung to Chungking, where for
forty days he talked with Chiang, the first time for nearly twenty
years that they had been under one roof. The Communist leader

in his public statements was all for peace and solidarity and it seemed a good omen when it was announced that an agreement had been signed on the great Republican festival of the *Double Tenth* (10 October 1945). This guaranteed the legality of all parties, the release of political prisoners, the disbanding of secret police and the convening of a People's Consultative Conference and pledged that the Nationalists and Communists together, under Chiang's direction, would strive to prevent civil war and that the Communist regular forces would be reduced from forty to twenty divisions. While the talks were going on, another auspicious ceremony took place at Nanking, where the Japanese Commander-in-Chief in China formally surrendered to the Nationalist Minister of War. Wang Ching-wei had died the year before, but his fellow collaborators were in custody and awaiting death or imprisonment.

Before the ink was dry on the Double Tenth agreement, it had to all intents and purposes become a nullity. The American carriage of Nationalist troops to take over from the Japanese had turned into what was described by General Wedemeyer as

the greatest air and sea transportation in history.

American troops, too, were landing at Shanghai and Tientsin, and establishing themselves at such inland cities as Peking and Nanking. The Communists exclaimed that they were being attacked; the outcry spread. In November 1945 a League against Civil War was organized in Chungking itself, while in Kumming thirty thousand students demonstrated in the streets.

In the following month, America anxiously appointed as special envoy to China one of its most distinguished soldiers, General George Marshall, and charged him with the mission of bringing about a truce and the formation of a coalition government. This time Chou En-lai represented the Communists in the negotiations, and it says much for General Marshall's persuasiveness, which was assisted by the prevailing climate of opinion throughout the country, that a truce was signed on 10 January 1946. On the same day the all-party People's Consultative Conference began a three-week session, during which it was resolved that a National Assembly should meet in May to draft a constitution and that a State Council, with half the members Nationalists, should administer government.

Superficially then, the first post-war year began well enough.

Government organizations, universities and vast numbers of individual refugees were happily engaged in returning from the western provinces to the Lower Yangtze Valley and North China. Chiang Kai-shek was welcomed as a national hero by all sections of the population, who had heard only rumours of the discontent accumulating during the war years in the areas under Chungking rule. The Americans too were hailed as liberators. Yet by the end of the year everything had changed. Conditions were worse in many respects than they had been under the Japanese. The Civil War had resumed, to end only with the destruction of the Nationalists, and General Marshall was packing his bags, all his hopes in ruins.

The Civil War Resumes

It cannot be denied that Chiang Kai-shek understood more clearly than his foreign allies the true purpose of Mao Tse-tung's talk of democratic coalitions. To be sure, the Kuomintang was bound, by its own principles, ultimately to replace its dictatorship or 'tutelage' by parliamentary government, but Chiang had no intention of seeing this metamorphosis assume the shape of a Communist-led 'new democracy'. On their side, Mao and his comrades would never permit their armed forces to come under the control of a national government in which they themselves lacked a preponderant influence. Yet although we must recognize Chiang's clearsightedness in this one particular, it is impossible not to agree with General Stilwell that his ignorance of the science of administration rendered him incapable of an intelligent use of power at such a juncture. His ignorance was buttressed after the defeat of Japan by an overwhelming stubbornness and self-confidence, for he assumed that in the last resort the United States would never fail to support him. Added to this was the lamentable state of the Kuomintang, which had lost some of its best men in Wang Ching-wei's defection, and had fallen more and more into the hands of the most reactionary or corrupt. To their dismay, the industrialists and businessmen of Shanghai, once the backbone of the party, found that the main areas of the economy were henceforward to be run by government monopolies over which the Four Great Families exercised undisputed hegemony. At a lower level, ordinary citizens found their daily affairs conducted by officials who in face of the constantly rising inflation could not seriously be expected to live on their salaries. The Americans, still omnipresent in the role of military advisers, although the bulk of their forces had been withdrawn, found themselves yet again outstaying their welcome. In December 1946 the whole country was convulsed with rage when a hysterical girl student in Peking accused a GI of rape. The whole evil brew of stupidity and malice was kept on the boil by the endless war of words.

The main centre of conflict was now in Manchuria. The Russians, as we have seen, had swept across the country without resistance, and immediately set to work at the great task of seizing booty. Japanese industrial equipment was dismantled wholesale and transferred to Siberia along with a multitude of military and civilian prisoners. Among these was the last emperor of China, and puppet ruler of 'Manchukuo', Henry P'u Yi. Handed over in 1950 to the Chinese Communists, and imprisoned by them to be brainwashed, he was released in 1959 and is now a minor functionary of the People's Government in Peking.

The Russians were pledged to withdraw by December 1945, but lingered until May 1946, by which time their zest for plunder had inflicted on Manchuria a loss estimated at two thousand million US dollars. Yet they so contrived that their delay in leaving was with the formal approval of the Chinese government. For after the Russian invasion, units of the Chinese Communist forces poured into Manchuria. In November 1945, American ships reaching the South Manchurian port of Yingkow with Nationalist troops found the place held by Chinese Communists, who refused them permission to land. The difficulties that loomed ahead were so intimidating that General Wedemeyer strongly recommended that any idea of reoccupying Manchuria in the near future should be abandoned. This was unacceptable to the Generalissimo, who was enough of a realist to see that the presence of the Russians was at least keeping Mao's followers from controlling the chief cities and communications. In spite of the looting Chiang agreed to their postponed departure. To preserve appearances, the Russians, when they did at last withdraw, allowed Nationalist units some restricted access by the ports whose control they retained, but for the most part Chiang's forces entered Manchuria overland through the pass at Shanhaikwan, and had to fight their way northwards against Communist opposition.

As the towns of southern Manchuria passed one after the other into their hands, Chiang was exultant; he was accomplishing what Wedemeyer had pronounced impossible. And why not? He was incomparably stronger than his rivals, capable of putting over four million men in the field, four times more than the Communists, without reckoning the vast difference in equipment. On 17 June 1946 the Nationalist Government ordered the Red Army to withdraw unconditionally from a whole list of 'liberated areas' reaching from Manchuria to the Yangtze. A week later an open attack was launched against Communist bases in Central China, and within a matter of days the country was plunged into a war not less destructive than the one from which it had emerged ten months earlier.

From then till the summer of 1947 Chiang enjoyed a series of intoxicating victories, as his armies swept over all the 'liberated areas' between the Yangtze and the Great Wall; beyond the Wall, besides South Manchuria, Jehol and Kalgan were occupied by government forces. The most spectacular triumph came in March 1947 with the capture of Yenan itself, for eleven years the Communist holy of holies. By then, hope of reconciliation had faded; Chou En-lai, who had lingered in Nanking to maintain liaison with General Marshall, had left for Manchuria in November 1946 and Marshall himself returned to America early in 1947. True, at the beginning of the offensive Chiang had promised that the Red Army would be wiped out within six months. This time limit expired at the end of 1946, but a little exaggeration was pardonable. The constitutional programme called for by the People's Consultative Conference at the beginning of 1946 was set in motion, but the proceedings were pure farce. When the National Assembly was convened in November 1946, no Communists attended, and the second largest non-Kuomintang Group, the Democratic League, was disbanded by government order in 1947, on grounds of public security. In these circumstances, the Constitution which was finally contrived would, if it had come into effect, simply have confirmed the existing supremacy of Chiang and the Kuomintang; in fact, however, the war made it a dead letter on the mainland, though the Nationalists were to carry it with them in their flight to Formosa.

The Communist Triumph

But General Wedemeyer's warning was soon vindicated. Already in June 1947 Communist guerrillas were back in the heart of the country and the old liberated areas were springing up again from Shantung to Shensi. By December, partisan warfare was raging across a vast area north of the Yangtze. Too late, Chiang Kai-shek understood what his American advisers had meant by urging him not to over-extend his lines into Manchuria. The guerrillas were equipped with Japanese rifles and ammunition which the Russians had spared for them; before long they were to be using even better weapons of American manufacture, taken from Nationalist prisoners. They had ideological arms as well. There was no pretence now of mealy-mouthed agrarian reform. This was a revolution promising rewards to the poorest of the peasantry, including the satisfaction of revenge for wrongs inflicted by the class enemy in the heat of the Nationalist triumph. Many of the peasantry responded with enthusiasm, and rallied to leaders who knew how to use them. By the middle of 1948, after a year of counter-attack, the Liberation Army, swollen by new recruits and deserters from the enemy, numbered two million eight hundred thousand soldiers, against three million six hundred and fifty thousand Nationalists.

There were those in the Kuomintang itself, especially men with old resentments against Chiang, who heard the knell tolling, and found pretexts for going to the safety of Hong Kong. In January 1948, they organized themselves into a Kuomintang Revolutionary Committee which declared itself an ally of 'the Communists and all other democratic parties' against the dictatorship of Chiang Kai-shek. The Democratic League, outlawed by Chiang, also found an asylum in the British colony, where it made a similar statement of policy.

North of the Yangtze, by the summer of 1948 Chiang's military control was even shakier than that of the Japanese had been. Like them, he was restricted to the large towns. His hold over the railways was feebler than theirs. In Manchuria they had had a solid foundation of power, whereas his armies held only the southern cities. In fact, it was from Manchuria that the final chapter of the war began. It would be tedious to go into details; the fate of

Nationalist China was determined in three great battles, each of which, in the number of men taking part, was on an enormous scale. The first of these was fought round Mukden from September to November 1948 and ended with a Nationalist withdrawal not only from that city but from the whole of Manchuria. In November–December occurred another vast struggle at Hsuchow, the important railway junction half-way between Tientsin and the Yangtze. No sooner were the Communists victorious there, than the attack on Peking and Tientsin began. The latter city fell on 12 January 1949, and then on 31 January the Nationalist general defending Peking with a garrison of two hundred and fifty thousand men surrendered the old imperial capital to the Liberation Army. In effect, the Communists held the country north of the Yangtze.

Across the river, Nanking and Shanghai, the very heart of Chiang's regime, waited apathetically for their fate. A few months earlier, in August 1948, the government, in a desperate bid to halt the inflation, had introduced a new currency and had decreed that all individuals and firms must hand over their holdings of gold, silver and US dollars in exhange. In Shanghai especially the edict was applied with shocking severity, headed by one of Chiang's sons in person. Many wretched businessmen and private citizens were summarily put to death for alleged infringement of the law. Terrified by the example, whole sections of the urban bourgeoisie gave up their life's savings in return for the new banknotes, which in a few weeks were as worthless as the old. It was whispered that the sole purpose of the transaction was to confiscate the people's wealth for the benefit of the Four Great Families, who promptly transferred the takings to safe custody overseas. Having thus alienated for good a numerous class of supporters, the government sought to defend itself by fear. Suspected Communists and others believed to be conspiring against the state were dragged before drum-head courts and then out to some public place to be shot through the back of the head. Scenes of this kind were of daily occurrence in Shanghai, the busiest street-corners being invariably chosen for the execution of the victims, who were nearly all young men. Photographs of the slaughter filled the newspapers. So long as the regime had a reasonable chance of survival, this bloodshed would have been accepted as an inevitable concomitant of the war, but the Americans were ostentatiously washing their hands of their former protégés, and by now even the most ignorant of the population could read the signs. The old belief in the Mandate of Heaven played its part in the crisis. An uninterrupted succession of catastrophes such as the present could only be attributed to some incurable vice in the ruler. From the chaos a new leader would emerge, whose victory would in itself be the best evidence of his authentic title to authority. By the beginning of 1949 one did not have to look far to discern him.

One last fantasy was entertained by Nanking in the early spring of 1949. The Communists paused for breath before crossing the Yangtze. Could they possibly be induced to stay on the other side of the river? Could China, after many centuries, again witness the coexistence of a Northern and a Southern Dynasty? Chiang Kai-shek thought this was the proper moment to go and tend the grave of his mother, leaving his Vice-President to take his place. Envoys went backwards and forwards, but the Communists were adamant; nothing would satisfy them but the annulment of the Nationalist state system and the substitution of a 'democratic' coalition with themselves in control, the reorganization of the reactionary armies, and high on the list of priorities, the punishment of Chiang and other war criminals. In the middle of April 1949 fighting was resumed and the Liberation Army crossed the Yangtze. Nanking fell before the end of the month, and Shanghai in May. At first, the government withdrew to Canton and throughout the summer and autumn Chiang, back in office, busied himself between there and the western provinces, anticipating that once again a stand might be made in the wartime fortress of Szechuan. But it was above all the island of Formosa that seemed to offer the safest refuge. The Nationalist political and military establishment was transferred there and though resistance of a kind dragged on in the vast spaces of the interior until the end of the year and even beyond, by March 1950 no Nationalist authority remained anywhere on the mainland.

Meanwhile, the Kuomintang dissidents and the men of the Democratic League thought it safe to quit the neutrality of Hong Kong for the new centre of power in Peking. They received a hearty welcome, and with Communist delegates and representatives of Overseas Chinese and minority groups, set to work to lay the foundations of a People's China. In June 1949 Mao Tse-tung gave them their directions. The new regime would be a democratic dictatorship 'led by the working class through the Communist Party'. Reactionaries would be deprived of all right of expression, which henceforward would be enjoyed by the people alone. The goal was the transformation of China from an agricultural to an industrial country, and from New Democracy to Socialism and then finally to the classless Utopia of Communism. In the last ten days of September, a new People's Political Conference, which because of the total absence of all opposition, was no more representative than the old one, assembled to give its rubber-stamp approval to the decisions of the Communist leaders. A Common Programme and an Organic Law for a Central People's Government, was adopted on 1 October 1949. Once more, Peking was the capital of China.

CHAPTER XXI

THE PEOPLE'S CHINA

'Liberation' – Russia and the West – Formosa and Korea – the Terror – the first Five-Year Plan – the 'Hundred Flowers' – the Great Leap Forward – the road to Bandung – the quarrel with Russia – China in the world – Communism and Chinese Tradition

---

'Liberation'

THE overwhelming majority of the Chinese people acquiesced in the Communist victory simply because in the first place it brought an end to the War. The more thoughtful set their hopes even higher. It was half a century since the country had last been effectively under one government, and the protracted disunity resulted in a pitiful backwardness of industrial development. The political doctrines of the new regime would, it was felt, be of trifling importance so long as it fulfilled its pledge to lead China forward to industrialization. To do this, functions of government would have to be carried further than those of previous administrations. In practice as well as in theory, its monopoly of force would have to be asserted, something which even the strongest dynasties had never achieved. In imperial times, the mandarins had as a rule, found it expedient to shut their eyes to the existence of separate jurisdictions within their administrative areas. The family or the clan often enjoyed virtual autonomy in its control of junior members. Under the Republic, the warlord system had vastly increased the opportunities for arbitrary power, while the breakdown of public order encouraged the proliferation of bandits and of freebooting soldiery. The first task of any government worthy of the name would be to put a stop to this anarchy. The Chinese Government must at last become master in its own house. If in so doing it had to use exemplary sternness against the enemies of society, certainly the population at large, so far from calling it tyrannical, would applaud its resolution. Thus the word 'liberation', used by the Communists to denote their seizure of a territory, seemed to many people by no means an unfair description of the events of 1949.

In the first twelve months few had reason to complain. After the great battles in the north and the crossing of the Yangtze, the attitude of the conquerors was noticeably milder and no attempt was made in the south and west to re-enact the severities which the richer landlords elsewhere had endured from the Liberation Army in 1947–8. So benign was the new dispensation that it was a commonplace down to the middle of 1950, for foreign observers to make admiring comparisons between this Chinese revolution and its precursors in France and Russia. Unless they had rendered themselves particularly obnoxious, the local functionaries of the Nationalist Government were not molested, and most of them continued in their posts.

In theory the authority of the regime was derived from the united-front People's Consultative Council, which until the Constitution of 1954 sustained the role of an elected National Assembly. In practice, the duty of the Council's non-Communist members was simply to approve the decisions of the Communist Party leaders and to co-operate in winning public support for Communist policy. The principal organ of rule was a Government Council chosen by the People's Consultative Council, and consisting of fifty-six members, mostly Communists and with Mao Tse-tung as Chairman and Head of State. Stemming from this parent body were the Central Administrative and Military Councils, the Supreme Court, and the supervisory Procurator-General's office. The military conditions of the 'liberation' and the inadequacy of communications made it necessary in the early days that many of the normal responsibilities of a Central Government should be parcelled out between administrative zones, each under its separate Committee: there were six of these, ranging from Manchuria to the south-west. They were merely a temporary measure and were abolished in 1954. Since then the whole administration has been centralized and there has been no intermediate body between the capital and the provinces.

Amid the general relief at the coming of peace, there were certain ominous tokens for the future. In the most stringent period of Kuomintang censorship, the Chinese reader had had access to a wide range of newspapers, one or two of which would have done credit to any country in the world. With liberation, everything was changed, and news, as we understand the word, was banished overnight from the press, which from that time on had space only for messages from Communist leaders, resolutions of conferences, and statistics about the production of pig-iron. It must be confessed that the deprivation, at least in the beginning, was not felt as very painful, even by the educated classes. Meanwhile the introduction of compulsory courses in Marxism at schools and universities was greeted with enthusiasm by the students, many of whom manifested in their behaviour signs familiar to Christian countries in the more hysterical cases of religious conversion: discussion groups assumed the atmosphere of prayer-meetings, and classmates during vacation would correspond at enormous length about the state of their souls. This phenomenon was particular to young people of education, but all ages and callings, with schooling or without, were pressed into taking part in rallies and demonstrations. It was very noticeable how in Shanghai, for instance, an office-worker of fifty, who at first cursed the busybodies for getting him out of bed in the small hours to assemble for a procession, would before the day was over be parading in front of the local hierarchy with the proud feeling of at last counting for something in the scheme of things.

It had been declared that Sun Yat-sen's policy of 'land to the tiller' was to be one of the primary goals of the new government, and after a breathing space of some months the programme was duly set in motion by the Agrarian Law promulgated at the end of June 1950. This measure soon gained for itself a notoriety which could not be attributed to its provisions alone, for these were markedly reasonable. The reign of terror, there is no other word, which surrounded its application was, like its prototype in Revolutionary France, justified, if not produced, by a foreign war. It is necessary therefore, before going further into the Communists' domestic policy, to take a look at their international relations.

Russia and the West

Even before the People's Government had come into being, Mao Tse-tung had announced its foreign policy. In June 1949 he informed the world that China could never choose the way of neutrality. She must 'lean to one side', and the side would be that of the anti-imperialist front and the Soviet Union. Russia recognized the new regime immediately on its foundation, and in December 1949 Mao went to Moscow. It was the first time he had left Chinese soil.

Stalin was on the eve of his seventieth birthday and had entered on the ultimate and not the least sanguinary phase of his career. Enraged by Tito's insubordination, he was striking out at all those around him whom he suspected of doubting his infallibility. The purge had spread to the satellite countries: in Hungary, it was said, more Communists were hanged by Stalin's disciples than had been slaughtered under Admiral Horthy's White Terror in 1919. The magazine *Bolshevik*, the mouthpiece of the Russian Communist Party, on the very day of Mao's arrival in Moscow denounced nationalism as the greatest threat to Communist unity.

Years later, after Stalin's death, China was to blame him for his tendency to 'Great Power chauvinism'. Yet at the time Mao seems to have found the atmosphere in Moscow quite healthy. He accepted that Russia was the leader of the Communist world, a fact reinforced by the explosion of her first atomic bomb three months earlier. There was much in Stalin's character that he admired, and he was ready to defer to the Georgian's seniority. But he had no intention of entering into servitude. When in February 1950 he signed a new Sino-Russian Treaty of Friendship, Alliance and Mutual Assistance, the negotiation of which was the purpose of his visit, he proclaimed that it was the first time for centuries that China had concluded such an agreement as a free partner.

In form the treaty was directed against aggression by Japan or any country allied to her, in other words the United States. Russia made certain concessions, consenting for instance to the restoration of the Manchurian railways and the naval base at Port Arthur to China not later than 1952. But she was more reluctant to say goodbye to Dairen, and Mao, like Chiang before him, had to accept the loss of Outer Mongolia. Financially, too, Moscow was not over-lavish with aid, granting a credit of only three hundred million dollars over five years, or less than had just been advanced to Poland. The creation of mixed Sino-Soviet companies for such enterprises as the exploitation of the mineral deposits of Sinkiang Province is open to stronger criticism. Russia, who contributed the capital and the technicians, demanded so exorbitant a share of the profits that some years earlier Yugoslavia had declined such an arrangement and even Stalin had admitted that it was not suitable between allies. After Stalin's death, Mao demanded and obtained the restoration to China of the Soviet share in these companies.

Bare statistics do not, however, give an adequate notion of the extent of Soviet help to the Chinese Communists. Apart from the fact that the Chinese revolution could never have succeeded without Russian inspiration, when Mao and his friends came to power they could look to the Soviet Union for models of every kind of political and economic institution. Then again, during the 1950s a multitude of Soviet advisers and experts gave incalculable assistance to the development of Chinese industry, and by all accounts conducted themselves with admirable modesty and discretion. Whatever quarrel now divides the two governments, these Russian citizens deserve Chinese gratitude.

The Western Powers were slow to appreciate the quality of the new Chinese regime. Indeed one extraordinary incident in April 1949 made one wonder whether Britain was really attuned to the twentieth century at all. In that month, when the opposing armies were separated by the Yangtze, the British authorities ordered HMS *Amethyst* to sail upstream to Nanking with supplies for the Embassy. While the vessel was on her way, the Communists launched their attack across the river and the *Amethyst* was trapped in the battle. Other ships of the Royal Navy were dispatched to her rescue but were repelled with heavy casualties. After months of captivity, the *Amethyst* succeeded in escaping, and in the natural jubilation at her exploit it was forgotten that before the whole episode had begun, nobody had thought it necessary so much as to notify the Communists that the ship was to be sent through the line of fire. Still, the affair blew over and in January 1950 Britain recognized the People's Government. But even this step was not simply the acknowledgement of a fact. There is no doubt that some British merchants and officials believed that China would respond to the gesture by granting all kinds of economic privileges. The thing was a damp squib. It was a long time before Peking would even bother to send a *chargé d'affaires* to London, and sixteen years later the two countries had not yet exchanged ambassadors.

In view of the violent hostility that was later to develop in the United States towards Communist China, it is worth remembering that the attitude of the American government in 1949 was very different. As we have seen, there had been for years much sympathy for the Communists among influential circles in Washington, and this sentiment, reflected in an increasingly critical appraisal of the Kuomintang, and a corresponding reluctance to throw good money after bad, contributed substantially to Mao Tse-tung's victory. When the Nationalists withdrew from Nanking, the American Ambassador, Dr Leighton Stuart, instead of following them southwards, remained behind with the obvious intention of establishing contact with their successors. This well-meant attempt ended disastrously. Dr Stuart, who had previously been head of the famous American-run Yenching University, a few miles outside Peking, was invited to attend a dinner given by some of his old pupils, and in a speech he urged them not to go into exile but to stay and exert their influence in the New China. To us this sounds harmless enough, but the Communist authorities, not it must be admitted altogether unfairly, interpreted it as an exhortation to try and dilute the prevailing Marxist policies with an admixture of liberal democracy, in other words as an encouragement to sabotage. So Dr Stuart was treated very rudely and soon afterwards left for home to the accompaniment of a chorus of invective from the newspapers. Nevertheless there was considerable opinion in Washington that it would be well to follow the British example and recognize the Peking regime, and even though this step was not taken at once because of the continued existence of the Nationalist Government in Formosa, it was thought that before very long this impediment would have been removed.

Formosa and Korea

The island of Formosa, or Taiwan, as the Chinese call it, was one of the territories which the Cairo Declaration had promised should be returned to China, and so at the end of the Pacific War it was occupied by Chiang's troops pending the signature of a formal peace treaty. Apart from an insignificant number of proto-Malayan aborigines, the eight million inhabitants were Chinese whose ancestors had come from the other side of the straits during the past two or three hundred years. After the cession in 1895, the Japanese

had exploited the economic resources of the island in a comparatively enlightened manner, and although the Chinese population
were treated as second-class citizens they enjoyed a standard of
living far higher than that of their countrymen on the mainland.
To them, the Nationalists who poured into the place in 1945 were
carpet-baggers of the most odious kind, and to all intents and
purposes foreigners, for the Formosans in general spoke the
Fukienese dialect of their ancestors and found standard Chinese
unintelligible. Ill-feeling grew, until in the spring of 1947 there
was an uprising which the Nationalist garrison crushed with
atrocious severity. Of course, the affair became an international
scandal, and was one of the things which alienated American
sympathy from the Kuomintang. Since then, Chiang had reformed
the administration, and in the spring of 1950 was solidly established on the island with the cream of his troops. Yet everybody
believed that the Communists would strike at any moment, and
when that happened no help would be forthcoming from America.
President Truman, on 5 January 1950, said:

> The United States will not pursue a course which will lead to involve-
> ment in the civil conflict in China. The United States will not provide
> military aid or advice to Chinese forces on Formosa.

The American disillusionment with the Kuomintang had consequences outside the borders of China itself. The peninsula of
Korea was another portion of the Japanese Empire wrested from
Tokyo after the war. The allies agreed that the country should
regain its independence, but as a temporary measure it was decided that it should be divided into two zones at the 38th parallel;
the southern half would be occupied by American troops to
manage the surrender and repatriation of the Japanese, while
Soviet troops would accomplish the same task for the northern
part. In a manner that was to become familiar elsewhere, what
was intended, by the Americans at least, as a short-term arrangement was transformed by the rapid deterioration of the wartime
Soviet-American understanding into a permanent state of affairs,
so that at the end of 1949 there were in effect two Koreas. In the
North, a one-party 'people's' regime, fostered by the Russians,
ruled over ten million subjects. In the South, a smaller territory
contained twice as many inhabitants. It was administered by the

government of the Republic of Korea, elected under the auspices
of the United Nations in 1948, and hoping in theory to embrace
the northern zone when free elections would be possible there. It
was recognized by America and her allies. In spite of the disparity
of the population, the North had by far the larger and stronger
army, to the formation of which the Russians had paid the closest
attention. Both Russian and United States troops had withdrawn,
except for groups of military advisers on the two sides.

The southern government was composed largely of representatives of the wealthier classes whose anti-Communist views had
recommended them to the Americans. At its head as President
was Dr Syngman Rhee, an elderly patriot who had spent many
years in exile to avoid Japanese rule, without thereby acquiring
any political wisdom, for compared with him Chiang Kai-shek
was a progressive and enlightened figure. All the maladies which
had corroded the Kuomintang flourished just as vigorously in
Korea, and to complete the similarity, Dr Rhee and his associates
were continually making bellicose gestures towards the North.
From time to time, clashes on the border accentuated the danger.
At last Washington considered it necessary to do some plain
speaking, and in January 1950, exactly one week after President
Truman's declaration of disinterest in Formosa, defined the limit
of American military defence in a way which seemed to put Korea
outside the pale; in other words it was hinted that the South, in
case of war, would look in vain for American help.

Apparently, this statement was taken literally in some quarters,
for on 25 June 1950 the northern forces launched a massive invasion across the border. Although, of course, one does not know
what degree of collusion existed between the Communist powers,
it is unlikely that China can have had any real say in the decision
to attack, for she was then almost without influence in North
Korea. The links between Russia and her recent zone of occupation were so close that it is inconceivable that the adventure was
begun in the absence of consent from Moscow. No doubt it was
imagined that South Korea would quickly collapse without exciting any international reaction more serious than some impotent
condemnation by the United Nations. The first half of this suppo-
sition was justified; the southern resistance was broken almost at
once and it was plainly only a question of days before the whole
peninsula would be united under northern rule. What ruined the

calculation was the speed and vigour of the American counter-measures, for President Truman without hesitation ordered his land and air forces to intervene. This was done with the full blessing of the United Nations; a Russian boycott of the Security Council enabled that body, free from the impediment of a veto, to name the North as the aggressor and to institute a United Nations Command in Korea. At the same moment, going back on his statement of six months earlier, President Truman ordered the American Seventh Fleet to neutralize Formosa for the duration of the Korean fighting; that is to say the Americans, while preventing the Nationalists from attacking the mainland, undertook in return to defend them against invasion.

For the Chinese Communists, then, an immediate result of the outbreak of the Korean war was that America had intervened to prevent the People's Government from assuming control over an integral portion of its national territory. And as, very soon afterwards, Washington went further and sent advisers and equipment to build up the Kuomintang forces, it was easy for Peking to represent to the Chinese people that the territory in question was actually under alien occupation, or in a word that America had begun an aggressive war against them. The events in Korea were interpreted in the same way; the South had been encouraged by the imperialists into attacking the North. When in due course the foreseeable happened, and United Nations forces under General MacArthur began to get the upper hand, the General Assembly gave them the task of extending operations to the North and uniting the two zones. This mission led them to advance towards the Yalu River, which separates Manchuria from Korea, and at the news old memories began to stir. Twice before, in the sixteenth century and then in the nineteenth, invaders from beyond the sea (in both cases Japanese) had entered China through this doorway. To be sure, the United Nations had proclaimed that the Chinese frontier would not be violated, but General MacArthur was bitterly anti-Communist, and his victory would establish an anti-Communist, and therefore anti-Chinese, regime as China's next-door neighbour. Throughout history, until the humiliations of the last hundred years, it had been an essential aim of Chinese policy that Korea should sustain the function of a buffer against the outside world, and it was hardly to be expected that China after her triumphant revolution would allow her ancient satellite to be turned into an enemy. Before the end of October 1950, Chinese troops began to pour across the Yalu.

It would be out of place here to describe the Korean War in detail. By the end of November, the United Nations force had been driven over the 38th parallel, and early in 1951 the Chinese opened an offensive against the southern zone. By April they had been checked and pushed back to the 38th parallel once more, and there, roughly, the line of battle remained for the next two years. Although the United Nations condemned China as an aggressor, the knowledge that General MacArthur held that the war should be carried to China herself by air-raids over Manchuria, caused a panic among America's allies. They feared Russian intervention on China's behalf, and it was agreed that not only should there be no reprisals against Chinese territory, but that the attempt to unite Korea should be abandoned. General MacArthur's dissatisfaction with these conditions caused his recall in April 1951. When an armistice was at last signed, in July 1953, the existing battle-line was taken as the boundary between the zones, which remained in size practically as they had been before June 1950.

The consequences of the war were far-reaching. The United Nations force was overwhelmingly American in composition, and the conflict was essentially one between China and America. The latter's losses were very heavy, and as they were inflicted by a country which she had saved from Japanese conquest only a few years before, and had elevated to the status of a Great Power, her resentment was correspondingly bitter. The Peking Government was seen as the most malignant of America's enemies, whose refusal to abide by the rules of international law made any talk of granting it recognition or of admitting it to the United Nations a dangerous absurdity.

To China the involvement in Korea meant increased dependence on Russia and Eastern Europe, especially since America and her allies instituted an embargo against the export of strategic commodities to the aggressor. As a result, commerce with the non-Communist countries which accounted for three-quarters of China's foreign trade in 1950, had by 1954 fallen to one-fifth, while dealings with the Communist bloc rose in proportion. Peking, too, found it expedient to let the Russians postpone their departure from Manchuria. But on the credit side was the immense accession of prestige gained by what seemed, in the eyes of the world, the successful Chinese defiance of the military power of the United States. Naturally too, the physical presence of her intervention set China in Russia's place as the predominant patron of North Korea. But over and above these things was the effect of the war on the Peking government's conduct of domestic policy. Although the fiction was maintained that the Chinese who fought in Korea were simply 'volunteers', the nation was not only summoned by its leaders to withstand the foreign enemy, it was also put on the alert against traitors within its gates who were plotting to bring back the Kuomintang and the imperialists.

The Terror

The enforcement of the Agrarian Law offered the first great example of this atmosphere of emergency. Promulgated at the end of June 1950, it was intended to 'release agriculture from feudal shackles and thus pave the way for industrialization'. It was not, therefore, devised as a measure of utopian egalitarianism; on the contrary it proposed for a time to tolerate even the richer peasants, in order not to disrupt the economy by too great precipitation.

A supplementary decree defined the standards of class status. First came the landlords, who did not labour and lived wholly by exploitation. Then there were the rich peasants, working on some of their land, but letting most of it. The middle peasant lived by tilling his own soil, while the poor peasant had to rent the land of others. Finally came the worker, without land or implements, and dependent entirely on the sale of his labour. The new law provided that the land, draught animals and implements of the landlords should be confiscated. The estates of monasteries and temples were to be requisitioned against compensation. The rich peasants would fare better, for besides the land they tilled themselves, they might be permitted to retain even a part of what they leased to others. This generosity was intended to calm any fears felt by the middle peasant who might otherwise believe that his turn for expropriation would come next. It was seen that the middle peasant in many cases had managed to keep himself on a sound basis because of his superior efficiency as a farmer and therefore even when he was a wealthy member of his class he was allowed to retain his land in its entirety. The two poorest classes shared in the division of confiscated property; this varied in amount from district to district. During the entire operation, down to the beginning of 1953, seven hundred million *mou* (a *mou* is one-sixth of an acre) were divided between three hundred million persons, an average of just over two *mou* per person. But in densely populated Eastern China, the average share was less than one *mou*. Regarded as a gain in productive power, this was quite clearly insignificant. The true purpose of the exercise, however, lay elsewhere.

Communist Party cadres had been left throughout the country-side in the wake of the Liberation Army, and they were now joined by more of their colleagues. Their duty was to observe the class structure in the villages, and to become familiar with the local personalities, in particular with those men and women who showed evidence of being potential 'activists'. From their find-ings, the cadres proceeded to organize the peasants into village associations; these elected some of their number into village con-gresses, which in turn chose delegates to county congresses, and so up the scale to the province and the Greater Administrative Area. The system thus constructed ensured the subordination of the masses to higher policy. Finally, to see to the enforcement of the Agrarian Law in each county, special People's Tribunals were set up which differed from the ordinary courts in that no appeal from their sentence was permitted once they had defined an accused person as a class enemy. The president and half the judges were elected by the peasants associations in congresses, and the tribunals went on circuit through the countryside.

Meanwhile, in the village meetings the cadres had encouraged the denunciation of such public enemies as specially rapacious landlords, and the miscellaneous bullies who had been their hangers-on. Sometimes the anger of the crowd was spontaneous; sometimes it required stimulation, and then the villagers were taken into the rich men's houses and shown the luxuries they con-tained, while tales of oppression and outrage were dinned into their ears. When the trial came on, feeling would be at its height, and the occasion would be a great orgy of hatred. Often an abject confession by the criminal, and his public humiliation would be considered sufficient, but in many cases he was shot out of hand; now and then indeed he was lynched by the spectators. Day after day the newspapers were filled with descriptions of these proceed-ings, in which the yells of the mob were reported in detail. The number of people put to death was enormous; the Nationalist figure of fifteen million or more is certainly exaggerated, but it is unlikely to have been much lower than one million. At the end not only had the power of the landlord class been totally eliminated, but the peasantry as a whole had been led into habits of obedience towards the new order.

In 1951–2 the People's Tribunals extended their activities to the cities, as an instrument in two separate campaigns of terror waged respectively against corruption in government officials and illegal practices, such as tax-evasion, in businessmen and industrialists. This latter purge bore so strong a resemblance to its counterpart in the villages that at first the capitalists who had foreseen a reasonable future for themselves in the New China, thought they were going to share the fate of the landlords. Cadres settled in among workmen and clerks and in the way which had become familiar incited them to denounce their employers. When accusations had been procured, life was made unbearable for the victims until they confessed their crimes; a common trick was to station outside their houses a lorry with a loud-speaker which roared abuse day and night. In cities like Shanghai and Canton, which were visited with particular energy, hundreds of people committed suicide. Those who confessed got off with heavy fines, for it was intended at this stage not to eliminate the bourgeoisie, but merely to cow it into submission and incidentally to replenish the Treasury, depleted by the needs of the Korean War. By the beginning of 1953, the terror in town and country was over, and the formidable Tribunals, their purpose accomplished, vanished from the scene. The best excuse for the bloodshed was the demonstrable fact that in spite of the strain and burden of the Korean War, inflation had been halted and that production, both industrial and agricultural, had returned to, and occasionally surpassed, the levels attained in the comparative peace of the years before 1937.

The First Five-Year Plan

It was now time to take the direct road towards socialism, and accordingly the first Five-Year Plan was launched, to cover the period 1953–7. The details were not clarified until the five years were nearly over, but the goal was evident from the start. China was to be industrialized, and as a prime necessity the labour of the people was to be dedicated, at whatever sacrifice, not to the immediate satisfaction of material wants, but to the building of a foundation for future development by the investment of the fruits of their toil in capital construction. One result of the years of chaos had been to render almost impossible the proper scientific investigation of the country's natural resources, but now the task could be undertaken. It is still in progress and whereas in the old days it was pessimistically assumed that apart from coal, and the prospect of hydro-electric power, China was not well endowed in this respect, the People's Government now claims to possess deposits of minerals, including substances like uranium, necessary for the creation of the most advanced modern industries. The point upon which foreign observers have expressed the most serious reservations concerns petroleum. In 1952 production was a mere four hundred and fifty thousand tons from Sinkiang and Manchuria, and even at the end of the first Five-Year Plan the figure reached no more than one and a half million tons annually. Industrial requirements could be met only by importation of oil from Russia. Then came a series of remarkable discoveries of oilfields in Manchuria, Kwangtung, Szechwan, and Chinghai, near Tibet. In 1959, the output had risen to over three and a half million tons and the Minister in charge revealed that he foresaw the day when China would be one of the great oil-producing areas of the world. The general dearth of statistics since 1960 makes it impossible to express any views on this prophecy.

But the most sensational report provided by the surveyors was in the matter of manpower. It was generally believed that the population of China was in the region of four hundred and fifty millions, so when the result of a census made in June 1953 – the first real trustworthy operation of its kind – showed that in fact there were five hundred and eighty million inhabitants, the astonishment was enormous. One might have imagined there would have been consternation as well, since this meant that for every three persons the planners had taken into account there had all along been a fourth lurking in the background. Yet the official reaction to the news was on classical Marxist lines, namely to welcome the fecundity as a valuable national asset. Some time later, to be sure, it struck home that the decline in the rate of mortality, with better hygiene and the end of civil war and famines, was raising the annual increase to over two per cent. It seemed likely that by 1980 there would be a thousand million mouths to feed. A birth control campaign took place for a few months in 1957. But it seems to have been distasteful to Mao Tse-tung both for doctrinal reasons and because of traditional prejudices. Although contraceptives remained procurable, the publicity was stopped at the end of the year. In the 1960s, the movement has apparently been resumed with greater moderation, helped by the encouragement of later marriage among young people.

To conduct the nation on its way to socialism, it was felt that a more efficient machinery of government was required than that which had served the purpose since 1949; one conforming more adequately to the doctrine of Democratic Centralism. In a word, it was hoped to convey the commands of the ruling power through the various strata of society with all the greater acceptance for appearing itself to be the creature of the popular will. By the Constitution of 1954, the ultimate authority is vested in a system of People's Congresses, in the pyramidal form with which we are already familiar. At the base, in each locality a Congress is elected by the inhabitants, men and women over eighteen, with the exception, amounting to several millions, of public enemies who are deprived of the franchise. There is a single list of candidates, who are usually voted for by a show of hands. The body thus formed in turn elects some of its members to Congresses at a higher level, until the supreme National Congress is constituted. The first was convoked in September 1954 and consisted of 1,226 deputies. It chose Mao Tse-tung as Chairman of the People's Republic and Head of State. In theory, the National Congress is elected for four years, which may be extended, and should meet once a year for a fortnight. For the rest of the time its functions are performed by a Standing Committee elected from its members. The highest administrative body is the State Council, headed by the Premier (Chou En-lai), which is responsible to the National Congress and is subject to the direction of the Chairman of the Republic. It is an elaborate complex of Ministries and Commissions. The judges of the Supreme People's Court are appointed by the Standing Committee of the National Congress, while judges of lower courts are appointed by local congresses of corresponding level. Any citizen over twenty-three is eligible to be made a judge; no legal knowledge is required. A system of People's Procuratorates supervises all judicial and administrative activities.

This government recognized itself as a dictatorship of the proletariat; to add some verisimilitude to this, the urban populations are more strongly represented in the National Congress than the peasantry, having one member for one hundred thousand persons, while the countrypeople have to be satisfied with one member for eight hundred thousand. In fact the whole structure is an instrument to carry out policy decided upon by the Communist Party, which controls every section of it. The dictatorship in theory is applied only to class enemies, while against the people proper democratic means should be used with full protection of the law. But the law is the collective expression of the will of the masses, a will which by definition can be understood only by the Party. Consequently, in any case of the slightest importance, the courts are enjoined first of all to seek the advice of the local Party representatives. In 1966 there was still no Civil or Criminal Code; it has been argued that economic relationships are being transformed at such a pace that any Civil Code would be out of date by the time it was promulgated; and although there is a substantial amount of legislation, plenty of scope exists for the exercise of uninhibited authority even by the lower echelons of officialdom.

The Constitution was at pains to emphasize the recognition of private property and of the capitalist section of the economy. During the redistribution of land, much solemnity had been made of the issuing of title-deeds to the new proprietors as an assurance of the Government's determination to defend their rights. Nevertheless, even while this was being done, steps were already taken to reverse the process and lead the farmers into collectivization. The first stage on this road was the encouragement of an institution known, in embryo form, to traditional China. This was the 'mutual-aid' team by which neighbours pooled their labour and equipment in the busy season; by August 1952 it was reckoned that thirty-five million households had been organized into six million such teams, while in the same year advances were being made elsewhere towards alternative and more permanent association into agricultural co-operatives. In these, though still retaining their private ownership of land, tools and draught animals, the peasants put them into a common stock and received a proportionate number of shares in what was produced.

Great efforts were made to explain to the people the obvious advantages of these measures and the waste and inefficiency of minute plots, each growing separate crops, where a large tract of land, devoted to one crop and run jointly, would be far more profitable to all concerned. At the end of 1953, the Government indicated its preference for the agricultural co-operatives over the mutual-aid teams, and from then the movement went on those lines. Yet it was a slow process, in the course of which cadres encountered much peasant stubbornness, production did not increase so quickly as had been hoped, and worst of all, signs were detected of 'spontaneous capitalism' in the countryside. This made a disappointing contrast with the position in industry and commerce, where during the years 1954–6 the private sector was to all intents and purposes eliminated in favour of nationalization. Odder still, it was maintained at the time that the urban capitalists in general sold out to the state voluntarily from an abundance of patriotic enthusiasm. Ten years later, however, a film on this theme was condemned for the heresy of attributing such virtuous sentiments to exploiters who yielded only when overawed by the might of the people.

Even allowing for the low level of the starting point, the period of the first Five-Year Plan saw a remarkable growth in industry, particularly in heavy industry. By the end of it, in 1957, China for the first time was in a position to manufacture tractors and cars, cargo-ships, and jet planes. A new and romantic world of activity offered itself to the young. Students who ten years earlier would never have dreamed of learning technical subjects saw that prestige was to be won not by international law or European languages but by engineering and chemistry. This alone points to a significant difference in educational emphasis between the People's China and most of her Asian and African sisters in underdevelopment.

Clearly agriculture could not be allowed to lag so far behind. In July 1955, Mao Tse-tung set a definite target. By the end of the first Five-Year Plan in two and a half years' time, half of the entire rural population, he said, must be organized into co-operatives, and he reproached some Party comrades for being

like women with bound feet, always complaining that others are going too fast.

The reassurance of the great man's views put fresh heart into the activists. The co-operatives most recommended were of the so-called 'higher' type. Only trivial strips of land, for the cultivation of vegetables, were allowed to be retained privately. Members' dividend was calculated more as wages for labour than as reimbursement for land contributed. Opposition spread and in many districts the peasants showed their resentment in the age-old manner by slaughtering livestock rather than handing them over to the common fund. No protests were allowed to delay the operation, which was carried on with such vigour that Mao's goal for 1957 was already achieved in March 1956. Less than a year later, in February 1957, over ninety per cent of the peasants were in the higher co-operatives, and Mao was able to declare that the task of reorganization had been successfully completed.

The 'Hundred Flowers'

Compared with the experience of Russia, the transition to collectivization had indeed been wonderfully smooth. Undoubtedly the awe in men's minds induced by the terror of five years earlier had its part in keeping opposition within manageable limits, and the Liberation Army was always in the background, but the direct use of force had not often been necessary. Was there in China some instinctive link of sympathy between Party and people? Mao, at least, thought there was, and that the phenomenon could be profited from. Already in the summer of 1956, he had put out the idea that the Party stood to benefit from the frank opinions of its multitude of friends, and a slogan, later to become famous, had been issued to the effect:

Let a hundred flowers bloom, let a hundred schools of thought contend.

So far it had aroused little attention, but the Hungarian Uprising in the winter of the same year had furnished a splendid example of what happened when a Communist regime got out of touch with the masses.

In the spring of 1957 Mao returned to the attack. It is suspected in some quarters that, in order to remove inhibitions, criticisms of the Party were deliberately planted here and there in the press. The result surpassed all expectations. A torrent of scorn and even hatred, pent up for years, poured out over the Government and

the Party leadership. Most of the criticism came from those intellectuals – university teachers and students, journalists, writers –
who had been chafing at the pretensions and authoritarianism of
what had become a new ruling class, and often enough they did
not attempt to distinguish between the system and its representatives but called for an abandonment of Marxist doctrine altogether.
It was later alleged that the malcontents were bourgeois in origin,
and regretted the loss of their old dignified status in society. Very
likely there is a solid kernel of truth in this; a demand for instance
such as that made by a number of lawyers for the reinstitution of
the Nationalist codes cannot have had the faintest interest for the
people at large. In other words, it would be unwise to exaggerate
the significance of the *Hundred Flowers* episode as an indication of
public opinion generally. Nevertheless, the affair was an unpleasant shock to the Government. In June 1957, after six weeks
of licence, it again imposed its censorship, remarking that it
wanted flowers not weeds in the socialist garden. The criterion for
separating the two was simple. Right words and actions

help to consolidate, not undermine or weaken, the people's democratic
dictatorship, and tend to strengthen, not to cast off or weaken, the
leadership of the Communist Party.

Those who had expressed themselves too freely now cursed their
foolhardiness. Branded as untrustworthy by the organized judgment of their colleagues, to which, if they were wise, they added
their own self-condemnations, they became social pariahs, whose
only hope was that they might rehabilitate themselves by austerity
and hard work. College teachers, for example, were transferred
from cities like Shanghai to some remote spot in Sinkiang or
Inner Mongolia.

The Great Leap Forward

This turn of the wheel was to the advantage of the strongly left-
wing members of the Party and Government, and enabled them to
carry the day against those of their comrades who felt that the time
had arrived for some relaxation of the ceaseless pressure upon the
people. A second Five-Year Plan was in process of being devised,
Liu Shao-ch'i, Chairman of the Standing Committee of the
National People's Congress, and a theoretician inferior only to

Mao himself, was convinced that a spectacular development of industry would occur, if only the faint-hearted would stop impeding those whose slogan was always 'Faster and Better!' and who knew the necessity of 'uninterrupted revolution'.

Meanwhile one vast reservoir of energy was lying to hand, almost untapped over most of the country. The peasantry, after the autumn harvest, had nothing to do till the spring sowing. In the northern provinces this idleness accounted for a good hundred days a year for every person. It was essential to turn this manpower to use, and during the winter of 1957-8, millions of men and women were put to work laying railways, building river embankments, digging canals and irrigation trenches. In February 1958, the National People's Congress heard of a design for 'a great leap forward', a phrase which in the technical vocabulary of Marxism meant that so much quantitative advance would be accomplished that the resulting transformation would be qualitative; in other words that China would emerge out of the period of transition into a socialist society. There was, it appeared, no profound mystery in this business of industrialization; once the people had put their minds to it their own native common sense would carry them to victory. The most characteristic phenomenon of the time was the 'backyard furnace' for making steel. By October 1958, there were said to be no fewer than six hundred thousand of these in operation. The official objective written up everywhere in the streets was to overtake Britain in steel production within fifteen years, but even this period was too long for the enthusiasm of the cadres, and it was hinted that ten years would be more than enough.

But the capital for this gigantic undertaking would have to come overwhelmingly from agriculture, and it was impossible to conceal the fact that collectivization was very far from bringing the abundance that had been expected. Floods and drought had been partly to blame and the shortage of chemical fertilizer could not easily be remedied but there were many complaints of inefficiency in administration. Mao Tse-tung's reaction to this challenge was, in the atmosphere of the time, predictable. Collectivization must assume even greater dimensions, and the people must be convinced, by every possible means of persuasion, that the era of plenty could be reached well within their lifetime. In April 1958, the news came that in Honan twenty co-operatives had merged into one. The example was followed in other provinces, and then in July the Honan enterprise absorbed even more co-operatives to form a Commune. The development was alleged to have occurred at the request of the peasants themselves; immediately afterwards it was approved by the Government for the whole country, and Mao made a tour of North China to advocate the scheme.

As compared with the co-operatives, which were concerned purely with agriculture, the Communes controlled not only farming, but industry, commerce, and education. Besides taking over the property of the co-operatives they had absorbed, the Communes digested the private-plots, fruit trees and livestock of their members, who were organized, both men and women, like soldiers ready for any duty they might be assigned. Mess halls and nurseries set housewives free for labour outside the home, and as a further convenience in some places men and women moved from domesticity into separate dormitories.

The speed with which the movement spread was almost incredible. By early November 1958, it was stated that ninety-nine per cent of the peasantry had been organized into twenty-six thousand odd Communes. The average territorial extent was ten thousand acres for five thousand households. Most frequently the boundary of a Commune coincided with that of an administrative district, and then the district government and the Commune government became one and the same. As we have seen, the official story was that the initiative sprang from the spontaneous enthusiasm of the people which drew Peking in its wake, but only a simpleton will credit this. The prevalent mood in the leadership, especially of Mao himself, was heavily behind greater collectivization, and this was communicated to the local cadres. True, the population allowed itself to be conducted along the road more readily than might have been expected, but the excitement was infectious and the harvest in that first summer of the experiment (1958) happened to be unusually good. One undertaking to capture the imagination of the world was the slaughter of that pest of farmers, the sparrow, in which from one end of the country to the other there was a mighty din of voices and gongs to frighten the birds from their perches and keep them on the wing until they fell to the ground exhausted, to make a tasty addition to the cooking pot.

And then began that season of delirium in which for a few

months it seemed as if a miracle was coming to pass and the People's Government had indeed subdued nature to its will. Agricultural production, it was said, was more than double what it had been the year before, and the same was true for iron and steel. Communist society was not a dream of the future but was in visible process of being born. Some of the Communes were announcing that already their members were being supplied according to their needs.

But by the end of 1958, Peking seemed to be having second thoughts. The great discovery was made that human bodies after all require some repose, and a special directive enjoined the cadres not to force the people to work more than twelve hours a day. Backyard furnaces were very well, but the novelty was apt to distract the peasants from what should be their chief preoccupation, the land. In any case, scrap metal was practically exhausted. It was premature to offer supplies according to need. Wages would prove an incentive; so too would the return of the small private plots. Then, as the spring of 1959 passed into summer, there were rumours that something else was amiss. These were confirmed when in August 1959 Chou En-lai confessed that the production figures for 1958 had been monstrously exaggerated by the boastfulness and incompetence of Commune officials, anxious to surpass their fellows. Grain output, for example, instead of three hundred and seventy-five million tons was only two hundred and fifty million tons. Steel amounted to eight million tons in place of eleven million. Targets for 1959 were cut accordingly; in the matter of grain, the quantity aimed at was revised from five hundred and twenty-five million tons to two hundred and seventy-five million. As a final encouragement to sanity, the weather during the summer of 1959 was disastrous, the first of three calamitous harvests in succession. At the year's end, it had to be admitted that the goal for grain had not been achieved; to be sure, it was stated that the deficiency was of merely five million tons, which would still have meant an increase of twenty million tons over the 1958 production, but it is extremely doubtful whether the claim is true. No figures were issued for 1960 but it is thought, in view of the bad weather, that the whole agricultural output could not have been much in excess of the 1952 figure. In 1961, China had to go abroad for its food, and bought ten million tons of grain from Australia, Canada and elsewhere.

So much noise had been made by propaganda about the 'Great Leap Forward' that not surprisingly there was a tendency in the outside world, on hearing this news, to suggest that a better name for the thing would have been the 'Great Leap Backward'. This is an error. Much in the experiment was wrongly conceived – the disregard of human factors especially – but in some respects striking results were obtained, and the catastrophe of the three bad harvests, though inflicting great hardship on the people, at least did not cause famine, as would have occurred in the past. Then also it is fair to acknowledge that the Communist leaders did not shrink from exposing themselves to ridicule by confessing they had been deceived, something very hard for a dictatorship to stomach. Almost certainly there were members of the government who did not share the extreme optimism of Mao Tse-tung; Chou En-lai, who gives a perhaps misleading impression of moderation, is often named as one of these. But there seems no reason to suppose that Mao's retirement at the end of 1958 from his post as Head of State and his replacement by Liu Shao-ch'i signified that he was beginning to lose influence because of the failure of his policy. Liu himself was fully as committed to the Great Leap as Mao, and had throughout been Mao's most zealous supporter. Mao kept his grip on the reality of power by retaining his leadership of the Party, and his influence as Sage and Teacher has gone from strength to strength.

There have, then, been some necessary shifts in emphasis. Priority today goes to agriculture as the indispensable foundation of the economy, and the infirmity of man's nature is consoled by devoting a fair proportion of industrial activity to the manufacture of consumer goods. In practice the peasants have reverted to the Collectives as before 1958, with possession of small personal plots and the right to market the produce from these. The family group has re-asserted its integrity over the dormitory and the mess-hall. But the ideal of the Commune has never been repudiated. On the contrary, as late as 1960, when the movement was being slowed down in the countryside, there was an attempt to introduce it to the cities, and to organize places like Peking and Shanghai into Urban Communes for the better co-ordination and control of the inhabitants' activities. This at any rate has not been pushed very far, but the Rural Commune remains, on paper, the basic social institution, the framework within which the nation's manpower is assembled for such duties as militia service, and it may well be that the present eclipse of its economic function is merely temporary.

The Road to Bandung

These domestic vicissitudes were matched by equally dramatic changes in foreign relations. The initial months of the first Five-Year Plan in 1953 witnessed the death of Stalin and the armistice in Korea. Both events appeared to bring Russia and China even more cordially together. In October 1954, Bulganin, Khrushchev and Mikoyan, in Peking to celebrate the fifth anniversary of the foundation of the People's Government, agreed to extend a further credit of one hundred and thirty million dollars and to assist in more industrial undertakings. At the same time, joint Russo-Chinese companies, objectionable because of their infringement of Chinese sovereignty, were broken up, with the Russian shares going to China. Another Russian withdrawal was in Manchuria, where Soviet troops finally quitted Port Arthur and transferred their installations to China without compensation.

It seemed then that something approaching a partnership had been concluded between the two giants. China, already basking in the glory of having rescued North Korea from the Americans, had her prestige enhanced still further by the armistice in Indo-China (1954), where Ho Chi Minh's victory over the French was certainly due to Chinese help. At the Geneva Conference that summer, which decided on the partition of Vietnam, Chou En-lai emerged as a statesman of world rank.

China was ready to profit from this favourable atmosphere by modifying her own attitude. In 1949, when she declared her total adherence to the socialist camp, her contempt for all neutralists, whether in Asia or elsewhere, was open and undisguised, and Pandit Nehru in particular was lampooned in the Chinese press as a lackey of imperialism. What was more important, the question of Tibet had seemed for a moment as if it might turn Indian opinion against the New China from the very beginning.

Like Outer Mongolia, Tibet formed part of the Manchu Empire, and on the fall of the dynasty, Chinese garrisons were expelled from both territories by their inhabitants who seized the opportunity of asserting their liberty. But whereas Outer Mongolia could rely on the patronage of Russia, whether Tsarist or

Soviet, Tibet never obtained foreign support for its claim to independence. True, at a conference held at Simla in 1913–14 between Britain, Tibet and China, it was agreed that, although all Tibet lay under Chinese suzerainty, the part of it nearer to India, called Outer Tibet, should enjoy internal autonomy, but the Chinese government at once repudiated the agreement, which it never signed. In the next three decades, successive regimes, warlord and Nationalist, insisted that both Outer Mongolia and Tibet were included in the Chinese dominions though temporarily out of control. As we have seen, it was with the utmost reluctance that Chiang Kai-shek, under American pressure, consented in 1945 to placate Stalin by recognizing the independence of Outer Mongolia.

There were special reasons why the People's Government should have been anxious to re-impose Chinese authority in Tibet as soon as possible. British influence in the area was considerable, and in 1950 there were signs that America, having washed its hands of China proper, might be inclined to support Tibetan independence. Certainly a briefing had been prepared for American troops who might eventually go to Tibet. Furthermore, the condition of Tibetan society, a peculiarly benighted form of religious feudalism, was abhorrent to Marxist notions. In October 1950, it was announced that the liberation of Tibet was under way. India protested to Peking, but when the United Nations seemed likely to be invoked, it was found that Chiang Kai-shek was just as firm as Mao Tse-tung on the question, and the matter was dropped. Meanwhile, the Dalai Lama was made to see the necessity of co-operating with his new overlords, who promised to respect the Lamaist religious institutions, and as time went on even Nehru seemed reassured. By 1954 friendship between Delhi and Peking had gone so far that a Sino-Indian Trade Agreement recognized Tibet as 'the Tibetan region of China'.

But it was the conference of Afro-Asian states, held in 1955 at Bandung in Java, which set the seal on China's claim to leadership in the East. By general consent Chou En-lai's performance was masterly; amiability in person, he charmed all who met him, and when he and Nehru proclaimed the Five Principles of Peaceful Coexistence, it seemed that Asia had put the West to shame.

The Quarrel with Russia

In February 1956, the cordial relations between Moscow and Peking were subjected to something of a strain by Khrushchev's famous denunciation of Stalin at the 20th Congress of the Russian Communist Party. It is almost certain that Mao was angered at not having been consulted in advance about a step of such importance, but for the time being he swallowed his annoyance and seemed to share Khrushchev's views. During the Hungarian crisis at the end of the year, China came out as a strong partisan of the USSR. In November 1957, Mao made a second visit to Moscow for an international gathering of Communist Parties and in a speech at the University declared that the Socialist camp must have a head and the head was Russia. The sentiment was undoubtedly sincere; a few weeks earlier the launching of the Sputnik overwhelmed the Chinese leaders with admiration of Russian science and technology. 'The East Wind,' said Mao, 'is prevailing over the West Wind.' This conviction played a large part in inducing the enthusiasm in Peking for the Great Leap Forward. It is highly significant, for example, that the very first Commune, founded in July 1958, was christened 'The Sputnik'.

But Moscow was far from being enchanted by these tokens of esteem. The Great Leap Forward, Peking was boasting, would carry China into a Communist society ahead of Russia, although to Khrushchev, leaving aside the implied threat to Soviet leadership, the whole notion was ill-conceived and impracticable. Nevertheless, provided China came to her senses, it was important to keep her friendly. In December 1958, Peking had to begin, in principle, to acknowledge the difficulties that stood in the way of the practical working of the Commune plan, and Russia was sufficiently reassured, early in 1959, to agree to an exchange of goods, worth over one billion dollars, for the period of the second and third Five-Year Plans, that is to say down to 1967. But it soon became clear that Mao had recanted nothing. Nor was that all. Khrushchev's denunciation of Stalinism had another side; he genuinely hoped to reach an accommodation with the United States. Mao on the contrary judged that Russia's technical triumph with the Sputnik had made all compromises unnecessary.

The intransigence was not confined to words. In Tibet, the rate of Chinese immigration began to provoke sporadic uprisings from 1956 onwards, the revolt gathered momentum and in March 1959 the Dalai Lama fled to India where he was given asylum. About the same time the Indian public became aware of what was already known in Delhi, namely that China not only laid claim to a considerable tract of frontier territory asserted by the Indians to belong to their own country – there was no mystery on this point, because Chinese maps marked the territory as Chinese – but were in such effective occupation of that part of it which lay in Ladakh (Kashmir) that they had for the past two years been using a military road built across it to link Tibet with Sinkiang. It may be thought that the fact such a road could escape notice for so long hardly suggests the region was under regular Indian administration, and indeed it cannot be denied that the Chinese claim, both to the twelve thousand square miles in Ladakh in the northwest, and to the forty thousand square miles of the North-East Frontier Agency at the opposite end of the Himalayas, has formidable evidence in its favour. The latter area was assigned to India by that same Simla convention which the Chinese refused to ratify in 1914. But when to the news from Tibet there were added reports of frontier clashes, the impression was given that a threat to Indian security was being built up in the northern mountains.

Moscow had been at pains to cultivate Indian friendship with exchanges of state visits, loans exceeding in amount those made to China, and technical aid to Indian industries, and now at this juncture Russia let it be seen that she maintained neutrality in the Sino-Indian dispute. In October 1959 Khrushchev, immediately after a visit to the United States, went to Peking, ostensibly to celebrate the tenth anniversary of the People's Government, but really, if we judge from a speech he made, to deliver a warning. He said:

We must do every thing possible to avoid war as a means of settling questions. The fact that we are strong does not mean that we should test the capitalist system by force.

The month following, Nehru told the Indian Parliament:

I doubt if there is any country that cares more for peace than the Soviet Union. I doubt if there is any country that cares less for peace than China.

It was in the spring of 1960 that the dispute between China and Russia began to assume the doctrinal form which it was henceforward to retain. On Lenin's ninetieth birthday (22 April) Lu Ting-yi, a member of the Politburo, in an address to the Central Committee of the Chinese Communist Party reminded his listeners that Lenin had long ago declared American imperialism to be the most vicious enemy of the people of the world. Today Eisenhower was its chieftain. But modern revisionists, betraying the spirit of Marxism-Leninism, were camouflaging imperialism and describing Eisenhower as a peace envoy. As against these renegades, Mao Tse-tung's thinking

integrates the universal truth of Marxism-Leninism with the concrete practice of the Chinese revolution.

Since Khrushchev was at that moment preparing for a summit conference with Eisenhower, a meeting from which China would be excluded, the message was plain.[1]

In the event, Khrushchev cancelled the summit conference, on the grounds that American planes were spying over Russian territory, and there are those who believe that he was deterred by the strength of Chinese opposition. This does not seem very probable, since in June 1960 Moscow retorted to Peking by applying to 'present day Leftism' Lenin's term 'an infantile disorder'. At a congress in Bucharest in the same month, Khrushchev said that

only madmen and maniacs can now call for another war.

Then he struck the most wounding blow he could. In August 1960, Russian technicians in China were ordered to return home and to take their blueprints with them. Undaunted, the *Peking People's Daily* said:

Let us rely on our own strength. If we do not have this revolutionary will, we shall forever be bullied by others.

There ensued attempts by Communists throughout the world to reconcile the two titans and prevent the scandal of a schism which must tear the movement apart. Now and then it looked as if these efforts might succeed, but always the recriminations broke out, worse than before. In the past, there was a decent convention that the protagonists should not name each other in public, but that abuse from China should be ostensibly directed against Yugoslavia, while Moscow poured contempt on Albania. Now even that thin disguise has been abandoned, and every Chinese or Russian who reads the paper or listens to the radio is told of the quarrel. When Khrushchev fell from power in 1964, it was thought at first that the great cause of offence had been removed. Certainly there was deep personal dislike between him and Mao; to the latter, venerating the majestic simplicity of Stalinism and recognizing that he himself was cast in that mould, Khrushchev was a moral and intellectual nonentity, whose policies if allowed to go unchecked would reduce Marxism to a nauseous pettifogging mishmash. But it soon became apparent that the enmity transcends mere personal incompatibilities, and is nothing less than a struggle between Peking and Moscow for the leadership in two distinct arenas of power. In the first of these, the international Communist movement itself, Moscow may in the nature of things expect to retain its supremacy, since only a tiny number of national parties will find it rewarding to change allegiance, but in every Communist Party throughout the world, there is a section of varying importance which finds the Peking doctrine to its liking. The second is the so-called Afro-Asian bloc, which in the late 1950s and early 1960s received a massive accession from the newly independent states of Africa. Here the appeal is of an openly racialist kind; for instance, Peking seeks to exclude the Soviet Union from participation in international conferences on the grounds that Russia is essentially a white European power. At first, hostility to the West was in itself sufficient to guarantee sympathy from peoples just liberated from colonial rule, especially when Peking made most flattering efforts to cultivate their goodwill, but by 1966 there were many signs of disenchantment.

China in the World

In the eyes of India especially, China has emerged as a most dangerous enemy. To be sure, the frontier war of the autumn of 1962 is not readily explicable in simple terms of Chinese aggression. Even in the Indian version of the story, the government of New Delhi, finding that diplomacy could not induce the Chinese to withdraw from Indian soil, launched a military offensive to drive out the invaders. The attack was repulsed and the Chinese pursued the retreating Indians a considerable distance within what is indisputably Indian territory before returning in triumph to their line of occupation. There was nothing to prevent their advancing a great deal further, and the episode is most reasonably intelligible on the assumption that they genuinely believed in the justice of their claim and intended to give the Indians notice of their determination to retain what in their view belongs to them. On the whole, though, the Chinese case was inadequately represented in the international press, and when in September 1965, during the fighting between India and Pakistan, China made a warlike demonstration on the frontier, the gesture of solidarity towards Pakistan–for disputes with India had brought Karachi and Peking into the warmest friendship –was taken by the world at large as yet another proof of the Chinese lack of interest in the preservation of peace. Meanwhile, the saying of Chou En-lai, that Africa was ripe for revolution, was beginning to have an ominous sound to some African nationalist leaders who guessed that the words were not directed merely against the few surviving colonialist regimes. But the clearest evidence of all was provided by the abortive *coup d'état* in Indonesia in October 1965, when China, by encouraging a Communist attempt to seize power, alienated one of her most faithful supporters. Even in Latin America, where according to trustworthy reports China-trained activists are already making their presence felt, it looks as if Peking may be overreaching itself.

On the other hand, if the Maoist doctrine of world revolution makes China a troublesome member of the international community, especially when we bear in mind the Chinese communities throughout South-East Asia, and the emergence of predominantly Chinese Singapore as a sovereign state, it must be conceded that in some questions closely affecting her security and prestige she has behaved with decided circumspection. For a country marked out by nature and by history as a Great Power, it must be galling in the extreme to witness the events in Vietnam, where on her own doorstep and in an area traditionally acknowledging her cultural and political suzerainty the Americans seem to have committed themselves to propping up a regime which symbolizes everything most odious to her. Yet although American bombs were falling within a few miles of her frontier, there was nothing in the spring of 1966, when these words were written, to suggest that China was preparing to intervene. Similarly, few people imagined, on the formation of the People's Government, that seventeen years later Hong Kong would be allowed to remain as a thriving British colony. The fact is that the need for foreign exchange has for the time being overcome national pride, and as it would be undignified to take back Macao while leaving Hong Kong undisturbed, the tiny Portuguese possession survives as a grotesque anachronism.

It is often surmised that the one way to bring China into a more amenable temper would be to replace the Nationalist delegation in the United Nations with representatives from Peking. Certainly it is hard to believe that American opposition will be able to delay this step for much longer. It is more than doubtful, however, whether Peking will see the advantage of accepting such an invitation. At any rate, Chinese leaders have let it be known they will require as a preliminary that the United Nations should withdraw, and apologize for, the condemnation of China's intervention in the Korean War. Yet, typically, their indignation has not prevented them from maintaining one tenuous link with Washington, namely the regular conversations between American and Chinese diplomats that have been going on for ten years, first at Geneva and then in Warsaw.

Taiwan itself is of course a great stumbling-block in the way of any lessening of tension. It is almost certain that the majority of people on the island, those whose ancestors came from the mainland before the Japanese annexation, would like nothing better than to be independent, but the Nationalist refugees agree with the Communists that Taiwan is inseparably part of China, and it is doubtful how much international backing there would be for a Free Formosa movement. The most probable solution may be that when Chiang Kai-shek has disappeared from the scene his successors will find the Nationalist content of the Chinese Revolution sufficiently attractive to bring them back to the fold. An augury of this was discernible in the return to Peking, in the summer of 1965, of Li Tsung-jen, Vice-President of the Nationalist Government, after sixteen years of exile in America. One may assume that the province of Taiwan would be rewarded for its loyalty by being indulged for a while with its special administrative and economic structure.

Communism and Chinese Tradition

The People's Republic thus enclosed and insulated seems to many who look at it from abroad to have more than a superficial likeness to the Manchu Empire described at the beginning of this book. If we leave aside the international field, where the resemblance is most apparent, to what extent have the Communists after their victory accepted the domestic legacy of Chinese tradition? On this question, it is enlightening to see what they have made of one of the basic social institutions, that of marriage.

As in France and Russia, so in China the revolutionary regime addressed itself from the first to the reform of the marriage laws. A statute on the subject was among the earliest legislation of the Kiangsi Soviet in 1931, but here it is sufficient for us to deal with the current Marriage Law promulgated in May 1950. Some months earlier it had been declared that all Nationalist laws were abrogated, though when one considers the trifling effect of the abolished codes on Chinese society as a whole, this was not so drastic a step as might be supposed. The mass of the population had always regulated their lives by the old customary law, and it is clear from the words of the new enactment that the Communist legislators recognized that to all intents and purposes their task was the extirpation of 'feudal' institutions. Of these the most immediately obnoxious, as well as the easiest to deal with, was concubinage. Unions of the sort already in existence were left untouched if the parties had no complaints, but for the future all such arrangements were totally prohibited. The agrarian reform, and the elimination of the landlord class, which followed on the heels of the Marriage Law, wiped out the most odious form of polygamy, by which wealthy families would have the pick of any desirable girls born to their tenantry. Indeed, even in those cases where concubines taken before 1950 were satisfied with their lot and were in theory to remain undisturbed, when the concubine was a young woman it must have been hard for her to resist the social pressure which would inevitably be employed to persuade her into abandoning so undignified a way of life. The result is that concubinage survives today merely as a relic of the past among certain people over middle age.

A more widespread evil, though not exciting such class hatred as polygamy, was the traditional system of arranged marriages without reference to the will of the parties. Over much of the countryside this was almost as strong as ever. Even where a modern education might be supposed to have emancipated young people, the thought of the trouble and disgrace which the repudiation of a childhood betrothal would bring to their families frequently outweighed any aversion they felt towards the partner chosen for them. On the other hand, 'modern' marriages contracted outside family control often resulted, especially to the wife, in hardship of a different kind. The Nationalist Civil Code, in an attempt to safeguard the parties' freedom, required in the way of ceremonial merely that the man and woman should publicly and in the presence of at least two witnesses manifest the intention of taking each other as husband and wife. Divorce by consent was just as speedy, being effected without the intervention of the state by a declaration in writing signed by the parties and by two witnesses. The result was that among urban intellectuals in particular marriage was treated with decided flippancy, and many a woman of this class, abandoned with her child, found it difficult to prove that she had ever been a legal wife. The obvious remedy was to impose government control by making registration a necessary formality in all marriages. A provision to this effect was included in the Marriage Law of 1950, and in addition it was stipulated that the groom must be at least twenty, and the bride eighteen. Parental consent was not required, nor would such consent enable younger persons to marry.

The benefits of compulsory registration are undeniable. Not only is free choice secured, but a simple and effective procedure discourages the waste of money on ostentations ceremonial to pay for which peasant families used to burden themselves with debt. Nevertheless, the innovation encountered some unexpected obstacles. In the first enthusiasm of the reform it was declared unequivocally that in future no unregistered marriage would be recognized as valid or enjoy legal protection. Yet before many months had gone by it was found that the country people, to whom government intervention in matters of the family was still a totally alien concept, persisted in marrying without help from the registrar, and that to withhold recognition from such unions would be not only unjust but impracticable. In 1953, a Legal Committee of the People's Government ruled that a marriage defective merely through non-registration would be recognized, and it became clear that if a party to such a marriage later went through the form of registration with a third person, the registration would be not only void but might be punished as bigamy. Even so there is no doubt that the concession is temporary, and that in due course the intention of the 1950 Law will be carried out in full.

In the 1920s and 1930s, the great majority of 'progressive' Chinese, whether Nationalists or Communists, were in conscious revolt against traditional institutions. Confucian society, as we have seen, was based on the notion of duties, but for two decades and more the cry among intellectuals was for the right to personal freedom, especially in the domestic sphere. These people considered it intolerable that anybody's social or cultural development should be hampered by an unsuitable spouse from earlier days, and the feelings of the repudiated husband or – as was far more frequently the case – wife were not taken into consideration. Instances have already been cited from the careers of Sun Yat-sen and Chiang Kai-shek. Many observers believed that the Marriage Law of 1950 would reinforce this tendency. True, for the first time a decree was made necessary even for divorce by consent, but it was laid down that, once it was established that both the parties genuinely wished to put an end to their marriage and that satisfactory arrangements had been made for the welfare of children and the division of property, the local Ward Office must grant the request. In the case of an application by one of the parties, the Nationalist Code had required the presence of certain specified causes, but this necessity was removed by the new Law. From now on, whenever there is a unilateral application for divorce, the Ward Office must try to reconcile the parties. If it fails, the matter is referred to the County or Municipal Court, which also attempts a reconciliation. If this in turn is unsuccessful, the Court proceeds to give judgment. As the classic doctrine of Marxism holds that the function of a Court in such circumstances is not to terminate a marriage, but rather to put on record that a marriage has in fact come to an end by itself, it was assumed that perseverance in demanding a dissolution would inevitably be effective. Indeed, one edition of the Marriage Law, published in Shanghai in 1950, actually contained a printer's error which made it appear that after failing to reconcile the parties the Court would render not simply 'judgment' but 'a decree of divorce'. All the greater was the disillusionment when it became plain by the middle of the 1950s that the authorities were more and more often shutting their ears to pleas for marital freedom. In April 1957, during the brief license of the 'Hundred Flowers' episode, the *People's Daily* of Peking carried an article in which one critic complained that the People's Courts seemed to be ignoring the original Marxist teaching and refusing to acknowledge that a marriage had failed, if the failure could be attributed to the fault of the party seeking relief. 'This attitude' he said, 'is as absurd as for a surgeon to refuse to operate for appendicitis if the patient has brought the trouble on himself by overeating.' But opportunity for expressing such opinions was soon lost, and the critic was denounced as an advocate of bourgeois corruption. Phrases like 'incompatibility of temperament' were held to stink of reaction. Throughout the 1950s it is certain that a large number of marriages were what is called 'half-arranged', or in other words the parents or family heads first contrived the introductions and the parties then gave their consent. This seemed to some people too reminiscent of the old days, but when such husbands or wives repented of their bargain and sought their freedom, they were as often as not sent away with a lecture from the Court on the danger of bourgeois ideas. With the passage of time and increased opportunity for young people to meet one another at work and elsewhere, these 'half-arranged' marriages naturally grew fewer. The stern attitude of the authorities towards anything savouring of sentimentality in the relationship between husband and wife remains as formidable as ever, and in this respect it may be thought that 'proletarian' morality does bear the imprint of tradition.[2]

The most effective way the Communists could have broken with the past would have been the replacement of the Chinese ideographs by alphabetic writing. During the 1930s, many of the clandestine pamphlets and news-sheets circulating among left-wing students were composed in this 'latin script', and after the victory of 1949 some powerful voices were raised in favour of a root-and-branch substitution. The consequences of such a change would have been enormous. If the old characters went out of daily use and were no longer taught in primary schools, few students would undertake the task of learning them later on, and in a couple of generations even educated people would become cultural geldings, surrounded by the incomprehensible monuments of their national history. By 1960 the likelihood of such a step was receding ever further into the background, and the roman letters were taught not as a substitute for the ideographs but merely as the handiest means of indicating correct pronunciation, for the spread of the standard national language was being vigorously encouraged. As regards the ideographs, it was considered sufficient to introduce simplified forms for those most frequently in use, and to cut out unnecessary classicisms in ordinary writing. The study of the old literature was patronized more than it had been for years, and books long out of print were issued in modern editions. Add to this the care and protection bestowed on antiquities and works of art, and it might appear that here also old cultural values are re-asserting themselves.

Such a suggestion would be strongly repudiated by the leaders of the People's China, who omit no opportunity of proclaiming that they are in process of building a totally new society. So far, national sentiment as much as anything else has secured the acquiescence of the country at large in the policies of the government. Any Chinese is to be pardoned for being convinced by the history of the last hundred and thirty years that a militarily weak China constitutes an irresistible invitation to foreign aggression, and this impression is confirmed today by the ring of hostile bases around her borders. Great hardship is endurable for the sake of self-preservation – how great may be gauged from the fact that so poor a country has been willing to bear the cost of manufacturing nuclear bombs, of which the first was exploded in the autumn of 1964. But as her strength grows, and in particular as an increase in prosperity gives the mass of her people an interest in the maintenance of peace, will China, like Russia, shed her revolutionary zeal? To prevent such a catastrophe is now Mao's main purpose in life for he and his ageing companions cannot expect to survive much longer. His teachings, already accepted as canonical, have in recent years been sanctified still farther into a corpus of doctrine – the so-called 'Thought of Mao Tse-tung' – which is held to contain the key to all human activities, from science and industry down to the winning of a pingpong match, and from which only the basest renegade would deviate by a hair's breadth. A campaign of propaganda, unparalleled in intensity, seeks to guarantee that the faith shall be handed down whole and entire to future generations.

The unusually high proportion of young persons among the population who either have no recollection of the years before 1949 or who remember them vaguely as a period of chaos and misery makes it easier for the government to convince its listeners that pre-Communist China was a hell on earth, where the nation as a whole was ruthlessly exploited by imperialists and class enemies and from which only Mao Tse-tung and the Communist Party were able to bring liberation. It is not permissible for a teacher of history to credit earlier regimes with any improvement of social conditions. Let one example suffice. The rickshaw, introduced into Shanghai in the 1870s, and during the first half of the twentieth century a common feature of every Chinese town, is now on the mainland seen only in museums, where it is exhibited as a particularly odious example of the inhumanity to which the Communists put a stop. Yet the fact is that by 1949 the rickshaw was everywhere in full retreat before the pedicab, a sort of passenger tricycle pedalled by a driver, and now generally in use in China and South-East Asia. This more efficient and more humane vehicle was introduced from Indo-China to Shanghai and other cities under Japanese occupation during the early 1940s. Fairly considered, the Communist victory in this as in some other things simply accelerated a development which was already well advanced.

All pre-Communist culture, then, is to be viewed with varying degrees of suspicion. The literary value of an old novel may entitle it to a place in the national heritage, but the mere fact that it was appreciated by the former ruling class shows that it is bound to have political faults against which the modern reader must be on his guard. However, here as in the domain of marriage, there is little doubt that the real danger in Mao's eyes is not 'feudalism' but bourgeois liberalism. By 1965 this had become plain from the violent attacks organized in the press against a group of scholars and writers, many of them members of the Communist Party, and all of them notable during thirty years and more for their advanced left-wing views. It was now declared that their works were infected with bourgeois corruption all the more insidious from the way it was camouflaged. But if men whose services to the regime can hardly be called in question are thus treated as pariahs, it can be imagined how strict is the quarantine against intellectual contamination from Western Europe and America. For practical reasons considerable attention is paid to western languages but British and French lecturers in Chinese universities as a rule find themselves confined to translations of Maoist texts, while the few Chinese students sent to London and Paris are segregated from the contagion of their surroundings. True, the five million Chinese Christians, of whom three and a half million are Roman Catholics, though their beliefs are officially derided, are permitted to practise their religion. But foreign missionaries have been expelled, and Catholicism, its links with Rome severed and under a hierarchy many of whom have been consecrated in defiance of the Holy See, appears to be drifting into schism.

In this survey of China since 1949 one factor has been omitted. For fifty years, between 1895 and 1945, Japan had a vast influence, political, economic and cultural, upon her neighbour, but from the end of the Pacific War she has played no part at all in continental affairs. Today, the Tokyo government follows Washington in recognizing the Taiwan regime, but a numerous section of the Japanese public, whether businessmen resentful of impediments to trade, or intellectuals rebelling against bourgeois ideals, is casting wistful glances across the China Sea. It is impossible to predict what form the future relations between China and Japan will take, but the confrontation, when it comes, will be laden with consequences for the two countries and for the world.

REFERENCES

CHAPTER I

1. *Speeches by the Right Honourable T. B. Macaulay, M.P.*, p. 213. London 1854.
2. Thomas De Quincey: *Confessions of an English Opium Eater, together with Selections from the Autobiography*, p. 333. London 1950.
3. *Confucian Analects*, Bk II, Chap. 5. (James Legge: *The Chinese Classics*, Vol. I, p. 147. Oxford 1895.)
4. *Mencius*, Bk IV, Pt I, Chap. 26. (James Legge: op. cit., Vol. II, p. 313.)
5. *Taiwan Shihō*, Reference Vol. II, Pt 2, pp. 186–7. Tokyo 1910.
6. N. Niida: *Chūgoku hōsei-shi*, pp. 217–18. Tokyo 1952.
   The *Observer* newspaper of London, on 24 September 1815, after describing the public auction of a wife, remarks: 'this degrading custom seems to be generally received by the lower orders as of equal obligation with the most serious legal forms.'
7. Father Pierre Hoang, S.J., quoted in *Gendai Chūgoku Daijiten*, p. 469. Tokyo 1950.
8. Ting Fu-pao: *Fo hsüeh chih-nan*, p.1. Shanghai 1919.

CHAPTER II

1. G. E. Morrison: *An Australian in China*, pp. 209–10. London 1895.
2. Sybille van der Sprenkel: *Legal Institutions in Manchu China*, pp. 76–7. London 1962.
3. *Hung Lou Meng*: Chap. IV.
4. Tai Yi: *Chung-kuo chin-tai shih-kao*, Vol. I, p. 39. Peking 1958.
5. Tai Yi: p. 20.
6. *Taiwan Shihō*, Vol. II, Pt 1, pp. 222–5. Tokyo 1910.
7. H. McAleavy: *That Chinese Woman*. London 1959.

CHAPTER III

1. Chiang T'ing-fu: *Chung-kuo chin-tai shih*, pp. 8–9. Hong Kong 1954.
2. Tai Yi: p. 69.
3. Lo Erh-kang: *T'ai-p'ing t'ien-kuo shih-kang*, pp. 15–16 (4th ed.). Shanghai 1938.
4. Tai Yi: p. 71.
5. Chiang T'ing-fu: pp. 13–14.
6. Tai Yi: p. 73.

7. Tai Yi: p. 75.
8. Tai Yi: p. 73.
9. Chiang T'ing-fu: p. 19.
10. Chiang T'ing-fu: p. 25.
11. Tai Yi: p. 95.
12. Tai Yi: pp. 102–4.

CHAPTER IV

1. Tai Yi: p. 117.
2. Lo Erh-kang: p. 40.
3. L. Pfister, S.J.: *Notices Biographiques et Bibliographiques sur les Jésuites de l'ancienne mission de Chine*, pp. 930–1. Shanghai 1932.
4. Lo Erh-kang: p. 52.
5. Lo Erh-kang: p. 53.
6. H. McAleavy: *A Dream of Tartary*, pp. 29–33. London 1963.
7. Lo Erh-kang: p. 58–60.

CHAPTER V

1. Lo Erh-kang: pp. 64–6.
2. Tai Yi: p. 267.
3. Jung Sheng and others: *T'ai-p'ing t'ien-kuo ko-ming chan-cheng*, p. 69. Peking 1962.
4. Tai Yi: p. 299.

CHAPTER VI

1. Tai Yi: p. 314.
2. Wu Hsiang-hsiang: *O-ti ch'in-lüeh Chung-kuo shih*, p. 30. Taipeh 1954.
3. Wu Hsiang-hsiang: p. 48.

CHAPTER VII

1. Lo Erh-kang: p. 95.
2. Hu Pin: *Mai-kuo-tsei Li Hung-chang*, pp. 16–17. Shanghai 1955.
3. Hu Pin: pp. 17–18.
4. In the 1960s, certain Communist historians have attempted to blacken Li Hsiu-ch'eng's memory, not only by alleging that when captured he offered to serve the Manchus if they spared his life, but also, and more typically, by condemning his generosity towards his enemies. According to these critics, only a class traitor would, for instance, give dead foemen an honourable burial, as Li did.

CHAPTER VIII

1. Chiang T'ing-fu: pp. 57–8.
2. Mou An-shih: *Yang-wu yün-tung*, p. 24. Shanghai 1956.

3. Chiang T'ing-fu: p. 53.
4. Hu Pin: pp. 21–3.

CHAPTER IX

1. Chiang T'ing-fu: p. 9.
2. Hu Pin: p. 44.
3. Hu Pin: p. 50.
4. Chia Yi-chun: *Chia-wu Chung-Jih chan-cheng*, p. 6. Shanghai 1955.
5. H. B. Morse: *The International Relations of the Chinese Empire*, Vol. III, p. 11. London 1918.
6. Chiang T'ing-fu: p. 90.
7. Hu Pin: op. cit., p. 78.

CHAPTER X

1. J. O. P. Bland and E. Backhouse: *China under the Empress Dowager*, pp. 132–47. London 1910.
2. Wang Shih: *Yen Fu chuan*. Shanghai 1957.
3. Hu Pin: *Wu-hsü pien-fa*, p. 25. Shanghai 1956.

CHAPTER XI

1. L. Richard: *Geography of the Chinese Empire*, Eng. ed., p. 342, Shanghai 1908.
2. Pierre Loti: *Les derniers jours de Pékin*, pp. 81–2. Paris, no date.
3. Chiang T'ing-fu: p. 106.
4. Chiang T'ing-fu: p. 106.

CHAPTER XII

1. Feng Tzu-yu: *Ko-ming yi-shih*, 3rd ed., Vol. I, p. 1. Shanghai 1947.
2. Li Han-ch'iu: *Kuang-ling ch'ao*, Chap. 20. Shanghai, no date.
3. M. Ikeda: *Chūgoku gendai seijishi*, pp. 77–8. Tokyo 1962.
4. Wu Yu-chang: *Hsin-hai ko-ming*, p. 97. Peking 1962.
5. H. McAleavy: *Su Man-shu*. China Society, London 1960.
6. Wang Shih: pp. 81–6.

CHAPTER XIII

1. T'ao Chu-yin: *Pei-yang chun-fa t'ung-chih shih-ch'i shih-hua*, Vol. I, pp. 156–7, 162, 177–8 (n. 6).
2. Wang Shih: p. 94.

CHAPTER XIV

1. *Shina mondai jiten*, p. 190. Tokyo 1942.
2. For the career of P'u Yi, see Henry McAleavy: *A Dream of Tartary*. London 1963.
3. Wang Shih: p. 96.
4. Wang Shih: p. 95.

CHAPTER XV

1. Quoted in Hua Kang: *Wu-ssu yün-tung shih*, pp. 74–6.
2. Hua Kang: p. 110.

CHAPTER XVI

1. T'ang-jen (pseud.): *Chin-ling ch'un-meng*, 7th ed., pp. 3–15. Hong Kong 1961.
2. Ch'en Po-ta: *Jen-min kung-ti Chiang Chieh-shih*, p. 21. Shanghai 1949.

CHAPTER XVII

1. Ch'en Po-ta: p. 26.
2. M. Ikeda: pp. 263–4.

CHAPTER XVIII

1. Arnold J. Toynbee: *Survey of International Affairs, 1932*, p. 479. Oxford 1933.
2. M. Murata, in *Tōyō Bunkashi Taikei*, Vol. III, p. 247. Tokyo 1939.

CHAPTER XIX

1. B. Schwartz: *Chinese Communism and the Rise of Mao*, p. 166. Harvard University Press 1952.
2. M. Ikeda: p. 323.
3. Ssu-ma Lu: *Ch'u Ch'iu-pai chuan*, pp. 95–7. Hong Kong 1962.
4. M. Ikeda: pp. 343–4.
5. Howard L. Boorman: *Wang Ching-wei, China's Romantic Radical*. Political Science Quarterly, Vol. LXMIX, pp. 504–25, at p. 515. New York, December 1964.

CHAPTER XX

1. Howard L. Boorman: p. 517.
2. Chang Ch'i-chun: *Chung-hua Min-kuo shih-kang*, 2nd ed., Vol. V, p. 10. Taipeh 1956.
3. Dan N. Jacobs and Hans H. Baerwald (3e.): *Chinese Communism – Selected Documents*, pp. 60–77. Harper Torchbooks, New York 1963.

CHAPTER XXI

1. The text of Lu's speech is in Jacobs and Baerwald, pp. 168–77. For the Sino-Russian dispute generally, see the same work, pp. 158–214.
2. This information on the marriage law is drawn chiefly from N. Niida's essay *Chūka Jinmin Kyowakoku Koninhō* (Shin Nikaku Koninhō, ed. K. Miyazaki, Vol. I, pp. 1–110, Tokyo 1960) and the pamphlet *Li-hun wen-t'i lun-wen hsuan-chi* (Peking 1958).

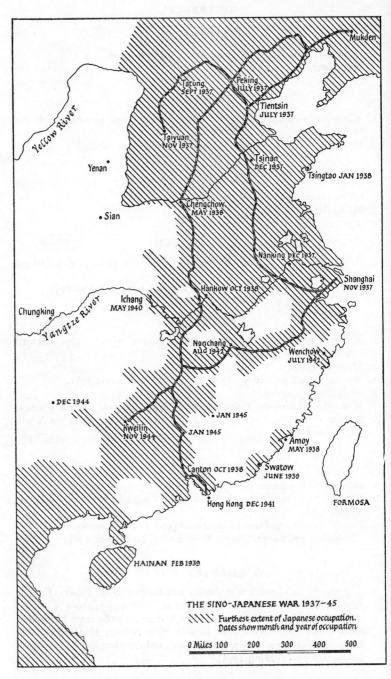

Tatung SEPT 1937
Peking JULY 1937
Mukden
Tientsin JULY 1937
Taiyuan NOV 1937
Yellow River
Yenan
Tsinan DEC 1937
Tsingtao JAN 1938
Chengchow MAY 1938
Sian
Nanking DEC 1937
Hankow OCT 1938
Shanghai NOV 1937
Ichang MAY 1940
Chungking
Yangtze River
Nanchang AUG 1942
Wenchow JULY 1942
DEC 1944
JAN 1945
Kweilin NOV 1944
JAN 1945
Amoy MAY 1938
Canton OCT 1938
Swatow JUNE 1939
Hong Kong DEC 1941
FORMOSA
HAINAN FEB 1939

THE SINO-JAPANESE WAR 1937-45

///// Furthest extent of Japanese occupation.
Dates show month and year of occupation

0 Miles 100   200   300   400   500

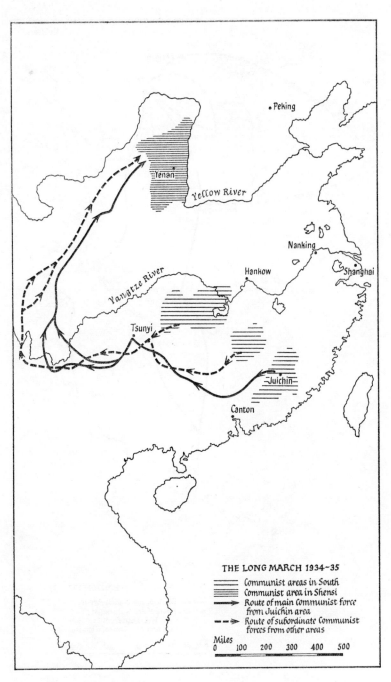

THE LONG MARCH 1934-35

Communist areas in South
Communist area in Shensi
Route of main Communist force
from Juichin area
Route of subordinate Communist
forces from other areas

Miles
0   100   200   300   400   500

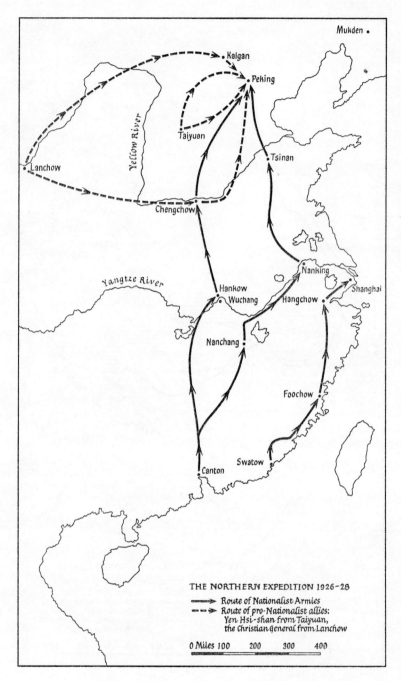

Mukden

Kalgan

Peking

Yellow River

Taiyuan

Tsinan

Lanchow

Chengchow

Yangtze River

Hankow
Wuchang

Nanking

Shanghai

Hangchow

Nanchang

Foochow

Swatow

Canton

THE NORTHERN EXPEDITION 1926–28

→ Route of Nationalist Armies
⇢ Route of pro-Nationalist allies:
    Yen Hsi-shan from Taiyuan,
    the Christian General from Lanchow

0 Miles 100   200   300   400

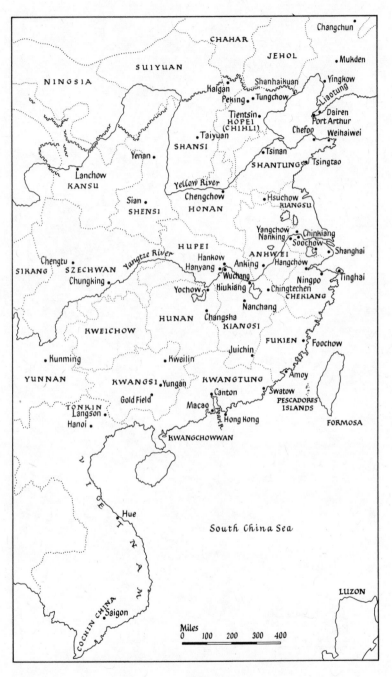

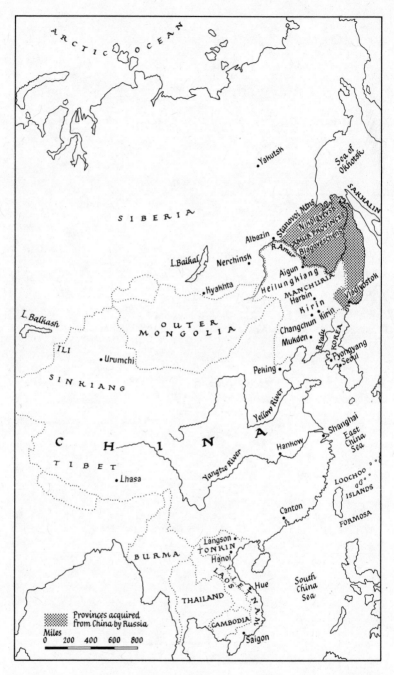

ARCTIC OCEAN

SIBERIA

Yakutsk

Sea of Okhotsk

SAKHALIN

Stanovoi Mtns.

Albazin

R. Amur

Nikolayevsk

AMUR PROVINCE

Blagoveschensk

Nerchinsk

L.Baikal

Aigun

Heilungkiang

MANCHURIA

Harbin

Kirin

Vladivostok

Kyakhta

OUTER
MONGOLIA

Changchun Kirin

Mukden

Yalu

KOREA

Pyongyang

Seoul

L.Balkash

ILI

Urumchi

Peking

SINKIANG

Yellow River

C   H   I   N   A

Shanghai

East
China
Sea

TIBET

Hankow

Lhasa

Yangtze River

LOOCHOO
ISLANDS

Canton

FORMOSA

Langson

TONKIN

Hanoi

BURMA

LAOS

Hue

South
China
Sea

VIETNAM

THAILAND

CAMBODIA

Saigon

:::::::: Provinces acquired
:::::::: from China by Russia

Miles
0   200 400 600 800

374

SUGGESTIONS FOR FURTHER READING

General

A Short History of the Chinese People (Boston and London, 2nd ed. 3rd imp. 1962) by L. Carrington Goodrich is highly readable. *Imperial China* (London and New York 1966) by Michael Loewe is an excellent account of political and social institutions from 221 BC to the collision with the West in the nineteenth century. C. P. Fitzgerald's *China: A Short Cultural History* (London and New York, rev. ed. 1958) is a useful survey of the main achievements of Chinese civilization.

A History of Chinese Literature by Lai Ming (London 1964) is good and up to date, but lacks the charm of H. A. Giles's book of the same title, which though unrevised since its appearance in 1901 and therefore marred by many errors is a delight to read and thoroughly deserved its paper-back edition (New York 1958). Both Lai Ming and Giles provide long extracts from the authors they discuss. Of old Chinese novels in English, probably the most enjoyable is *All Men are Brothers* (New York and London 1933), Pearl Buck's version of a picaresque masterpiece which seems to have influenced the thinking of Mao Tse-tung. The most famous of all Chinese novels is the eighteenth-century *Dream of the Red Chamber*, of which the fullest English translation is that by T. and I. McHugh, from the German of Franz Kuhn (London and New York 1958). Cyril Birch's *Stories from a Ming Collection* (London 1958, Bloomington, Ind. 1959) and *Strange Stories from a Chinese Studio* by H. A. Giles (4th rev. ed. Shanghai 1936) contain some typical specimens of the shorter tale, and together with the novels above mentioned convey to the foreign reader the flavour of the traditional Chinese world.

Arthur Waley is of course the principal western interpreter of Chinese poetry, and *Chinese Poems* (London, 5th imp. 1964) is the most representative of his works. Another good anthology is A. C. Graham's *Poems of the Late T'ang* (Penguin Books 1965). Waley's *Yuan Mei: Eighteenth Century Chinese Poet* (London and New York 1957) gives an interesting picture of literary society two generations before the Opium War. Similarly, *My Country and My People* by Lin Yutang (New York and London, rev. ed. 1939) is a brilliant description of some pre-Communist attitudes to life by a modern equivalent of the traditional Chinese man-of-letters.

For many centuries, Chinese society was organized and governed in accordance with Confucian doctrines. Few readers will have either the time or the inclination to consult James Legge's celebrated translation of *The Chinese Classics* (Oxford, 2nd ed. rev., 8 vols. 1893–5). *Chinese Thought from Confucius to Mao Tse-tung* by H. G. Creel (Chicago 1953 and London 1954) is a sound work of interpretation. For Confucius himself, H. C. Creel's *Confucius, the Man and the Myth* (New York and London 1951) or a study by a Japanese scholar, S. Kaizuka's *Confucius* (translation by Geoffrey Bownas, London 1956) will fill in the background, while Arthur Waley's *The Analects of Confucius* (London and New York, 5th imp. 1964) is a standard version of the great man's collected sayings. Of the classics of Taoism, the famous *Tao Te Ching* has enjoyed numerous translations. Arthur Waley's *The Way and its Power: A Study of the Tao Te Ching and its Place in Chinese Thought* (London, 5th imp. 1965) or a more recent version *The Tao Te Ching* by D. G. Lau (Penguin Books 1963) will be found interesting.

The greatest work of sinology ever undertaken is Joseph Needham's *Science and Civilization in China* (Cambridge 1954: in progress) which has brought to the attention of the world an aspect of Chinese culture too little valued even in China itself. In spite of the highly technical nature of much of his material, and the impression given here and there that a case is being overstated, Dr Needham's volumes abound in passages of the most engrossing interest.

The Western Impact and the Fall of the Empire

Europe and China: A Survey of their Relations from the Earliest Times to 1800 by G. F. Hudson (London and New York 1931) is an agreeably written history of the first contacts between the two great civilizations. Those who want to put themselves in the place of the victims of the initial British aggression ought to read *The Opium War through Chinese Eyes* by Arthur Waley (London 1958, New York 1959) while the affair is seen from the winning side in M. Collis's *Foreign Mud* (London 1946, New York 1947). *The Opium Wars in China* by Edgar Holt (London 1964) is the clearest account of the military operations not only of the war with Britain in 1839–42, but also of the intermittent hostilities against the Anglo-French allies between 1856 and 1860.

F. Michael's *The Taiping Rebellion* (Univ. of Washington, Vol. I, 1966) is well recommended. *The Rebel Emperor* by Lady Flavia Anderson (London 1958, New York 1959) is a romanticized biography of the Taiping leader Hung Hsiu-ch'uan. *The Chinese and Their Rebellions* (Stanford, Academic Reprints 1954) is a first-hand account, originally published in 1856, by T. T. Meadows of the British Consular Service.

Tseng Kuo-fan and the Tai Ping Rebellion by W. J. Hail (Yale University Press 1927) relates the exploits of the famous statesman, whose efforts together with those of others like him to rebuild the Manchu dynasty are described in a most valuable book by Mary C. Wright, *The Last Stand of Chinese Conservatism: The T'ung Chih Restoration, 1862–1874* (Stanford University Press 1957). *China under the Empress Dowager* by J. Bland and E. Backhouse (London, Heinemann 1910), rich in anecdotes of the Court of Peking, is a classic of its kind and deserves reading if only for entertainment. Victor Purcell's *The Boxer Uprising* (Cambridge University Press 1963) is a detailed investigation of the famous anti-foreign movement, of which the episode best remembered abroad is vigorously described in *The Siege at Peking* by Peter Fleming (London and New York 1959). A lively book by Emily Hahn, *China Only Yesterday* (New York 1963, London 1964), though going from the Opium War to 1949, is especially strong on nineteenth-century personalities. Some curious byways of social and political life are explored in *That Chinese Woman* (London 1959, New York 1960), a translation by Henry McAleavy of a biography of Sai-chin-hua (1874–1936), the most famous courtesan of the time, who at the age of fourteen went to Berlin as concubine of the Chinese Minister and in 1900 became the mistress of the German Field-Marshal Count Waldersee, the Commander-in-Chief of the Allied Expeditionary Force sent to suppress the Boxers. The outstanding authority on this whole period is still H. B. Morse's *International Relations of the Chinese Empire* (London, 3 vols. 1910–18) while English readers may study the official Communist point of view in *Imperialism and Chinese Politics*, by Hu Shen (Peking, Collets 1957).

The intellectual reaction to the foreign impact is described in *China's Response to the West* (Oxford University Press for Harvard U.P. 1954) by J. K. Fairbank and Ssu-yu Teng, and in J. Levenson's *Confucian China and its Modern Fate* (Berkeley, Calif. and London, 3 vols. 1958–65). Two influential leaders of Chinese thought are discussed in *Liang Ch'i-ch'ao*, also by J. Levenson (London 1959) and in B. Schwartz's *In Search of Wealth and Power: Yen Fu and the West* (Oxford University Press for Harvard U.P. 1964). *Wang T'ao* by Henry McAleavy (London, China Society 1953) is a short sketch of one of the most active of nineteenth-century Chinese journalists.

The Early Republic

Lyon Sharman's *Sun Yat-sen* (John Day 1934) is an unbiased history of the rather ineffectual patron saint of Chinese nationalism. Jerome Ch'en, a leading authority on the republican period, has written in his *Yuan Shih-k'ai* (London 1961) an excellent biography of the greatest of the warlords. The twelve years between Yuan's death and the overthrow of the Peking regime by the Nationalists are among the most chaotic in Chinese history. The founding of the Chinese Communist Party, and the Kuomintang-Communist alliance are described in some of the books given under the next section, but the political and social history of the militarists still awaits its own chronicler. Meanwhile readers should consult *Twentieth Century China* (Columbia University Press 1964) by O. E. Clubb, an American consul long resident in the country, while something of the atmosphere of life in those days may be found in the first volume of Han Suyin's autobiography *The Crippled Tree* (London and New York 1965). The tale of the last Manchu Emperor, P'u Yi, for years the centre of intrigue, who has survived a puppet reign in Manchuria and consequent imprisonment by the Communists to become a minor official under the People's Government, is told by himself in *From Emperor to Citizen* (English translation by W. J. F. Jenner, 2 vols.: Peking, Collets 1964-5). P'u Yi's English tutor, Sir Reginald Johnston, describes his unusual experiences in *Twilight in the Forbidden City* (London and New York 1934). Henry McAleavy traces a less reverent picture of the Manchu imperial family under the Republic in *A Dream of Tartary* (London 1963).

The Nationalist Period and the Emergence of Mao Tse-tung

The Tragedy of the Chinese Revolution (rev. ed. Oxford University Press for Stanford U.P. 1951) by H. Isaacs is a detailed study of the break between the Kuomintang and the Communists in 1927. T'ang Leang-li, himself a follower of Wang Ching-wei, in *The Inner History of the Chinese Revolution* (London and New York 1930) describes the struggle for power within the Kuomintang. Chiang Kai-shek and his entourage receive sympathetic treatment in two books by Emily Hahn: *Chiang Kai-shek, an Unauthorized Biography* (New York 1955) and *The Soong Sisters* (New York 1941, London 1942). The Generalissimo's political ideals are set out in *China's Destiny*, a work written by one of his followers but expressing his views and published under his name (New York and London 1947). His autobiography, *Soviet Russia in China: A Summing-up at Seventy* (New York 1957) is less rewarding. Edgar Snow's *Red Star Over China* (New York 1944, London 1951) which first brought Mao and his friends to the notice of the world, remains an indispensable guide to early Communist history. A more recent work on Mao's career down to 1949 is Jerome Chen's *Mao and the Chinese Revolution* (Oxford University Press 1965). The development of an indigenous Chinese Communism outside Russian direction is best traced in *Chinese Communism and the Rise of Mao*, by B. I. Schwartz

(Oxford University Press for Harvard U.P. 1951). The Sian Mutiny of 1936, which forced Chiang to end the Civil War and form a united front with the Communists against Japan, is the subject of a brilliant piece of reporting, *Crisis in China* (London 1937, issued in the U.S. as *First Act of China*, New York 1938) by James Bertram. *Journey to a War* by W. H. Auden and C. Isherwood (London and New York 1939) relates the personal experiences of the two well-known authors during a visit to China in the first months of the conflict with Japan, while the deterioration of the Nationalist administration towards the end is exposed in *Thunder out of China* by T. H. White and A. Jacoby (New York 1946, London 1951). Herbert Feis in *The China Tangle* (Oxford University Press for Princeton U.P. 1953) tells of the fruitless American efforts to achieve peace between Communists and Nationalists after the surrender of Japan. J. Belden's *China Shakes the World* (London and New York 1949) is an eye-witness's account of conditions in the Communist areas of North China shortly before Mao's victory. Readers who want authoritative sociological works should turn to *Peasant Life in China* (pre-war) by Fei Hsiao Tung (London and New York 1939) and *Chinese Family and Society*, by Olga Lang (Oxford University Press for Yale U.P. 1946).

The People's China

To sum up the Communist advance to victory, read C. P. Fitzgerald's *The Birth of Communist China* (Penguin Books 1964) and consult *A Documentary History of Chinese Communism* by C. Brandt, B. I. Schwartz and J. Fairbank (Cambridge, Mass. and London 1952). Mao's own *Selected Works* (London 1954–) are indispensable to anybody who wishes to understand the ideals and policies of China's present rulers: *The Political Thoughts of Mao Tse-tung* (New York and London 1963 and paperback) edited by S. R. Schram provides a good introductory volume. Events since the creation of the People's Government have been described in a multitude of books, all too often written for the purpose of propaganda from one side or the other, while the impossibility for foreigners of travelling freely in China and meeting Chinese people without supervision has resulted in a dearth of authentic information on many aspects of daily life and society. Kuo Ping-chia's *China – New Age and New Outlook* is an eminently fair book by one who, as a former Nationalist official living in America, cannot be charged with undue sympathy for the Communists (London 1956 and Penguin Books). Two further books by C. P. Fitzgerald, *Revolution in China* and *Flood Tide in China* (London 1952 and 1958 respectively), are valuable studies by a scholar well acquainted with Chinese history, though perhaps inclined to over-emphasize the traditional, at the expense of the

Marxist-Leninist, element in Maoism. *Commonsense about China* by Guy Wint (London and New York 1960 and paperback) makes some useful comparisons between the old China and the new, while T. Mende's *China and Her Shadow* (London 1961, New York 1962) gives a sound appraisal of the first stages of the Chinese experiment against the general Asian background. *The Economic Development of Communist China* by T. J. Hughes and D. E. T. Luard (2nd ed. Oxford University Press for Royal Institute of International Affairs 1961) is trustworthy and covers the famous Communes. A short work specially devoted to these is *The Chinese Communes* by Richard Hughes (London 1960). *The Hundred Flowers*, edited by R. MacFarquhar gives an interesting picture of the famous debate of 1957 which gripped the attention of the world (Paris, Stevens 1960).

How the Communist victory affected the lives of some intellectuals is revealed in *The Umbrella Game* (New York 1954) by Maria Yen who was a Peking University student at the time of the change of regime. An even more sensitive study of the same theme is *China in Crisis*, by S. Lindquist, a Swede who also spent some time as a student in Peking in the 1950s (London and New York 1965). Of the numerous books by travellers *The Long March* by Simone de Beauvoir (London and Cleveland 1958) is predictably sympathetic, but through the author's intellectual distinction is filled with interesting passages. Very sympathetic too are *The Wall has Two Sides* by F. Greene (London, 2nd ed. 1963) and *The Other Side of the River* by E. Snow (New York 1962, London 1963), an enormous book in which Mao's old chronicler revisits China after many years.

The Chinese quarrel with Russia may be studied from the original documents in W. E. Griffith's *The Sino-Soviet Rift* (Cambridge, Mass. and London 1964): the more general cultural and historical background to the dispute is described in K. Mehnert's *Peking and Moscow* (New York 1963, London 1964) and H. Schwartz's *Tsars, Mandarins and Commissars* (Philadelphia and London 1964). A well-balanced account of the origins of the conflict with India is *The China-India Border* by Alastair Lamb (Oxford University Press 1964).

In conclusion, the following books are recommended for their information about the Chinese societies existing beyond the control of Peking: *Formosa Today*, edited by Mark Mancall (New York and London 1964); *The History of Hong Kong* by S. B. Endacott (Oxford University Press 1957); *The Overseas Chinese* by Lois Mitchison (London 1960) and Victor Purcell's *The Chinese in South-East Asia* (2nd ed. Oxford University Press 1965). A masterly introduction to this last topic is a pamphlet by M. Freedman, *The Chinese in South-East Asia: A Longer View* (London, The China Society 1965).

AUTHOR'S NOTE

This book was finished in the spring of 1966, a few months before the Red Guards burst upon the Chinese scene, and on going to press it seemed better to leave the text as it had been written, without adding any description of that boisterous phenomenon. The Great Proletarian Cultural Revolution is in all probability the ultimate stage in the canonization of Mao's doctrines referred to in Chapter XXI. There it was suggested that Maoism is decidedly more hostile to liberal or 'revisionist' ideas than to Chinese tradition and in spite of some widely publicized vandalism by Red Guards against monuments of the national past, I see no reason to alter this opinion. Meanwhile higher education is for the time being at a standstill, pending the reorganization of the universities which is promised for the middle of 1967. How can a country so desperately in need of technical skills afford such a loss of time? How much of the Red Guard movement is a contrivance serving personal ambitions within the Chinese Communist Party? Will the Peoples Government eventually be riven asunder by feuds? These are questions which will occur to everyone, but which at the moment it is still too early to answer.

I must not omit to thank Mr Peter Quennell and Mr Alan Hodge, Editors of *History Today*, for their courtesy in allowing me to reproduce material from articles I have contributed to their magazine.

INDEX

Abahai, 21, 22
aborigines, 62, 66
actors, 34
administration, Manchu, 26ff.
adoption, 5, 6
Africa, 356ff.
agrarian reforms, 330, 338, 359
agriculture, 158
Aigun, 90, 92
Aigun, Treaty of, 1858, 92, 96
Airways Corporation, Chinese National, 268
Airways, Eurasian, 269
Alcock (British Consul), 84
Alexander II, Tsar, 91
Amethyst, HMS, 332
Amherst, Lord, 43
Amoy, 41, 51, 53, 54, 218, 271
Amur River, 2, 21, 39ff., 89ff., 148
ancestor worship, 5
Anfu clique, 209
Anglo-Japanese Alliance, 168
Anhwei, 48, 76, 109ff., 123, 124, 191, 248, 306
Anhwei Party, 208ff.
Anking, 109, 110
An Te-hai, 107, 121ff., 143, 147
Anti-Footbinding Society, 155
Arab merchants, 16
armaments, 37, 48, 54, 90, 111, 116, 124, 127, 324
Army of National Protection, 199
Arrow, the, 87
arsenals, 116–17, 127, 135, 182
assassination, political, 176
assemblies, provincial, 179–80
astrology, 12
astronomy, 37, 118
Australia, 227, 349
Austria-Hungary, 194

Baltic, the, 39
Baltic Fleet, Russian, 169

Bandung Conference, 1955, 352
banks, 158
bannermen, 21, 23, 25, 120, 171
banners, Manchu, 21, 23, 50
Belgium, 194, 270, 271
Bengal, 44
Bergson, Henri, 221
Berlin, Chinese legation at, 34
birth control, 342
bishops, status of, 164
'Black Flags', 134, 142
Blucher, Vassily, 235
Blue Shirt Society, 272, 291
Bodhisattva Manjusri, 22
Bolshevik, 331
Bonham, Sir George, 83ff.
Borodin, Michael, 233–4, 240ff., 248ff., 277
Botany Bay, 28
Bourgeois, Father François, 64–5
Boxer rising, 161–70
brewing, 32
bride-piece, 9
Britain, 1, 2, 41–3, 54, 83ff., 91, 108, 111ff., 116, 117, 126, 130, 132, 133, 141, 150, 155ff., 159, 161ff., 184, 191, 194, 216ff., 226, 238, 245, 256, 270, 271, 302, 307ff., 332, 352
Bruce, Mr, 95ff.
Buddhism, 3–4, 14–16, 23, 59, 75
Bulganin, 351
Burgevine (American commander), 111
burial, 8, 12
Burma, 2, 3, 14, 133, 134, 135, 151, 155, 309ff.
Burma Road, 302, 307ff., 312, 315

Cairo Conference, 316, 333
calendar, preparation of, 37
Campbell, Mr, 135
Canada, 226, 349
Canton, 4, 16, 32, 36, 38, 41ff., 46–8, 49ff., 54, 56ff., 60ff., 87ff., 155, 172,